1/06

Calling the Shots

How Washington Dominates Today's UN

By Phyllis Bennis

Foreword by Erskine Childers
Updated and with a new Introduction
by Denis Halliday

OLIVE
BRANCH
PRESS

An imprint of Interlink Publishing Group, Inc.
New York • Northampton

For my various and sundry sisters:
Judy Bennis, Jeanne Butterfield, Ellen Kaiser, and Nancy Parson

Updated edition first published in 2000 by

Olive Branch Press
An imprint of Interlink Publishing Group, Inc.
99 Seventh Avenue • Brooklyn, New York 11215 and
46 Crosby Street • Northampton, Massachusetts 01060
www.interlinkbooks.com

Library of Congress Cataloging-in-Publication Data

Bennis, Phyllis, 1951–
Calling the shots: how Washington dominates today's U.N./
by Phyllis Bennis; foreword by Erskine Childers
p.cm
ISBN 1-56656-353-4 (pbk.)
1. United Nations—United States. 2. United Nations—Management
3. United Nations—Finance. I. Title.
JX1977.2.U5B46 1996
341.23 73—dc20   95-39385
                                                   CIP
Printed and bound in Canada

CONTENTS

ACKNOWLEDGEMENTS

Numerous people helped provide the various kinds of support that made this project possible. I am grateful to Fran and Bob Boehm, and the Boehm Foundation, for their assistance and confidence in this work.

A residency at the Blue Mountain Center and backing from the Center's magnificent staff provided the space for much-needed concentration and focus in the last push to finish the manuscript.

I am especially grateful to my thoughtful and perceptive editor and colleague, Michel Moushabeck of Interlink Publishing, for his commitment to this project. Tim Watson, my hardworking copy-editor, deserves many thanks, as do the Interlink staff. Several other people gave generously of their time and ideas, reading early drafts of parts or all of the manuscript, questioning, criticizing, and providing provocative new approaches and ideas. They include Marc Raskin, Jeanne Butterfield, Ellen Kaiser, Marv Gettleman, Samer Farraj, and Clovis Maksoud, as well as the Blue Mountain gang, Anne McClintock, Rob Nixon, Esther Hyneman, Amy Chen, and Nancy McKenzie.

My family, colleagues, and numerous friends provided unstinting help and support. They include Vicki Alexander, Judy Arnow, Janet Bruin, Ping and Carol Ferry, Laura Flanders, Connie Hogarth, Peter Hogness, Art Kamel, Rochelle and Sid Kivanoski, Samori Marksman, Mario Murillo, Jerry Persky, Ellen Sacks, Vivien Stromberg, and David Wildman. I relied more than I should have on journalists Jim Zarroli, Bart Ziegler, Terry Allen, and Joe Lauria for helping me find crucial access to information, documents, and computer solutions as well as for broader encouragement. Discussions with Alejandro Bendaña, Noam Chomsky, Richard Falk, Jim Paul, and the staff of the South Center in Geneva provided unexpected ideas, approaches, and direction.

A number of UN-based diplomats, especially from countries of the South, as well as UN staff, provided crucial ideas, information and analysis, documentation, and other kinds of inspiration. My deepest thanks go once again to Erskine Childers, not only for his insightful foreword, but as well for his vision and the confidence that this UN issue really does matter. And I remain grateful to Andreas Zumach for creative help with the title, as well as for his support.

—P B.
Brooklyn, New York

AUTHOR'S PREFACE TO THE NEW EDITION

There have have been extraordinary changes in the world since the first edition of this book was published. Certainly some of the developments have been horrifying — NATO's war in Yugoslavia, the brutal wars in Chechnya, the Congo, Sudan and elsewhere, the continuing slaughter of Iraqi children by the weapon of U.S.-led economic sanctions. Hopes have been raised and then dashed in Palestine where negotiations foundered because they were not based on justice, in Kosovo where claimed concerns about human rights and ethnic pluralism dissolved in the smoke of NATO's depleted uranium bombs, in East Timor where the triumph of independence was crushed by Indonesia's U.S.-backed military and its militia supporters.

But some of the changes have been in a more hopeful direction. An international mobilization against NATO's Kosovo war in Yugoslavia turned into a global search for alternatives to bombing to solve humanitarian and human rights crises. Despite delays, UN action is beginning the long effort to rebuild the war-ravaged, but newly independent, East Timor. Tireless movements against the sanctions in Iraq are visible and active not only in the Middle East and Europe but across the U.S. as well. In August 1999 the first group of congressional staff traveled to Iraq since the Gulf War, to examine the humanitarian impact of sanctions, and in February 2000 seventy members of Congress urged President Clinton to lift the economic sanctions. In the fall of 1999, the combination of a broad coalition of environmentalists, trade unionists and human rights advocates protesting in the streets of Seattle, together with the dozens of impoverished southern countries who refused to accept being marginalized, succeeding in derailing the World Trade Organization's plans to increase globalization's power at the expense of the poor. The call of many, after the battle in Seattle, was to increase the role of the United Nations in regulating the global economy in the interest of the most vulnerable countries and peoples, while diminishing the power of U.S.-led corporate-driven globalization.

In fact, the increased centrality of the United Nations in the strategic and visionary thinking of so many social movements, non-governmental organizations, analysts, and activists around the world has brought new life and reality to the possibility of creating a new internationalism with the UN at its center. Speaker after speaker at the April 1999 conference of the Hague Appeal for Peace called for strengthening the UN as a centerpiece of the international effort to bring an end to war. Even in the U.S., where the World War II generation's understanding of the vital importance of the United Nations never was passed on to the next generation, the Vietnam generation, interest in and respect for the UN is rising among young people. And significantly, Senator Jesse Helms' efforts to convince the American people that the UN represents some kind of threat to U.S. national security or sovereignty has failed.

There have been many changes as well among friends and colleagues whom I had counted on for support in writing *Calling the Shots*. Several are now gone—Ping Ferry and Janet Bruin, and Samori Marksman, the heart and soul of my old radio station WBAI, who died so unexpectedly on the eve of the Kosovo war. Erskine Childers, whose sudden death within moments of finishing a brilliant speech excoriating U.S. undermining of the UN, haunts those of us with him in Luxembourg at the time. And Eqbal Ahmad, the scholar of the South whose searing poetry of analysis sets a standard for us all, the firebrand of unshakeable principle of heart, who died on the eve of the Hague Appeal for Peace, remains sorely missed.

New friends and co-conspirators have made Washington DC a more bearable place to live, despite the staggering levels of segregation and corrosive political culture. Mona Younis and Khaled Mansour each have given me more than they know. Peter Lems kept our Iraq sanctions work focused. My work on the United Nations has been greatly assisted by my co-workers at the Institute for Policy Studies, where I have been working as a Fellow in charge of the New Internationalism project since 1996. Marc Raskin, in particular, continues to provide insight, great jokes and a supportive political opponent. James Early helps me keep my political bearings on track. The Transnational Institute in Amsterdam, most especially its keen-eyed director Fiona Dove, has provided me with another political home and colleagues to help sort out the world.

And I have been privileged to be able to work with and later to call friends some of the key actors in the UN's constant drama. Former

Assistant Secretary-General Denis Halliday, the UN's first humanitarian coordinator in Iraq to quit in order to protest the UN's inability to protect Iraqi civilians from the ravages of U.S.-led economic sanctions, came to Washington immediately after leaving his position. We met testifying in Congress, and shortly thereafter undertook a six-week, 22-city speaking tour across the United States. It gave us an extraordinary opportunity to meet a wide array of students, faith-based, Arab-American and other peace activists across the country, learning from them as well as from each other. In the fall of 1999, when I accompanied the congressional aides to Iraq, Denis' successor, Assistant Secretary-General Hans Von Sponeck, made his time and his staff generously available to them, and provided by far the most nuanced, comprehensive and useful information to the delegation. Hans Von Sponeck asked to be relieved of his job in February 2000, citing the same reasons as Denis Halliday: he refused to continue implementing a sanctions regime that was killing civilians and shredding Iraq's social fabric.

Denis and Hans, along with Jutta Burghardt—the World Food Program's director in Baghdad who quit her job one day after von Sponeck for the same reasons of principle—represent the moral core of the United Nations, the reason I believe there is hope for returning the UN to its role as the centerpiece of a new internationalism.

—Phyllis Bennis
Washington, DC

INTRODUCTION TO THE NEW EDITION

This is an important book for students of international affairs, for those who care about the United Nations, and for Americans involved in U.S. foreign policy work. It is equally important for those Americans not involved, but who know they should be better informed, consistent with the democratic obligations of citizenship. It is a good read for all diplomats attached to UN Missions and for staff members of the Secretariat who serve the inter-governmental bodies of the Organization.

It is important as a tool, not for those intent on tearing down the United Nations, but for those who, after its more than fifty years of endeavor, its astonishing successes and its dismal failures, wish to repair its creaky stays, which were always anchored to soft ground by creators of questionable motives.

Phyllis Bennis forces the reader to question those very origins of the UN organization, something many of us would perhaps prefer not to face at this late date in its history. It is unsettling to be reminded that this United Nations of ours, with its Charter of high ideals, is built on the vested interests of a very few. It is uncomfortable to be reminded that the five victorious nations of the Second World War in 1945 created an instrument designed to sustain their newly won power through the entirely undemocratic and North-dominated machine termed the Security Council. And we have seen and experienced the consequences of the Council's inequitable nature, its lack of global representation and antediluvian veto power.

The book reminds us of the second class status of the more representative General Assembly, and the effective redundancy of the International Court of Justice. It provides the reader with an understanding of the influence and control flowing from those permanent members that dominate and manipulate the Security Council through raw military and economic power. We learn how this has impacted the great majority of member states, especially the poorest, in the General Assembly as well as the Economic and Social Council and throughout the many bodies and entities of the Organization worldwide.

Much of the violence in the world today results from either the neglect by the powerful member states of the Security Council, or from actions designed to protect their vested interests. The cozy deal—let's not embarrass each other, chaps—among veto-wielding member states that allows the destruction of Chechnya to unfold before the eyes of the world without getting on the agenda of the Council, appalls. The self-protective hesitancy of the U.S., UK, and China as Indonesian army-supported militia slaughtered thousands in East Timor, disgusts. The blatant use of Chapter VII of the UN Charter to attack carefully chosen enemies under hastily raised UN umbrellas, while protecting allies guilty of equal or even worse depredations, presents a double standard of approach that calls into question not only the integrity of the member states concerned, but far worse: the very credibility of the United Nations worldwide. The manipulation of the Council by the U.S. in regard to the former Yugoslavia during the Kosovo crisis, the illegal, Charter-violating bypassing of the UN to allow instead NATO's murderous military aggression, has left in Europe and throughout the South sincere questioning of the viability of the future existence of the Organization.

Calling the Shots is what it is all about. The amusing yet tragic spectacle of UN-bashing Senator Jesse Helms addressing the Security Council to threaten the member states with U.S. withdrawal from the Organization—if American national security were to be threatened by the UN!—has brought Washington's abuse of the UN to what is hopefully its all-time low. The buffoonery of that moment may have served to warn the Washington establishment that the nonsense must stop, that the black helicopters must be landed, and that the U.S. must recognize that even the world's sole remaining superpower requires the United Nations. And maybe Washington will start to recognize that global participation, even democratic change (incompatible though that seems in the context of U.S. foreign policy), is the only way to go for a hyperpower (as the French say) whose global reach will not last indefinitely.

Washington needs an effective United Nations; that is the bottom line. No one state, not even the U.S., can effectively police the world, nor take unilateral responsibility for breeches of international law, humanitarian crises, or wide-spread human rights violations. In addition, as Phyllis Bennis has said, the U.S. is itself the key rogue state with which we need to concern ourselves. Setting a rogue to catch a rogue cannot benefit international peace and security.

Let us hope that the anecdotes of this fascinating book and the lessons that can be readily drawn by its readers, will lead to a more effective Organization, in which all member states regardless of size are respected for their contribution, and where the most powerful member states will learn to respect the provisions of international law. The U.S. cannot remain forever outside international standards of behavior and must learn to comply like other states. All member states of the Security Council must protect the provisions of the Charter in applying its various provisions. They can no longer be allowed to undermine the very foundation of the Organization, as, for example, they do today with genocidal impact, by sustaining economic sanctions on the people of Iraq.

The Council is obligated to respect Articles 1 and 2 of the Charter. Article 1 identifies the purpose of the United Nations as first, "to maintain international peace and security...and to bring about by peaceful means and in conformity with the principles of justice and international law, adjustments or settlement of international disputes." And second, "to develop friendly relations among nations based on respect for the principle of equal rights and self-determination of peoples, and to take other appropriate measures to strengthen universal peace." Article 2 states that the UN is based "on the principle of the sovereign equality of all its Members," and calls on members to "settle their international disputes by peaceful means in such a manner that international peace and security, and justice, are not endangered. All members shall refrain in their international relations from the threat or use of force...in any other manner inconsistent with the Purposes of the United Nations."

The Council is also obligated to act in compliance with the Universal Declaration of Human Rights. And it must consistently apply the requirements of international conventions without double standards, including those prohibiting the targeting of civilians and civilian infrastructure; those that defend and protect the rights of children, who have been the most frequent victims of the economic sanctions in Iraq; those protecting the rights and aspirations of women; and those that defend the basic human rights of all peoples regardless of their nationality, race, color or beliefs.

The sustained economic sanctions imposed on the people of Iraq since 1990 demonstrate the corruption of Security Council decision-making and its disregard for the UN Charter and other international

Conventions. Their full knowledge that these sanctions kill thousands of Iraqi children every month makes the member states, and especially those like the U.S. and the UK who force their unpopular views on the rest of the UN, guilty of genocide. That the governments were and are fully aware of the consequences of their sanctions policy, was confirmed by the infamous 1996 statement of then-UN Ambassador, now Secretary of State Madeleine Albright, that the 500,000 deaths of children the sanctions caused were "worth it" to contain President Saddam Hussein.

After thirteen months in Iraq as the UN's Humanitarian Coordinator overseeing the oil for food program, I resigned from the UN in late 1998 in order to speak publicly about this outrage, this crime against humanity, being committed by the member states in the name of the Security Council and even worse, in the name of the United Nations itself. My successor, Assistant Secretary-General Hans von Sponeck, has similarly asked the Secretary-General to release him after a little over one year heading the UN same humanitarian program in Iraq. He has said that he cannot work with the new provisions and constraints of the latest Security Council decision on Iraq, Resolution 1284 of December 1999, which talks only of possible future short-term suspension of economic sanctions, vastly insufficient after almost ten years of crippling deprivation, and sets ill defined requirements that Iraq is unlikely to be able to satisfy.

In the meantime, the unnecessary deaths of children and adults, combined with widespread social, intellectual, economic and other damage to Iraq, will continue. In fact, this seems inevitable when one considers that Washington and London, heedless of UN requirements, have said repeatedly that they will not lift economic sanctions as long as President Saddam Hussein remains in power. It is my hope that the resignation of two sequential Assistant Secretaries-General from the position of UN Humanitarian Coordinator residing in Baghdad, two people with combined UN service in development and humanitarian careers of more than sixty years, will be recognized as part of the continuing indictment of the crime against humanity that the Security Council, in continuing economic sanctions against the people of Iraq, is committing.

This book would do a great service to the United Nations if it could be read as a guideline for a different future: for ending the undermining of the Charter by the Security Council, for changing the gross inadequacy of representation of the South; and for forcing Washington to understand the importance of the United Nations as an integral part, but not a tool, of its foreign policy. We need to see the powerful member states of the UN subordinating their short-term national ambitions to the greater good of humankind in the longer term. In this interdependent and rapidly-changing world, surely it is time to transform a United Nations dominated by the five aging victors of a distant war of half a century ago.

—Denis J. Halliday

Assistant Secretary General Denis Halliday resigned from his post as Humanitarian Coordinator in Iraq, and from the United Nations, in the fall of 1998. He testified, along with Phyllis Bennis, in Congress on the humanitarian crisis caused by economic sanctions in Iraq, and in the winter of 1999 Halliday and Bennis travelled together on a 22-city speaking tour across the United States. He has continued to speak, write, and organize against the economic sanctions.

FOREWORD

Two of America's finest UN hours during the founding period of the world organization were in the hands of women. As Phyllis Bennis suggests, by no means all American women assigned major roles at the UN have creditably served their country and the organization. But when, in 1945, Virginia Gildersleeve got her hands on the then-existing draft of a Preamble to the Charter of the proposed new institution, she gasped in disappointment at the stuffy League of Nations-style opening ("The High Contracting Parties...") and totally rewrote the text into the inspiring Preamble that was ultimately adopted in San Francisco. Unfortunately neither Ms. Gildersleeve's role, nor the product of her efforts, are even close to well enough known in the U.S. — the country from whose constitution she adopted the UN Charter's opening words, "We the peoples of the United Nations...."

The second early finest hour was in 1948, when Eleanor Roosevelt emerged from her two years of indefatigable negotiation as Chair of the UN Human Rights Commission, and strode to the General Assembly podium to present the completed Universal Declaration of Human Rights. In the ensuing decades, as that Assembly became fully representative of all humankind, its image was transformed in U.S. foreign policy and media establishment language from "parliament of the world" to "useless talking shop." But it steadily built on what Eleanor Roosevelt and her colleagues achieved, until we now have some 70 detailed instruments covering virtually every aspect of economic, social, cultural, civil, and political human rights —the first-ever *magna carta* of all humanity.

It is, however, yet again all too symptomatic that Mrs. Roosevelt is far better known and far more revered for her contribution to the fundamentals of the UN's goals everywhere *else* in the world than she is in her own country. At the end of this quite extraordinary book, which I feel extremely privileged to introduce, Ms. Bennis discusses the ultimate question about a democratization of the UN in the face of its multifaceted domination by the United States, and asks, "what is the call for progressives and democrats and civil society?" Well, to begin with, it could be to remind their fellow-citizens that their country is not just a member of the UN, not just a very powerful member, but (at least at time of this writing still) is the *Host Country* to the United Nations.

Consider it. After forty-nine years of having this unique privilege and responsibility, the United States has assuredly earned a place in the *Guinness Book of World Records* under the rubric of "Worst Host to a Public Service Institution." For the U.S. is certainly the only host to a public service institution that has repeatedly violated that organization's charter; that has almost succeeded in bankrupting the organization by deliberately and illegally refusing to pay its share of membership dues; and most of whose establishment leaders and media have consistently vilified the organization while grossly disinforming their citizens about it.

As one who worked for eleven of my twenty-two years of UN service at the world seat in Manhattan, I am a personal witness to this shameful record. I would open the major newspaper of the Host Country and find that its editors did not hesitate to allow contributors to its op-ed page to use language against the UN — the language of putrefaction, the worst gutter epithets — that they would not permit about any other public body. One worked as though behind barricades of siege — as though hostaged in the U.S., not hosted.

More importantly, however, when I would venture outside the barricades and go to speak to ordinary Americans across the continent, I would invariably find a very high level of basic public support for the United Nations, that this year's polls have again confirmed — 67% support, down only 9 points even after a year of the most virulent right-wing demagoguery. It was truly as though I had traveled to speak in a different country from the one whose political leaders, claiming to represent the people I would talk with, still continued traducing them day in and day out about the evils of the UN. Those leaders ignored the fact that the UN belongs to the American people, along with the other 95% of humankind — not just to the U.S. government.

The world was bound to be more, not less, dangerous when Cold War constraints and neglects of the causes of upheaval and conflict ended. The detailed analyses of UN responses that make this book so valuable, emerge in the context of a basic deprivation of information and resources that no American citizen could possibly realize if one were to rely solely on Senator Jesse Helms' mendacities about the UN "draining billions of dollars from American taxpayers."

The entire budget of the UN and its specialized and technical agencies for the world of 5.7 billion people, including funds for development, peacekeeping, and humanitarian relief, is about $11 billion a year. That is about what Americans spend in a year at beauty parlors and health clubs. It represents just under $2.00 per human being alive on Planet Earth, while governments are still spending about $150.00 per capita of humankind on military establishments. The U.S. *makes* over a billion dollars a year out of hosting the UN and out of UN procurement awards to U.S. companies.

Americans are continuously informed that the civil service of the UN system is a "vast, sprawling, swollen bureaucracy" — and tax free as well. Certainly the UN civil service needs overhauling, but it numbers only 52,000 people, at all levels, worldwide. That is less than the civil servants in the State of Wyoming (population 450,000), and less than the district health staff of Wales in Britain. And all staff pay income tax to their own governments.

The grim truth is that, under relentless U.S. demands to *cut* its staff, the UN is perilously under-resourced in relation to the tidal waves of challenges that pound in upon it from every part of the spectrum of human need and endeavor — of which the high-profile peacekeeping operations represent only a fraction. But how many Americans — the citizen *hosts* of the world organization —know any of this?

Thus, a serious part of the problem Ms. Bennis addresses throughout this remarkable study — the problem of a UN that indeed reflects all of humankind but that is denied its democracy by the U.S. and its compliant Northern allies — is a problem in American democracy itself. Her book is certainly a finest hour in American writing about the United Nations. It deserves reading by every American who remembers another phrase from a founding U.S. document — "with a decent respect to the opinions of mankind."

—Erskine Childers

INTRODUCTION

At the moment the Gulf War began, the UN Security Council was in a meeting. The consultations had been going on for most of the day and it was already dark outside, although in the windowless hallways and alcoves of the United Nations building it was hard to tell. It was the night of January 16, 1991.

The diplomats inside the Council chamber were exhausted. They had been sitting around that table for months. Throughout the late summer, from August 2, 1990, when Iraq invaded Kuwait and the U.S. ambassador to the UN called the Council into special session, they had been trying to figure out how to reverse Iraq's invasion while avoiding all-out war in the Gulf. They had been meeting virtually round-the-clock, but so far they had failed. Since December, the Council had unofficially agreed not to consider any alternative proposals until after the U.S.-imposed January 15th deadline had passed. War seemed inevitable.

Correspondents waiting outside the Council chamber on that January night were worn out too. They had been there most of the day and, like the diplomats, had been worn down by the continual meetings, the long delays, and the late-night parleys. There was a rumor, and some press corps grumbling, that the still deadlocked Council meeting might be adjourned until 10 p.m. so delegates could attend a reception planned at the Canadian mission and then return to headquarters. The meeting probably wouldn't start again till 11:00 or so. That meant another all-nighter. Some reporters, tired of waiting, went upstairs to their offices to catch up on work or check the wires.

Shortly after 6:30 that evening, a few journalists came running back down to the second-floor Council chamber. "Something's going on in the sky over Baghdad," one said. "It's not clear what it is." Another asked if any of the Council members, or Secretary-General Perez de Cuellar, had come out of the meeting yet. No, no one's been seen. One of the UN security guards, who had overheard the press people talking, quickly headed inside, into the Council meeting. Another reporter came down the escalator, three steps at a time. "They're bombing Baghdad," he called out. "It's on CNN."

Moments later, the envoys began streaming out of the Council chamber. In the foyer, where correspondents traditionally wait to interview the diplomats, the tables were turned, as Council ambassadors and their aides quizzed the journalists about what was going on. No one knew for sure, and everyone — diplomats, UN officials, and reporters alike — responded to the same instinct. They scattered to offices throughout the UN headquarters to find TV sets tuned to the real-time coverage of Desert Storm, just launched half a world away. The Security Council had to learn from a UN security guard and CNN — not from the UN's military Staff Committee or the secretary-general or even the U.S. ambassador — that the "UN's war" had begun.

One small group of people sought out the television in a cramped press office two floors above the Security Council chamber. They crowded around, watching wordlessly as wave after wave of massive explosions shuddered across the screen. No one knew what to say. Among them was Ambassador Ricardo Alarcon, then representing Cuba on the Security Council. "The chickens have come home to roost," he said after a long silence. "Now we can only wait to see what happens."

Throughout the world many others watched and waited too, on that singular night. Many millions looked to the UN, waiting for the Security Council to take control of, or at least monitor, the assault raging over Baghdad, hundreds of miles away from Iraqi-occupied Kuwait. But no one at headquarters suggested such a move.

This was a war authorized and annointed with international credibility by the United Nations, but in fact the global organization had no say in decisions about how, when, where, and for how long the war would be wagged. The thousand points of light flashing in Baghdad's sky were the U.S. bombs dropped by U.S. planes flown by U.S. pilots guided by U.S. radar systems.

The United Nations was at centerstage of world attention as U.S. troops stormed across the desert. The rhetoric was of a grand international coalition. But in terms of real decision-making, the "coalition" was a fraud and the UN was out of the loop. Washington was calling the shots.

The end of the Cold War had transformed the possibilities and potentials of the UN. Earlier, during the long years of decolonization and the East-West split, the Security Council was largely paralyzed, and the UN had been relegated to the margins of U.S. policy.

Washington's disdain for the organization reached its peak during the Reagan administration, when the UN was rountinely excoriated as a bastion of Third Worldism and a center of socialist bombast. The U.S. stopped supporting many of the UN's agencies and programs; U.S. dues went unpaid and arrears piled up, reaching hundreds of millions of dollars.

By the end of the 1980s, Soviet weakness and the winding down of the Cold War created a new political terrain. The East-West conflict no longer divided the world, but in the new era of ruthless economic expansion by the West, the suddenly visible North-South chasm between rich and poor nations emerged to challenge Washington's claims that a "new world order" meant peace and prosperity for all. The U.S., shorn of "fighting communist expansionism" as a legitimizing international framework, needed a new instrument to justify its new foreign policy. White House and State Department analysts figured that in these changed conditions UN diplomacy could be played out very differently. The UN quickly became a viable tool. Key players in seemingly intractable regional conflicts began looking to the UN for help in resolving problems. Negotiated diplomatic solutions suddenly became possible, as the superpower support for warring factions dried up. Longstanding conflicts in Afghanistan, El Salvador, Namibia, Cambodia, and in between Iran and Iraq all saw some kind of UN-orchestrated end in sight. While those successes won the 1988 Nobel Peace Prize for the United NAtion's blue helmet peacekeepers, they did little at first to reverse Washington's disdain for the UN.

But by 1990 the Gulf Crisis pushed even a reluctant White House to reconsider the value of the once-despised global organization. The crisis exploded at a time when the U.S. urgently needed a new set of slogans and justifications for its foreign policy initiatives. With U.S.-Soviet rivalry nearly at an end, Washington needed a new global framework to articulate its role — that of a superpower without a sparring partner. Its message was that despite the collapse of its strategic competitor, the U.S. remained very much a player in the superpower game; it had no intention of taking its marbles and going home.

President George Bush and his advisers soon realized that the UN held new potential for U.S policy. The Gulf crisis made it possible for Bush to seize the initiative. The genuine unanimity of UN censure in response to Iraq's invasion, given global voice through the first Security Council resolution condemning Baghdad's move, set the stage for the U.S. to claim further — this time falsely — that the same "consensus" supported Washington's military showdown. The ploy worked, thanks to the carrots and sticks pulled from the seemingly bottomless bag of U.S. diplomatic tricks. So when U.S. officials announced that Desert Storm was a war of "the world" against Saddam Hussein, few diplomats or journalists or policy analysts were willing to disagree.

What Washington did was to plan, arm, and launch the Pentagon's own war against Iraq using the UN's credential as a multilateral shield, while spin-doctors hailed "the international coalition" against Saddam Hussein. What the U.S. didn't do was to share actual decision-making authority, either strategic or operational, with the UN, or even with its so-called "coalition."

But while the real levers of power directing Desert Storm remained in Washington, the Gulf crisis did bring the UN to new visibility in global politics. The end of the Cold War and the Soviet Union's collapse had left the U.S. a strategically unchallenged superpower. But emerging regional tensions and new power alignments demanded that the U.S. at least maintain the appearance of multilateralism. In this new era, U.S. unilateral interventions would not be denounced as projections of naked power, and perhaps violations of international law, but rather would be sanctioned by an invented international "consensus" voted in the UN.

Ensuring UN endorsement for Washington's policies and initiatives therefore became a high priority for U.S. diplomats. The standard was set by Ambassador Tom Pickering, President Bush's brilliant UN operative. Tall and affable, rarely seen without his trademark State Department-linked cellular phone clamped to his ear, Pickering's all American informality of style masked an iron resolve. Over and over during the long months of the Gulf crisis, he forced the Council to his will as another might mold a lump of clay.

In the months and years that followed the Gulf War, the UN remained a crucial player in U.S. responses to local and regional crises around the world. The East-West divide faded into the past and hopeful visions arose in the U.S. and elsewhere of the United Nations leading a new and peaceful world into the new century. Perhaps now the soaring but unfulfilled words of the UN Charter, calling for an end to "the scourge of war," the reaffirmation of "faith in fundamental human rights," and the promotion of "social progress and better standards of life in larger freedom," could come closer to reality.

But the hopes of a new and peaceful post-Cold War world soon turned out to be illusory, as restive North-South fault lines divided rich and poor nations, developed and abandoned countries, haves and havenots. Virulent new nationalisms and xenophobic ethnic hatreds, fueled by economic and political disempowerment, exploded within as well as across the borders of new and reconfigured states. Overnight wars popped up like poison toadstools after a storm of acid rain. More and more the U.S. and its allies in the North turned to the UN as their agent to make, keep, or enforce the peace in these proliferating zones of crisis, almost all of them in the South.

But turning over responsibility to the UN did not mean providing the organization with the resources needed to do the job; too often "the job" itself was only recognized when longstanding incremental problems exploded into shocking violence or humanitarian catastrophe. With more and more crises dumped in its under-financed, understaffed, and under-equipped lap (especially when CNN-driven public pressure forces an otherwise reluctant Washington and its partners to act), it has surprised no one that the UN has largely failed.

This is because ultimately, for the White House, support for or projection of the UN is simply a convenient tactic to be used or abandoned at Washington's whim. According to President Bush's own Under-Secretary of State for International Organizations, John Bolton, the State Department's linchpin of connection to the UN:

> There is no United Nations. There is an international community that occasionally can be led by the only real power left in the world, and that is the United States, when it suits our interest, and when we can get others to go along .... The success of the United Nations during the Gulf War was not because the United Nations had suddenly become successful. It was because the United States, through President Bush, demonstrated what international leadership, international coalition building, international diplomacy is really all about ... When the United States leads, the United Nations will follow. When it suits our interest to do so, we will do so. When it does not suit our interests we will not.[1]

And as independent UN activism has fallen short, the U.S. has changed its view of what the organization should be and do. The Clinton administration's asserted commitment to "aggressive multilateralism" collapsed with the first U.S. casualties in Somalia.

Like its role in the Gulf War, the UN's function in the years since has increasingly become one of authorizing and facilitating the unilateral interventionist policies of its most powerful member states — especially those of the U.S. Despite the emergence of a "new world order," at its fiftieth anniversary in 1995 the United Nations remains a player on the margins, a dependent actor in world affairs, whose ability or impotence to fight to "end the scourge of war" remains contingent on the scraps of power and dregs of resources bestowed on or denied it by Washington and its Security Council allies.

This book grew from a concern that political and media campaigns blaming "the UN" for failures more accurately attributable to Washington were in danger of succeeding. The U.S. uses the UN as a scapegoat for its own failures, expects it to clean up global crises abandoned by or of little interest to the U.S. and its allies, and denies it the political and financial support to carry out even a modicum of the work the UN was asked to do. And yet too many, in the U.S. and elsewhere in the North, accept Washington's notion that "the UN" is responsible when things go wrong on a global scale.

Some time after the Gulf War, the U.S. public television network re-broadcast the extraordinary series, *Eyes on the Prize,* about the history of the civil rights movement. It opened with an old black-and-white film clip, apparently from the early 1950s, showing a small group of Black sharecroppers marching, somewhere in the deep South. They could have been almost anywhere in the world: they were ragged, they were badly educated, they were desperately poor. They carried with them a few crudely-drawn signs, asking for justice, for the right to vote. And they carried a single flag, the blue and white banner of the United Nations. It represented their hopes, at a time when their government offered no hope at all for a better life.

One wonders whether, nearly fifty years later, there are still poor and disempowered and desperate people, whether in Mogadishu or Sarajevo or Kigali, or in Alabama, who would think of the post-Cold War UN, under Washington's relentless thumb, as a font of hope.

Notes

1. Under-Secretary of State for International Organizations, John Bolton, speaking at Global Structures Convocation, Washington, D.C., February 1994.

1

The Founders, The History

The UN Charter is filled with stirring rhetoric that seizes the heart and captures the imagination. Written for a world so recently threatened by the slaughter of fascism, it called for countries to come together in a new organization. Nations would unite to "prevent the scourge of war ... to reaffirm faith in fundamental human rights, in the dignity and worth of the human person, in the equal rights of men and women, and of nations large and small ... to promote social progress and better standards of life in larger freedom."

But the founding of the United Nations wasn't only a victory of moral principles and the triumph of democratic values. Behind the high-minded phrasing was the hardball world of diplomatic power-plays and forced, reluctant compromises. While the drafters of that remarkable document included some of the best democracy- and justice-oriented minds of the Western world, some of their governments in Washington, London, Moscow, and Paris had goals in mind far more primitive than world peace and shared equal development. For the Allied powers, the goal was to insure, through diplomatic means, that the governments that had won the war would continue to rule the post-war peace.

The founders were a strange blend. The official U.S. delegation, and its parallel advisory team, included political analyst-activists and diplomats of various stripes, most of whom shared a commitment to internationalism, as well as academics and intellectuals seeking a form for a new peace-oriented global body whose mandate would be to prevent future wars, insure economic development, and create some modicum of social justice. They included brilliant minds and committed people. Many of them believed that the UN would truly represent a step towards a one-world government, an agency that could, if not challenge directly, at least provide an alternative to the continuation of economic, political, and strategic domination by any one power. The UN, they hoped, like no organization before it, would project the derivative

1

power of joint U.S., European, and Soviet backing while simultaneously upholding the world's collective interests. It would enjoy the unassailable credential of internationalism and provide an independent
voice in global affairs.

But the democratic-minded activists and academics were the Third
Deputy Secretaries and the Staff Assistants and the behind-the-scenes
grunt workers, who toiled over successive drafts without fancy titles or
job descriptions. They weren't the ones making the final decisions.
The U.S. government controlled the bottom line, and its representatives, headed by Secretary of State Edward R. Stettinius, had not
traveled to Dumbarton Oaks, and later to San Francisco, only to talk
about peace and justice and internationalism; Washington's agenda
was power.

LESSONS OF THE LEAGUE

The 1945 San Francisco meeting, officially known as the Conference
on International Organization, had learned a number of lessons from
the UN's predecessor, the League of Nations. Founded after World
War I, the League had failed to create a more harmonious world, and,
most crucially, had failed to prevent the rise of fascism and the out-
break of another world war. The U.S., then emerging as a global superpower, had refused to join the League.

There was a strong isolationist current in U.S. political culture, and
it was dominant after World War I. President Woodrow Wilson, while
a strong supporter of the League's stated goals, was unable to win Senate endorsement for U.S. membership. In the Congress, and throughout the political echelons of U.S. policy-making, League membership
was suspect. Rejection of League membership, corresponding to popular opinion, was couched in the more diplomatic language of a threat to
U.S. sovereignty.

But for Washington, beyond electoral concerns mandating isolationist rhetoric, the real fear was that joining the League would somehow
result in a significant loss of international power and influence. There
were no sufficient protective guarantees, Washington policy-makers
believed, to insure that League decisions would always be taken in accord with U.S. policy and interests.

The League's claims to represent a truly global organization faced a
number of daunting contradictions. First and foremost, for all its high
ideals, the League was a creature of, by, and for Europe and, to a lesser
degree, Europe's Western allies. Its concerns regarding Europe's colonies, the rich lands and impoverished populations of Africa, Asia, the

Middle East, and Latin America, primarily focused on keeping them that way. The League's leadership by the colonial powers also helped institutionalize the conflicts and competition between them.

The absence of the U.S. further undermined any chance the League might have had to operate in a broader multilateral fashion. Ultimately, colonial rivalries and competition among the European powers set the stage for World War II. The League of Nations was powerless to stop the Nazi juggernaut. It soon faded into irrelevance, and its formal dissolution in 1946 was almost forgotten in the excitement surrounding the new United Nations.

But years before the San Francisco conference that brought the United Nations to life, the League's limitations and the need for a truly empowered global organization were already clear. Throughout the horrifying years of World War II, efforts towards creating a new multilateral body were underway. The 1941 Inter-Allied Declaration issued a resounding, if vague, call for international cooperation after the war. Roosevelt's and Churchill's Atlantic Charter, that same year, provided the first sign of U.S.-British intentions to establish a replacement to the failed League. The Washington Declaration of January 1, 1942 first used the term "united nations," and included 26 countries as signatories. Allied conferences in Moscow and Tehran, in late 1943, actually began to lay the political foundations for a new organization, and the Dumbarton Oaks conference in mid-1944 was finally assigned the task of crafting a structure.

It was in Dumbarton Oaks, outside of Washington, D.C., that the Proposals for the Establishment of a General International Organization were adopted by four of what became the Permanent Five members of the Security Council: the U.S., the Soviet Union, Britain, and China. A few months later, in February 1945, after the end-of-the-war Yalta Conference, de Gaulle's Free French government joined in and the Five worked out a conflict-resolution formula; it was the first step towards the creation of the Security Council. Only weeks later, the San Francisco conference would be convened.

THE NORTH'S POWER TAKES HOLD

The San Francisco meeting brought together representatives of 50 nations — primarily the industrialized countries of the North, mostly European and North American. The cornerstone was the five-power alliance of the U.S., the Soviets, the French, the British, and the Chinese — the victors of the war, with their allies. There were a few U.S.-dominated Latin American states, plus still-colonized India, Egypt,

Iran, French-controlled Lebanon, Saudi Arabia, Turkey, and the U.S.-dependent Philippines. (Poland was a signatory, bringing the number of original signers to 51, but did not have a representative to the San Francisco conference.) The overall balance was at least 35 countries closely allied to the U.S., five close to the Soviet Union, and only ten non-aligned.

The drafting of the Charter in San Francisco posed numerous vexing questions. Most of them were shaped by the constant tension between democracy and power. How could an organization be created that would end war, protect the smaller and weaker countries, encourage egalitarian access to resources and development, improve human rights and standards of living — all while quietly insuring that the richest and most powerful countries remained in control?

For the U.S., there was no question whether power or democracy would carry the day. And there would be no taking chances on decision-making. Recently released intelligence documents clearly demonstrate that for months prior to, as well as during, the San Francisco founding conference, U.S. intelligence agencies were bugging the offices and rooms of the other delegations, and intercepting and breaking coded diplomatic messages — including those of Washington's closest allies — in an operation known as "Ultra." The intercepts allowed the U.S. team to know ahead of time what were the positions, special concerns or interests, potential pressure points and vulnerabilities of competitors and allies alike. The spying worked. By the end of the conference, the U.S. delegation had won support for structural, economic, and mandate decisions that effectively guaranteed Washington's domination of the UN for years to come.

According to historian Stephen Schlesinger, who has analyzed the long-classified files, the secret information allowed the U.S. team to indulge "not only in altruism but also in national self-interest .... The U.S. apparently used its surveillance reports to set the agenda of the UN, to control the debate, to pressure nations to agree to its positions and to write the UN Charter mostly according to its own blueprint."[1]

The U.S. organizational blueprint, among other things, included special privileges for itself and its powerful allies. Specifically, this meant permanent seats on the Security Council; Security Council control over all vital issues of international peace and security; and, of enormous tactical significance, a veto over any proposed Council action by any of the five permanent members. The veto was of special concern to President Roosevelt, who feared he would be unable to win congressional support, and crucial ratification from a Senate still influenced by isolationism, without it.

The Soviet Union was committed to a veto as well. There were few illusions on either side about the tenuousness of the wartime anti-Hitler alliance, and Stalin was convinced that without the veto, his anti-communist adversaries would carry the day unconditionally. His fears were not entirely groundless; the overwhelming numerical advantage of the U.S. and its allies first gave rise to the Soviet demand for additional General Assembly votes for its constituent republics and later efforts to veto the membership applications of some new U.S.-backed members.

So the veto rationales for the U.S. and the Soviet Union were slightly different. Moscow wanted to insure that it had some sort of weapon to compensate for its numerical disadvantage; its goal was to prevent the U.S. and its allies from gaining complete control over Council decisions. Washington's motivation was simpler: it wanted to insure its own power to do just that. But both agreed the veto was required.

According to Australia's foreign minister, Gareth Evans, the creation of the veto "was justified largely on the grounds that it saved the Security Council from voting for commitments it was incapable of fulfilling, namely enforcement action against one of the five permanent members or the imposition of sanctions against the will of one of those states. In other words, to convince the permanent members that they should adhere to the Charter and the collective security framework embodied therein, a deliberate decision was taken to establish a collective security system which could not be applied to the permanent members themselves."[2]

Eventually, all of the major powers agreed on the necessity of the veto. It was part of the viewpoint of the U.S. and its World War II allies that they alone would determine the nature of the post-war peace. There was no illusion that smaller countries, let alone nations still colonized by the great powers, would have an equal voice. According to UN historian Innis Claude, "all of the sponsoring powers — meaning the big five, essentially — insisted on the veto and made it very clear that they were going to have a veto or there wouldn't be an organization. In fact there were some cases of something very much like diplomatic blackmail at the conference, when an occasional small state would be fussy about the veto, when a spokesman of the great powers would say 'you either take the veto, or we'll dissolve the conference right now.'"[3]

Under Roosevelt's prodding, Great Britain, the Soviet Union, and China had agreed at Dumbarton Oaks to accept the U.S.-initiated and U.S.-defined veto-power into the UN structure. As Schlesinger describes it, the veto decision "reflected F.D.R.'s belief that the Security Council would actually run the United Nations, and that, since these five nations were the only ones that possessed the forces to police the world, this prerogative was required. Extending the veto to all nations (as had been done for the Executive Council of the League of Nations) would invite gridlock and inaction. Four months later, at Yalta, Churchill and Stalin, at F.D.R.'s insistence, completed voting procedures reflecting this veto system for the United Nations."[4]

The Ultra documents also expose some of Washington's own thinking about the significance or merits of decolonization. France worried that the U.S. effort to establish a Trusteeship Council within the UN, couched as it was in rhetorical commitments to the colonies' evolution towards autonomy or even independence, threatened Paris's post-war control of its own "overseas departments." While the British government, who hoped to rely on its own colonies for a return to economic power after the war, initially shared those concerns, London was quickly reassured by the U.S. Then, seeking to persuade the French that Washington had no real anti-colonial intentions, British Foreign Secretary Anthony Eden reminded France's provisional foreign minister, Georges Bidault, that although the trusteeship plan was an American one, it was not really designed to challenge colonialism at all, but in fact to "permit the United States to lay hands chastely on the Japanese islands in the Pacific. The system is not to be applied to any region in Europe nor to any colonies belonging to the Allied countries."[5]

(In fact, the European concerns were right. Soon it became clear that the efforts of the new, rising superpower U.S. to open up all the world's markets were coming into conflict with British and French attempts to keep some control of their dwindling colonial empires. When decolonization began to take hold throughout the 1960s and into the 70s, U.S. control of ostensibly "independent" post-colonial governments gave Washington important new leverage over its old-fashioned colonial allies.)

Thus encouraged that Washington had no greater commitment to decolonization than its colony-holding allies, and in fact intended to establish its own quasi-colonial control over former Japanese-controlled territories, France relaxed and accepted the creation of the Trusteeship Council. A concomitant result was the French backing away from their chosen role of champion of the smaller (European) powers against the Big Four. Once Paris was induced to accept its own veto-wielding permanent seat on the Council, its opposition to the veto, and to the concentrating of UN power within the Council, collapsed. A Turkish warning to French diplomats, also revealed through Ultra interceptions, that "the small states are inevitably going to be reduced to the status of satellites of the great," proved prescient.[6]

For Washington, the triumphal founding of the United Nations was made possible thanks to a mixed bag of tricks, including honest diplomacy, cloak-and-dagger codebreaking, and when necessary, the crude assertion of virtually untrammeled power.

But a triumph it was. And from that moment in 1945, one historical reality has remained unchanged: the United Nations was created, and continues to exist half a century or more later, in order to consolidate and strengthen — not to challenge — the global reach of its most powerful member-states, most especially that of the U.S.

THE FOUNDING: WE THE NATIONS OF THE NORTH

But however narrow the power-limned goals of the U.S. and its allies throughout 1945, the stated aims for the new United Nations organization were wide-ranging and socially ambitious. The Charter declared the organization and its constituent institutions were to become a "center for harmonizing the actions of nations" in achieving international peace. Perhaps even more significantly, the founding document acknowledged the integral links between the political, socio-economic, and military aspects of peace, recognizing "conditions of stability and well-being [as] necessary for peaceful and friendly relations among nations."

That meant creating a complex system responsive to a wide variety of political, economic, cultural, and human needs. On paper, the new UN system did just that. As noted UN scholar Erskine Childers describes it:

> Taken together, the constitutions of the System gave humanity a comprehensive international social contract for the first time. The constitution of the new Food and Agriculture Organization of the United Nations (FAO) committed governments "to contribute to the expansion of the world economy and to liberate humanity from hunger." That of the World Health Organization (WHO) declared that "the health of all peoples is fundamental to the attainment of peace and security." Approaching the same web of problems with another causal insight, the constitution of the UN Educational, Scientific and Cultural Organization (UNESCO) avowed that "since wars begin in the minds of men it is in the minds of men that the defenses of peace must be constructed."[7]

(Childers goes on to note that the UNESCO reference is "one occasion in a UN document when the word *men* is entirely apposite.")

But despite the lofty words, that social contract was far from universal in its application. Like the fraying social contracts of liberalized and globalized corporate economies of the mid-1990s, entire populations were written out of the social equation, marginalized or deemed fully expendable. In 1945 that meant, largely, the populations of the still-colonized nations of the global South. Their representatives were not, in the main, present among those united nations who together created the UN; neither did they form a collective *eminence grise* to hover over the consciousness of the founders.

What those founders built was a global structure responsible not only for maintaining international peace and security (as defined by the Northern powers), but for implementing a broadly formulated worldwide political and economic system that would be imposed, operated, and controlled by the victors of World War II. "Worldwide," in this context, referred to the decision-making capitals of the North — the world of the industrial and military powers.

Decolonization, as an inevitable historical impulse, was not on the founders' agenda, except for the tactical concerns of the major powers about protecting their existing or future colonial holdings. The United Nations of 1945, made up of only 51 countries, dominated by the U.S. and Europe, was overwhelmingly white and virtually all male. The founders, giving instructions to the architects drafting plans for the new UN headquarters on New York's East River, knew that other countries would some day join the organization. They had the magnanimity to order the architects to build an Assembly hall big enough to hold, eventually, a total of 70 delegations (not even close to the 185 missions crowding the hall in 1995).[8] It was anticipated that the rest of Europe, Scandinavia, Switzerland, maybe even the Vatican would sign up. It apparently didn't occur to anyone that the rest of the world might also want to join the party.

DECOLONIZATION AND THE RISE OF THE SOUTH

The General Assembly, repository of the most democratic impulses of the UN system, had been created on the basis of one-country, one-vote. One can assume that the representatives of power and privilege present in San Francisco crafted it with themselves and countries "like themselves" in mind; after all, at that time voices of the vast populations of the colonized South were largely unheard in the North. But those Northern powers later paid a price for their unthinking assumption that the democratic club would remain the province of the white, the rich, the industrial, and the powerful. The UN Charter did not, in fact, specify a requisite level of Westernization or wealth for new countries seeking to qualify for membership. And so join they did. In many cases the first, and highly symbolic, act of a desperately poor, weak, but proudly (even if only nominally) independent new government, following the defeat of its colonial overseer, was to send a delegation to New York to take its seats in the General Assembly before the eyes of the world.

Within a decade of the UN's founding, the composition and face of the Assembly quickly began to change. While the U.S. could be assured of virtually automatic majorities in the General Assembly throughout the 1950s, the process of decolonization had already begun. In 1955, 16 new member states were admitted, including Cambodia, Jordan, Libya, Nepal, and Sri Lanka (as well as several Eastern European countries). In 1960 alone, 16 African nations joined the United Nations. By the early 1960s, Assembly membership had climbed over 100, and the South — the countries of Africa, Asia, Latin America, and the Middle East — claimed a new majority. The Assembly hall was now dominated by yellow, black, and brown faces, surrounded by a rainbow of national costumes. The powerful countries didn't try to stop the process and keep these newly independent nations out of the UN; after all, in most cases colonial occupation had been replaced by less overt but no less complete control, using political and economic rather than military means, by the same countries who now also controlled the Security Council. Further, the UN Charter had been drafted in such a way that usually no debate was required for the admission of new members. While U.S. and Soviet diplomats sometimes tussled over membership rights for countries deemed hostile to one or the other superpowers (most often the Soviet Union), there was a strong democratic current in access to UN membership, and, politics aside, in most cases countries were admitted regardless of population, size of treasury, military capacity, or form of government. The transformation of the General Assembly was one of the processes that seemed to take place almost organically, without the conscious intervention of any controlling political forces.

As Childers describes it:

> The arrival in the early 1960s of a new majority from the South was an epochal development in world history. Yet the profound implications for the position of the Northern minority in the new, at least legally liberated world and in the now universal United Nations, were not debated. The Charter itself, with a one-nation one-vote principle that had been inscribed only for what had originally been perceived as its limited membership, ironically made the UN's transformation too

easy. Many decent, world-minded Northern citizens would remain unaware that their leaders would go right on trying to run it: a minority of governments (and population) determined to retain control while preaching democracy to the majority.[9]

It should be noted that the broadened, South-dominated Assembly did not spell an immediate end to U.S. influence over GA decision-making. Washington did lose, despite a massive campaign, its effort to keep the People's Republic of China out of the UN; the U.S. found itself in the minority of the Assembly's 1971 vote to admit Beijing in place of the discredited Taiwanese government of Chiang Kai-shek. But as late as 1974, Washington still managed, through intensive lobbying and high-pressure tactics, to maintain the fictitious credibility of maintaining U.S. troops in South Korea under the UN flag.

The "too easy" transformation of the General Assembly, and the lack of public debate about the phenomenon in the countries of the North, was to exact a costly price. The U.S. and European founders, learning the political lessons of the League of Nations' failures, had worked hard to mobilize broad public support within each of their countries. In the U.S., that supportive public opinion played a key role in legitimizing and strengthening the early UN's place in U.S. foreign policy. But absent an ongoing educational campaign, or even debate, over the rapidly changing composition of the UN, the South's majority slipped in without much acknowledgment by the organization's U.S. boosters.

When the right-wing ideologues and Washington isolationists later turned on the UN with full force, it was too late. The UN constituency's base had not expanded; it was rooted in a World War II generation who had come to understood the need to defend internationalism. But its mobilization remained stalemated.

Ultimately, as it turned out, the perceptions of U.S. activists and analysts didn't really matter. By the time the trajectory of decolonization was underway and the Assembly's make-up had been transformed, the Cold War's chill had set in. The U.S., Britain, and France were far too preoccupied mobilizing an anti-Soviet coalition to be much concerned with the consequences of the "Third Worlding" of the General Assembly.

FORCING THE WORLD TO "UNITE FOR PEACE" IN KOREA

With the Security Council largely paralyzed by Cold War and colonial interests, the General Assembly was Washington's agency of choice in 1950 in obtaining the UN's credential of multilateralism to go to war in Korea. Following the attack on South Korea by the North, the U.S. took the initiative to bring the question to the UN. Under the terms of Chapter VII of the Charter, the Security Council holds the ultimate power of deploying UN military force. But the Council, by this time, was already locked in a paralysis born of Cold War and colonial interests' conflicts, so it was deemed an unlikely agency to provide Washington with the desperately sought international endorsement. In fact, luck, in the form of fortuitous timing, was on the Americans' side. At the moment the U.S. tabled a resolution in front of the Council, its Soviet nemesis was temporarily boycotting Council meetings, in protest over Washington's refusal to accept the People's Republic of China as the legitimate representative of China, ousting the Nationalist government on Taiwan.

U.S. diplomats grabbed the chance to gain the Council's imprimatur. The result was that all countries sending troops to support South Korea were asked to put them under a unified command under the United States — but all those troops would fight under the UN flag. When the Soviets returned to the Council a few weeks later, Washington turned to the Assembly, introducing the Uniting for Peace resolution authorizing the GA to meet on short notice in an emergency in which the Security Council could not act, and to recommend collective measures including the use of armed force. Inevitably, the pliant, predecolonization Assembly passed the U.S.-sponsored resolution. The result was that, despite the Soviet position that the Council's action was illegal, and the active Soviet opposition that followed in the Council, the U.S. relied on the Assembly resolution to legitimate its claim that its own involvement in the Korean War was somehow mandated by the international community.

TAKING CONTROL:
THE BRETTON WOODS INSTITUTIONS ABANDON THE UN

Along with the Charter and the broad issues of war and peace, the genesis of the UN in San Francisco had included the creation of a set of agencies designed to reshape the economic order of the post-World War II Western world, in the image and interests of Washington, London, and Paris. The main economic organs established were the World Bank Group, the International Monetary Fund (IMF), and the General Agreement on Tariffs and Trade (GATT), which in the mid-1990s was to become the World Trade Organization (WTO). Known as the Bretton Woods institutions from the site of the 1944 New Hampshire conference that gave them life, they were officially supposed to be, and to function as, part of the UN system — they were designated specialized agencies accountable, ultimately, to the General Assembly.

But from the beginning they operated separately from, and without oversight by, the UN organization. The ostensible mandate of the IMF, for example, was truly global, designed to cover all countries, rich and poor. On paper it was clear: "To carry out surveillance of the member states, to ensure that they maintained stable exchange rates and to provide a temporary facility that could enable a member state to overcome cyclical balance of payment deficits."[10] But in fact the Bretton Woods group never represented or served the interests of the whole world — it responded to the imperatives and demands of its powerful members.

The result was an extraordinary myopia in Washington, in which a narrowly defined interest in controlling local markets dominated U.S. strategy in the South, and the State Department showed little interest in serious study of the causes of economic underdevelopment:

> The U.S. and U.K., the two dominant powers in the immediate aftermath of the war, went about conceiving and putting in place institutions that were aimed at reconstructing war-devastated market economies of the North .... The spirit of free enterprise giving full play to market forces had to be preserved .... Two individuals close to their respective establishments, social scientists and thinker economists in their own right — Dexter White for the U.S. and John Maynard Keynes representing the U.K. — were to lead negotiations as discreetly as possible, with the purpose of constructing the post-war edifice to promote common perceived interests .... It is quite clear that the Bretton Woods institutions were never equipped to understand the deep-rooted causes of underdevelopment, let alone to examine them closely enough to realize the Herculean tasks that faced humankind. The assumption that membership of these institutions will make up for lost time can charitably be described as myopic. The equilibrium of asymmetry based on power play is here to stay.[11]

Voting systems within these institutions, weighted according to financial shares held by member states, are explicitly anti-democratic, consciously aimed at insuring control by the wealthiest states. Those states are then in a position to dictate terms to impoverished developing countries.

So the Bretton Woods group never functioned as truly multilateral UN agencies through which the interests of all countries could be mediated. Instead, they remained functionally outside the UN system and UN oversight, and the General Assembly emerged as the central organ for discussion and often heated debate over the direction of international economic and social policies. This was in an historical period in which, despite the devastation of Europe and especially of the Soviet Union caused by World War II, the inequitable division of wealth between the industrialized and the once-colonized developing countries was profound.

As a result, the General Assembly emerged as the venue for the newly independent governments' efforts to craft macro-economic programs designed, in their grandest form, to fundamentally challenge the asymmetrical access to wealth and power between rich and poor, industrialized and newly independent, countries. ECOSOC, the UN's Economic and Social Council, was to be the implementing agency for these plans.

THE NON-ALIGNED MOVEMENT: THE ASSEMBLY OF THE SOUTH CHALLENGES THE COUNCIL OF THE NORTH

In 1955, the Bandung Conference in Indonesia created the Non-Aligned Movement (NAM), grouping those developing and mostly newly independent countries not members of Western or Soviet-led military pacts. But while the organizational definition categorized those countries as outside the two Cold War blocs, the actual unifying feature of the NAM was the effort of post-colonial states to create new, truly independent nations, based on national sovereignty and the right to economic and social development. As the South emerged from its colonial past from the late 1950s and through the 1960s, the NAM group in the General Assembly emerged as the engine of GA activity, especially in economic and development planning.

Ironically, while the Uniting for Peace resolution on Korea had taken into account the Assembly's legitimate role in responding to international crises, it was not to become much of a precedent. After Korea, the Assembly was largely excluded from issues of peace and security (especially those occasions for military intervention that proliferated so quickly in the 1990s). But during the 1950s, when the U.S. could still depend on an almost automatic majority, the Assembly did become the venue for some actions that would in later years be deemed the sole province of the Security Council.

It was the General Assembly that organized the UN's first peacekeeping operation, in Egypt following the Suez crisis of 1956: the UN Emergency Force (UNEF). The fighting had begun when Israel, France, and Britain attacked Egypt after Cairo's nationalization of the Suez Canal. The Assembly was drawn in, meeting in emergency special session, because the involvement of France and Britain in the fighting insured that the Security Council would be unwilling to act.

The Assembly's Suez response, unlike Washington's more tactical approach to Uniting for Peace, reflected a more serious reading of the UN Charter than came to be the norm in later years. While the consequences of colonial powers holding the veto may have initially caused the Council's inability to respond, the assertion of responsibility by the General Assembly was clearly called for under terms of the UN Charter often ignored in later years. Specifically, Article 11 of the Charter mandates the Assembly to "consider the general principles of cooperation in the maintenance of international peace and security; *the General Assembly may discuss any questions relating to the maintenance of international peace and security* brought before it by any Member of the United Nations ...." (emphasis added). Article 35 goes on to state that "any Member of the United Nations may bring any dispute, or any situation ... which might lead to international friction or give rise to a dispute, in order to determine whether the continuance of the dispute or situation is likely to endanger the maintenance of international peace and security ... to the attention of the Security Council or the General Assembly."

After Suez, the Assembly gradually lost influence in security affairs. Following the Soviet intervention in Hungary the same year, and later the Lebanese crisis of 1958, Security Council paralysis linked both to Cold War pressures and to the continuing influence of the colonial powers prevented any serious results. But the Assembly, despite some efforts, was similarly affected by the superpower stalemate, and failed to craft a serious response to either crisis.

While the much larger and more representative Assembly continued to hold nominal sway over broadly-defined UN policies, its resolutions still lacked the force of international law bestowed on Council decisions. By the early 1970s the major powers had succeeded in consolidating virtually all major UN decisions and agenda items in the Security Council, where there was no bothersome illusion of democracy.

U.S. and its allies' efforts to influence Assembly votes continued, although bigger bribes and more serious threats were required to assure Assembly compliance with those issues of serious concern to the Western powers. But Washington remained largely indifferent to most of the issues actually galvanizing the Assembly. The GA, Washington believed, could be left largely to its own devices. Because GA resolutions, no matter how strong the consensus, lacked (and still lack) any enforcement mechanism, the efforts of the Assembly (and especially the Non-Aligned Movement within it) to organize opposition to the North's global domination could be ignored without much peril.

Those efforts crystallized in 1974 with the Assembly's convening a special session, at Algeria's initiative, to take up the question of accelerating economic and social development in the South. The hopeful goal was that the Assembly could begin the challenge of narrowing the vast income gap between North and South. The special session led eventually to the call for a New International Economic Order (NIEO). For the Non-Aligned diplomats who crafted it, the NIEO was an enormous accomplishment. The document wove together issues of development, North-South economic relations, social justice, debt relief, national sovereignty, and self-determination. It was a clarion call of the impoverished South against the privileges of the North, a call for the justice of equity, of fairness, requiring nothing less, finally, than the re-orchestrating of the iniquitous underpinnings of the entire economic structure of the planet.

For the North, especially for the U.S. (whose early years of controlling GA decision-making had led to taking its supremacy in the General Assembly for granted) the NIEO was a wake-up call. And it was frightening. Although the Assembly was still powerless to impose its will on any countries of the recalcitrant North, the public perception of near unanimity in the Assembly in opposition to their interests was not something Washington or London or Paris relished. In fact, it appeared that the U.S. only realized for the first time, after the special Assembly session was called and the process of drafting the NIEO had begun, the degree of influence and level of mobilization of the Non-Aligned Movement within the Assembly.

Once the Assembly was recognized for what it was, an increasingly independent voice of the disenfranchised South, the U.S. had no intention of leaving it alone — rather, it would be brought swiftly to heel. It was largely in response to the NIEO, in the mid-1970s, that anti-UN fever kicked in with a vengeance among mainstream forces in the U.S. (Earlier campaigns, including the John Birch Society's famous "Get the U.S. Out of the UN and Get the UN Out of the U.S.!" bumper stickers, were led by and had appealed largely to extremist fringes of the right-wing. While isolationists of various stripes, and many conservatives in both major parties, held no great love for the global organization, UN-bashing didn't become a national sport for another ten years.)*

Once the Non-Aligned efforts were targeted, a venomous campaign began in U.S. political circles, excoriating the UN in general and the

---

* It is perhaps no accident that the mid-1990s version of anti-UN mobilization, centered on right-wing militia groups spreading tales of "black helicopters" leading UN troops to occupy U.S. land, bears a striking resemblance to much of the campaign style of a generation earlier. A key difference lies in the parallel mainstreaming of anti-UN sentiment, based less on black helicopters than on a unilateralist vision of intervention against a multilateral one, promulgated by leading Republican and Democratic Congresspeople and strategists.

General Assembly in particular, as hotbeds of socialism, as bastions of Third Worldism, and as ungrateful centers of rampant anti-U.S. sentiment. By the late 1970s, this crusade was in full swing. And by 1980, with the final adoption of the NIEO, anti-UN rhetoric became a potent weapon within the larger attack on the South launched by the "Reagan Revolution" in the U.S. (and mirrored by that of his friend and colleague Margaret Thatcher in Britain).

In Washington, backed by London, the campaign included the projection of the "responsible" Bretton Woods institutions to take over the role the activist, Non-Aligned Movement-dominated General Assembly had assumed in global economic planning and policy-making. It drastically escalated the process of imposing what came to be called "structural adjustment programs," in which desperate governments in the South were forced to impose brutal social cutbacks against their impoverished populations as the price for receiving World Bank loans or IMF guarantees or assistance.

The depth of the anti-UN campaign was perhaps best symbolized by Reagan's appointment of arch-conservative Jeane Kirkpatrick, a brilliant academic and powerful diplomat, as his ambassador to the United Nations. From all appearances, Kirkpatrick's overarching goal was nothing less than bringing down the entire organization to which she was seconded.

It was during Kirkpatrick's tenure at the UN that the cry of "U.S. double standards" began to be heard much more often. The NIEO had placed the question of the unequal distribution of wealth and power squarely on the world's agenda. In the UN context, even beyond the general effort to craft a diplomatic framework for narrowing that gap, two specific issues spotlighted the inviolability of U.S. power. One was apartheid South Africa, officially a UN-designated pariah state, to be excluded from normal diplomatic discourse, but in fact long treated with kid gloves by Washington and its Northern allies. The other, perhaps even more explosive, was Israel's continued occupation of Palestinian land, especially after the 1967 war.

The U.S. led its Western allies to defend a gradualist approach to isolating South Africa and forcing an end to apartheid; by the 1980s that approach had been codified as "constructive engagement" with the racist regime. The South, on the other hand, especially the African states, viewed the government in Pretoria as a rogue state, and demanded, largely in vain, more serious sanctions and tighter implementation of existing ones. The Assembly established numerous programs designed to provide active support to the anti-apartheid struggle, including establishing the Special Committee Against Apartheid and the

Centre Against Apartheid within the Secretariat itself. The Assembly in fact expelled South Africa from its own ranks in 1974, and granted credentials to the African National Congress and the Pan Africanist Congress as the authentic representatives of the South African people. The Security Council passed resolutions on occasion, but its porous arms embargo, declared in 1963, remained officially voluntary until 1977. It was widely believed, even after 1977, that the U.S., Britain, and other Western countries, especially Israel, were covertly collaborating with South Africa for purposes of commercial transactions and even arms sales. Assembly-sponsored resolutions and international conferences throughout the 1970s and 80s had, in fact, called for Chapter VII enforcement (meaning armed action) of anti-apartheid sanctions. The 1977 resolution making the arms embargo mandatory was in fact taken under the terms of Chapter VII, but the Council never showed any intention of imposing armed enforcement methods. And the committee established by the Council in 1977 to examine implementation by UN member states of that mandatory embargo never resulted in action against Israel, known for its nuclear collaboration with South Africa.

Israel's occupation of Arab lands, first and foremost Palestine, but after 1967 also parts of Egypt (until the Camp David Accords), Jordan, Syria, and (from 1978) Lebanon, was another sore spot in relations between the Assembly and the Council. Beginning in 1967, and continuing through the mid-1990s, the U.S. backed Israel in standing alone in countless near-unanimous Assembly votes of every other member state on resolutions condemning Israel's continued human rights violations, its occupation of Palestinian land, especially Jerusalem, its commercial, military, and especially nuclear ties with South Africa, its violations of the Fourth Geneva Convention requirements for treatment of civilians living under occupation, etc. Resolution 242, mandating an exchange of land for peace and calling on Israel to withdraw from lands seized during the 1967 war, was passed by the Security Council. It remains the centerpiece of peace efforts of the 1990s, but like other resolutions making demands on Israel, it was never enforced.

In 1974 the Assembly recognized the "inalienable rights of the Palestinian people in Palestine" to self-determination, national independence, and sovereignty. The Palestine Liberation Organization was invited to participate in the work of the Assembly and other UN activities as an observer. In 1975 the Assembly established the Committee on the Exercise of the Inalienable Rights of the Palestinian People, and later the Division for Palestinian Rights within the Secretariat. For years, annual Assembly resolutions called for an international conference under the auspices of the permanent members of the Security

Council and involving all parties, including Israel, the PLO, and other Arab governments, as holding out the best potential for solving the perennial crisis in the Middle East. Only the U.S. and Israel opposed the plan. But U.S. opposition was enough to prevent it from ever coming to fruition, and when the regional (explicitly *not* international) peace conference was planned for Madrid in 1991, Israel withheld its agreement to attend until the U.S. had guaranteed that the UN would not be allowed to participate.

In fact, when the Assembly invited PLO Chairman Yasir Arafat to address its members following the PLO's November 1988 Declaration of Independence, Washington, in what many viewed as a violation of its obligations as host country, announced it would not grant an entry visa (even the most limited kind, valid only within 25 miles of UN headquarters, granted to UN visitors from countries or organizations the U.S. deems hostile) to the Palestinian leader. The result, at a time of growing financial pressure on the UN, was a forced transplanting of the entire General Assembly, members, secretariat staff, secretaries, security guards, translators, etc., to Geneva for the one-day special session.

Tel Aviv, and many in the U.S., have often claimed that Israel is singled out for special hostility in the UN. But to the contrary, despite numerous resolutions criticizing or condemning or demanding a halt to its violations of international law and/or UN resolutions, Israel remains the only country, of the many facing such consistent criticisms, that has blithely avoided even the threat of serious enforcement. Its ally in Washington has seen to that.

U.S. OUT OF UNESCO

Throughout Ronald Reagan's years in office, especially during the tenure of his formidable Ambassador Kirkpatrick, the UN was scorned in U.S. policy circles. The U.S. first delayed, then reneged completely on its financial obligations to the organization, and its UN dues fell into serious arrears. Washington's positions, in the General Assembly and anywhere in the UN system outside the Security Council, were becoming increasingly isolated, and while important decisions were still largely limited to Council discussion, it could escape no one's attention that the UN's agencies and departments, outside the Council chambers, held to views quite at odds with the U.S. and its closest allies.

One of the agencies long associated with the South and the Non-Aligned Movement was UNESCO, the UN's Educational, Scientific and Cultural Organization. Charged with promoting collaboration and cooperation between countries, using science, education, communication, and culture as means of advancing peace and security in the world, UNESCO served as a key instrument of South-South communication, and a voice for North-South dialogue on questions of development and access to technology. For the U.S., UNESCO provided a convenient target for all that was wrong with the UN. After years of criticizing UNESCO, including charges of mismanagement, direct criticism of long-time Director-General Amadou Mahtar M'Bow, and finally the dreaded charge of "politicization" of the agency,* the U.S. withdrew its membership from the agency in 1984. (In fact, what appears to have pushed Washington to take the final step of renouncing its membership, was the agency's invitation to the PLO to participate as an observer in its cultural and educational work.)

By the time Reagan's second term was finished in 1988, Washington's UN dues were already over $1 billion in arrears. The money shortfall played a major role in the UN's continuing financial crises throughout the 1990s. Bush did very little to pay overdue assessments. And the Clinton administration, despite some efforts to make good on U.S. back debts, remained $1.2 billion in combined regular and peacekeeping arrears to the world organization as late as July 1995.

APRÈS LE DELUGE ...

But two things (at least) had changed during the eight long years of Reagan's revolution. In the world, we saw Soviet power on the verge of collapse. U.S. policy no longer needed to be — and indeed no longer could be — based on a scaffold of anti-Sovietism. Something different was needed.

And back at home, Reagan's successor, George Bush, came to power (unlike *his* successor Bill Clinton) with a strong interest in foreign policy. Significantly, Bush had himself been ambassador to the UN in the early 1970s, during the Nixon administration.

Multilateral initiatives were not exactly Nixon's strong suit. Stuck at the UN representing a White House which defined bombing Vietnam back to the stone age as the essence of foreign policy, while obsessed with Enemies Lists at home and about to implode over the Watergate scandal, Bush likely had plenty of time to observe the UN unhindered by a terrible press of work.

Certainly he couldn't have liked what he saw: decolonization well on its way towards ending colonial occupation of much of the South,

---

* This claim was often used as a catch-all reference to any UN effort to include national liberation movements in its work, to consult with, or to provide aid to those challenging U.S.- backed governments largely in the South.

the rise of the Non-Aligned Movement and its support for the Soviet Union because Moscow backed the Movement, the first stirrings of what would become the call for a New International Economic Order, all these were shaping the activist voices of the UN. But much of that existed only in unmet General Assembly goals; much of it, despite Assembly efforts, never fully reshaped UN programs. Bush watched the UN, and saw something else: possibilities.

Almost two decades later, the world would have irretrievably changed. George Bush would be president, and (despite being afflicted with wannabe Reaganism), he would remember the UN. Almost two decades later George Bush would have his chance.

Notes

1. Stephen Schlesinger, "Cryptanalysis for Peacetime: Codebreaking and the Birth and Structure of the United Nations," *Cryptologia* vol. 19, no. 3 (July 1995), pp. 219-220.
2. Gareth Evans, *Cooperating for Peace: The Global Agenda for the 1990s and Beyond* (St. Leonards, Australia: Allen & Unwin, 1993), p. 20.
3. Professor Innis Claude, University of Virginia, National Public Radio, June 26, 1995.
4. Schlesinger, "Cryptanalysis for Peactime," pp. 220-221.
5. Ibid., p. 224.
6. Ibid., p. 227.
7. Erskine Childers, "Introduction," in Childers (ed.), *Challenges to the United Nations* (New York: St. Martins Press, 1995), p. 3.
8. Ibid., p. 2.
9. Ibid., p. 4.
10. Amir Jamal, "The IMF and World Bank," in *Challenges to the United Nations*, p. 53.
11. Ibid., p. 53.

2

Center Stage:
The Role and Power of the
UN in Washington's Gulf War

THE PROLOGUE

By the late 1980s, the Soviet Union was already in the throes of crisis. Glasnost had opened up Soviet society to the West, and the lure of wannabe capitalism had proved overpowering. *Perestroika*'s effort to restructure Soviet society and especially its economy to meet those new illusions proved insufficient to guarantee the survival of the Soviet state and the unity of the numerous republics.

Responding to multi-faceted crises, the Soviet government turned inward, and the inter-superpower tensions of the Cold War began to fade. Moscow's support for its long-time friends in regional proxy-wars across the South began to dwindle, and once vexingly irresolvable conflicts suddenly seemed to have an end in sight. By the time George Bush was elected president in 1988, multilateral intervention aimed at settling these longstanding conflicts, rather than fueling them, seemed a real possibility.

United Nations involvement in overseeing or encouraging negotiated settlements had already begun, even in those regional conflicts most clearly tied to the Cold War (such as Nicaragua or Angola). But once the easing of strategic tensions between the superpowers had become an irreversible trend, an active role for the UN, and in many instances specifically for then-Secretary General Javier Perez de Cuellar, moved to the top of the international agenda.

The secretary-general himself, writing in the UN's own analysis of peacekeeping, noted, seemingly with surprise, that "in 1988 and 1989 the United Nations Security Council set up five new peacekeeping operations. This doubled, in two years, the number of operations in the field, a striking increase when it is remembered that only thirteen such operations had been established during the previous 40 years." His warning, that "it *is* an expensive activity; in 1989 the peacekeeping budget was almost as great as the Organization's regular budget,"[1] sounds almost laughable in the mid-1990s era of peacekeeping budgets far outstripping the UN's regular budgets. But increasing UN involvement served the needs of both Washington and Moscow, as it allowed the global organization to take over responsibility for crafting the logistical and detailed bases for peace negotiations or agreements in arenas where, for the local forces' sponsors, the overriding strategic purposes of the conflict had already ended. The UN was not, in these cases, imposing the political basis on which settlements should be reached; rather, the UN would be called in to write the texts, to satisfy as much as possible the domestic political needs of both sides, to provide ceasefire line monitors, election training and officials, humanitarian support to both sides including to newly demobilized soldiers from both the government and rebel sides, to oversee and encourage the accommodations required to attain what the U.S. and its Northern allies, at least, would be satisfied to call "peace."

By 1988, settlements, or at least significant motion towards settlements, had been achieved under UN auspices in Afghanistan, Namibia, and the decade-long devastating Iran-Iraq war. That same year, Perez de Cuellar accepted the Nobel Peace Prize on behalf of the UN's Blue Helmet peacekeepers. In 1989 and 1990 agreements were signed leading to settlements in Nicaragua, El Salvador, and Cambodia.

The UN was seconded to respond to that new potential, it did not create it. And in virtually all of those cases, the U.S. simply allowed the UN to organize the trajectory towards peace; Washington did not play an aggressive role in initiating the UN's new assignments,* and did not appear to view the UN as a major new U.S. partner in international affairs.

The unanticipated emergence of the UN as a useful instrument in institutionalizing agreements made possible through the winding down of the Cold War appears to have caught the Reagan administra-

---

* The partial exception was in Namibia, where the real negotiations leading to the withdrawal of South Africa and the independence of the country took place in lengthy three-party negotiations involving the U.S., South Africa, and Cuba, and focused primarily, in Washington's view, on insuring the withdrawal of Cuban troops from Angola. Once that was assured, South Africa, where apartheid was also close to defeat, had no support from Washington to remain in Namibia. The UN was given an unprecedentedly broad mandate of not only verifying the Cuban withdrawal, but, in Namibia, setting up a virtual quasi-government, whose brief included everything from overseeing elections to training police officials to creating a national government and educational and justice systems in the former colony.

tion unawares in its last weeks and months. Though playing the determining role, of course, in ensuring that U.S. domination would emerge unchallenged from the end of the U.S.-Soviet contention, Reagan's State Department did not on its own initiative turn to the UN as a significant player in the end-of-an-era drama.

When President George Bush was inaugurated in January of 1989, the collapse of the Eastern European socialist states was already imminent. The focus of foreign policy for the new administration lay in claiming credit for and laying the groundwork for maximizing the U.S. benefit from the new political terrain being created in Europe, and in hastening the demise of the Soviet Union. The U.S. was now a superpower without a sparring partner. And to the degree that multilateral organizations were anywhere among the priorities of the new administration's policy-makers, the economic behemoths of the International Monetary Fund and the World Bank, both already slated for major roles in shaping post-Cold War life in Eastern and Central Europe, were far higher on the agenda.

In the Middle East, the Bush administration had continued the cordial ties of its predecessors with the Iraqi leader Saddam Hussein. Viewing Iraq as a critical balance against a resurgence of Iranian power in the oil-glutted region, Washington had, through several subsequent administrations, essentially encouraged the Iran-Iraq war to rage unchecked, as millions were slaughtered. The tilt had been towards Iraq, certainly, viewed not so much as a lesser evil but as a more compliant one.

Of the two parties, Iraq was far more desperate for military assistance. The Pentagon viewed its pro-Iraqi tilt, and the military largesse provided to Baghdad as a result, as necessary to keep the war alive. Throughout the Iran-Iraq war, the Pentagon had shared satellite information, including highly advanced intelligence material obtained from overflights by AWACS (Airborne Warning and Control Aircraft Systems) planes, with Baghdad's military.

Washington was increasingly worried about Baghdad's ability to withstand the Iranian onslaught. "We cannot stand to see Iraq defeated," Assistant Secretary of Defense Richard Armitage had testified in 1987.[2] For Washington, as compared to the perceived threat of an Iranian resurgence, Iraq's own regional ambitions were of little consequence. In her famous tête-à-tête with Saddam Hussein on July 25, 1990, just a few days before Baghdad's attack over the border into Kuwait, U.S. Ambassador April Glaspie told the Iraqi president that "I have a direct instruction from the president to seek better relations with Iraq .... We have no opinion on the Arab-Arab conflicts, like your

border disagreement with Kuwait .... James Baker has directed our official spokesmen to emphasize this instruction."[3]
Then came August 2nd. And nothing was the same.

CRISIS MODE

From the beginning of the Gulf crisis, it seemed the United Nations was at the center of the whirlwind. Meetings went on around the clock, decisions were made, and, in the eyes of the world, it was the international organization that took the world to war. From the first nearly-unanimous Security Council vote on resolution 660, condemning the Iraqi invasion and laying the groundwork for comprehensive anti-Iraq sanctions, through the precedent-setting resolution 678 granting UN authorization for the use of force against Iraq, to the harshly punitive ceasefire terms set out in resolution 687, it was the United Nations that was at the center of decision-making. It was the Security Council that imposed deadlines on Iraq, and refused to delimit the Pentagon's jurisdiction to launch the battle and carry it out however and wherever it saw fit. It was the United Nations' war.

But by the end of the first stage of the crisis, by the spring of 1991, the international organization was already identified, in many quarters, especially in the South, as one of the key victims of Washington's Gulf War. UN independence, UN integrity, and the UN's peace-making identity all were undermined by Bush administration coercion.

UN involvement in the crisis began on the very first day, on August 2, 1990. Within hours of the Iraqi invasion of Kuwait, U.S. Ambassador to the UN Thomas Pickering called for an emergency session of the Security Council. While the sudden urgency of the U.S. response raised a few eyebrows around UN headquarters (after all, the fact that Iraq had enjoyed Washington's backing through much of the eight-year Iran-Iraq war was public knowledge, and the Glaspie statements to Saddam Hussein were only eight days old), there was certainly little support for the Iraqi move. Baghdad's invasion clearly represented a violation of international law and the Charter of the United Nations. Ambassador Pickering had no difficulty orchestrating a 14-0 Security Council vote of condemnation. (Yemen, the sole Arab country on the Council, declined to participate in the vote.)

The U.S. ambassador's high-profile role in directing the Security Council, and his continued insistence on imposing, at virtually any cost, unanimity in Council decisions, were to become hallmarks of Bush administration strategy throughout the Gulf crisis. And the imprimatur of the United Nations on Washington's military build-up in the Gulf quickly emerged as a critical component of George Bush's "new world order."

In the U.S., and throughout the North, there was the rhetoric and appearance of an international organization mobilizing the world to confront and punish an international outlaw. But the reality was far different. On the eve of the war, Middle East scholar Eqbal Ahmad spoke at a teach-in broadcast across the U.S. and called it "the use of a multilateral instrument to carry out a unilateral war."[4] It was, ultimately, a clear U.S. exercise of what one United Nations official privately called "raw power."

SOVIET DECLINE BRINGS UNIPOLARITY

George Bush's selection of the UN as his favored instrument to legitimate his sudden war against Iraq did not reflect a new-found respect for international law and multilateral diplomacy. Of far greater influence in that choice was the demise of the Soviet Union as a superpower capable of challenging U.S. intervention around the world, leading to the emergence of what Bush dubbed the "new world order," shaping the new terms of U.S. domination.

White House and State Department spin-masters went to work, and a public relations campaign of global proportions was created. It would rely not on the outmoded image of the superpower U.S. battling its Soviet counterpart, but instead on the vision of the U.S. as the leader of a brave new free world coalition, even including the Soviet Union, operating against tyranny in the name of all the nations of the world. New legitimacy and importance for — matched by enhanced U.S. control of — the United Nations would be a critical tool.

For Washington, the stakes were high. Bush insisted that his military build-up in the Gulf was on behalf of a grand international coalition, of the "whole world" against Saddam Hussein. And gaining the support of the Security Council was crucial to carrying out his strategic agenda. He needed the vote on resolution 678, authorizing the use of force against Iraq, to counter potential resistance both from wary allies, especially in the Middle East, and from a nascent congressional unease. And he was desperate for the vote to be unanimous.

The Bush administration's need for a military confrontation, and a clear military victory, had far less to do with Iraq's ostensible regional threat than with a broader global goal of insuring Washington's continuity as a full-fledged strategic superpower — implying worldwide military reach as well as economic and political power. With the Cold War already winding down, Bush was determined that there be no uncertainty about whether the one remaining superpower had any intention of folding its tents. U.S. domination of international political, military, and strategic relations, would grow even stronger in the absence of its superpower contender. Post-Cold War Washington might be a superpower without a sparring partner, but it would remain a superpower nonetheless.

That meant a military outcome was virtually inevitable from the moment the U.S. decided to turn what might have remained a containable regional crisis, into a global conflagration. Simply ending Iraq's occupation of Kuwait through a negotiated solution would not be sufficient for the far-reaching American goals. For the U.S. aim was not only, or even primarily, an end to Iraq's occupation of Kuwait and its control of Kuwaiti oil. The real goal was the reaffirmation of U.S. strategic power; the vital oil-rich Middle East was a traditional center of U.S. hegemony that Washington was not about to abandon "just" because the long-time raison d'être of U.S. intervention in that region, the threat of Soviet competition, had collapsed.

Internationally, the Arab regimes allied with Washington all faced varying degrees of instability. Lack of democracy and/or autocratic near-feudal monarchies characterized all of the Arab components of the anti-Iraq coalition. It was not surprising that most of those governments showed tremendous ambiguity about joining an alliance that could exacerbate challenges to their continued rule.

Egypt's impoverished 55 million people, for example, largely opposed sending troops to the Gulf, and the resulting street confrontations seriously destabilized Hosni Mubarak's government, despite the billions of dollars in debt relief paid to Egypt to assure its backing. Syrian President Hafez al-Assad found his militarily-buttressed legitimacy undermined, with his historic role of leader of the "confrontation states" arrayed against Israel fading as his troops moved into the desert to join those of Israel's superpower sponsor. Even the wealthy and pliant citizens of Saudi Arabia and the oil-bloated Gulf statelets began to whisper a few concerns about how long the alien troops would be present to pollute the soil of the sacred lands of Islam. In some areas, most notably in Saudi Arabia itself, nascent movements for democracy emerged with embarrassing questions for the heretofore unchallenged princes of the royal family. For all of these governments, broad multilateralism was a requisite cover factor in joining the U.S.

Domestically, despite Bush's claims of a broad American consensus backing his build-up to war, Congress remained sorely divided. Few opposed the goal of forcing Iraq out of Kuwait. But many in both the House and Senate had serious misgivings about going to war and shedding American blood before sanctions had been given a decent chance to bring Saddam Hussein to his knees.

Further incentive for the U.S. to turn to UN endorsement as a legitimating factor centered on the Soviet Union. The threat of Cold War vetoes had often left the Security Council paralyzed. But now economic and political crisis overwhelmed Soviet President Mikhail Gorbachev, and Moscow's European allies were undergoing massive transformations and new alienation from their one-time sponsor. The resulting demise in Soviet global reach meant that a Soviet veto of U.S. plans had become an impossibility. The Soviets were now too dependent on U.S. and Western economic aid, and too committed to a strategy of co-operation in order to get that aid, even if it meant collapsing under Washington's demands. Imposing an anti-Iraq mandate on the now compliant Council would be almost too easy; for the White House it was an irresistible lure.

In just two or three years, the world had become uni-polar. So, for the first time, U.S. strategic clout in the Security Council was unopposed. On the night of January 16, 1991, during the first hours of the U.S. bombardment of Baghdad, a few journalists caught up with then-Soviet Ambassador Yuliy Vorontsov as he headed up a UN escalator. Since the Soviet Union has no troops in the Gulf, he was asked, aren't you concerned about the Pentagon alone making all the decisions for a war being waged in your name? "Who are we," he answered sadly, after a long pause, "to say they should not?"

Over the years the U.S. had used its Council veto with a vengeance — most notably and consistently to prevent passage of resolutions criticizing Israel. Since 1967 alone, the U.S. vetoed over 40 such resolutions. And in the UN generally throughout those years, Washington remained a grudging and half-hearted participant in multilateral diplomacy. The Bush administration's 1990 decision to re-seize control of the UN as a crucial part of U.S. diplomacy can best be viewed in the context of changes in international power as a whole. The Security Council of the 1990s reflects less the West's domination over the East, than the sharply evident Northern domination of the South. With the Soviet Union and its Russian heir unable to challenge U.S. interventionist aspirations and largely willing to tacitly back them in the name of cooperation, at least four of the five permanent Council members function within the U.S.-led Northern power alliance.

Only China remains a question mark. Beijing's need for economic assistance and its desire to establish a more legitimate and influential role in international diplomatic circles make it unlikely to stand against U.S. interests. It still faces Third World development challenges, however, but its skyrocketing economic growth and billion-strong market potential give Beijing, in the mid-1990s, new buffers against the North's pressure.

BACK AT HEADQUARTERS

When the August 2 emergency session of the Security Council convened, there was little disagreement with condemning Iraq's invasion and demanding its withdrawal from Kuwait. Yemen's refusal to participate in the Council's vote, however, marked an early challenge to the U.S. search for unanimity. Yemen had only recently, and still precariously, been unified, merging the northern pro-Western and near feudal Republic of Yemen and the socialist-oriented People's Democratic Republic of Yemen in the south. Sana'a took seriously its responsibilities as the sole Arab country serving on the Council, to represent as far as possible the broad collective interests of the entire Arab world. Yemen's position reminded the Council that the United Nations Charter requires that regional solutions be relied on first, before looking to international intervention to solve regional crises.

At the time of Iraq's invasion, the Arab world viewed the problem largely as an intra-Arab, regional, and very likely containable crisis. When Iraqi tanks rolled into Kuwait, an Arab League meeting in Cairo was about to go into session. Jordan's King Hussein, a long-time friend of President Bush from the period when Bush headed the CIA and the king was an asset of the agency, called the White House. He pleaded for time, for the Arab League to find an Arab solution, a regional solution. You've got 48 hours, Bush replied.

It surprised no one that the Arab League could not resolve the crisis in two days. An assembly of widely diverse governments, the regional group could hardly agree on lunch in 48 hours. King Hussein contacted Bush again, this time bolstered by a plea from Egypt's Mubarak. They pleaded for more time. No dice, came the White House answer; we're sending the troops.

After an early, and half-hearted, warning against the danger of foreign intervention, Egypt shifted to full support for an Arab League vote against Iraq, opening the way for League support for the U.S. military build-up. Under intense pressure from Cairo as well as from Riyadh and the now-exiled Kuwaiti royals, the Ministerial Council of the Arab League debated a resolution to condemn Iraq, and a jagged split divided the organization. Egypt, Syria, Lebanon, Morocco, Somalia, Djibouti, and the six states of the Arab Gulf voted to condemn Iraq. Opposition came only from Iraq and Libya. Jordan, Algeria, and

Yemen abstained, while Palestine (which is a full member of the Arab League), the Sudan, and Mauritania "expressed reservations." Tunisia did not participate.

The summit meeting scheduled in Riyadh for the following week was canceled. In response to the League's inability to resolve the crisis, and the weakness it indicated in Arab unity and the Arab state system as a whole, the Arab League's long-time ambassador to the United Nations, Clovis Maksoud, resigned his position

But the political and diplomatic efforts within and by the Arab League had little impact on the global stage of the UN Security Council. The UN Charter (Article 52) calls on regional organizations to "make every effort to achieve pacific settlement of local disputes through such regional arrangements or by such regional agencies before referring them to the Security Council." It goes on to mandate the Security Council itself to "encourage the development of pacific settlements of local disputes through such regional arrangements or by such regional agencies either on the initiative of the states concerned or by reference from the Security Council." In this case, of course, the regional organization never had a chance. It is certainly not clear whether further negotiations by the Arab League might have led to a solution ending Iraq's occupation of Kuwait. What is clear is that the organization was denied a serious opportunity to try.

By August 6, only four days after Iraq's troops entered Kuwait, resolution 661 was adopted, imposing harsh economic sanctions against Iraq. Yemen and Cuba abstained, expressing concerns about both the legal implications of imposing sanctions (technically viewed as an act of war under international law), and about the impact of the sanctions on civilians in Iraq.

Other resolutions followed in rapid succession. Every one was drafted by the U.S. delegation, and lobbied for at the highest levels. For every one, nothing short of unanimity would satisfy the tireless Pickering and his aides. Resolutions 662 (August 9) rejecting Iraq's claimed annexation of Kuwait, and 664 (August 18) calling for the release of third-country nationals held in Iraq and Kuwait, were both adopted unanimously. Resolution 665 (August 25), tightening the economic embargo with a naval blockade, passed with Yemen and Cuba again abstaining. Resolution 666 (September 13) tightened the embargo again with greater restrictions on food and medical supplies imported to Iraq; Yemen and Cuba opposed. Resolutions 667 (September 16) and 669 (September 24), both passed unanimously, called on Iraq to restore protection to embassies and diplomatic personnel, and took responsibility for the increasing requests for financial assistance from countries affected by the anti-Iraq embargo. Resolution 670 (September 25) expanded the blockade to aircraft; only Cuba voted no. Resolution 674 condemned Iraq's treatment of foreign nationals, claimed other instances of violations of prior resolutions, and called on the secretary-general to use his good offices to help resolve the conflict; Yemen and Cuba abstained, concerned here about the double standards implicit in the resolution. Resolution 677 (September 28) condemned Iraq's effort to change the demographic composition of Kuwait; it passed unanimously.

But all those resolutions were merely a run-up to the big game itself, the hard-won Security Council endorsement of a U.S. war against Iraq. Throughout the autumn, that was the prize eagerly sought by Pickering and his team. The Bush administration's efforts to construct strong majority momentum in the Council for the escalating anti-Iraq build-up seemed to be working. Support for a military solution was broadening. Carrots and sticks were wielded, more and more carrots were accepted. There seemed to be only one major glitch in the operation: the question of Palestine.

The U.S. need to maintain the loyalty of its hesitant (and sometimes new) Arab allies in its anti-Iraq build-up meant that it could no longer routinely veto resolutions criticizing or condemning Israel for actions against Palestinians in the occupied territories. But those new conditions did not mean that Israeli treatment of Palestinians improved, or that Palestinian efforts to stop the repression through UN action would be halted.

The killing of more than 20 Palestinians by Israeli troops in Jerusalem on October 8, 1990 set in motion a two-and-one-half-month-long process in which Non-Aligned members of the Council, the secretary-general, and the Palestinians battled the U.S. and Israel over whether, or how, the Council should respond to the persistent violations of Palestinian rights inherent in Israel's continuing occupation. (See chapter 9.)

In a context of U.S. efforts to maintain support from sometimes reluctant Arab allies for its military build-up against Iraq's occupation of Kuwait, the double standard evident in Washington's refusal to condemn Israel's much longer occupation of Palestine, its rejection of "linkage" as it was called, created a serious challenge for the U.S. diplomatic team at the UN.

THE UNITED NATIONS GOES TO WAR

But the long and painful debate over the Palestine resolution also served to divert some international attention from the fundamental goal of Washington's UN strategy during that fateful autumn.

With the military build-up well under way, the Bush administration turned to diplomatic weapons in its Gulf arsenal, and the UN became the venue of battle. While UN watchers' eyes were on the Palestine debate, long-range U.S. eyes remained focused on the Gulf. The ultimate UN goal was a resolution authorizing Bush's war-in-the-making against Iraq, to allow him to wage that war in the name of the United Nations. The vote was planned for the end of November, the month in which the U.S. held the Council presidency.

It would not be enough, in these circumstances, to win a bare-bones nine-vote Council (the minimum needed for passage of a Council resolution); that would look embarrassingly equivocal. So to assure a vote that could be spin-mastered to look like an overwhelming endorsement, U.S. diplomats went to work with every economic and political weapon in their considerable diplomatic arsenal.

Ironically, while the diplomatic/financial campaign was waged relentlessly throughout August, September, October, and even later, culminating in the November 29th vote, the most concentrated U.S. efforts at coercing and/or buying support came during one of the most highly acclaimed UN conferences ever held: the 1990 World Summit for Children. Held at UN headquarters in New York at the end of September, the summit provided a convenient venue for Pickering's team to plead its case, whisper its threats, and sell its wares to a broad high-level audience concentrated in one place. When the summit was hailed as an example of the possibilities of post-Cold War global cooperation, only a few journalists pointed out that its seeming concord was rooted in the complete absence of deadlines and enforcement mechanisms in the final document, effectively leaving the wealthy countries to implement whatever they liked, and walk away from the rest. Virtually no one pointed out that beneath the appearance of the conference's international concern for children lay a far colder, far harsher, and far more power-driven agenda: U.S. officials were on the prowl, wrapping up commitments from one country after another to insure the appearance of unanimity for war.

Some of the economic bribes were dispensed to countries not even on the Security Council, as part of a campaign to win the recipients' support for *their* allies on the Council to vote with the U.S. The $7 billion in debt relief to Egypt was one such example of U.S. largesse. Saudi Arabia wiped out another $4 billion of Cairo's debt. The U.S. used its considerable leverage with the World Bank and the International Monetary Fund to dispense bribes to a wide range of countries, aiming at broadening Washington's international support. Both institutions made loans to Jordan, Turkey, and Egypt on unusually favorable terms; the World Bank allocated some soft-loan funds to several African countries to buffer the effect of higher oil prices caused by UN sanctions against Iraq.

Virtually every developing country on the Security Council was offered new economic perks in return for a vote in favor of the U.S. war: Colombia, impoverished Ethiopia, and Zaire (already fully in thrall to the U.S.) were all offered new economic aid packages from Washington, access to World Bank credits, and in some cases rearrangements of International Monetary Fund grants or loans.

Military deals were cut as well. Ethiopia's government was given access to new military aid after a long denial of arms to that civil war-wracked nation. Unstable Colombia was also offered a new package of military assistance.

China was the sole member of the Perm Five not yet toeing the U.S. line. It was common knowledge among UN-based journalists that China was looking for two major concessions in return for allowing the U.S. resolution to go through without a veto. One was Washington's support for Beijing's return to international diplomatic legitimacy after 18 months of post-Tienanmen Square massacre isolation. The second was economic development aid (since Tienanmen, only emergency assistance and humanitarian aid had been offered). On November 28, the day before the vote authorizing the use of force against Iraq, the White House announced a high-profile meeting between President Bush and Chinese Foreign Minister Qian Qichen, the first since Tienanmen Square, to be held the day after the vote. It was designed to officially welcome Beijing back into the international diplomatic fold. China duly abstained on the use of force resolution. And less than one week later, the World Bank announced that China would be given access to $114 million in new economic aid.

But carrots were not the only tool; sticks were used too. The U.S. would see that those countries who opposed the U.S. resolution, Cuba and Yemen, would, as much as possible, pay a high and very public price.

Against Cuba the U.S. had few options. Washington's 30-year-long diplomatic and economic blockade against Havana meant the State Department had few new diplomatic or economic weapons available to it. But in an interesting example of just how far the U.S. was willing to go to try to gain support for its resolution, Washington agreed to its first foreign minister-level meeting with Cuba in over 30 years. The brief meeting between Secretary of State James Baker and Foreign Minister Isidoro Malmierca was held at an East Side hotel in Manhattan on the eve of the November 29 vote. The encounter received little publicity, and officially was belittled by U.S. diplomats as nothing more than an ordinary meeting between the Council president and a Council member. (With the U.S. holding the Council presidency in November, Baker had come to New York to preside personally over the vote on the use of force resolution. He had asked all other Council foreign ministers to attend the session as well.) But the unprecedented meeting appeared designed for Baker to assess close-up whether there might be any possibility of convincing Cuba to stop its efforts to win other countries away from Washington's war. To no one's surprise, the effort failed.

AUTHORIZING WAR

The operative language of Security Council resolution 678 "authorizes Member States cooperating with the Government of Kuwait ... to use all necessary means" to implement prior resolutions "and to restore international peace and security in the area." The resolution passed by a vote of 12 to 2, with one abstention. It was introduced and sponsored by the U.S., the Soviet Union, Great Britain, and Canada. The negative votes were cast by Cuba and Yemen; China abstained.

The resolution was designed to give Washington a free hand in beginning hostilities against Iraq. Taken under the provisions of Chapter VII of the Charter, which authorize the Council to use force against threats to international peace and security, resolution 678 did not make even a pretense of requiring further UN consultation, let alone UN or multilateral control, for the launching of a war in the Gulf.

And even as the war moves escalated, the U.S. continued deploying its diplomatic weapons. Yemen, the one Arab member of the Council, voted against resolution 678. Since its unification in the late 1980s, Yemen had maintained cordial ties with Washington. But now the small and impoverished country was to be made the example to the world of the consequences of violating a U.S.-ordered consensus. Within minutes of the Council vote, Yemen's Ambassador Abdallah Saleh al-Ashtal was informed by a U.S. diplomat, in full earshot of the world via the UN broadcasting system, that "that will be the most expensive 'no' vote you ever cast." Three days later the U.S. completely cut its $70 million aid package to Yemen, one of the poorest countries in the region. The cut-off significantly exacerbated the economic crisis in Yemen caused by Saudi Arabia's expulsion of hundreds of thousands of Yemeni workers, as punishment for their government's refusal to back the U.S.-led troop build-up in the Gulf.

But even beyond the pay-offs and threats to the developing countries, the crucial new relationship the U.S. had to forge in the Council was with the Soviets. If the Bush-Baker strategy of using the Security

Council to create the appearance of an international consensus was going to work, the world would have to see Moscow fall into line as part of the U.S.-orchestrated new world order. And the strategic weakness rooted in the escalating political and economic crises facing Mikhail Gorbachev and the Soviet leadership made it possible. The arrangement was sweetened with a $4 billion aid package the U.S. negotiated for the Saudi government to pay to Moscow, but it was the Soviet collapse as a superpower capable of influencing events around the world, at least able to check U.S. ambitions, that set the new terms.

After the passage of resolution 678, authorizing the use of force against Iraq after January 15, activity quieted down around the United Nations. A majority of the Council had agreed not to meet formally again until after the deadline, to avoid giving Iraq the appearance of weakness. In the last weeks before the deadline, several other diplomatic initiatives were explored. Iran attempted a negotiated solution, supported by the Soviet Union, and another framework was proposed by a group of non-aligned leaders led by Daniel Ortega of Nicaragua, India's Rajiv Gandhi, and the German Social-Democrat Willi Brandt. There were others. Some approaches seemed to have a plausible chance of averting war, some seemed foolhardy. The Iraqi response to several was relatively forthcoming. But each time there seemed to be a potential way out, Washington played a new round of "move the goalposts," insuring that each new diplomatic effort would fail. It was clear that neither the UN-sponsored nor other diplomatic moves would be allowed to divert the U.S. march towards war.

On the eve of the January 15 deadline, UN Secretary-General Javier Perez de Cuellar made a high-profile last-minute trip to Baghdad to meet with the Iraqi president. When he returned, he closeted himself behind closed doors with the Security Council to report that he had failed to bring peace, that Saddam Hussein had refused to withdraw from Kuwait. The UN refused to release the minutes of Perez de Cuellar's hours-long meeting with Saddam Hussein.

Obtained through diplomatic channels, a copy of the secret transcript sheds some light on the SG's reluctance to go public. In a crucial section of the Perez de Cuellar-Hussein meeting, the Iraqi president discusses U.S. influence in the Security Council. The following exchange takes place:

> *Hussein*: We have said and still assert that we seek peace and that we are prepared to shoulder our responsibilities as part of the universal family of the United Nations. But are the others ready to shoulder their responsibilities on the same basis? Are they willing to apply international legality and international law on Mid-

dle East issues and on each issue on the basis of its background and the justice and fairness that characterize each of these issues? Note what the President of the United States said: He is talking about procedural matters which do not touch the substance. The substance is of interest to us because we are a vanquished nation. He is talking about the possibility of withdrawing "ground forces" once the "crisis is over." He did not mention anything about withdrawing air or naval forces. He is talking about the possibility of easing "some" economic measures, and did not talk about the economic measures, all of them.

Perez de Cuellar: These were not my decisions, but the resolutions of the Security Council.

Hussein: These are American resolutions. This is an American age. What the United States wants at present is the thing that is passed; and not what the Security Council wants.

Perez de Cuellar: I agree with you as much as the matter involves me.

That acknowledgment by the secretary-general, that "what the U.S. wants" is what gets passed in the Council, would likely have been a source of embarrassment for the 71-year-old Perez de Cuellar. But of even more significance was the general tone of the conversation as a whole, and especially the remarks of Saddam Hussein. The Iraqi leader's statements, while not making explicit promises, did not reflect an absolute rejection of diplomatic possibilities. There was a certain amount of flexibility, an apparent willingness to consider diplomatic alternatives based on an Iraqi withdrawal from Kuwait, possibly linked with a broader regional settlement. Whether these possibilities might have become realities will never be known; all that is certain is that the unequivocal "no" indicated in the SG's report to the Security Council is not reflected in the meeting's unauthorized transcript.

MOVING TOWARDS WAR

The January 15 deadline passed quietly. The following evening, the Security Council was again in session late, again debating a resolution focused on Israeli actions against the Palestinians. It was almost 6:30.

Someone came down and told the cluster of journalists that they had seen "something" on television upstairs. "Something" seemed to be going on in the skies above Baghdad. News was scant.

The UN was taking the world to war, but the UN had nothing to say about it. The thousand points of light in Baghdad's sky were from U.S. planes flown by U.S. pilots dropping U.S. bombs. The United Nations was out of the loop.

During the weeks of the air war, some diplomatic efforts continued. The Soviet Union and Iran attempted to forge a settlement before the ground war began. The U.S. and Great Britain remained committed to a no ceasefire, no withdrawal, nothing-less-than-surrender scenario. But within the U.S.-led coalition and among some members of the Security Council, particularly the Soviet Union, opposition to the Washington-London no-compromise axis was growing.

Moscow was willing to support Iraq's agreement to withdraw from Kuwait under the terms set by resolution 660. The U.S.-British position at the time was that that wasn't good enough anymore, that Baghdad now must accept and implement all resolutions simultaneously. Soviet Ambassador Yuliy Vorontsov stated that while he was "in favor of Iraq accepting all 12 UN resolutions, 660 is the one we started with."

When Moscow indicated an openness to accepting Iraq's withdrawal, the U.S. added new terms, dashing any hope of avoiding a ground war. Bush demanded that the statement regarding withdrawal be made personally by President Saddam Hussein, that the statement simultaneously accept all relevant UN resolutions, and, significantly, that withdrawing Iraqi troops must leave their weapons behind. Otherwise, Bush stated, there would be no ceasefire and retreating soldiers would continue to be targeted by U.S. and allied forces.

Saddam Hussein answered with a 3 a.m. speech calling on his forces to withdraw from Kuwait, but throughout the day Iraqi soldiers trying to retreat were bombarded with U.S. cluster-bombs.

In the closed-door all-night Security Council meeting on February 28, some discussions apparently focused on the question of a ceasefire. Soviet officials in Moscow at the highest level went on record in support of an immediate ceasefire. Deputy Foreign Minister Alexander Belonogov stated that "we would like to hope that such a declaration of the Security Council would be unanimous and that it would facilitate the speediest possible end to bloodshed and an end to hostilities." In the early morning hours Gorbachev's spokesman, Vitaly Ignatenko, supported the ceasefire idea, saying that "it is in everyone's interest that the war end today; Saddam Hussein has practically thrown out the white flag, he has capitulated." Gorbachev himself suggested that superpower relations were "still very fragile," and hinted that U.S.-Soviet relations might be at stake in the settlement of the Gulf War.

This apparent Soviet commitment to a ceasefire revived talk at the UN about the possibility of splits within the U.S.-led anti-Iraq coalition. Western diplomats, including several usually genial press attaches, were aggressively outspoken throughout the day in defending the no-ceasefire position. Sir David Hannay, Britain's ambassador, described the situation as one in which the "good news is that Iraq accepts 660; the bad news is that it only accepts 660." At the end of the day, the Security Council capitulated and the U.S. carried the day. Diplomacy was left behind, and the air war took to the ground. Yemen's ambassador Abdallah Saleh al-Ashtal, dismayed with the UN failure to reach a political solution, noted, "This is the only time the Security Council has been reluctant to facilitate the withdrawal of an occupying force in compliance with its own resolution."

THE NON-CEASEFIRE "HALT IN HOSTILITIES"

The "UN war" came and went, with the UN having very little to say about it. The center of gravity remained in Washington. Resolution 678 had been designed to give Washington a UN credential but impose no UN control in its war against Iraq. The use of military force was unlimited by UN oversight in duration or destructiveness.

In early March, the U.S. introduced resolution 686, calling for a temporary halt in hostilities. But it explicitly did not call for a ceasefire, and there were rumors of some discontent among Council members. A now-familiar pressure campaign swung into action. New bribes and old threats were the order of the day.

The vote had been expected throughout the late afternoon hours of March 3, and as the meeting stretched into the early evening, journalists and diplomats alike were growing impatient. It appeared that the ambassadors of both Zimbabwe and Ecuador, two important Non-Aligned members of the Council, were late.

When they finally showed up, the vote took place quickly. Both Zimbabwe and Ecuador voted with the United States. According to knowledgeable diplomatic sources, both ambassadors were late because they had been closeted at their respective missions, getting last minute instructions on how to respond to Washington's latest pressure tactics.

In Quito, the Bush administration's ambassador to Ecuador brought to bear the classic kind of coercion so often used against Latin America: a meeting to remind ranking Ecuadoran officials of the unspecified devastating political and economic consequences that would result from a vote against Washington's non-ceasefire resolution.

Against Zimbabwe, the bribe offer was made in New York, to Harare's UN diplomats. The pressure came in the form of a promise of new assistance, specifically access to low-price oil supplies that the impoverished African country so desperately needed. The oil was to be guaranteed by the just-restored government of the Kuwaiti emir, in return for a pro-U.S. vote.

The pressure worked. The resolution passed.

Finally, resolution 687, drafted by the U.S. and calling for a stringently regulated ceasefire, was put on the table on April 3.

The resolution did not hold out much of a promise for peace. As Yemen's Ambassador al-Ashtal described it, "We want a situation of peace — with this ceasefire we are still in a state of war. We need peace."

The resolution imposed drastic controls on post-war Iraq. Along with the expected destruction of Iraq's chemical and biological weapons, it continued indefinitely an absolute international embargo against all arms sales to Iraq, apparently meant to include such standard items as bullets for sidearms carried by Baghdad's police officers.

Much of the opposition to the resolution centered on its failure to place arms control in a regional context. While the preamble refers to "the objective of the establishment of a nuclear weapons-free zone in the region of the Middle East," the resolution's binding terms refer only to Iraq's weapons. No mention was made of the 200 high-density nuclear bombs possessed by Israel, the only nuclear power in the region.

Significantly, tight economic sanctions also remained in place, insuring that Iraq remained impoverished and financially dependent. The resolution harshly restricted Iraq's oil exports. When exporting oil was finally to be allowed, a major percentage of the income was designated to pay compensation for Iraq's war-generated debts. While easing some controls on food and medicine, the resolution did not allow Iraq access to vitally needed consumer goods and the equipment needed to rebuild the country's devastated infrastructure. Further, by denying Iraq the right to sell its oil, the resolution insured its inability to purchase badly needed food and medical supplies.

One of the most hotly contested portions of the U.S. draft, of special concern to the Non-Aligned caucus within the Security Council, was the question of the Iraq-Kuwait border. Resolution 687 demanded that the two countries accept a border described in the minutes of a bilateral meeting in 1963, which had never been ratified and remained in dispute. Iraqi diplomatic sources, as well as Non-Aligned members of the Council, stated the view that the appropriate venue for resolving such conflicts must be the International Court of Justice, not the Security Council. It wasn't until 1994, during a small-scale flare-up of U.S.-Iraqi tensions, that Baghdad would accept the new border.

There was a great deal of unease in the Council about the precedent the resolution would set. Never had the UN been put in the position of guaranteeing a disputed border not accepted by the two parties.

Cuba introduced a series of amendments, all of them ultimately unsuccessful, many of which were designed to frame a post-Gulf War settlement in broader regional terms. For example, it added language to the U.S. resolution that would have placed demands for Iraqi disarmament in the context of being "a first step towards the full elimination of weapons of mass destruction and weapon systems incompatible with the aim of achieving a comprehensive, just, and lasting peace in the Middle East."

The overall impact of the resolution was to keep Iraq economically dependent and militarily vulnerable, but territorially more or less intact. And by leaving economic sanctions in place, the U.S.-drafted resolution virtually insured continued instability inside Iraq, as the population struggled to rebuild shattered lives.

But despite its unpopularity with the Council, the resolution passed easily. Only Cuba voted no. Even Yemen was only able to abstain, along with Ecuador. The rest of the Council voted yes.

THE POST-GULF UN

The passage and implementation of the ceasefire resolution embodied the end of the UN's center-stage role in the Gulf. While it would remain engaged in the post-war chaos engulfing the region, trying to orchestrate relief for the Kurds and verification of Iraq's weapon destruction, there was no longer the illusion of UN decision-making power.

The follow-up areas did, however, raise some new issues for future UN debate. The UN involvement with the Kurds clearly violated the Charter's prohibition against interfering in the internal affairs of a member state. A number of UN officials, led by some French diplomats, began to raise openly the question of whether that prohibition was not out of date, and whether an actual change in the Charter to authorize an international obligation to intervene for humanitarian protection would not be more appropriate. Related questions about peacekeeping vs. peacemaking would shape UN debates for years to come, as the organization struggled to respond to new kinds of conflicts in a world no longer bi-polar.

But from the start, while the issue simmered in the quiet corners of the delegates lounge, a number of countries, especially from the Non-Aligned Movement, expressed grave concerns about such a development. The issue of who (read: from the Northern powers) would make the determinations justifying multilateral intervention remained a serious concern to the South.

Much of the future of the United Nations still lay with the United States. Washington's high profile projection of the UN as a part of its global strategy in the Gulf was a new, almost experimental, approach. It would be some time before U.S. policy-makers came to any agreement on the strategic value of the UN — and after a couple of years of deeper involvement, their differences would emerge stronger than ever.

In the immediate post-Gulf period, the question of the UN's role in the world was on the front burner. Debates regarding selection of the next secretary-general to replace Perez de Cuellar, calls for changes in the composition of the Security Council, and other organizational issues remained unresolved. A challenge to Washington's double standard on enforcement of UN resolutions remained high on the Non-Aligned agenda, though expresssions of concern were muted.

The Bush administration succeeded during the Gulf crisis in holding the UN hostage to its drive towards war. In doing so, however, it also opened up the Pandora's box of UN potential — in a post-New World Order world of true multilateralism the possibility that the UN might take on the role that most, at least, of its founders envisioned: as an instrument to prevent war and preserve the peace.

BUSH CONSOLIDATES

After its 1990 star turn in the build-up to the Gulf War, the United Nations remained a central figure in Washington's foreign policy. A small part independent player, a much larger part multi-faceted tool of U.S. diplomacy, the international organization has served as a forum for winning both support (coerced or not) and legitimacy (however legally shaky) for U.S. goals ranging from Desert Storm to the anti-Libya embargo to sending the Marines to Somalia to the fierce missile attacks against Iraq in the last days of the Bush administration.

With the organization's prominence in the new world order reaffirmed by the punishing ceasefire it imposed on Iraq, the UN became mirror as well as venue for the vast changes sweeping the world. Bush's emphasis on the UN's significance, so starkly contrary to Reagan's dismissive, often condemnatory attitude towards the world body, reflected Washington's goal of creating an international consensus (or the illusion thereof) to legitimate its international domination. The U.S. claim remained based on its unchallenged military-strategic power; while Japan and the EC, especially Germany, were competing with it economically, U.S. strategic superiority remained undisputed.

That superiority also insured Washington's power to determine not only how, but whether and when the world organization would respond to emerging crises. In the first two years following the Gulf War, newly public accusations of Western and especially U.S. double standards became a permanent cloud hovering over the UN. When Iraq violated international law with its invasion of Kuwait, the U.S. created a putative coalition that took the UN to war to reverse the wrong and punish Baghdad. Shortly after, when questionable allegations arose regarding Libyan involvement in the terrorist attack on Pan Am flight 103 over Lockerbie, the U.S. rammed through punishing sanctions against the Arab state.

But when other countries, including Serbia and most consistently Israel, violated UN resolutions with impunity, including Security Council decisions that ostensibly carry the force of international law, the U.S. did nothing, and allowed the UN to do nothing, to enforce them.

The double standard showed up especially overtly when Israel expelled over 400 Palestinians for a two-year exile in a no-man's-land on the Lebanese border in December 1992. In that pre-Oslo Agreement period, when the stumbling Madrid talks between Israel and the PLO seemed to be swimming through quicksand, the impact of the expulsion, on a larger scale than at any time since the 1967 war, was instantaneous and dramatic across the Arab world and throughout the South. There was an immediate demand for the Council to act, not just to condemn but to reverse this clear violation of the norms of international law guaranteeing every person's right to remain in their own country.

The subsequent Council resolution condemned the expulsions and demanded that Israel immediately allow all 400 of the Palestinians to return home, but Washington blocked the inclusion of any enforcement mechanism as a price for allowing the resolution to pass. At first Israeli officials believed that after an initial flurry, the media attention would fade away and the expellees would, like others before them, gradually be absorbed into Lebanon's teeming Palestinian refugee population. But instead, Lebanon threw the Israelis a curve. For many years, Israel had often flown expelled Palestinians in ones or twos, or small groups, by helicopter over the Lebanese border and deposited them just outside the Israeli-occupied zone of south Lebanon. Welcomed first as heroes, then as brothers (there were no Palestinian women expelled to Lebanon; many were, however, expelled to Jordan), the new exiles were usually able to remake their lives among the impoverished but politically vibrant communities of Palestinian refugees. But in 1992, just barely emerging from 15 years of a devastating civil war, the precariously unified Lebanese administration unexpectedly resisted the Israeli move. Struggling for governmental cohesion in Beirut, and most likely less than thrilled with the prospect of 400 Islamist activists being heralded as heroes among dispossessed Palestinian and poor Lebanese communities alike, Lebanon deployed its reborn national army to prevent the Palestinians from leaving their windswept, isolated, and soon snow-bound tents on the edge of the Israeli-occupied zone of Lebanon.

Even on first arrival (during an early spring 1993 visit) the Palestinian encampment was a made-for-the-media spectacle. Rows of Palestinian flags and Islamic banners lining a dirt roadway greeted visitors, ending in rows of small tents only recently dried out from the harsh winter snows, and lines of Palestinian men kneeling on prayer rugs. A series of Lebanese and Syrian army checkpoints rigorously enforced a blockade of all but the most basic supplies — although generators, medical equipment for the use of the numerous doctors among the expellees, and eventually even a cellular phone all made it to Marj al-Zahour on donkey-back, supplied by local villagers. The Israelis stood tough, and widespread international condemnation of Israel followed.

Tel Aviv simply announced it had no intention of implementing the UN resolution. In response, instead of calling for sanctions against Israel or even quietly urging its key ally to accept the UN conditions, Washington jumped to orchestrate a "compromise." The Clinton administration announced proudly that Israel would allow 100 of the exiles to return right away, the other 300 after one year. President Clinton's Secretary of State Warren Christopher announced the arrangement during his first appearance at the United Nations, claiming that the expulsion of 300 instead of 400 Palestinians, for one year instead of two, somehow was "consistent" with the Council resolution's explicit and unequivocal demand that Israel allow the *immediate* return of *all* expellees.

The deal included a U.S. promise to veto any sanctions resolution, and Washington made perfectly clear it would view with extreme disfavor any move by Non-Aligned or other Council members even to discuss such an idea. As a result, the draft sanctions resolution even then being discussed in the Non-Aligned Caucus of the Security Council was shelved. Led by its Muslim members, Morocco, Pakistan, and Djibouti, the Caucus agreed that the Council would simply express its belief that the U.S.-Israeli compromise represented a positive step, and its hope that all the expellees would be released soon. In what many observers believed to be a craven effort to win points from the Clinton administration, Morocco's ambassador, as Council president, took the lead in arranging the diplomatic steps, and relayed the message to his Israeli counterpart.

WASHINGTON REACHES FOR THE GLOBE

As countries fell and new nationalist passions rose with the massive changes of 1991, the UN remained at center stage of global clean-up operations. The UN's apparent centrality in the Gulf War segued to newly prominent efforts to resolve civil and inter-ethnic wars and conflicts, some of longstanding duration, often rooted in Cold War realities (El Salvador, Angola, Mozambique, Afghanistan, Haiti); others creating newly "cleansed" swaths of death and destruction (Croatia, Bosnia, Rwanda, Nagorno-Karabakh, Somalia).

Throughout 1992, UN activism remained at an all-time high. Despite continuing criticism of double standards of enforcement, peacekeeping missions expanded. Debates proliferated over the nature of the UN's military role. The French heated up the debate by suggesting the legitimacy of "humanitarian intervention" that would bypass considerations of national sovereignty and send troops without the consent of governments to protect populations deemed by some outside force to be at risk. By early 1993, the UN was fielding 13 separate peacekeeping operations, more than ever before. Some, like the operations in Cambodia and the former Yugoslavia, included tens of thousands of UN military and civilian staff.

The new secretary-general, Boutros Boutros-Ghali played a central role in the effort to redefine the nature of peacekeeping, at times going beyond what even his Council backers were prepared to accept. In his *Agenda for Peace*, drafted at the request of a high-profile January 1992 Council summit, he outlined a bold plan to dramatically expand UN interventions. While traditional UN peacekeeping was based on troops deployed to monitor ceasefire lines with the consent of both parties, Boutros-Ghali's 1992 plan called for preemptive UN deployments to prevent or limit disputes; peacemaking, designed to force parties to agreement, if possible through "peaceful" means such as boycotts (and presumably through military means if not); peacekeeping, identified as "hitherto" requiring the consent of all parties; and peace-building following conflicts.

Perhaps most contentious, he also called for a permanent UN military force to be established and placed under the command of the Security Council, noting that the end of the Cold War had created the political environment to make such a multilateral force possible. His call inevitably drew new attention to the longstanding refusal of the U.S. ever to place its troops under any UN or multilateral command. Even during the Gulf War, the SG reminded the world, the Council only authorized member states to go to war against Iraq; it did not call for a direct UN attack.

As the organization's resources were spread thin in peacekeeping and peacemaking efforts around the globe, failures emerged from the shadows. After a high profile claim of success in ending the 13-year civil war in Afghanistan, the UN withdrew, leaving behind an even more brutal intra-*mujahedin* war. The hard-fought UN-brokered peace agreement in El Salvador was threatened by the government's refusal to demobilize the worst human rights violators within the military. Cambodia's UN-imposed peace accord, threatened from the beginning by U.S. and UN acquiescence to Khmer Rouge "legitimacy," was undermined even further by Pol Pot's organization's refusal to participate in UN-sanctioned elections. And in Angola, despite a clear victory for the ruling MPLA in UN-sponsored elections, long-time U.S. ally Jonas Savimbi's UNITA rebels rejected the results and relaunched the civil war.

As the UN is stretched thinner and thinner in hot spots around the world, it has become easy to blame "the UN" for failures in disaster situations, often while praising as an alternative the arrival of a few platoons of red-blooded young U.S. Marines.

When the simmering post-Cold War crisis in Somalia suddenly saturated Western television screens in the summer of 1992, the Security Council finally agreed to take action. But the UN deployment of 500 Pakistani peacekeeping troops was far too small and its mandate far too limited to accomplish anything against the civil war and famine ravaging Somalia. The Council members, including the most powerful, did nothing to ensure the deployment would be able to function. To no one's surprise, the UN mission failed — and provided a dramatic triumph-by-contrast for the U.S. Marines' media-enshrined landing at Mogadishu. The ultimate U.S. judgment on intervention in Somalia — whether U.S. or UN orchestrated — will likely be based on the deaths of the 18 U.S. Rangers, fighting under U.S., not UN command, killed in Mogadishu in October 1993.

But what too often gets lost is the reality of who determines success or failures for the UN. Certainly the 500 Pakistani troops sent to Somalia in the summer of 1992 arrived too late, stayed too close to the airport, accomplished very little and quickly failed. But who determined that their mandate should only include defense of the Mogadishu airport? Who decided only 500 should be sent? Why did they have to wait over six weeks because their own logistics people did not have the requisite equipment and no other country would provide it? And given the predominance of U.S. influence in the Council, can a full distinction between "UN" and "U.S." responsibility be made?

While the Somalia operation was underway, the former Yugoslavia was already in flames. A massive UN troop deployment and joint UN-

EC-sponsored talks to resolve the Serbs' war of "ethnic cleansing" in Bosnia-Herzegovina did nothing to staunch the brutality of wanton rape and murder. The UN's credibility there, already perilously low, continued to dip even further as the UN's declared "safe zones," including Sarajevo itself and five mostly Muslim-populated towns completely surrounded by rebel Serb forces, continued to face virtually unchallenged shelling. The promise of protection for those areas, declared in early 1993, remained hollow. And by May 1995, in response to a suddenly stiffer NATO resistance effort including air strikes against Serbian positions, the Bosnian Serbs took over 400 UN peacekeepers and other observers hostage. Television footage of French, Ghanaian, British, Polish, and other Blue Helmets chained or handcuffed to poles outside of likely military targets was seen around the world. The U.S., which unlike its NATO allies had no troops in Bosnia, had nonetheless demanded the air strikes. (See Chapter 6 for more on the UN role in Bosnia.)

The Clinton administration had little to say when the strikes resulted in a humanitarian and policy debacle all too easy to have foreseen — and the UN's shredded credibility plummeted once again. The last tatters of Western — and, derivatively, the UN's — legitimacy in Bosnia were probably destroyed in the summer of 1995, when rebel Bosnian Serb forces overran, with horrifying brutality, two of the six "safe havens," Srebrenica and Zepa. That the UN as an organization, rather than its most powerful members, was made to take the blame for the horrors of the Bosnian war, made the global organization only one of the many victims of U.S. and European Bosnia policy.

Notes

1. Javier Perez de Cuellar, "Foreword," *Blue Helmets: A Review of United Nations Peacekeeping*, (New York: United Nations, 1990), pp. xv, xvii.

2. Joe Stork, "Reagan Re-Flags the Gulf," *Middle East Report* (September-October 1987), p. 4.

3. "The Glaspie-Hussein Transcript," Appendix B, Phyllis Bennis and Michel Moushabeck (eds.), *Beyond the Storm: A Gulf Crisis Reader* (New York: Olive Branch Press/Interlink, 1991), p. 391.

4. Eqbal Ahmad, speaking at "Countdown to the Gulf" teach-in, broadcast from New York's Nuyorican Poets Cafe, January 13, 1991, by WBAI/Pacifica Radio.

3

Who Rules? The Struggle for UN Democracy

The United Nations is a complicated organism. Even its name recalls ambiguity: a singular noun used for an extraordinarily plural subject. Decision-making and structure within the organization have, from its founding, struggled for that uneasy balance between democracy and power.

On paper, the interplay between the two looks great. The General Assembly, the highest decision-making body and the only UN agency comprising the full membership of the organization, works on the fully democratic basis of one-country-one-vote, regardless of size of army, number of nuclear warheads, wealth of national treasury, or form of government (though also without taking into account geographic or population size). It provides the broadest overview of the wide range of global opinion, and therefore is widely viewed as the ultimate repository of UN credibility and legitimacy. The Economic and Social Council, ECOSOC, is responsible for economic and social policy planning, and for coordinating the work of the myriad specialized agencies. The Security Council, made up of the most powerful member-states along with a rotating, regionally-representative sampling of others, holds the brief for international peace and security, and provides the strategic muscle to impose it. The International Court of Justice is supposed to hold jurisdiction over interpretations of international law, and member states are obligated to comply with its decisions in any case to which they are a party. The UN Secretariat provides the organizational scaffolding and technical support to implement the broad agenda and priorities set by the Assembly; its chief, the secretary-general, accountable to the Assembly and the Council, manages the system and serves as the voice and personification of the UN to the world.

But in the real world, the carefully crafted system of checks and balances never existed. It couldn't: the very nature of the United Nations (reflected in its real, if unofficial, structure hidden beneath the ever-so-democratic flow-chart facade), as well as the primary raison d'être of its founders, had far more to do with maintaining the power of the World War II victors than with extending democracy, whether political or economic, across the globe. The brilliant scholar George F. Kennan, author of the U.S. containment doctrine against the Soviet Union, understood better than most of his colleagues the harsh reality of the U.S. position after the end of World War II:

> We have 50% of the world's wealth, but only 6.3% of its population .... In this situation we cannot fail to be the object of envy and resentment. Our real task in the coming period is to devise a pattern of relationships which will allow us to maintain this position of disparity .... We should cease to talk about the raising of the living standards and democratization. The day is not far off when we are going to have to deal in straight power concepts.[1]

Control of the United Nations gave the U.S. as an emerging superpower the opportunity to do just that.

While Cold War tensions and the colonial legacies of many of its members essentially paralyzed the Security Council for most of the first 45 years of UN history, decolonization and especially the end of U.S.-Soviet competition transformed the terrain. With the end of the Cold War, Washington moved to reassert its relatively dormant dominance.

According to one Non-Aligned diplomat with many years experience at the UN, U.S. control emerges partly through what he terms "psychological pressure on the South." Some of the pressure emerges from U.S. control over the Bretton Woods institutions. "Sometimes all it takes is for a poor country's ambassador to be asked, pointedly, 'Don't you have a loan pending?' for them to get the message." Every year, a few months before the General Assembly convenes, he recalled, the U.S. Mission to the UN publishes a compendium of issues. It includes a clear statement of which issues Washington considers priorities, and what the U.S. position is on each. "So without direct pressure," he said, "the U.S. is telling all the other countries, especially the South, how they are expected to act."[2]

The vulnerability of any country to that pressure, of course, stands in direct correlation to its economic precariousness and dependency on outside aid. For that reason, Latin America, traditionally within the U.S. sphere of influence, and Africa, faced with deep and systemic impoverishment, are far more often targets of U.S. pressure campaigns than the more rapidly developing economies of Asia.

But the U.S. has never been content to rely solely on psychological pressure. Since its tactical embrace of the UN to internationalize Desert Storm, Washington has worked diligently to reshape the organization's components in its own image.

The Bush administration moved in, using the Gulf crisis campaign to assert Washington's dominance in and over the UN. That strategy included the generally successful efforts to centralize overall UN power in the Security Council, while sidelining the General Assembly and diminishing the authority of other structures within the UN organization, including the International Court of Justice.

These power shifts from the more democratic (especially the Assembly) to less democratic, more U.S.- and North-dominated components of the UN (especially the Council) mean that the Assembly, once the most vocal sector within the organization, is increasingly marginalized. Its resolutions, which unlike those of the Security Council do not hold the force of international law, are increasingly ignored. Although an Assembly oversight function is mandated in the Charter,[3] by the mid-1990s the Assembly had essentially abandoned any monitoring of Council proceedings.

SECURITY COUNCIL TO THE FORE

From 1989-1992, there were significant power realignments inside the Security Council reflecting the end of the Cold War and the Soviet Union's collapse. The "Perm Five" power center of the Security Council's permanent members, once dominated by the overarching contention between Moscow and Washington, shifted to "Big Three" cooperation between the U.S., Britain, and France.

The Council orchestrated its own post-Soviet composition largely by acting as if the Soviet collapse had never occurred. When the Soviet Union's flag was lowered over the Kremlin for the last time on Christmas Day, 1991, the Security Council and the United Nations as a whole did not institute any sort of serious proceeding. The UN Charter, in Article 23, states that the permanent members of the Security Council shall include "the Union of Soviet Socialist Republics." It does not state that any self-proclaimed successor would be accepted without Council and Assembly debate and approval. While the results of such a process were probably never at issue,* the means of changing the composition of the Council should have been taken seriously, as seri-

---

* It is interesting to speculate on the possible result if the new Russian government, instead of simply announcing that the shaky but (at that time) more or less functional Confederation of Independent States "supported" its grab for the former Soviet seat, had actually worked to craft a collective CIS representation. Besides being more exemplary of the vast populations and land of the once-Soviet Union than Russia alone, it might have set a precedent for collective European involvement, through the European Union, in a dramatically reformed post-Cold War Security Council.

ously (if perhaps less contentiously) than the earlier debate over trans-
ferring China's seat from Taipei to Beijing. Instead, the ambassador of
the new Russian Federation (conveniently enough, the same Yuliy
Vorontsov who had long represented the Soviet Union at UN headquarters) simply relayed a letter from the newly-elected president of
the Russian Federation, Boris Yeltsin, to the Security Council, stating
that Russia would take over the Soviet seat and the Soviet veto in the
Council. There was never a vote, either in the General Assembly or in
the Council itself. A round of applause greeted his announcement, followed by business as usual.

Having taken over the USSR's permanent seat, Russia soon became
a Western "wannabe" that, like China, was desperately dependent on
keeping Western goodwill to insure access to Western aid. As a result,
both Russia and China largely foreswore an opposition role to U.S.
domination of the Council, to follow the demands of Western money.
Council debates soon reflected the courteous new relationships. While
Non-Aligned countries serving two-year terms on the Council occasionally grouped together to challenge a Big Three proposal, the structure of the Council, with its attendant veto privileges for the North,
insured that a unified Northern position never faced serious threat
from the countries of the South. And even when Russia and/or China
may have disagreed with the Big Three's initiatives, they were rarely
prepared to antagonize their desperately needed donors.

Divisions among the Big Three, between the U.S., France, and Britain, emerged sharply over Bosnia, framing uncertainties over how the
UN and NATO should interact in a post-Soviet Europe. But while disagreements were frequent (most often between Washington and Paris),
they were usually quite tactical, not calling into question the fundamental commitment to maintaining the Council's command and control over UN resources and decision-making. Thus, by the first days of
1992, U.S. endorsement of the UN and consecration of the Council's
role within it had reached its zenith. The announcement of a high-profile Security Council summit was a clear indication that the UN had
proved itself far too valuable a weapon in Washington's diplomatic arsenal to be tossed aside after the Gulf War. The unprecedented summit
brought together the heads of state of all 15 members of the Security
Council to discuss the future of the United Nations. On the practical
level it was not much more than a photo op. (The imperial British ambassador, Sir David Hannay, rotating president of the Security Council
for January, insisted that the hastily called meeting be held before
January 31. A less diplomatic British diplomat, asked why the telegenic
conference couldn't be delayed till February, when the U.S. would be

presiding over the Council, reportedly quipped, "because our elections come before yours.") But beyond the hype, the UN summit was designed to cement the transformation of the world body into a credible implementor of U.S.-orchestrated Northern policy, and to reassert the Council as the engine-room of UN activity. To a large degree it worked. The Council summit requested that the secretary-general draft a complete analysis of the UN's peacekeeping role in the no longer bi-polar world: *Agenda for Peace*, with its sweeping rewrite of the rules of traditional UN peacekeeping to encompass "peacemaking," "peace-enforcement," "peace-building," and a whole array of interventionist approaches, was the result. Crafting a viable international response to the rapidly escalating North-South division separating rich and poor nations and peoples did not appear so high on the Council's program. In response to fears about the primacy of Council attention and funding going towards peacekeeping, the General Assembly requested the secretary-general to provide a parallel plan for the UN's development work. But Boutros-Ghali's *Agenda for Development*, when it appeared eighteen months later, was widely viewed by UN-watchers as skimpy on new ideas and narrow in focus. It received little international diplomatic or media attention. Even the UN Secretariat itself seemed dismissive of the effort: unlike the much-hyped *Agenda for Peace*, published quickly in slick book form, widely distributed through the UN's bookstores and information centers, *Agenda for Development* was for months available only by special request, in poor-quality photocopy form.

In the new era of UN centrality, especially with its new presence in international peace and security issues, the Council was to be the locus of authority. And though backed by Britain and France, the U.S. was the indisputable power within the Council. A key U.S. goal, during that post-Gulf War period, was to clarify for the international community that within the UN system, crucial decisions would be made by the Security Council; secondary or tertiary agencies would be granted only limited briefs, and allowed even more limited authority. In broad political/strategic decisions, they would be kept out of the loop altogether.

It wasn't always easy; the official structures of the UN have, on paper at least, a partial system of checks and balances more or less designed to divide power between various agencies. So Washington was faced with having to force the issue. The Bush administration's handling of the Gulf crisis, in which Council decisions escalating sanctions and ultimately the approval for war were enforced without serious involvement of the General Assembly, set the stage. In the next step, the Council's preeminence had to be institutionalized.

To do so, in the spring of 1992, the U.S. reactivated its simmering anti-Libya crusade. The pretext was Washington's effort to force Libya to turn over two of its nationals for trial in the U.S. or Britain on charges of involvement in the 1988 Lockerbie disaster. Noting its lack of bilateral extradition treaties with either London or Washington, Libya refused to send the two for trial in either place. Instead, as required by the 1970 anti-hijacking Montreal Convention, Libya volunteered either to put the men on trial itself, or send them for trial in Malta or another neutral country. Tripoli requested a finding from the International Court of Justice to determine whether its proposed action constituted sufficient compliance with the Convention. The Court agreed to hear the case, and took it under review.

But although the case was already being heard before the ICJ, the U.S. forced the Security Council to debate and vote on the imposition of preemptive, punitive sanctions against Libya, refusing to wait for the Court's decision. It was not a popular move. The severity of Washington's post-war anti-Iraq sanctions, along with its refusal to allow any UN pressure on Israel to win compliance with international conventions protecting Palestinians living under occupation, led to continuing charges of U.S. double standards. As a result, despite a new flurry of diplomatic carrots and sticks, the U.S. faced widespread unease, and in many cases downright opposition, to the proposed sanctions from Council members. Further, Washington was prepared to expend far less political and financial capital on its anti-Libya crusade than it had used to gain support for Desert Storm, and the results were far less decisive. The final sanctions vote was for a far less punishing set of restrictions, primarily a commercial air traffic embargo against Libya; the U.S. demand for an oil embargo was not accepted. Further, only ten of the fifteen Council members voted for the sanctions, just one more than the minimum required for passage; five Non-Aligned countries abstained.

But the stage was set. Whispered fears grew louder that the U.S. effort was designed not just to punish Col. Qaddafi, but to concentrate UN power solely in the hands of the North-weighted Security Council, stripping the authority of all other UN institutions — even of the usually non-controversial International Court, let alone the sometimes unruly democracy of the General Assembly.

Zimbabwe's Ambassador Simbarashe Mumbengegwi noted the threat to UN integrity posed by that concentration of power. "The Security Council only consists of 15 members," he said after the sanctions vote. "There are 160 [UN] members who are not part of the Security Council. Therefore it would be a serious mistake to want to create a situation where 15 members can want to argue that they are much stronger as a body than the 160 who are not in that body. That would really undermine the very basis of the United Nations, which is basically democratic, [and based on] equality of states. And if the Security Council were to be seen in that light, it would undermine its authority for the rest of the members' confidence in it as an institution which can protect their interests."[4]

The post-Cold War period saw a shift in the use or threat of Security Council vetoes: away from using vetoes to reflect Cold War antagonisms, to the "new world order's" effort towards forcing consensus, or at least the appearance of consensus, in Council decision-making. The Soviet Union was gone, and Russia had neither the interest nor the will nor the economic strength to veto Western initiatives; the U.S., without a strategic challenger and facing only smaller-scale disagreements with its Northern allies, no longer had much need. Until May 1995, when it reverted to its traditional vetoing of resolutions critical of Israel (in this case, vetoing a 14-to-1 vote demanding that Israel stop its imminent seizure of a large tract of Palestinian land in Jerusalem to build Jewish settlements), the U.S. had essentially stopped relying on its Council veto power since the end of the Cold War.

The veto had always been a form for playing out Cold War rivalries. In the UN's earliest years, the Soviet Union exercised far more vetoes than did the U.S. — primarily in (ultimately futile) efforts to deny membership to numerous countries backing Washington. Use of the veto by all powers began to decline in the 1960s and 70s. But in the period between 1973 and 1990, the balance between the U.S. and the Soviet Union dramatically reversed, with the U.S. casting 65 vetoes, to only eight by the Soviet Union. On the question of the Middle East, efforts by the Council to condemn Israeli occupation of Palestinian land or Tel Aviv's violations of human rights were routinely vetoed by Washington. The U.S. vetoed 27 separate Middle East resolutions during that time; the Soviet Union vetoed one. Even more telling, perhaps, of the twenty resolutions vetoed aiming at responding to the crises in southern Africa (including South Africa's occupation of Namibia, issues of apartheid, and the situation in then-Rhodesia), the U.S. cast every one.[5]

Since the end of the Cold War, everything (except perhaps U.S. intransigence on Israel/Palestine) is different. When tactical divisions emerge (for example, the 1994 Iraq crisis pitting Russian and French willingness to consider lifting sanctions against the American and British refusal to even discuss such a possibility), they tend to be smoothed over with the appearance of unity broadly in support of U.S.

positions. (The 1994 sanctions crisis ended without consideration of lifting the oil embargo, and a statement asserting that any diplomatic efforts would have no impact on existing sanctions.) The possibility of a veto is rarely taken seriously.

Certainly the end of regular vetoes has strengthened the Council's ability to concentrate broader UN authority by enabling it to speak with one voice.

A WEAKENED ASSEMBLY

As the Council moved into ever greater prominence and power, the relationship between the Council and the Assembly was severely strained. Traditionally, the Assembly had been the centerpiece of the broadest, most democratic discussion and debate within the UN system. While the Assembly had almost always been excluded from decisions involving peacekeeping and the use of force, throughout the decades of the Cold War, that didn't matter too much, since those activities were neither the most common nor most significant of the UN's work. Issues of economic development, decolonization, democratization of technology access, control of multinational corporations, fighting for a more equitable international division of resources — all of these were far more vital to the Assembly's mandate.

In that context, the role of the Non-Aligned Movement had been central. Representing the vast majority of the world's population, and only the tiniest sliver of the world's financial or political clout, the NAM (functioning in the UN as the Group of 77) provided the energy and leadership for Assembly decisions reflecting the interests of the South. But throughout the 1980s, the NAM had seen a steady erosion of its influence and of its internal unity. By the time the Soviet Union had collapsed and the U.S. had fought the Gulf War with a number of Non-Aligned countries helplessly endorsing its actions, the NAM was floundering for direction. In a speech ending his chairmanship of the Assembly's Group of 77, the Non-Aligned caucus, Colombia's Ambassador Luis Fernando Jaramillo described the desperate plight facing the South:

> In contrast to the euphoria created by the end of the Cold War, the changes in Eastern Europe, the reforms of economic liberalization, the new concepts of sustainable development and the conclusion of the Uruguay Round of GATT, the developing nations continue to face, at the dawn of the twenty-first century, a hostile international environment and a loss of economic and political standing in the so-called new world order .... In the new balance of power, the relative situation of the developing world has worsened. Any dissent of our countries from the position of the countries of the North is now la-

beled as confrontational, even by ourselves. In practice, we have less political influence and less priority in the international agenda .... We are fragile to pressures and weak to the appeal of particular interests and aspirations. Many a time we fall in the temptation of rhetorical discourse as a pretext for not harming resource flows from the North or bilateral preferential treatments. The industrialized countries and their institutions know this vulnerability and this ambivalence very well .... The disadvantage of the developing countries ultimately resides in the lack of a firm political platform.[6]

The political disempowerment of the South, combined with the increased economic pressures brought on by the aggressive structural adjustment policies imposed by the IMF and the World Bank, severely undermined the vibrancy that had once characterized the General Assembly. With growing rich/poor divisions emerging within countries of the South, governments found themselves actively seeking, or at least quiescently accepting, U.S.-orchestrated (even if officially multilateral) Northern intervention in the form of stringent social cutback programs to insure loan guarantees or foreign investment. The *New York Times*, describing fears in developing countries of being ignored by the U.S., asserted that, "It isn't that theoreticians of Third World politics have suddenly embraced the idea that the United States should tell them what to do. Rather, it is that with only one truly global bankroll, diplomatic corps and military left, it is American money they want (to help them develop), American pressure (to help control unruly neighbors) and American military force (to give weight to peacekeeping operations)."[7]

While the opinion of the lower — and much larger — strata of the populations of those Third World countries was not sought in drawing those conclusions, it is certainly true that national governments throughout the global South had, by the mid-1990s, put forward few options other than acquiescence to U.S. control. The now unchallenged nature of U.S. domination seriously undermined the ability of Southern governments, or the Group of 77 or Non-Aligned Movement within the Assembly, to assert any new strategic approaches to development at odds with those of Washington. Further, the impact of the dissolution of the Soviet Union on the changed geopolitical configurations and balances of power in the Assembly was profound. Fifteen new member-nations joined the Assembly, suddenly defined as "emerging democracies," and competing with the South for increasingly scarce aid and assistance.

The shifts and realignments also pointed up the anachronistic nature of the Cold War-defined regional groups, through which many

UN agency votes and appointments, including rotating Security Council seats, are apportioned. Those groups, Africa, Asia, Latin America, Eastern Europe, and "Western Europe and other States," reflect clear Cold War political considerations, not anything reflecting geographic or demographic realities. The Western European group, for example, includes Canada, Australia, and New Zealand. And the Middle East is splintered, with Egypt and the North African Maghrebi states with Africa, while Syria, Jordan, Lebanon, the Gulf states, and Yemen all part of the Asia group. Israel belongs to no regional group.

The shift in attention from an East-West to a North-South conflict meant the continued marginalization of the South in terms of economic and political-strategic power relative to the North. It was difficult for many countries of the South to find enough hard currency even to send sufficient delegates to represent the country in different UN agencies (many of them scattered around the world).[8] The need for a collective grouping of countries of the South, like the Group of 77, remained strong, but political unity among the developing countries was seriously strained by economic pressure from the North, which decimated already weakened political independence and imposed new levels of South-South competition for scarce aid.

As a result, the Assembly itself seemed to lose its moorings, uncertain of its role in a new era in which the UN as a whole was re-emerging as a key player in international affairs, but within which the U.S.-dominated Council held tight reins over the rest of the organization. The Assembly tried to raise the level of attention and resources devoted to a number of crucial socio-economic issues of vital concern to the South, especially with the sequence of high-profile international conferences scheduled (following the 1990 Summit for Children) for 1992-1995. Beginning with the 1992 UN Conference on the Environment and Development (UNCED, known as the Earth Summit) in Rio, followed by the 1993 Human Rights Summit in Vienna, the 1994 Population Conference in Cairo, the 1995 Social Development Summit in Copenhagen, and the obstacle-filled International Women's Conference in Beijing in 1995, all were planned and held under the nominal sponsorship of the General Assembly.

But in virtually all of these conferences, generalized Northern unease about potential Southern initiatives was resolved by straightforward U.S. refusals to sign on to legally binding obligations that came even close to meeting the desperate needs of the South.

The Earth Summit provided perhaps the sharpest example, one which served as a model for international conferences to come. In what the *Los Angeles Times* called a "tactical tour de force,"[9] the Bush administration beat back the environmental concerns of Europe and the developing countries alike. Washington held the line on limiting its commitment to environmental goals, and in doing so, reasserted U.S. hegemony over the countries of the South. (See chapter 8 for more on the conferences.)

Other, more direct U.S. pressure on the Assembly has emerged as well. As part of its post-Desert Storm diplomatic offensive in the Middle East, Washington promised its Israeli allies that a key goal of its UN agenda would be the scrapping of the 1975 General Assembly resolution which identified political Zionism as a form of racism and racial discrimination. In fact, the Bush administration committed itself to winning that repeal as one of the conditions to assure Tel Aviv's participation in the Madrid peace conference; it was included in the U.S.-Israeli Memorandum of Understanding setting forth the terms on which Israel agreed to come.

The 1991 General Assembly session, the first since the end of the Gulf War, saw a succession of heads of states, including President Bush, extolling the UN's role in the "new world order." For the Bush administration, that meant bringing the Assembly to heel to reflect those new international realities. By November, once the Assembly's ceremonial parade of presidents, kings, emirs, and prime ministers had ended, U.S. diplomats took off, criss-crossing the globe using Gulf War-tested methods of bribing and threatening other nations to win support for the repeal effort.[10]

Washington's position was that the repeal vote must be taken without discussion, without debate. The original resolution's identification of Zionism as a form of racism and racial discrimination was understood to reject the Israeli claim that a 4,000-year-old theological assertion somehow granted modern Jews from anywhere in the world the right to expel the indigenous Palestinian inhabitants from their homeland, as well as to criticize the ethnic/racial privileges allotted only to Jews in Israel. Member states were not to have the opportunity to discuss whether they believed Israel's occupation had fundamentally changed, or whether they believed the resolution was rendered moot by changing diplomatic realities since the Gulf War, or whether they in fact believed now they had been wrong sixteen years before. The vote, instead, was to be swift, unequivocal, and as overwhelming as possible.

(It should be noted that the resolution was repealed in the midst of Israel's most severe escalation of West Bank/Gaza repression in months. Numerous towns, villages, and refugee camps, only recently released from the Gulf War's 40-day curfew, were once again under 24-

hour-a-day curfew imposed by the Israeli occupation authorities, and arrests, land confiscations, and forced expulsion of Palestinians from their homes were at that time all on the rise.)

On December 16, 1992, just three months after President Bush had promised to get the repeal passed, the General Assembly voted. Washington's bribes, threats, and persuasion worked, and virtually without substantive discussion the Assembly voted overwhelmingly to overturn the resolution.

On the immediate level, the vote was clearly part of U.S. efforts to smooth relations with Israel at a time when Tel Aviv had announced its anger at a number of perceived slights by the Bush administration, and amid an Israeli unease that in orchestrating control of the post-Gulf War Middle East, the White House was turning towards the Arabs. In fact, the repeal vote presented Israel with its first prize as Washington's most favored nation of the new world order.

But more broadly, the vote — 111 countries for repeal, 25 countries opposing repeal, and 13 abstentions — provided a clear look at the emerging alignment of power and influence in the new world order's United Nations.

U.S. diplomatic pressure quickly pushed the number of co-sponsors of the repeal resolution past 50. Less than ten days before the final collapse of the Soviet Union, and given still-President Gorbachev's desperate search for Western aid, Moscow's support for repeal was unsurprising. More revealing was the division the U.S. was able to forge within the Non-Aligned Movement and other developing countries: longstanding critics of Israel's occupation, including nations such as India and Mozambique, voted for repeal, Angola and Laos abstained, and only Cuba, Vietnam, and North Korea stood with the Arab and Islamic opponents of repeal.

What was also a telling testament to Washington's heightened levels of influence in the region was the number of Arab countries whose ambassadors ducked out of the Assembly hall or who refused to participate in the vote. Among those non-participants (which also included China) were Bahrain, Egypt, Kuwait, Morocco, Oman, and Tunisia — all Arab states that supported the U.S. during the Gulf War and that maintained a realistic hope of significant upgrades in political, military, or economic aid from Washington. While Saudi Arabia voted against repeal, Saudi Ambassador Samir Shihabi (a Palestinian by birth), who was then president of the General Assembly, was himself absent for the vote. A lower-ranking and lower-profile Saudi diplomat cast the vote, and the Assembly session was presided over by its vice-president, the Honduran ambassador.

THE GOLD STANDARD

For the U.S., a key task of the post-Gulf War new world order was to consolidate the relegitimized United Nations as a respected part of U.S. diplomacy. During the Gulf crisis, Washington raised the organization's stature, but it remained unclear whether that rehabilitation was to be a one-time tactic to claim international credibility for Desert Storm, or whether the U.S. intended to continue to project the United Nations as the instrument and legitimizer of its policies.

Once the more lasting value of the UN was accepted in Washington, the next step was to insure that the organization itself could be reshaped in the image of its new sponsor. One means of exerting control would come from a not unfamiliar aspect of U.S. hegemony: the power of the purse. Begun during the Reagan administration, but continued for years after, the affirmative as well as laissez-faire U.S. decisions to withhold UN dues have had a serious impact on important UN programs, as well as on efforts towards UN democracy.

In the UN's Regular Budget (distinguished from both the separate peacekeeping budget and the voluntary contributions that fund specific agencies), the U.S. is assessed 25% of the total. Countries' shares are determined on an "ability to pay" basis, taking into account such factors as national income, population, level of debt, etc. The U.S. is billed at by far the highest rate; Japan, which is second, is assessed at 12.4%, Russia at 6.7%, and Germany at 8.9%. The least developed, poorest countries are assessed at 0.01% of the budget.

The system is based on the understanding that it is equally difficult for Cameroon, for example, to find the few tens of thousands of dollars (and it must be paid in U.S. dollars, thus further pressuring the poorest countries without access to hard currency) required of its 0.01% assessment, as for the U.S. to pay the multi-million dollar 25% assessment. The idea was to insure that larger contributors would gain no benefit in influence or power as a result of their higher dues. There has been a longstanding concern in the United Nations that control of such a large percentage by any one country in effect holds the world organization hostage to the whims of that country.

Washington politicians often complain about the high rate of the U.S. assessment. In 1985, the late Swedish prime minister Olaf Palme proposed that no individual country be allowed to pay more than 10% of the total UN budget. "A more even distribution of the assessed contributions," he told the General Assembly the following year, "would better reflect the fact that this Organization is the instrument of all nations."[11] India, leading advocate of non-alignment and generally viewed as critical of the U.S. at that time, quickly endorsed and led the support for the proposal. The European countries, concerned that they would have to make up much of the difference, were against imposing such a limit, at least until Washington had paid up its back debts. But it is especially ironic to note that it was the U.S. itself that led the opposition to the new lower dues structure: U.S. policy-makers were clear that paying less dues would mean a lessening of political leverage at the UN.[12]

By June 1995, the UN faced a back-dues shortage totalling $2.75 billion; of that, $904 million was owed to the regular budget, $1.85 billion to the peacekeeping account. Despite claims by the Clinton administration that it intended to pay back debts and keep its UN dues current, the U.S. still led the UN's scofflaws by better than two to one over the next highest debtor. Washington's debt totalled $1.18 billion: $575 million in unpaid regular dues, and $652 million in unpaid peacekeeping assessments. (The next highest debtors were Russia, owing $598 million, Ukraine, owing $217 million, and South Africa, $113 million.)

But U.S. control of the United Nations is not only an economic enterprise; it is highly ideological as well. According to one ranking Non-Aligned diplomat with many years UN experience, domination of the Secretariat is the "most egregious" way in which the U.S. holds sway in the UN. "Washington has been imposing a number of corporate-style policies and mechanisms on the UN," he said, "dealing with the organization as if the UN were a corporation and Boutros-Ghali its chief executive officer, and the U.S. its majority stockholder."[13] But, he went on to say, "the UN is of a different character from a corporation; its goals and purposes are very different, and so the administrative and financial structures should not be seen in the same way as a corporation."

In fact, much of the U.S. effort towards UN "reform" was and remains shaped by a corporate-style effort at downsizing the Secretariat staff (in which effort the "bloated bureaucracy" rhetoric plays a key role) and in sharply limiting the scope of UN work programs. The restrictions are aimed primarily at those UN programs and agencies viewed as giving a voice to, or providing a serious opportunity for collective decision-making among, the countries of the South, and at providing some monitoring or control of North-centered corporate initiatives.

For example, the closure of the Center on Transnational Corporations, one of the first acts taken by the new secretary-general in February 1992, was widely viewed as both a concrete example of where UN resources would not be allowed to go, but also as an unmistakable signal about where the priorities of the post-Cold War UN would and would not lie.

Insuring control of the Secretariat also meant insuring that the individuals holding the highest relevant policy positions were proponents of the U.S. approach to international affairs. Much of the most direct U.S. influence is reflected in the U.S. authority (granted by the secretary-general) to appoint (officially to "recommend" a candidate for the SG's consideration) the key position of under-secretary-general for administrative and budget affairs. During the Bush administration's early 1991-92 effort to enhance the UN's role, U.S. appointee Richard Thornburgh played a major role in defining, and thus narrowing the scope of, the UN's "crisis" as one of management and budget, rather than of power and politics. By the time Thornburgh left office in early 1993, his report placed virtually all emphasis for necessary reforms of the UN in a framework for upgrading management and administrative systems.[14]

SPIN DOCTORS AND THE NEW TOP-GUN

If the option of projecting a high-profile UN was to continue, it was vital to change the nature of the third potential power center in the organization, after the Security Council and General Assembly: the secretary-general.

Towards the end of 1991, the five-year term of the diligent but uninspired and lackluster Secretary-General Javier Perez de Cuellar was coming to a close. What Washington and its allies needed in his replacement was a combination of seemingly incompatible characteristics: a secretary-general who was both skilled in managing (read: downsizing) the "bloated bureaucracy" and in projecting the organization's centrality in world affairs, while remaining fully accountable to the sometimes quarrelsome powers in the Council and never wavering on a strategic commitment to the North's agenda.

It was a tall order, and at least on the assertiveness side would be quite a contrast to what had gone before. One respected British newspaper described the legacy of excessively pliable secretaries-general. "From Trygve Lie to Perez de Cuellar, some ... have been too easily intimidated by the strongest gang on the East River block."[15]

By UN tradition, the SG cannot be a citizen of one of the five permanent members of the Security Council. Also by tradition, the regional groups within the General Assembly rotate the right to nominate from among their own member states the new candidate. So following the Peruvian Perez de Cuellar, Austrian Kurt Waldheim, and Burmese U Thant, as well as the earliest European SGs, Scandinavians Trygve Lie and Dag Hammarskjold, it was understood to be Africa's turn. And that presented a problem. A Third World-oriented secretary-general, speaking from and for the Non-Aligned countries and th South, could do much to thwart U.S. efforts to achieve the appearance of unanimity in the UN behind its grand coalitions.

The Africa Group and the Organization for African Unity (OAU) began the process of culling through lists of possibilities. Early rosters of candidates were all headed by the longstanding chairman of the Organization of African Unity and advocate of non-alignment, Salim Ahmad Salim. The U.S. immediately let it be known that the articulate Tanzanian was unacceptable.

In the next round, diplomats focused on the former Nigerian president Olusegun Obasanjo as the most likely African candidate. Also on the list was Zimbabwean finance minister Bernard Chidzero. Of the two, Obasanjo was far more palatable to Washington and its Security Council allies. At that time, Nigeria's pro-Western political direction, along with the free market policies and IMF/World Bank liberalized orientation of its economy, made its representative much less challenging to Western domination than those of other African countries. Zimbabwe, on the other hand, had remained a partisan of the Non-Aligned Movement. In its post-independence struggle out of colonial-imposed economic crisis, it was more open to Western involvement than earlier in its history. But Chidzero would still have been an uncomfortable choice for Washington and its allies, in what they hoped would be an era of increased UN involvement in stamping out flare-ups of North-South conflicts.

In the meantime, in this "new" UN, longstanding UN traditions, including the significance of regional rotation of secretary-general candidates, underwent new challenges. Rumblings were heard around UN headquarters that perhaps in that critical time of the organization's history, an African SG was not the most "appropriate" choice.

Right-wing *New York Times* columnist William Safire joined the fray early on, making his own proposal for a three-person "UN troika" to replace the position of secretary-general. His combination of choice: former Soviet foreign minister Eduard Shevardnadze, former British prime minister Margaret Thatcher, and experienced UN diplomat (then serving as coordinator of UN refugee work in the Gulf) Prince Sadruddin Aga Khan.

The first step towards realizing Safire's self-defined "revolutionary" proposal was to "put Africa on hold; promise it the next secretary-general after this one. Next, drop the informal agreement not to appoint a national of any of the Big Five nations to head the UN Secretariat." Then, he went on, "with that underbrush cleared away," the Western world could get on with the business of finding a person or group of people really capable of running the UN — not just "some other local [African] pol with regional clout [who] will be appointed to his decade of global publicity and institutional impotence."[16]

The inability of the African countries to unite behind a single candidate was a major stumbling block in the effort to assure election of an African SG. The vast disparity in African economic and social systems had kept functional African unity out of reach. But the antagonism of the Western powers to an African UN leader in the "renewed" UN of the post-Gulf War world remained the most powerful barrier.

So the list of potential candidates moved far afield from the African diplomats. A highly-publicized poll conducted in the fall of 1991 by the United Nations Association/U.S.A. offered sixteen candidates, of whom only five were from any African country. Salim Salim, by far the leading candidate for many Africans, was not even included in the list.[17]

By October, possibilities still ranged all over the map. Aga Khan was a perennial favorite of the U.S., which had supported his candidacy over that of Perez de Cuellar in 1981, until Soviet opposition forced the U.S. to accept the Peruvian instead. Born in Paris to Iranian parents, raised in the West, Aga Khan was not viewed as being directly accountable to a specific government. But his broad Western orientation — and accountability — was unshakable.

But soon there were strong indications emerging that Washington's preference was settling on Egypt's Boutros Boutros-Ghali. Developing his political position in the post-Nasser period in Egypt, Boutros-Ghali reflected the strong pro-Western orientation of Anwar Sadat, his mentor. In late October, the Security Council took several straw polls to gauge the relative popularity of the candidates. Two African contenders emerged to lead the rest: Chidzero and Boutros-Ghali. In the first poll, the two Africans won ten and eleven positive votes respectively, with two negative votes for Chidzero and one for Boutros-Ghali. But since the balloting was secret, it remained uncertain if the negative votes had been cast by one of the veto-wielding powers, whose thumbs-down vote would end that candidate's chance to be named for approval by the Assembly.

Three days later, the five permanent members were provided with blue ballots, to distinguish their votes from the white ballots of the non-veto members. In that count, Chidzero edged ahead of the Egyptian, with eleven positive votes to Boutros-Ghali's ten (nine positive votes are needed to win). Neither candidate received a negative vote by any veto-carrying member of the Council.

Boutros-Ghali remained the U.S. favorite. But while he was one of the eight African candidates officially endorsed by the Organization of

African Unity, it was widely understood that only an accident of geography had placed him on that list. Most African and other diplomats from the South believed that only a representative of a sub-Saharan country was likely to be truly accountable to African needs and Africa's agenda. So the chance that a representative of Egypt, a country politically, historically, and culturally situated far more in the Arab Middle East than in Africa, and additionally a country whose foreign and domestic policies were shaped by its close ties to and dependency on the U.S., could be responsive to an African agenda seemed low.

But Boutros-Ghali's candidacy proved too enticing to the West. Besides diverting potential African objections, Boutros-Ghali also allowed Washington to promote a pro-U.S. Arab candidate, thus bolstering its post-Gulf War credibility among its sometimes reluctant Arab allies in the Middle East and other developing countries. Of course Egypt's post-Camp David foreign policy, buttressed by billions of dollars a year in U.S. aid, loyally defended U.S. Middle East interests. Who could be better trusted to continue that same political trajectory from the SG's office on the UN's 38th floor? At the end of the day, the combined resistance of the African and some Arab nations was not enough to overcome the power and influence in the Security Council of the U.S. and its allies. Egypt's accident of geography provided a free gift for U.S. spin-masters concerned about bolstering Washington's legitimacy as a backer of "UN democracy." With France playing the role of his sponsor in the Security Council, Boutros-Ghali's election was assured, and U.S. influence in the organization seemed higher than ever.

The new SG quickly made his own priorities and accountability known. He stated that the UN "must remind the world of the needs of the Third World," and asserted that "at this moment it is critical that the secretary-general again come from the Third World. He must help these lands to achieve a new self-awareness, a new confidence. He is also a sign that they are respected."

But in the next sentence, he made sure there were no illusions that he would support a reordering of North-South access to resources. "To make it absolutely clear to the Western public: I am not all that concerned about financial or technical assistance to the Third World." And in case anyone in Washington had second thoughts about selecting a "man of the South" for the all-important post, Boutros-Ghali quickly laid their fears to rest: "Believe me," he said, "I would rather travel to Dusseldorf or Paris than to Harare, Addis Ababa, or Khartoum. I was fortunate enough to get a European education. I like Europe, and I feel at home there."[18] While the new secretary-general had been embraced for his activist approach, he soon faced criticism by diplomats and staff alike for an aloof and arrogant style. Shortly after taking office, Boutros-Ghali also angered some of his erstwhile sponsors by refusing to remain silent in the face of Council inaction. The Council wasn't used to an SG who talked back. As one French diplomat lamented, Perez de Cuellar had been "more consensual," and "when the Council wanted something the secretary general was at their disposal."[19]

By the summer of 1992, as Somalia's crisis worsened with no serious UN response, the secretary-general's famous July 23, 1992 condemnation of the Council's narrow focus on "the war of the rich" in the former Yugoslavia further antagonized the U.S. and European Council members (although it did help spur international public interest in Somalia).

Tensions between the SG and the Council mounted. The *New York Times,* in an August 3, 1992 article headlined "UN Chief's Dispute With Council Boils Over," quoted diplomats describing Boutros-Ghali as "petulant," "disingenuous," and "inflexible." *The Guardian* (August 2, 1992) headlined the question: "The Boot for Boutros?". But while acknowledging that some of the criticism might be unfair, *The Guardian* still described how he "began to behave erratically," on the former Yugoslavia, and analyzed the "decline and fall of Mr. Boutros-Ghali."

Going even further in annoying the Western powers, Boutros-Ghali wondered publicly whether the criticism and attacks were "maybe because I'm a wog."[20] In the formal hot house of the UN, where race and racism are denied and national origin only delicately mentioned, such blunt language, recalling both racism and colonialism, caused quite a stir.

But Boutros-Ghali did not either decline or fall; he described the controversy as "quite exaggerated" and "healthy." Ultimately, despite being provocative, something he himself characterized as "my job," he remained a key player in the U.S. and Western effort to remake the UN into a newly central player in post-Cold War diplomacy. While the SG's conflicts with the Council raged in overheated language, Boutros-Ghali's actions spoke far more eloquently of his real goals and accountability. One of his first organizational moves, soon after taking office in January 1992, was the closing down of the Center on Transnational Corporations. The Center, based at UN headquarters in New York and considered by many in the South to be an important example of how UN resources could be mobilized on behalf of the Third World, had monitored the behavior of multinational corporations, and the social and economic impact of their actions. It was the only multilateral agency charged with such a mission that held the imprimatur of UN legitimacy. And while Boutros-Ghali's action officially called for "merging" the Center into the already-imperiled South-oriented UN

Conference on Trade and Development (UNCTAD) in Geneva, neither North nor South could mistake his message: scarce UN resources would not be diverted to monitor or manage the activities of the wealthiest institutions of the industrial North.

Ambassador Luis Fernando Jaramillo, chair of the Assembly's Group of 77 throughout 1993, used the example of the closing of the Center on Transnational Corporations to show how Boutros-Ghali was not only "downgrading" some of the UN agencies that were seen as championing interests of the South, but "he is also trying to finish off some of them. I am very much disappointed with the actions of the secretary-general," Jaramillo said.[21] Another example was Boutros-Ghali's effort to merge the Nairobi-based UN Center for Human Settlements (Habitat) with the fledgling and still struggling UN Environmental Program (UNEP), which Jaramillo asserted reflected an attempt to downgrade UN attention to homelessness, one of the major social problems facing the South. (The General Assembly voted in January 1994 to prevent the merger.)

Jaramillo said that the far-reaching changes introduced by the SG, under the guise of organizational restructuring, were not in the interests of the South. They were also, he noted, not in the interest of UN democracy: "We have seen changes in UN institutions either without the authority of the General Assembly or even the inter-governmental bodies themselves," he said.[22]

At the end of March 1995, as the multilateral UN mission in Haiti took over the peacekeeping brief from the U.S. troops who had first overseen the ouster of the military junta in Port-au-Prince, the U.S. president had lunch with the UN secretary-general. Boutros-Ghali offered a toast. "The United States, under your leadership, Mr. President, has played the critical role that only it can play. The United Nations, as the instrument of its Member States, stands ready to carry this mission onward. If the world seeks a model for the future, it may find one here."[23]

At that moment Boutros-Ghali may have been referring to U.S.-UN cooperation in hot spots such as Haiti. But in describing the world organization as standing ready to carry the U.S. mission onward, the UN's highest official spoke a truth far broader than simply praise for a hand-over of command.

REWRITING THE UNITED NATIONS

Despite the passage of 50 years, Boutros-Ghali's words reflect a continuity of UN orientation: it continues to reflect, rather than challenge, the basic priorities set by its most powerful member states. Resources are still scarce, and while virtually every country's representative at the General Assembly can be expected to endorse greater UN activism in stemming poverty and famine, providing medical and children's assistance, and broadening development aid, the stark reality is that the only UN programs being expanded are those involving military forces or other peacekeeping efforts; development programs face continual budget shortfalls, lack of attention from the most powerful UN members, and a generally low position on the UN's list of priorities. In a world where the vast majority of conflicts now rage *within*, rather than between, nations, that increased UN activism may be the only viable alternative to the world standing in mute witness to mass slaughter. But the new definitions may hold dangerous portents as well. The call in some quarters for the UN to "take over" running the violence-wracked and governmentless Somalia, for example, might resonate more positively if the UN truly represented the interests of all the world's peoples, as opposed to the strongest of the world's *states*. In the reality of a U.S.-dominated UN, a "take-over" by the world body cannot be proposed lightly.

Since its founding, the United Nations has borne far more responsibility for answering the needs of the world's poor than for acting as a military arm of its major powers. While it has never succeeded in narrowing the vast chasm between rich and poor in the world, the effort to do so has shaped the UN's operative global definition of "all the peoples" referred to in the Charter. But since its founding, the disparities between the world's rich and poor have grown enormously.

In its 1994 Human Development Report, the UN Development Program analyzed global economic disparities by looking at the distribution of economic activity (gross national product as well as factors of world trade, commercial lending, savings, and investment) between tiers, each made up of one-fifth of the world's population. In graphic form, the image is that of a cheap champagne glass: imagine a wide shallow bowl topping a tall slender stem. The richest fifth, filling the wide bowl, accounts for a whopping 84.7% of the world's GNP. The long, narrow stem is made up of the other four-fifths of the world's population. And at the bottom, the poorest one-fifth of all humanity reaps the dregs of the champagne, accounting for only 1.4% of the global GNP, a mere 0.9% of world trade.[24]

It is the need to reverse that stark reality that shapes what the UN's role in economic and social development work might look like.

But from the vantage point of the U.S., the work of economic policy and financial issues is not to reside in ECOSOC, the UN's Economic and Social Council, despite its mandate from the UN Charter. Article 62 calls on ECOSOC to "make or initiate studies and reports with respect to international economic, social, cultural, educational, health and related matters and make recommendations with respect to any such matters to the General Assembly, to the Members of the United Nations, and to the specialized agencies concerned." But ECOSOC is a broad agency, and, by UN standards, relatively democratic. Decisions of the 54-member Council are taken on a one-country-one-vote system.

BRETTON WOODS

So instead, the U.S. looks to the much narrower, North-controlled Bretton Woods institutions to take care of economic policy. As analyst Chakravarthi Raghavan points out, "As early as the 1950s the United States had resisted any UN role in economic, monetary and financial issues, favoring instead the concentration of these issues in the World Bank and the IMF which are run and controlled by the major industrial nations on the basis of 'one-dollar-one-vote.' "[25]

From their origins, and despite the organizational flow-charts defining them as specialized agencies of the UN, situated squarely inside, the triad of IMF, World Bank, and General Agreement on Tariffs and Trade (GATT — in the process of being replaced by the new World Trade Organization) have remained outside of and completely unaccountable to the UN system or UN democracy. Their funding bears no connection to the hat-in-hand methods other UN agencies are often reduced to, being based on a "buying shares" system of funding — and, not unrelated, a voting system weighted on the basis of those shares. Staff recruitment, salaries, and perks bear no resemblance to the much lower salary strata of the UN's own international civil service; the men and women who staff the Bank and the IMF (especially the men who fill the highest posts) are viewed as representative of, and are compensated as, the elite of the North's global economic interests.

That divergence from UN accountability, however, does not mean separation from or disinterest in what the UN is doing. To the contrary, it has long been Washington's policy for the Bretton Woods triad to reduce the UN's economic policy-making work, and then to take over that vital brief. The goal is to replace the authority of the UN's own macro-economic policy coordinating agency, ECOSOC, with that of the Bretton Woods group. In July 1992, the managing director of the IMF told an ECOSOC meeting that the United Nations as a whole should be considered merely a "fourth pillar" (after the IMF, World Bank, and GATT) in the international system, and that the UN's main contribution could be in issues of sustainable and social development.[26]

Even Secretary-General Boutros-Ghali himself, ostensibly the defender of the UN's mandate, was reduced to weighing possible "complementarities" between the UN, the IMF, and the World Bank, as if they were all of equal status and legitimacy.[27]

As the Bush administration began from 1990 to recreate a United Nations simultaneously prominent, compliant, and limited to certain designated arenas of concern, the newly public roles of the IMF and World Bank fit right in. With the Gulf crisis, the White House showed the world how the UN would be used in a future of U.S.-orchestrated prominence. It would be, in this scenario, primarily involved with military or quasi-military activities: the emphasis would be on peacekeeping, with a vastly expanded definition of what that entails, and the UN would function either as active participant (as in the UN's own Rwanda operation or in Bosnia), or as legitimizer of the activities of major powers (as with the U.S. in Iraq, France's Operation Turquoise in Rwanda, or the Russian mission in Georgia), or as a combination of both (as with U.S. operations in Haiti and Somalia).

Economic and social development, environmental protection, macro-economic policy analysis, human rights — all of these would be less important, would be lower on the list of U.S. priorities and would receive lesser access to UN resources. The Bretton Woods institutions would be relied on instead of those UN economic agencies "plagued" (according to Northern estimates) by overly-democratic or worse, South-dominated, decision-making structures. The UN would be kept to a large degree out of the macro-economic business.

Instead, noted Colombia's UN Ambassador Luis Fernando Jaramillo:

> The strategy of the developed countries continues to be clearly directed at strengthening more and more the institutions and agencies that operate outside the United Nations system. Many subjects that are vital for the international community and the Third World are kept out of the purview of said system and taken to closed decision-making circles. Such is the case of the Group of 7, a forum in which the interests of the developing countries have either been taken into account marginally or been completely ignored .... *
>
> We all know the nature of the decision-making system in such institutions. Their undemocratic character, their lack of transparency, their dogmatic principles, their lack of pluralism in the debate of ideas

---

* The Group of 7, or G-7, is the grouping of the wealthiest industrialized states which collectively determine intra-capitalist economic strategy in annual summits. They include the U.S., Great Britain, France, Canada, Italy, Japan, and Germany. Russia has attended the G-7 summit as an observer for the past two years.

and their impotence to influence the policies of the industrialized countries ....

This also seems to be applicable to the new World Trade Organization. The terms of its creation suggest that this organization will be dominated by the industrialized countries and that its fate will be to align itself with the World Bank and the International Monetary Fund. We could announce in advance the birth of a New Institutional Trinity which would have as its specific function to control and dominate the economic relations [imposed on] the developing world .... [28]

PEACEKEEPING'S "NON-DIVIDEND"

This U.S.-supported shift from a development to peacekeeping emphasis impacts negatively on broader UN goals, which put global priority on sustainable development and social and economic stability. Jaramillo described how "the internal functioning of the [UN] Organization is also subjected to continuous demands to devote greater efforts to peacekeeping operations and security in detriment of its functions and responsibilities in the area of economic and social development."[29]

It should not, of course, have been surprising: the UN's move away from social protection emerged in tandem with similar changes in the U.S. domestic political scene. The UN shift represented, at bottom, the same call for privatization and rewriting of the longstanding social contract underway in Washington, now instituted on a global scale. In international terms, that meant, among other things, increased reliance on private investment by multinational corporations as a response to North-South income disparities and the South's economic crisis, to replace the understanding that direct government-provided, development-oriented assistance is desperately needed in the South, and that the wealthier Northern countries have some responsibility to provide that help.

In September of 1992, only six weeks before losing his re-election bid, President Bush spoke to the General Assembly. Turning to the world's economy, he claimed a renewed commitment to the G-7 process that maintains the U.S., Japan, and Europe as the unchallenged powers in setting the world's economic agenda. Then, in terms aimed directly at the South's diplomats, filling the Assembly hall, Bush turned to a more ominous note. "Foreign aid, as we've known it, needs to be transformed," he said. "The notion of the handout to less-developed countries needs to give way to cooperation in mutually productive economic relationships."[30]

With which poorer countries did Bush foresee such productive economic relationships? That was easy. His proposed $1 billion "growth fund" (carefully avoiding the sticky issue of where the money would come from) would not be directed to the poorest countries. Instead, it would furnish "grants and credits to support U.S. business in providing expertise, goods, and services desperately needed *in countries undertaking economic restructuring.*" And within the U.S. itself, foreign aid would be shifted to "building economic partnerships among our private sectors."

The transformation from a development to a peacekeeping organization is closely tied to the UN's financial crisis, both as reflection and cause. Legally, UN regulations forbid any direct linkage between the peacekeeping and regular budgets, and the UN is further forbidden to borrow commercial or other funds even for brief periods to cover cash-flow emergencies. But nonetheless, the Security Council's proliferation of brushfire-oriented peacekeeping operations still come first. In general, unless countries are unwilling to commit troops at all (as in Rwanda early on), at least partial deployments of Blue Helmets mandated to go to troubled areas are in fact sent, despite chronic shortfalls in the peacekeeping accounts.

One result is that troop-contributing or equipment-contributing or airlift-contributing countries, whose costs are supposed to be covered from funds in the peacekeeping budget, are often not paid back, or are paid very late. In many cases, they may respond by cutting their voluntary assessments for general/development/humanitarian funds of the UN, as well as allowing payment of their regular dues to lapse or be delayed.

The effect is the exacerbation of already-serious financial problems in those non-peacekeeping areas. Reduction in peacekeeping funds create other problems, especially because of the consistent U.S. debt to the peacekeeping as well as the regular budget. New moves in the 1995 U.S. Congress to further restrict dues paid for and contributions to peacekeeping threaten further paralysis of UN peacekeeping.

These problems arise not because development or other funds are used to provide peacekeeping troops, but because much of the UN's most critical economic development work is funded through voluntary, not mandatory, contributions. The UN Development Program (UNDP), for example, represents the linchpin of the organization's overall system of economic and technical assistance to developing countries. Its funding depends on voluntary contributions from relatively wealthier countries, whose own governments determine levels of support. According to UNDP sources, total cuts in funding available to the agency have reached about 30% since 1992.

Funding cuts for the "core" programs of UNDP have been even more dramatic. In 1992, program funding reached $1.77 billion. By

1994, it was down to $934 million. The impact is felt especially drastically in developing countries, whose own economic planning for development activities is based on anticipated assistance from UNDP outlined in five-year increments. Countries were told they would receive so much money over the next five years, and then are faced with receiving only 70% of those funds when across-the-board cuts are necessitated by UNDP's shortfall.

The U.S., since 1966, had been the largest donor to UNDP (with the exception of one year in which Sweden pulled slightly ahead). By 1995, even before the dramatic cuts mandated by the Republican Congress that year had gone into effect, its position had already dropped to fifth or sixth place — and not because other countries had dramatically raised their own contributions.[31] (Although it should be noted that a number of rapidly-developing countries in the South, including Brazil, India, Malaysia, and others *have* significantly increased their own contributions to UNDP.)

There is a certain irony to the U.S. role in undermining UNDP's ability to function. According to one ranking and disillusioned UNDP staff member, "In the past, it was the U.S. position to maintain organizations like UNDP because the U.S. dominated them. Now the U.S. is shooting itself in the foot, undermining its own credibility in the UN, letting other countries become major players in the UN. Latin America is transforming, there are big investments going to China and India, but ... Africa's situation is very precarious. Those situations can lead to Bosnias and Rwandas, so it's a big risk for the U.S. to take .... For an experienced U.S. observer like me, it's quite devastating to see the U.S. doing this."[32]

Some cuts were imposed more directly, joining the very real economic crisis to "reforms" taken in the name of "streamlining the work of the Secretariat," or "improving efficiency," or ending the "bureaucracy's bloat." The results have been more explicitly political cutbacks. In the spring of 1995, Senate Foreign Relations Committee Chairman Jesse Helms called for cuts of $100 million per year in funding U.S. membership in the International Labor Office, the UN Industrial Development Organization, and other agencies. He went on to recommend "terminating or greatly reducing" funds for virtually every UN organization (UNICEF being the sole exception). Helms' "hit list" included UNDP, the UN Population Fund, the UN Environment Program, the UN Development Fund for Women, the World Food Program, and many more.[33]

These proposed cuts, and others already imposed, were aimed at some of the UN organs less well-known in the North, but agencies viewed as crucial by policy-makers, diplomats, scholars, and much of civil society in the South. In particular, the across-the-board organizational restructuring imposed by Boutros-Ghali in the first months of his term reflected the corporate orientation of his U.S.-selected administrative officials.

According to Chakravarthi Raghavan, chief editor of the *South-North Development Monitor*, what was

> officially described as "the first phase of restructuring and streamlining" was viewed with deep concern not only by Third World delegates but also by some from the North as one involving a major erosion, if not a dismantling, of the role of the UN in international economic cooperation and development. The programs and activities of the Office of the Director-General for Development and International Cooperation, ... the Department of International Economic and Social Affairs, the Department of Technical Cooperation for Development, the UN Center on Transnational Corporations and the Center for Science and Technology for Development — all created after considerable debate and discussions, and negotiations and decision by the UN General Assembly — have just disappeared and been put under the new "Department of Economic Development."[34]

Raghavan went on to wonder whether the absence of the word "cooperation" from the new bureaucratic description in fact reflected the shifting focus away from development assistance towards an emphasis instead on the internal domestic politics and policies of the countries of the South.

The broadest impact has been felt on the work of those agencies with the widest areas of responsibility for the South: the UN High Commissioner for Refugees (UNHCR), the UN Development Program (UNDP), the Human Rights Commission, and others. In particular, the cutbacks in resources (both financial and in staff resources) have been especially damaging in the UN Development Program. There has been an additional spill-over impact as well, since the UNDP, aside from its own crucial projects throughout the world, provides part of the funding for the work of numerous specialized agencies of the UN, which get additional funds through both assessed contributions of member states and voluntary contributions to projects.

While certain programs were scheduled to be taken over by other departments, some entire agencies were especially hard-hit. These include the Center on Transnational Corporations, as discussed earlier, as well as the UN Educational, Scientific and Cultural Organization (UNESCO), the UN's Conference on Trade and Development (UNCTAD), and the UN Industrial Development Organization (UNIDO).

UNCTAD AND UNIDO

The effort to "restructure" UNCTAD in early 1992 was widely viewed as an effort to undermine the agency's work. Since its creation in 1964, and especially with its 1973-74 re-emergence or reactivation as part of the General Assembly's work on the call for a New International Economic Order, UNCTAD had served as a key resource center for the South. It provided analysis of how the poorest countries were faring, policy assessments, and, crucially, a vehicle from which the South could orchestrate multilateral North-South negotiations from a relatively unified position. But when Boutros-Ghali began his reorganization, UNCTAD was on the chopping block. During UNCTAD VIII, held in February 1992 immediately following Boutros-Ghali's selection of Richard Thornburgh as his Undersecretary-General of Administration and Management, the Conference was dramatically reshaped.

In a generally supportive description of the process, UNCTAD's Secretary-General Kenneth Dadzie asserted that the 1992 reforms "encompass a *redefinition of the functions of* UNCTAD, a restructuring of its intergovernmental machinery, a comprehensive reorganization of its substantive work, and an overhaul of its methods of work .... They have been hailed as a model for institutional reform elsewhere in the UN."[35]

But Dadzie himself was forced to go on to acknowledge the impact of that "redefinition of the functions" of his agency. Beyond the structural changes, the reform campaign was designed to transform UNCTAD into an ineffectual discussion group for the South, stripped of any advocacy role. As Dadzie rather delicately described it, "the new methodology of work in particular has been criticized by some developing countries for appearing to downgrade the negotiating process [read: North-South bargaining] from its central place in UNCTAD's work in favor of analysis, reflection, and progressive consensus-building."[36] The "consensus" presumably was to be between the competing interests of the North and the South, without effort to transform the profoundly asymmetrical access to power dividing the two.

To take the UN Industrial Development Organization (UNIDO), one of the agencies clearly oriented towards the needs of the South, as another example, the impact of UNDP's budget cuts has been devastating. UNIDO's Technical Cooperation Projects, the backbone of its mandate to assist developing countries with access to industrial technology, electricity generation, etc., are funded through a combination of voluntary and assessed contributions, as well as through contributions funneled through UNDP. The massive reductions in UNDP funds and in voluntary contributions by member states led to the slashing of the projects budget by almost one-third, from about $159 million in 1989 to about $106 million by 1994. Within UNIDO, it is understood that the cuts are directly reflective of the increased assessments for proliferating peacekeeping operations.[37]

The weakening of such agencies as UNCTAD, UNIDO, and UNDP through cuts in funding, especially because of chronic U.S. underpayment and outright resistance to some dues structures, strips away some of the key institutions once available to developing countries for South-South dialogue and strategic planning. The combination of the "proliferating peacekeeping operations" and resulting drastic underfunding of UN agencies and projects supporting development in the South, along with the increased power accruing to the Bretton Woods institutions, insures an even more dramatic disempowerment of the South within the international community overall.

Fifty years after the UN's founding, its democracy remains a victim of the U.S.-led North's comprehensive victory over the South.

Notes

1. George Kennan, Director of Policy Planning, State Department papers, 1948.
2. Interview with author, May 1995.
3. "The General Assembly may discuss any questions or any matters within the scope of the present Charter or relating to the powers and functions of any organ provided for in the present Charter." United Nations Charter, Article 10.
4. Statement to author. (By 1995 there were 185 member states.)
5. Anjali V. Patil, *The UN Veto in World Affairs, 1946-1990* (New York: UNIFO/Mansell, 1992).
6. Statement by Ambassador Luis Fernando Jaramillo, Permanent Representative of Colombia to the United Nations and Chairman of the Group of 77, at the formal handing over of the chairmanship of the Group of 77 to the Republic of Algeria, New York, January 14, 1994.
7. Barbara Crossette, "Look Who Wants U.S. As a Leader," *New York Times*, February 12, 1995.
8. Erskine Childers with Brian Urquhart, *Renewing the United Nations System* (Uppsala, Sweden: Dag Hammarskjold Foundation, 1994), p. 51.
9. Rudy Abramson, "U.S. Flexes Its Muscle Before Earth Summit," *Los Angeles Times*, May 30, 1992.
10. Information from Non-Aligned diplomatic sources.
11. Statement to General Assembly during commemoration of 40th anniversary of the UN, October 21, 1985.
12. Paul Taylor, "Reforming the UN System: Value for Money," *The World Today* vol. 44 (1988), p. 122; cited in Childers with Urquhart, *Renewing the UN* System, p. 154.
13. Interview with author, May 1995.
14. Richard Thornburgh, "Report to the Secretary-General of the United Nations," March 1, 1993, unpublished; cited in Kenneth Dadzie, "The UN and the Problem of Economic Development," in Adam Roberts and Benedict Kingsbury (eds.), *United Nations, Divided World: The UN's Role in International Relations*, second edition (New York: Clarendon Paperbacks/Oxford, 1993).
15. "The Boot for Boutros?" *The Guardian*, London, August 2, 1992.

16. William Safire, "Reviving the UN," *New York Times*, March 21, 1991.

17. "Selecting the Next UN Secretary-General: A UNA/U.S.A. Membership Poll," UNA New York. The poll included six African diplomats: Bernard Chidzero, UNCTAD secretary-general Kenneth Dadzie, Boutros Boutros-Ghali, Olusegun Obasanjo, president of the International Peace Academy Olara Otunnu. Other candidates included were Sadruddin Aga Khan, Indonesia's Ali Alatas, Costa Rica's Oscar Arias Sanchez, Norway's Gro Harlem Brundtland, former U.S. president Jimmy Carter, Sweden's Jan Eliasson and Pehr Gustaf Gyllenhammar, Singapore's Tommy Koh, then-Soviet Eduard Shevardnadze, Canada's Maurice F. Strong, and former British prime minister Margaret Thatcher.

18. Interview with Boutros Boutros-Ghali, from *Die Zeit*, Hamburg, cited in "The New Boss Will Work for the Third World," *World Press Review*, February 1992.

19. *New York Times*, August 3, 1992.

20. Ibid.

21. Interpress Service/IPS, Thalif Deen, January 12, 1994.

22. Ibid.

23. Boutros-Ghali's toast at ceremony handing over U.S. Haiti operation to UN operation, March 31, 1995; UN press release.

24. United Nations Development Program, *Human Development Report* (New York: Oxford University Press, 1994), p. 63.

25. Cited in Third World Network, "UN Becoming Tool of U.S.?" *Third World Resurgence* (Kuala Lumpur, Malaysia), no. 20, spring 1992, pp. 27-28.

26. Statement at ECOSOC meeting, July 7, 1992 in New York. IMF press release 92/14, Washington D.C.

27. Report of the Secretary-General, "Enhancing International Cooperation for Development: The Role of the United Nations System," UN document E/1992/82/Add.1, June 26, 1992. Cited in Childers with Urquhart, *Renewing the United Nations System, p. 72.*

28. Statement by Ambassador Luis Fernando Jaramillo, Permanent Representative of Colombia and Chairman of the Group of 77 at the formal handing over of the Chairmanship of the Group of 77 to the Republic of Algeria, January 14, 1994.

29. Ibid.

30. President George Bush, address to 47th session of UN General Assembly, September 21, 1992.

31. Interview with UNDP staff, May 1995.

32. Interview with UNDP official, May 1995.

33. Thomas W. Lippman, "Helms Targets UN Programs for Cuts," *Washington Post*, May 6, 1995.

34. Chakravarthi Raghavan, "UN Influence Erodes," *Third World Resurgence* (Kuala Lumpur, Malaysia) no. 20 (spring 1992), p. 29.

35. Kenneth Dadzie, "The UN and the Problem of Economic Development," in Adam Roberts and Benedict Kingsbury (eds.), *United Nations, Divided World: The UN's Roles in International Relations* (New York: Oxford University Press, 1993), p. 318.

36. Ibid.

37. UN Secretariat sources, on not-for-attribution basis.

4

Peacekeeping, Intervention, and a Whole New World Out There

The enhanced visibility of the United Nations, and its new centrality within U.S. foreign policy since the end of the Cold War, are viewed by many largely through the prism of peacekeeping. Any assessment of UN success, therefore, is also filtered through the grim view of peacekeeping failures.

The word itself is a term of art; "peacekeeping" does not appear anywhere in the UN Charter. Although a Truce Observer Force had been in place in Palestine since June 1948, the term "peacekeeping" was first used in 1956 by UN adviser Lester Pearson and then-Secretary-General Dag Hammarskjold. It was crafted in response to the Sinai crisis, and the resulting UN Emergency Force, or UNEF, became the first actual UN peacekeeping operation.

Since that time, supporters and opponents alike of UN interventionism claim that "the founders" intended things their way. But whatever the real intentions of that often-cited but elusive group, any serious understanding of UN peacekeeping in the last decade of the twentieth century (let alone the role of the U.S. within it) has to begin with an examination of the changes in the global political terrain within which it occurs.

The conflicts that have emerged with horrifying intensity since 1990 did not spring into existence without any pre-Cold War history. Some, such as those in Afghanistan, Somalia, and Bosnia, emanated directly from specific changes resulting from the demise of the Soviet Union and the socialist bloc, and the resulting end of the East-West conflict — the collapse of the Soviet-backed Kabul government and subsequent fighting between anti-Kabul *mujahedin* factions; the instability fueled by left-over Cold War weapons that followed the collapse of the artificially-created state apparatus of U.S.-backed dictator Siad Barre in Somalia; and the severe economic crisis and social uncertainty in the former Yugoslavia that took largely regional (redefined as "ethnic" or "national") forms.

Other conflicts, such as in Rwanda, reflected longstanding competition for power and resources, first created during decades of colonial rule, and kept simmering, despite nominal independence, as colonialism's cruel legacy. Or, like in Haiti, the pattern of U.S. domination and the resulting political terror and economic inequity superimposed on horrific poverty created ongoing social instability that had nothing to do with the end of the Cold War.

The new, post-Cold War balance of forces, especially the emergence of the U.S. as an unchallenged superpower, meant that longstanding assumptions about national rights, sovereignty, "spheres of influence," and domination were suddenly up for grabs.

For politicians, the media, and much of the public, in the U.S. and the rest of the North, the end of the Cold War seemed an unmitigated blessing — an end to the threat of nuclear confrontation between the U.S. and the Soviet Union. But for the South, the perceived threat to national independence actually increased with the disintegration of the East-West conflict. During the years of the Cold War, it was understood that even if a small country's (or, more accurately, its government's) superpower sponsor dominated its political decision-making, at least it was protected from being attacked and/or swallowed up by the opposing superpower.

Now everything has changed. For small and weak countries, for poor countries, especially in the South, the absolute defense of national sovereignty remained a consistent hallmark of foreign policy despite the global changes. But now the legitimacy of national rights is being challenged, the nature of nationalism itself is in the process of transformation.

NEW NATIONALISMS

Of crucial importance in that shift is the changing role of nationalism in popular consciousness in both North and South, and the shifts in nationalism's voice in political and strategic discourse.

The last decade of the twentieth century is still part of the age of nations. The world is still divided into states defined largely, although by no means solely, by national identities. But increasingly those identities, and the passions they engender, are creating the basis for long-term dissidence and conflict on a very different basis than in earlier periods.

The post-World War II years, before and during the Cold War, were the era of decolonization. Anti-colonial struggles were the defining events of the time. In many of those battles, the struggle against colonial domination, or, in the later years, forms of slightly more subtle neo-colonial control, was waged in the name of independence, in concert with the battle for economic and social justice.

That intersection, between the calls for national rights and those for an end to economic exploitation by outside powers, created a progressive mobilization point in the demand for national self-determination. Nationalism was largely the province of former colonies asserting their independence from great-power control.

By the 1990s nationalism looked very different. Decolonization had largely succeeded, and virtually all the former colonies had won at least nominal independence. Nationalism in the mid-1990s emerged, or perhaps re-emerged, not as a rallying cry against colonial or colonial-style domination, but as an inward-directed, ethnically-defined, xenophobic isolationism, as insidiously fashionable in the North as the South. And the "national" and "ethnic" definitions and justifications covered a wide range of contests for power.

In Somalia, factional fighting brought Mogadishu to its knees. Despite the fact that Somalia is one of Africa's most homogenous societies, in which virtually all Somalis share a single ethnic, linguistic, and religious identity, the dispute over power was billed as "ethnic" or "tribal." The actual battle, fought with enormous caches of high-tech weapons left over from Somalia's days as a Cold War flashpoint, was over deteriorating power and decreasing access to food and money; it was waged among and between narrowly-distinct rival clans and subclans. As a result of the fighting, the capital and much of the rest of the country were brought to the brink of starvation and social collapse.

In Rwanda, colonial-era competition between the majority Hutu people and the minority Tutsi had broken out into fighting numerous times over the years. After independence, the Hutu-dominated army clashed repeatedly with the Tutsi-controlled government. The anti-Tutsi and anti-moderate Hutu genocide of 1993 resulted from the sharp deterioration in the economic conditions of the country, and the escalating battle over increasingly insufficient land, food, and cattle. Given the colonial history of Rwanda, and Belgium and France's persistent exacerbation of tribal divisions to facilitate their control and economic exploitation, it was not surprising that the fight for scarce resources took a brutally tribal form.

There is a certain irony, given the racist and nationally chauvinist assumptions of so many in the North, that it has been Europe where the rivalries of 1990s-style ethnic and nationalist hatreds are being played out so viciously. The images of the majestic city of Sarajevo, shell-shocked after years of Serbian bombardment, as well as the brutality of Serbian (and, to a lesser degree, Croatian) "ethnic cleansing" in Croatia and especially in Bosnia, shocked the nations of the industrialized North, unused to scenes of wanton destruction outside of the Third World, at least since World War II. The destruction of the historic Bosnian capital by Serbian gunners on the hills ringing the city came to symbolize the brutality of ethnic conflict.

SPHERES OF INFLUENCE

Nationalism was certainly not the only, or even the primary, cause of instability in the South after the Cold War. The lack of any strategic challenge to the U.S. has meant that the threat of unstoppable U.S. domination looms over small countries with a neutral or (in a dwindling number of cases) antagonistic stance towards Washington.

And the threat is not an idle one. With the end of global bi-polarity, the domination of regionally-defined spheres of influence became largely the province of the U.S. Washington led its allies in the North on a voracious quest for economic expansion. Economic influence, especially over weak post-colonial states in the South, was replacing more blatant forms of political domination. And the U.S., despite the problems at home caused by its deficit spending and international debtor status, gained more and more economic clout through its control of the new regionalized and globalized economic institutions, such as NAFTA and the Asia-Pacific Economic Cooperation organization (APEC), as well as GATT and its replacement World Trade Organization. Without missing a beat, even the not-quite-the-top-dog U.S. economy built up its international influence to match Washington's strategic reach.

And further, U.S. preeminence within the Bretton Woods institutions provided unparalleled global economic influence, as the IMF and the World Bank assumed greater roles themselves in setting the political as well as financial terms for the very survival of developing countries. After the demise of the Soviet Union, Washington, operating through these various multilateral institutions, quickly absorbed virtually all of the South into a vastly expanded sphere of influence — though with different levels of intensity and differing reactions from Washington's competitors in the North.

Despite their presence on UN flow charts as "specialized agencies" of the world organization, the International Monetary Fund and the

World Bank have never functioned with any accountability to the UN. Their wealth-weighted, one-share/one-vote voting systems insure that the South remains disenfranchised. The result is that the institutions are used to impose economic sanctions on poor countries (known as "structural adjustment programs") designed to strengthen North-friendly regimes able to head off popular instability. While not an acknowledged part of their mandates, the IMF/World Bank hold on national economic planning and priorities in the South serves essentially as the first stage of international "peacekeeping" in poor countries — a role ultimately more intrusive and domestically interventionist, perhaps, than the stationing of UN Blue Helmets on the border of a country facing economic crisis and resulting instability.

Certainly the end of the Cold War did not immediately bring about economic, social, and political stability in the world, and especially not in the South. Most of the regional instability that flared during the Cold War was rooted in concrete economic and political injustice and disempowerment, far more than in ideological skirmishing. While local disasters were often fanned by, and certainly were exploited for, Cold War purposes, the Cold War's end did not mean those conditions themselves disappeared. Indeed, the realities that originally gave rise to local conflicts — unfair political systems, denial of equitable access to basic resources or education, widening gaps between rich and poor even within largely impoverished countries — all changed little, except for the worse, after the Cold War.

With the end of superpower confrontation, serious humanitarian and political crises continued to emerge. What was new was not those crises themselves, but how, why, and whether the "international community" responded to those crises. In the past, Washington and Moscow immediately backed one side or the other in local or regional conflicts, thus taking control out of local hands while escalating the military level and raising the global political and strategic stakes. Often the local or regional realities that gave rise to the conflict in the first place were hidden under layers of bombastic Cold War rhetoric. Once Soviet support for partisans in these battles collapsed, the U.S. began to view most of the conflicts as either irrelevant, perhaps passé, or as some kind of minor diplomatic annoyance, significant only for their embarrassing domestic consequences for political leaders in the media-saturated North.

Some crisis-ridden countries were simply abandoned by their erstwhile superpower sponsors when they had no more value as proxies (like Somalia or Afghanistan). In others, brewing disasters were left to fester until they exploded, because competing Northern powers supported or at least leaned towards different sides, or disagreed on strategy, and because Washington did not have a clear enough strategic interest to impose its will on its bickering allies (like the former Yugoslavia).

WHOSE "HUMANITARIANISM"?

The challenge of responding to what often first appeared to the North as humanitarian emergencies (meaning violence had already broken out) led to the creation of a term somewhat new in the UN's lexicon: "humanitarian intervention." The phrase had been heard before, but its use by the French foreign minister in 1992 signaled the coming erosion of the UN's commitment to sovereignty above all. It represented, for those directly involved and from the vantage point of the South, a threat to the Charter's longstanding respect for national borders. But it also reflected the increasing frustration of the U.S. and its allies with their inability to deal with post-Cold War local or regional conflicts by traditional means. By appending "humanitarian" to the age-old notion of a more powerful nation invading a weaker one, the interventions that were to follow sounded appropriate and benign.

There is a way in which "humanitarian intervention" is an appealing concept. When the existing state structures collapsed and social anarchy threatened famine and epidemic, as in Somalia; when uncontrolled genocidal outbursts threatened the lives of an entire population, as in Rwanda; when terror campaigns of "ethnic cleansing" killed scores of thousands and displaced hundreds of thousands more, as in the former Yugoslavia, it was clear that some kind of outside involvement was required. But exactly what kind of involvement wasn't so apparent. It was in the face of that uncertainty that the concept of "humanitarian intervention" began to sound less oxymoronic than it might have under different circumstances.

The real problem, however, is that "humanitarian" describes (whether disingenuously or not) only the claimed motives of the intervention — not its longer-range strategy or approach or level of understanding of the underlying problem. Thus a "humanitarian" intervention does not necessarily have any better chance of success than an old-fashioned gunboat diplomacy-style invasion.

And even the definition of "success" remains obscure. To the degree that any intervention, or "peace operation" — whether carried out by Blue Helmet UN peacekeepers or by camouflage-bedecked U.S. Marines — is solely military, its value must be questioned. Even if it is narrowly aimed at assuaging the human catastrophe facing the civilian population (or at convincing those watching CNN that it is doing that), it can sometimes actually prolong the underlying strife. Even before the accusations that UNPROFOR, the UN Protection Force in the former Yugoslavia, was actually helping to extend the Bosnian crisis, for example, some in the UN recognized the danger: "It is right for the Security Council to ask itself from time to time whether the peacekeeping operation has 'become part of the problem' by protecting the parties from the consequences of their negotiating stands." [1]

Further, a fundamental issue unmentioned in the concept of "humanitarian intervention" is the disparity of power between those countries capable of intervening across the globe, and those countries who might be the potential target of unwanted and/or unaccountable interventions. The North-South divide shapes every aspect of the debate: Who determines when a looming disaster qualifies as needing international intervention? Who decides which victims qualify? Who decides which government or other forces should be consulted — and whether or not their opinion about the potential intervention should matter? What form of intervention should be used? Who sets the terms for the scope and scale of the intervention?

Australia's foreign minister, Gareth Evans, acknowledging that "in extreme cases" a "right of humanitarian intervention" should be recognized, has proposed the following conditions as a minimum standard before any such intervention might even be considered:

- there is a consensus that not just any human right but the most basic, the right to life, is under direct and widespread threat;

- there is no prospect of alleviation of the situation by the government — if there is one — of the state in question;

- all non-force options have been considered, and all non-forcible means to alleviate the situation have failed;

- there is a report from an impartial and neutral source, such as the International Committee of the Red Cross (ICRC), that the humanitarian crisis can no longer be satisfactorily managed;

- there has been consultation reflecting ... the views of external and internal parties involved ...

- there is a high degree of consensus on the issue between developed and developing countries; and

- hard-headed assessments have been made about the international community's capacity, in terms of human resources, finance, and organizational skills, to follow through from addressing an immediate crisis to helping the affected state regain its viability as a functioning sovereign state able to take care of its own citizens .... [2]

Evans makes a far more advanced assessment of the complex impact of "humanitarian" interventions than most other Western analysts. His reference to the need for "a high degree of consensus on the issue between developed and developing countries," in particular, would represent a critical defense mechanism for the South in a democratic UN. But the problem remains, unmentioned even by Evans: who asks the questions, who decides on the sufficiency of the answers, and what happens if North and South disagree? At root is still the stranglehold of power politics in UN decision-making.

It is significant that even such a nuanced understanding as Evans' runs up against the insurmountability of U.S. and other great power domination of the UN. After further discussion, including reference to the general cost-benefit equation of potential peace enforcement actions put forward by former U.S. Chairman of the Joint Chiefs of Staff Colin Powell, Evans poses a list of criteria for the actual decision to launch a "humanitarian" intervention. The list is similar to his baseline guidelines. But a key distinction is that in the final judgment, Evans leaves no room for insuring, or even seeking, consensus with the South. In his view, congruity of opinion between "developed and developing" countries is simply not one of the standards that can realistically be relied on in determining the appropriateness of an intervention.

Given the complications in determining the appropriateness of UN interventions, how can the more difficult assessment of success or failure of peacekeeping operations be made? In general, a UN mandate should be drafted in a way that anticipates the long-term impact on the subject country if the operation is a success in fulfilling its specific short-term goals. The problem of most peacekeeping mandates is that they are much too narrowly defined, or too military in emphasis, often ignoring the longer term social/political/economic roots of the immediate crisis.

An example of a too-limited mandate was the UN's first Somalia mission, UNOSOM I, in which a mere 500 Pakistani troops were deployed with a mandate that effectively limited their presence to protection of the Mogadishu airport. An additional 2,500 troops were authorized but never sent. Any evaluation of peace operations must also take into account the overall effect on the general situation in the country — in terms of peace, economic stability, and other conditions — after the UN mission has left the area.

(The officially U.S.-controlled UNITAF military intervention [known as Operation Provide Hope], and the UN's own [though also U.S.-dominated] follow-up UNOSOM II in Somalia, together provide another dismal example. Although the immediate famine and health crisis had largely abated by the time the last UN troops were withdrawn, social conditions continued rapidly to deteriorate. The once-marginal and relatively non-influential military leadership of the clan and sub-clan structure — their credibility and power increased through their designation as heroes or villains by the U.S. — emerged to trample the fragile and struggling traditional leadership [especially of women and clan elders] and civil institutions.)

As it stands now, the concept of "humanitarian intervention" remains largely a military concept. Its implementation speaks of the rationale or legitimacy of sending troops; it says nothing about the underlying inadequacy of military deployments, sent when it's too late for almost anything else, to respond to complex social, political, and economic crises. Evans mentions that the "greater use of civil police rather than military personnel could also assist the UN,"[3] but in this context even police forces represent a quasi-military answer. When a region or country sinks into a poverty-driven morass of tension and political instability without assistance from the rest of the world community, it is questionable whether any closing-the-barn-door military response can legitimately be called "humanitarian."

In foreign policy analysis, it must be taken for granted that any government's decision-making will be guided by the perceived interests of that government (and whatever political or economic forces it represents), not by broader, more evanescent, sound-bite concerns of internationalism or humanitarianism. That being the case, it becomes possible to strip away the euphemistic veneer of "humanitarianism" to recognize and confront the more sinister reality of international power that undergirds it.

In the real world, any UN decision to intervene, or any UN decision to legitimize or endorse any country's unilateral intervention against another country, will reflect the dominant power of the intervening side and the relative impotence of the subject nation. It is certainly true that civil society may be suffering enormous hardships while government or military forces fight for dominance, but anyone who believes that the real motivation for outside governmental military intervention (UN-endorsed or otherwise) is the alleviation of civilian hardship is suffering from a serious delusion of benevolence.

While the term "humanitarian intervention" quickly dropped out of favor in UN circles, the concept, at least as a public relations frame, has remained in use. And the questions posed by "humanitarian" definitions have remained on the table, although during the real-world interventions carried out by the U.S. and its allies with the UN's powerful imprimatur in Somalia, Haiti, Rwanda, Georgia, and elsewhere, none of the powerful countries felt the need to provide answers. The question of UN intervention and local/regional/national crises is complex and nuanced, and it is difficult to take an absolutist position. Certainly there are occasions that require some level of outside military involvement — Rwanda was one example where its absence stands as the failure. But two realities must be kept in mind: first, by the time the situation has deteriorated to the point where the deployment of foreign troops seems to be the only alternative, the international community has already failed — so such deployments, whatever their immediate outcomes, should *never* be pointed to with pride; second, and perhaps most fundamental, is the nature of the UN itself. A multilateral military move agreed to by a truly representative and democratic United Nations would be widely viewed as reflective of an international consensus and presumed necessary, however tragic. But as long as the UN remains caught in a U.S. stranglehold, even its "own" Blue Helmet operations remain fraught with illegitimacy and the taint of old-fashioned U.S. gunboat diplomacy.

AGENDA FOR PEACE

In January 1992 the Security Council convened as a high-profile summit meeting, with heads of state and heads of government leading their delegations to the UN. It was an unprecedented statement of support for the world organization by the highest echelons of the most powerful governments. The meeting took place at a heady time, when what was billed as the "UN's victory" in the Gulf War was still fresh in people's minds, when the possibilities of a new kind of activist world body still showered a thrill of excitement over the UN's jaded headquarters.

The Gulf War, fought by the U.S. with a Security Council-signed permission slip allowing unlimited force, presaged the new kinds of activism that would define the post-Cold War UN. Overwhelmingly, that defining activism would be military. The UN in 1992 stood on a threshold of transformation. This was an organization whose greatest accomplishments had been in the areas of victory over smallpox, the fight for literacy, and the battle against under-development. Soon its identity would be bound up instead with military missions sent far afield to (mostly) ineffectual ends, and with anointing old-fashioned invasions, aimed at stabilizing poor countries and reabsorbing them into (also old-fashioned) spheres of influence, as examples of a new style of internationally credentialed humanitarian intervention.

The linchpin of this militarization of the United Nations would be called "peacekeeping."

That militarization of the UN had the effect it had in the U.S. in the 1980s and 90s: military spending was the only budget category going up, and all programs involved in education, health, development, culture, and democracy suffered massive cutbacks. In 1988, for example, the UN deployed 1,516 international civil servants in its missions around the world; that same year it deployed 9,570 military personnel. Six years later, in 1994, there were 73,393 UN Blue Helmets on assignment, an eight-fold increase, and the UN had established the first UN military installation, contracting with the Italian government "for a permanent logistics base in Brindisi to support peacekeeping and humanitarian operations."[4] The number of civilians sent abroad on peacekeeping assignments had increased by only 700, to 2,206 (the number was identical to the 1992 civilian count).[5]

While the costs of peacekeeping kept rising, cuts in staff and resources and crucial attention from political leaders were imposed in virtually all the UN programs in health, education, development, culture, and democracy. The process would be called "downsizing."

The Council met that January of 1992 to define a new role for the UN around the world. It was before U.S. military actions would make the existing crisis in Somalia worse and lead to the deaths of U.S. Rangers, numerous UN peacekeepers, and hundreds of Somalis; it was before the U.S.-led Council would withdraw its pitifully few UN peacekeepers from Rwanda just as the slaughter began; it was before the inability of the U.S. and its allies to agree on strategy would lead to the humiliating failure of the UN to stop the ravaging of Bosnia. It was before the Clinton administration would demand (inexplicably, given the U.S. veto over any peacekeeping operations) that "the United Nations must know when to say no."[6]

The Council convened with its newly elected secretary-general, Boutros Boutros-Ghali. The French-educated Egyptian seemed exactly the right person for the job. Especially in contrast to his cautious and lackluster predecessor, the courtly Peruvian Javier Perez de Cuellar, Boutros-Ghali fit the bill as an aggressive, activist figure, broadly accountable to the North's agenda while maintaining his credentials as a man of the South.

Flush with what was called "success" in the Gulf War, and eager to enlarge the UN's role and visibility in responding to the proliferating crises popping up around the world, the Council asked the SG to prepare a report on the existing and potential capacity of the United Nations in peace operations. It was a wide-ranging request, based on a vision of how UN military activism might look in a changed world. For decades international peacekeeping efforts had to be balanced against the right of nations to maintain their sovereignty. But now it was evident that respect for borders and national sovereignty were no longer considered sacrosanct.

Boutros-Ghali's response was as wide-ranging as the Council's request. His proposals, codified as *Agenda for Peace*, expanded the range of potential UN roles, military and quasi-military, in crisis conflicts: preventive diplomacy, peacemaking, peacekeeping, and post-conflict peace-building. His view of UN interventionism was no longer circumscribed by longstanding requirements of UN peacekeeping, such as the need to obtain consent of the warring parties. In one of the earliest sections, Boutros-Ghali made the first of a series of astonishingly bold statements. He defined peacekeeping as "the deployment of a United Nations presence in the field, *hitherto* with the consent of all the parties concerned"[7] (emphasis added).

With the addition of that single qualifier, the secretary-general acknowledged that *Agenda for Peace* marked a turning point in the UN's relations with *hitherto* sovereign states. From now on, his statement asserted, if the Security Council chose, "consent of all the parties concerned" would no longer be required for the UN to send its troops to Council-designated trouble spots. The Charter's assurance of respect for the primacy of national borders had been seriously weakened, perhaps abandoned.

Boutros-Ghali's report also backed the UN's use of peace-enforcement activities based on UN military force (which had never, at that time, actually been deployed). He supported UN force when peaceful methods failed, on the grounds that the option of using force was "essential to the credibility of the United Nations as a guarantor of international security."[8]

It was in this context that the secretary-general called for member states to make troops available to the UN on a quick-reaction basis. That call appeared originally in the UN Charter but was never implemented because Cold War tensions prevented the Military Staff Committee (supposedly responsible for the mobilization of troops) from even meeting after 1948. It would be possible for the Military Staff Committee to function now, the SG asserted. Therefore, "the mission of forces under Article 43 [those made available by countries to the UN] would be to respond to outright aggression, imminent or actual."[9]

But planning and executing that kind of troop disposition to UN command, the SG understood, would take some time. So even before such a rapid reaction force might be available, Boutros-Ghali also called for a UN response to situations in which "ceasefires have often been agreed to but not complied with, and the United Nations has sometimes been called upon to send forces to restore and maintain the ceasefire. This task can on occasion exceed the mission of peacekeeping forces and the expectations of peacekeeping force contributors. I would recommend that the Council consider the utilization of peace-enforcement units." Those units would be "more heavily armed than peacekeeping forces" and the "deployment and operation of such forces would be under the authorization of the Security Council and would, as in the case of peacekeeping forces, be under the command of the Secretary-General."[10]

What is startling about the scope of the secretary-general's proposal is the degree to which he blithely suggested deploying UN troops not only between, but *within* states, with or without their governments' consent. In a paper supplementing *Agenda for Peace*, Boutros-Ghali was even more specific. Discussing problems of financing peace operations, the secretary-general suggested that the operations "might be included in the regular budget and the existing provision for unforeseen and extraordinary activities might be enlarged to make it available for preventive and peace-making activities in internal conflicts, as well as international ones."[11] So much for national sovereignty.

Boutros-Ghali's vantage point was clearly that of an activist leader eager to assume a much greater role in world affairs. He acknowledged that the "Security Council has not so far made use of ... action by military force foreseen in Article 42" of the Charter. Instead, in the case of Iraq, the Council chose "to authorize Member States to take measures on its behalf."[12]

It is clear that the secretary-general was not content with this kind of UN endorsement of U.S. or other individual nations' military actions; he wanted the United Nations itself to play the military role. The form it would take would be through member states' provision to the UN of "armed forces, assistance, and facilities [made] available to the Security Council ... not only on an ad hoc basis but on a permanent basis." Boutros-Ghali went on to describe how, with "the political circumstances that now exist for the first time since the Charter was adopted, the longstanding obstacles to the conclusion of such special agreements should no longer prevail."[13]

In a moment of astounding candor, the secretary-general himself described his vision of a new UN: "The United States is not eager to play the role of the policeman of the world. So *the United Nations is there to do the job*"[14] (emphasis added). In just whose interests "the job" would be done needed no articulation.

It is interesting to note the critique of Boutros-Ghali's activism and call for direct UN (meaning the secretary-general's) control of military troops, by one of the leading analysts of his predecessor. Giandomenico Picco, who served as assistant secretary-general for political affairs during the term of Secretary-General Javier Perez de Cuellar, focused on the successes of the UN between 1988 and 1991, when those successes were based on negotiations, not on force. Citing the end to the Iran-Iraq war, Central America, Afghanistan, Namibia, and Cambodia, Picco noted that "in all those cases, the office of the secretary-general played a key role. Importantly, however, UN success was not secured by the use of force. The United Nations was engaged under the secretary-general's direction solely in negotiations and peacekeeping." He went on to note that the only successful use of force was that of the Gulf War, which was authorized by the Council with the secretary-general "de facto kept out." Decrying the move towards greater direct UN involvement in military activities, Picco described the diplomatic problems that can result from the top UN official being authorized himself to use force: "Having that power [to call airstrikes in the former Yugoslavia] hampered the secretary-general's ability to play the good cop negotiator, warning from time to time of what the bad cop Security Council might do if negotiations failed." Ultimately, Picco concluded, "the more the institution of the secretary-general tries to resemble a state, the more it will fade away and, most seriously perhaps, the United Nations will become no more than the sum of its members. In other words, an enforcing alliance, at times, a modern Congress of Vienna at best."[15]

But the outspoken Boutros-Ghali was not like his circumspect predecessor. It was as if the new SG was saying the Cold War is over, now there is no reason why the U.S. and the other Security Council powers should not turn over troops to UN authority on a permanent basis. "The ready availability of armed forces on call," he said, "could serve, in itself, as a means of deterring breaches of the peace since a potential aggressor would know that the Council had at its disposal a means of response."[16]

The one cautious note in Boutros-Ghali's proposal was directed to the Council's major military powers. Implicit in the SG's request for troops was his assurance to the U.S. and its allies that he well understood the limitations of any such force. The reality of the UN's derivative authority insured that "UN force" could not — could never — be used against the armed forces of one of the Perm Five. (A significant distinction thus dissolves: between the Perm Five as veto-wielding permanent members of the Council, and the Perm Five as the world's most powerful military and nuclear powers.) *Agenda for Peace* was quite specific on which countries might be considered appropriate subjects for UN intervention. UN forces "may perhaps never be sufficiently large or well enough equipped to deal with a threat from a major army equipped with sophisticated weapons," it states. "They would be useful, however, in meeting any threat posed by a military force of a lesser order."[17]

So the Perm Five's existing constraints on UN democracy were extended to the use, or threat of use, of Security Council-controlled military force. Only medium or small countries, not the major powers, would be potential targets of direct UN military interventions; the limits on the capabilities of the force itself would preclude even consideration of its use against the U.S. or another member of the Perm Five, no matter how egregious their potential transgression.

A UN ARMY?

Among UN diplomats and analysts, even the discussion of a UN quick reaction strike force was widely understood to represent the first step towards creation of a standing UN army. Boutros-Ghali's proposal engendered vastly diverse reactions; some countries of the South, especially those in a traditionally subordinate or antagonistic relationship to the U.S., were the most uneasy about the idea, understanding that they were among the most likely targets of any Council-initiated action.

The U.S., although for quite opposite reasons, was also less than enthusiastic. President Bush's September 22 speech to the General Assembly just three months after *Agenda for Peace* was released identified peacekeeping as one of the three "challenges" facing the UN. Given the high profile of UN peacekeeping operations and the scope of the proposals in *Agenda for Peace*, it was not surprising that Bush devoted the largest part of his speech to that arena. (Notably missing, however, was any indication of willingness to increase U.S. financial support for already skyrocketing peacekeeping costs. There was not even a commitment to pay Washington's long overdue peacekeeping arrears, then totaling over $209 million out of a total U.S. back debt to the UN of $733 million.)

Bush shaped his speech to appear to endorse Boutros-Ghali's call for enhancing UN peacekeeping capacities. But the substance represented a sharp rebuke to anyone who might suggest true internationalism in the use of multilaterally-sanctioned military force. Asserting that "for decades, the American military has served as a stabilizing presence around the globe," Bush reaffirmed he had no intention of placing U.S.

military personnel under a joint UN command. He described how "nations should develop and train military units for possible peacekeeping operations ... Effective multinational action will also require coordinated command-and-control and interoperability of both equipment and communications."[18]

By Washington's definitions, such concerns meant maintaining U.S. control of global military action, insuring its independence of action and command, while taking advantage of the UN's international credibility. Thus UN military decision-making would remain solidly in Pentagon hands. There would be no assignment of U.S. troops to a UN rapid response force. "Member states, as always, must retain the final decision on the use of their troops," Bush said.

Instead of instituting true U.S. multilateral cooperation in peacekeeping training, Bush spoke of creating "a permanent peacekeeping curriculum in U.S. military schools." And rather than, for example, strengthening U.S. support for the United Nations University or the University for Peace as potential instruction sites for peacekeeping forces, Bush announced that Fort Dix, in California, would be used for "multinational training and field exercises." This would not only perpetuate U.S. control of international peacekeeping efforts, but is likely to mean UN or other multilateral organizations will be forced to foot the Pentagon's bill for such training activities.

And of course, neither the U.S. nor any other member of the Perm Five even considered broadening and democratizing the decision-making process through which the United Nations might actually deploy troops. In other words, any control of UN military capacity would remain solidly within the Security Council. The worldwide representation of the General Assembly would remain out of the loop.

Boutros-Ghali, however, was not willing to wait for U.S. support before organizing a UN rapid response force. Nor was he content merely to toss out the proposal and wait for others to react. Relying on the broad terms of the UN Charter, but without explicit Assembly authorization, the secretary-general moved in early 1993 to begin implementing his own still unapproved *Agenda for Peace* proposals. His goal was to create, on his own initiative, the inchoate core of what he hoped would become a UN strike force. (This was, of course, two years before a not-quite-UN-mandated rapid response force would be sent to Bosnia to back up the near-failing UN Protection Force there.)

To implement his plan, Boutros-Ghali, on his own authorization, recruited a staff committee whose job it was to travel the world, cajoling commitments from governments to provide troops, equipment, transport capacity, and more for a near-future UN quick reaction team. The

Stand-by Elements Planning Team (SEPT) was made up of high-ranking military officers from seven different countries. Led by French Col. Gerard Gambiez, the officers were paid by their own governments, and the minimal support staff and rent were paid by special funds available for the secretary-general's use without specific Assembly authorization.

Their small office, its walls covered with maps and push-pins to identify target countries, was not located within the Secretariat building but was squirreled away on the seventh floor of a Manhattan office complex just outside the UN compound. The SEPT headquarters (and the overall operation) wasn't a secret, exactly — there was a uniformed UN guard posted down the hall. But yet, despite being based on one of the most highly-publicized UN peacekeeping proposals in history (and the brainchild of probably the most media-savvy secretary-general in UN history), until a series of April 1994 press conferences it was largely kept out of the everyday buzz of UN diplomatic and staff discourse or even gossip. As Col. Gambiez laughingly admitted, "Our work has no specific authority, but it's not forbidden."[19] On another occasion he told the press, "You want to know exactly the terms of the mandate that we had .... It is not very clear."[20]

The SEPT officers described their goals primarily in the negative. The stand-by force they were trying to construct, Col. Gambiez said, would not be a ready-to-go army, and not a UN standing army, but rather something close to a toy. "It's not somewhere having a standing army, this is not the problem. We have a bunch of lego blocks — you have been kids, or you have kids, and you know what the lego game is. So when we want to build a nice house for a new mission, we shall pick one lego in Botswana, two legos somewhere else, ten legos of the right color in China, in every country. And then we build this. So the standing army doesn't exist."[21]

They were telling potential troop providers that their soldiers could be involved in old-style peacekeeping, like MINURSO (the Western Sahara observer force) or Sinai, or regimes like UNTAC, the large political-military operation in Cambodia. It would not be an intervention force exactly, but something that could be used for peace-building. The troops might be involved in dealing with repatriation, disarmament, democracy, environmental problems. And the operation would be cost-effective. The stand-by force wouldn't, in other words, be used in missions like those of Bosnia or Somalia, where UN resolutions authorize the use of military force as part of peace enforcement.

The SEPT officers criss-crossed the globe throughout 1993 in search of commitments for needed troops, transport capacity, equipment, and services. The travel was expedited as much as possible, with visits to several countries coordinated on a regional basis — one officer visited Poland, France, and Denmark; another traveled to Jordan, Syria, and Spain. China, Japan, Russia, and Ukraine were on a third's itinerary. In each country, there would be explanations of what the stand-by force was and wasn't.

The explanation was simple, benign. "You can consider us as some Woolworth's managers," Col. Gambiez told the UN press corps. "We have a Woolworth shop, with many closets. Each closet is assigned to one country. In the closet you have a tag with the name of the country. And on the door of the closet, we have a file which is some inventory of what is inside the closet. And then when some of our friends from DPKO [the UN Department of Peacekeeping Operations] in charge of building a new mission come with their shopping list, they say, 'I need this, I need two of that, I need this, I need that,' we can know what might be available because it is in the inventory. And then we choose that they want the white, the blue, the red, or this one or that one, and then we go to the countries and we check that they accept to provide what they promised they might provide, because they keep the key to the closet. So you see there is no boobytrap."[22]

What was requested was tailored to the needs and capacities of each country: developing countries were asked for troops, wealthier countries for supplies and transport ability; all countries were asked to send doctors. Fifty countries had been visited within the first year of the SEPT's work; 23 had agreed to sign on, and pledges of at least 54,000 troops were in hand.

It was no accident that the head of SEPT, Col. Gambiez, was seconded from the French military. Paris had, from the beginning, been far more receptive to the idea of a UN rapid response force than had Washington. A difference in approach had already emerged between the U.S. and France over how to implement Security Council military involvement. Paris had offered a contingent of troops that would be made instantly available to the UN for peacekeeping operations, on condition that the Military Staff Committee, long moribund because of Cold War rivalries, be reactivated. That matched Boutros-Ghali's intention of shaping a newly functional Military Staff Committee largely to direct UN troops on behalf of the Council.

The U.S., however, wanted no part of such a joint military command structure. Its goal would be better met by Council endorsements of unilateral or U.S.-led "coalition" forces that could intervene or fight without UN interference in Pentagon command structures. A secondary U.S. goal was to have the UN help in mobilizing troops to be made available for implementation of Washington's own command decisions. A truly UN-controlled military force was anathema to Washington's political and military agenda.

But Col. Gambiez had not given up on getting a U.S. commitment to participate in the stand-by force. Dealing with Washington wasn't easy. He was negotiating simultaneously, he said in early 1994, with the Departments of State, Defense, and Interior. He had reassured Washington that the force would "only" be used for peacekeeping missions authorized under Chapter VI of the UN Charter, the old-fashioned kind in which all parties must give their consent. He reminded them further that every country has the right to withdraw its troops if a Chapter VII deployment (enforcement actions, including the use of force) is contemplated, and that in any event the initial commitment was only "one of principle" — any actual deployment of a country's troops could take place only after specific authorization for that mission had been granted.

Once Col. Gambiez had gone public (in what may have been a carefully designed plan to force Washngton's hand), the Clinton administration announced that it was considering specifying U.S. troops and equipment that might be made available for UN peacekeeping. Col. Gambiez indicated he was concerned that commitments of infantry troops seemed to be far easier to obtain than assurances of access to military necessities only the U.S. and a very few other countries could provide — like cargo planes, satellite links, communications and other logistics systems. In Washington, Col. Gambiez reiterated that "we can play without the U.S., but it would be a pity."[23]

It was perhaps emblematic of the problems facing truly multilateral UN military action that of the 23 countries that signed on with Col. Gambiez and SEPT to participate in a hypothetical future commitment of the quick reaction force, every one of them refused to send those troops to Rwanda when the crisis broke out within just weeks or months of their commitments. The UN tried and failed to get troops to Kigali in time.

However much the UN's role shifted within the broad parameters of U.S. foreign policy, at least one constant remained: Washington would insure that its own command and control of ostensibly multilateral "UN troops" would never be threatened by high-sounding ideas of multilateral force and internationalism.

Notes

1. *The Blue Helmets: A Review of United Nations Peacekeeping*, 2d edition, UN Department of Public Information, 1990.

2. Gareth Evans, *Cooperating for Peace: The Global Agenda for the 1990s and Beyond* (St. Leonards, Australia: Allen and Unwin, 1993), p. 156.

3. Ibid, p. 157.

4. Letter of Cesare Previti, Minister of Defense of Italy, to Secretary-General Boutros Boutros-Ghali, September 19, 1994.

5. Barbara Crossette, "UN Chief Chides Security Council on Military Missions," *New York Times*, January 5, 1995.

6. Address by President Bill Clinton to 48th Session of UN General Assembly, September 27, 1993.

7. Boutros Boutros-Ghali, *Agenda for* Peace (New York: United Nations, 1992), para. 20.

8. Ibid., para. 43.

9. Ibid., para. 43.

10. Ibid., para. 44.

11. Boutros Boutros-Ghali, "Position Paper: A Supplement to An Agenda for Peace," Executive Summary, United Nations, January 5, 1995.

12. *Agenda for Peace*, para. 42.

13. Ibid., para. 43.

14. Boutros Boutros-Ghali, answering author's question, UN press conference, February 1994.

15. *Foreign Affairs*, Fall 1994, cited in "Picco's Advice to Boutros Is, Don't Manage Use of Force," *Secretariat News*, September 23-30, 1994.

16. *Agenda for Peace*, para. 43.

17. Ibid., para. 43.

18. President George Bush, speech to UN General Assembly, September 22, 1992.

19. Interview with Col. Gerard Gambiez, April 7, 1994.

20. Col. Gambiez, Dept. of Public Information briefing, UN, April 14, 1994.

21. Ibid.

22. Ibid.

23. Eric Schmitt, "15 Nations Offer Troops for UN Force of 54,000," *New York Times*, April 13, 1994.

5

Washington Keeps
Its Own Peace

The U.S. had no intention of allowing the UN to play the peacekeeping game without its controlling hand. With the post-Cold War militarization of UN programs, Washington was squarely in the middle of directing and constraining the political trajectory of UN peacekeeping efforts. But that didn't mean that Washington was pleased with the moves towards what looked like an at least partly independent role for UN military activities. The U.S. goal remained control.

By the time the White House issued its official "Policy on Reforming Multilateral Peace Operations," in May 1994, its opposition had gone beyond rejection of a permanent UN force. "The U.S. does not support a standing UN army," the Clinton administration document stated, "nor will we earmark specific U.S. military units for participation in UN operations .... It is not U.S. policy to seek to expand either the number of UN peace operations or U.S. involvement in such operations."[1]

It was a major retreat. The Clinton campaign had made "aggressive multilateralism" a linchpin of Democratic foreign policy. One analyst described how "candidate Clinton made increased support for the UN a central tenet of his foreign-policy platform. He even proposed a standing rapid-deployment peacekeeping force. Once in office, however, his good intentions were soon thwarted."[2]

Even before the policy statement was released, the White House was calling for a reduction in the U.S. share of peacekeeping budgets. Washington was assessed about 31% of UN peacekeeping expenses, based on a complex formula linking ability to pay with the special military clout of the five Permanent Members of the Security Council. In early 1994, Clinton's national security adviser Anthony Lake called for its reduction to 25%. While other countries were willing to consider such a reduction, there was significant resentment among UN diplomats and staff (especially from a number of smaller countries with long histories of peacekeeping contributions) towards the U.S. for raising the issue while Washington remained over $1 billion in arrears in current UN peacekeeping obligations.

Lake's rationale for the budget reduction was simply that "the world has changed."[3] While that statement was no doubt true, it ignored the fact that one critical factor in the world had not changed — Washington's identity as a superpower, with all its attendant strategic and economic benefits intact. It also slid past the bottom-line reality that the existing 31% assessment represented less than one-quarter of 1% of the U.S. annual defense budget.*

Clinton's 1994 policy statement was written just six months after the Somalia debacle in which 18 U.S. Army Rangers (under U.S., not "UN" command) were killed in Mogadishu. It reflected the massive retreat from multilateralism that public opinion, responding to sensationalized media coverage and political spin-doctors, seemed to demand in its aftermath.

That post-Somalia abandonment of the claimed commitment to multilateral engagement led to a broad-stroke return to the Bush-era approach of a tactical use of the UN only as a tool serving unilateral U.S. interests. Clinton's "Policy on Reforming Multilateral Peace Operations" abandoned any pretense of full partnership with the UN in the military side of peacekeeping and ignored the need to redefine peace operations to emphasize a broader social and economic role. It supported a thoroughly instrumentalist approach to the UN, in which Washington would turn to it only when the world organization was deemed useful to help finance U.S. operations, or when the U.S. needed the UN's international credential to legitimize its own engagements.

In the autumn of 1994, Clinton's UN representative, Madeleine Albright, told the Senate Foreign Relations Committee that "where it is in our interests, the U.S. should support and sometimes participate in well-planned UN peace operations." She stressed that U.S. troops must be kept under U.S. command, falsely implying that they had not been in the past. "Under no circumstances should American servicemen or

---

* It is interesting to compare realities to the often astonishingly misguided perceptions of the U.S. public. An April 1995 poll by the Center for International and Security Studies at the University of Maryland, with the Independent Center for the Study of Policy Attitudes, found a general perception in the U.S. that about 40% of UN peacekeeping troops are Americans — as opposed to the actual figure of less than 4%. Half those polled believe that the U.S. spends about 22% of the entire federal budget on peacekeeping; in fact it is less than 1/4 of 1% of the military section of the budget. And while general support for UN peacekeeping had slid from its 1994 high of 84%, the 1995 figure was still a respectable 67%. (Barbara Crossette, "Poll Finds American Support for Peacekeeping by UN," *New York Times*, April 30, 1995.)

women be sent into situations where involvement in hostilities is likely in the absence of competent command and control. As a practical matter, this means that when large-scale or high-risk operations are contemplated, and American involvement is necessary, we will be unlikely to accept UN leadership."[4]

Albright walked a fine line between advocating UN engagement and attempting to pacify the anti-UN unilateralists in her own, as well as the Republican, party.* So on the one hand she reassured the Senate that every existing UN peace operation was necessary, while in the same speech she condemned "what looks like a growth industry in peacekeeping."[5]

CONGRESS OUT-UNILATERALS CLINTON

In the meantime, by early 1995, the new majority of conservative activists in the Republican Congress was shaping a thoroughgoing effort to restrict U.S. involvement in multilateral peacekeeping.

The congressional effort was aimed at restricting U.S. troop participation in UN peacekeeping efforts, and enforcing deep cuts in U.S. funding of UN operations. In the House, the effort came to the floor with the vote on the Republicans' "Contract With America," the list of right-wing priorities for the first 100 days of Congress. With the exception of a section trying to re-start the discredited Star Wars program (seemingly eliminated from the bill out of sheer embarrassment), the National Security Revitalization Act passed the House easily.

In the Senate, Majority Leader Bob Dole's Peace Powers Act started with the repeal of the Vietnam-era restrictions on a president's ability to deploy U.S. troops without congressional approval. "But even as it gives the president a freer hand to dispatch troops under U.S. command, it would substantially restrict the ability of a U.S. president to commit troops to a multinational force operating under a UN mandate. The 'peace powers act' would also require the administration to say how it will pay the costs of any new or expanded peacekeeping missions before voting for them in the UN."[6] Significantly, while cutting the U.S. share of UN peacekeeping assessments from 31 to 25%, the bill

---

* There has been a great deal of semantic obfuscation by all sides in the debate over UN participation and U.S. international intervention. Most opponents of Washingtons involvement with the UN are *not* in fact isolationists; they support U.S. domination around the world and active U.S. intervention to assure its continuity, but believe such actions should be taken unilaterally, without accountability to any broader agency. Similarly, UN supporters within the mainstream Democratic (or those few in the Republican) Party are rarely opponents of intervention, favoring instead a multi-country, though North-only, approach. Thus "unilateralism vs. multilateralism" is probably a more accurate framing of the debate than "isolationism vs. interventionism."

would also mandate the Pentagon to charge the UN for use of some of the equipment and services (such as transporting peacekeeping troops) that it previously provided without reimbursement.

The (mostly) Republican unilateralist assault was shaped by the Republican House Majority Leader Dick Armey's view that the U.S. "has gone too far in the direction of globalism," and Bob Dole's claim that UN peacekeeping is "out of control" and "must be reined in."[7] William Kristol, theoretician of the Republican right wing, condemned Clinton's "mushy, UN-centered multilateral foreign policy."[8] And, given their left-over Cold War nostalgia, it was not surprising that "the Republicans were isolationist on peacekeeping but expansionist on NATO."[9]

The (mostly) Democratic multilateralist opposition based its arguments on the claim that if the Republican crusade succeeded, UN peacekeeping would be defunded and functionally ended. The result would be that the U.S. could be forced to choose between doing nothing or doing everything in response to local or regional crisis points.

Certainly in economic terms the cost to the UN of such a U.S. defunding would be enormous. "Critics note that had the bill been law last year [1994], the U.S. would have withheld all of its UN payments and demanded $300 million in compensation. That is because the U.S.'s unbudgeted UN peacekeeping costs came to $1.8 billion, while its authorized share and its annual UN dues totaled $1.5 billion."[10]

The move would likely be followed by other contributing countries. According to Secretary of State Warren Christopher, it would "threaten to end UN peacekeeping overnight."[11]

In fact, it is probably true that the reduction in U.S. peacekeeping dues and the increased demand for UN payback for related costs would not have an immediately catastrophic impact on UN peacekeeping. For one thing, the U.S. has for years held the dubious distinction of being by far the largest debtor to the UN system, and the organization has learned to get around Washington's bad debts through short-term juggling.

But more significantly, the largest proportion of the additional "unbudgeted" costs refer to expenses for essentially unilateral (or "coalition") operations run under full U.S. military command and control, though undertaken in the name of or with the endorsement of the UN. The airlift or other transport, and other logistical assistance, to truly multilateral UN Blue Helmet operations is a much smaller amount. Oft-cited examples of circumstances in which the UN would end up owing huge amounts of money to the U.S. are enforcement of the no-fly-zones in Iraq and the Gulf War (with $50 billion owed for Desert Storm).[12]

Interestingly, no one points out that the no-fly-zones over both northern (Kurdish) and southern (majority Shi'a) Iraq were never legalized by UN mandates at all; they were imposed simply by Washington's fiat and enforced by the U.S. and its Desert Storm allies. The Gulf War itself, of course, though endorsed through a coerced "consensus" in the Security Council (see chapter 2), was from the beginning created to be a U.S. war; it was never designated a Blue Helmet operation.

So the essential fact is that both the Republican bills and the Democratic critique of them reflect the view that a UN seal of approval somehow includes a strategic blank check from the UN as well. Even the Bush administration never tried to get away with that one.

This blurring of definitions of UN financial responsibility in its own, as opposed to individual countries', military operations is a particularly important problem given the growing tendency of the Security Council to choose granting a UN credential to unilateral interventions, rather than mandating true UN peacekeeping operations. Just within a six-week period during the summer of 1994, the Council authorized three of these "half-half" interventions: France's unilateral "Operation Turquoise" in Rwanda, the Russian intervention in Georgia, and what was anticipated to be the U.S. "Restore Democracy" invasion in Haiti.

Under this theory, successful implementation of the Republican bills could mean the Pentagon, aside from billing the UN for $50 billion for Operation Desert Storm, or scores of millions for its invasion of Haiti, could actually bill "the UN" (as if it were a separate and independent entity) for things like President Reagan's 1983 invasion of Grenada, or President Bush's Panama raid, both of which included a couple dozen token CARICOM (Caribbean Community) troops.

But the story is even more complicated than that.

Both Republican and Democratic assessments miss a crucial fact: the U.S., with or without a cut in financial support for peacekeeping, remains by far the most powerful strategic determinant in UN decision-making. When the *New York Times* editorializes that "Mr. Dole could force the country into an uncomfortable choice: intervene alone in international trouble spots, or do nothing,"[13] their sentiment has merit but their analysis fails. U.S. domination of the UN to credential its own interventions, or to force Blue Helmet operations, goes far beyond direct financial backing of UN peacekeeping. The ability to veto initiatives, bribe or threaten for votes, and shape the limits of Council mandates, have far more influence on UN peacekeeping than even the prospect of financial cuts.

The ideological right-wing isolationist message in the Republican vote on the National Security Revitalization Bill and its Senate counterpart is undisputed. But the framing of the issue is so filled with straw people (such as the hysterical fear of U.S. troops serving under "foreign commanders" as if that was either common or significant) that it is hard to believe it reflects a clear political effort. Rather, the crusade seemed to link a broadly defined unilateralist preference for intervention (certainly not an isolationist distaste *for* intervention) with an effort to at least placate, if not win over, the kooks on the right-wing's fringe raving about "the UN's black helicopters" coming to establish a world government and the new world order.

WHOSE COMMAND, WHOSE CONTROL?

The U.S. was more ambivalent about direct involvement in UN peacekeeping and in the political debates over a "UN army" or broad criteria for peacekeeping mandates than it was over what to do when a peace operation was actually moving. In that case, the U.S. role was easier: try to train it, try to control it, try to command it, try not to pay for it, and (unless directly part of Washington's sphere of influence) try not to staff it. In most instances, the U.S. has succeeded.

Not surprisingly, the dramatic increase in the number of UN peacekeeping and peace enforcement operations meant that a certain amount of scrambling was required to find qualified troops. Moving from fewer than 10,000 peacekeeping troops in 1987 to almost 80,000 in 1995 meant that a lot of soldiers had to be found and trained — fast. The UN's peacekeeping chief Kofi Annan lamented that "we can't get troops because we haven't got the money to pay for them or the staff to manage them. And poorer countries can't afford to contribute if they have to pay themselves."[14]

Despite their long history of involvement in peacekeeping, the traditional troop-providing countries (especially the Scandinavian and South Asian countries, as well as Canada, Australia, and New Zealand) did not have large contingents of diversely-specialized troops ready for quick UN deployment. An internationally-accessible training mechanism was needed.

But international access did not mean international control. Here again, overwhelming U.S. military capacity, this time in the form of the Pentagon's wealth of training facilities and personnel, carried the day. Some of the training was organized on a non-specific, anticipatory basis, with fictional "countries" and scenarios played out according to computer-generated speculation. Other aspects were overtly targeted at specific existing, or at least already-mandated, peacekeeping missions, such as the UN's Haiti operation.

Although the White House remained uneasy about direct U.S. participation in UN peacekeeping, the U.S. military has gone ahead to raise the visibility and the importance of peacekeeping operations within overall U.S. military strategy. According to Lt. Col. Doug Coffey, a top military aide to the Army Chief of Staff, "When the Berlin Wall came down, we recognized the differences in the world. Last year we finished creating a new doctrine — not dogma, but laying out how we think about what we do. This is the first time an operations doctrine includes a chapter on 'operations other than war' — including peacekeeping, peacemaking, humanitarian assistance, disaster relief. It recognizes the world as much more complicated .... So the military must be trained. Our fundamental role is still to fight and win wars. But if you look at history, the army was involved in growth and the development of the country from the beginning. Robert E. Lee built dikes, General Sheridan helped in the Chicago fire."[15]

What Col. Coffey didn't say, of course, was that in a period of economic downsizing, the best protection for the Pentagon's bloated budget is the ability to describe its work with new relevance in the new post-Cold War era. Since the fall of the Soviet Union, it would be difficult to justify the trillions spent on maintaining an anti-Soviet strategic military force. Far more seductive was the notion of a humanitarian army, capable of fighting anyone anywhere anytime, but in the meantime prepared to stamp out forest fires and rescue global kittens out of trees. White House and Pentagon strategists alike believed that the image of a kinder, gentler military, prepared to keep the peace as well as prepared to wage catastrophic war, would have a better chance of winning public support for keeping the military's budget intact when all other public spending faced slash-and-burn cuts.

As a result of this new approach, Pentagon training procedures now include a vastly expanded peacekeeping curriculum for many more U.S. soldiers than ever before. "We have been involved in peacekeeping operations in the past, but we never gave them as much attention as now," Lt. Col. Coffey said. "Our joint training centers include scenarios built-in for all the troops rotating through them for training. We need soldiers who are more versatile, who can understand the nuances of rules of engagement. The situation in Haiti shows the result of that new understanding: we were prepared for the 82nd Airborne to go in and fight and take down the country. That plan was quickly scrubbed and replaced with a plan originally scheduled for three days after the invasion. We were able to be flexible. Almost all combat soldiers receive some peacekeeping training. In basic training, the training is [in] how to fight. After basic, then there's more learning, based on existing training. It's like Wynton Marsalis, who trained in classical music theory, then he can improvise."[16]

Peacekeeping operations, Col. Coffey agreed, are "the jazz of military strategy."

The most direct involvement of U.S. military personnel in UN peacekeeping tends to be at the level of the commander. In this fashion, operations carried out by a "UN force" are actually led, on the ground, by an officer trained by and — crucially — accountable to the U.S. military chain of command. When a U.S. officer puts on a blue helmet, the U.S. reaps a number of advantages. The U.S. soldier now holds all of the multilateral credibility of being a "UN officer" without having relinquished any of her or his access to U.S. intelligence, access to top political and policy-making officials, and, perhaps most important, accountability to U.S. military goals for the operation.

Two recent cases provided fascinating models. In Haiti, the U.S. seconded General Kinzer to serve as the "UN commander" for phase two of the operation, in which a "UN force" would take over after the U.S.-led force had prepared the ground. Similarly, in Somalia, U.S. Admiral Jonathan Howe was named Special Representative of the Secretary-General in phase two of the UN's Somalia campaign, UNOSOM II. He followed in the footsteps of another U.S. commander, this one in charge of the U.S.-controlled, non-UN military campaign (better known by its U.S. code-name Operation Provide Hope), and thus was able to continue Washington's militarized strategy in Somalia in the name of the UN.

In these increasingly popular two-phase peacekeeping operations (like those in Somalia and Haiti), the U.S. directly controls the initial military action, by insisting that it be carried out largely by U.S. troops (sometimes with a few token soldiers from other countries to make a "coalition") under direct U.S. command. So the phase one operation is authorized by the Security Council, but not under the command and control of the UN. Washington maintains complete authority.

In phase two, the U.S. is generally willing to support an officially UN-commanded multilateral force, but still generally insists on maintaining functional control of the operation anyway. It is in this context that offering a U.S. commander to head the "UN" operation plays a significant role. In areas deemed central to Washington's own sphere of influence, such as Haiti, the U.S. may also insist on providing a high percentage of the ground troops, as well as the commander. When planning for the second (UN-led) phase of the Haiti operation was underway, UN sources report that the U.S. first demanded that 75% of the troops be American GIs. Secretary-General Boutros-Ghali is said to have been outraged by the proposal, which in his view would have thoroughly undermined the legitimacy of the UN force. Negotiations continued on percentages, with the SG offering 33%, the U.S. countering with a demand for 50%, and a final compromise being reached at just under 40%.

Although the U.S. supports these parallel "UN" operations, it remains resistant to the creation of any even nominally independent permanent UN force, and continues to reiterate its refusal to allow U.S. soldiers to serve under non-U.S. commanders. That issue is largely a red herring, as actual U.S. troop participation in UN operations has almost always been predicated either on placing a U.S. commander at the head of the UN operation, or on keeping U.S. troops outside of the actual UN force, creating a parallel "support" operation to "back up" the UN (such as the Rangers' role in Somalia).

TRAINING FOR WHOSE PEACE?

Guaranteeing U.S. control of UN peacekeeping, while oscillating between officially UN-authorized "U.S." or "coalition" campaigns, and officially UN-commanded "Blue Helmet" operations, starts by insuring a U.S. commander for both types of action. After insuring accountability of the commander, U.S. control of training comes next.

In Haiti, the initiative to offer training came from General Borden Sullivan, the U.S. Army Chief of Staff. According to Pentagon sources, Gen. Sullivan proposed to U.S. Ambassador Albright that the U.S. offer to train the UN military staff for the Haiti operation. Amb. Albright agreed, and made the proposal to Gen. Kinzer. Once the Pentagon's man at the UN agreed, Gen. Kinzer quickly obtained UN approval to "request" U.S. training for the entire international (non-U.S.) military staff of the Haiti operation.[17] Another military spokesperson described the process somewhat less formally: "Someone said there was the same problem of lack of coordination and communication in the joint UN mission staffs. Why not suggest to the UN that we do the training? Someone at some political level, I suppose, suggested it, but then the UN said okay, please do the training."[18]

And the U.S. agreed to the "request" — what a surprise! The result was an arrangement in which U.S. Special Forces, Green Berets, did the training of the UN's headquarters staff before the hand-over from the U.S. operation to the "UN mission." So the phase two UN mission, UNMIH, ultimately included a U.S. commander, General Kinzer, about 40% U.S. troops, and staff officers (U.S. and international) trained to U.S. specifications by a Fort Leavenworth-based U.S. military team led by Col. Len Moore.[19]

The Pentagon describes the Haiti operation as the first time a "UN commander" (General Kinzer) requested and received UN approval for the U.S. military to conduct the headquarters staff training exercise in preparation for a UN operation. The headquarters staff was drawn primarily from U.S. military officers anyway, with some additional officers from Bangladesh and Canada. U.S. military strategists came to see the value of influencing UN command decisions. This first example set in place a pattern that would be repeated later as a key link in U.S.-UN relations.

The absurdities of some aspects of U.S. military control of the training of UN peacekeepers emerge sharply when examining the troops of the overall force, not just the officer corps. The forces trained for deployment to Haiti included one battalion from Guatemala, one from Bangladesh, and two mixed battalion-sized contingents from the CARICOM countries. Their training was conducted primarily by the U.S. Army Atlantic Command's Third Special Forces Group/Special Operations Command. The new UN troops were trained for three months at the end of 1994 in Puerto Rico by the Green Berets. According to military spokesmen, the purpose of the training was "to establish a common baseline of understanding of operations" (a baseline, that is, common to U.S. procedures).

The Green Beret training was in preparation for both the U.S.-led "coalition" force and the ostensibly UN-run second phase of the Haiti mission. The goal for the UN phase two (UNMIH), the military said, was "to bring coalition forces up to a standard level of training — things like challenge and password, etc. — aimed at achieving a common level of U.S. training for the mission." As one U.S. military spokesperson defined it, "Here at Fort Leavenworth it's one thing .... This is the U.S. Army conducting training for the UN. When they put on the blue berets it becomes a UN operation."[20]

What was perhaps more startling about the plan for the U.S. trainers was that the Green Berets were to "provide a cultural orientation about Haiti for the international forces, to teach them how people in Haiti live, how people in Haiti think .... "[21] This meant, then, that U.S. Green Berets would be attempting to teach people of the South — Guatemalans, Bangladeshis, and other Caribbeans themselves — "how people in Haiti think." The irony was apparently lost on the Pentagon — "lots of people" at Army headquarters were "very excited" about the plan.[22]

Certainly other UN peace operations were established both before and after the Haiti operation that did not involve this high a level of direct U.S. military involvement. Haiti's crisis emerged squarely within the unchanged tradition of the U.S. sphere of influence; thus the stakes were high enough to warrant a deeper investment, including the use of U.S. troops. In other cases as well, however, the U.S. military was given the opportunity to shape ostensibly multilateral UN operations in its own image. Once the Haiti precedent was set, the training program began to expand. According to the military, after Haiti the U.S. Atlantic Command was contracted by the UN to train the UN headquarters staff for the UN-supported Rwanda mission; that training was carried out in Stuttgart.[23]

Beginning in about 1993, the U.S. military has been engaged on a large-scale program of training the UN's own military staff and specially recruited mission-specific military forces. When asked whether U.S. strategy required a different training approach if the planned operation is anticipated to be multilateral rather than unilateral, a ranking Pentagon official stated that, "We expect in many peacekeeping operations there will be other armies and agencies involved. In our Fort Polk training center, we have created a Potemkin village, populated with role players. Depending on how the army unit is training there, the role players might be a pro- or anti-U.S. army. Then we overlay that scenario with terrorists, rebel forces trying to influence the population, as well as NGOs and PVOs [non-governmental and private voluntary organizations, referring to the various humanitarian relief agencies] supporting the military."[24]

Military sources claim that joint training programs with allied troops are more generic in nature than those involving only U.S. troops, unless they are in preparation for a specific multilateral operation actually underway. The training methods involve the creation of fictional countries with borders, populations, and levels of instability that mirror those of the real world. But of course the requirements of multilateralism mean that the obvious targets of intervention remain officially anonymous. "The scenarios might 'look like' Bosnia or some other country," Col. Coffey explained, "but we want to avoid the tendency for people to assume it actually *is* that specific country. So we create 'Timonia,' 'Atlantis,' or some others."[25] And no one ever guesses that Bosnia or Haiti are on the UN's interventionist agenda ....

Besides the Pentagon's U.S. peacekeeping training center at Fort Polk, there is a similar set-up in Germany. The Dutch government asked for U.S. training for their Marines before their deployment to Cambodia for participation in the UN's Transition Assistance Group there. Given Holland's much longer and more extensive experience in multinational peacekeeping operations than that of the U.S., the reasons given for their interest in U.S. training were notable.

Col. Coffey described how the training program "took real-time intelligence material from Cambodia, and plugged it into computerized training modes, so trainees experienced the same situation as those actually inside Cambodia. The U.S. brings technology and planning skills to military training scenarios .... We have had Canadians, Germans, British, and Dutch come for training. They paid $300,000 for a training rotation."[26]

In other words, the U.S. training is aimed (tuition aside) at making peacekeeping operations as high-tech and computer-dependent as possible. While ostensibly willing to train other countries' military forces in this technically innovative approach to UN operations, the reliance on advanced technology insures that only the wealthiest countries of the North will be able to put it to use in their own military systems. (An additional financial boon for Washington may emerge in the form of follow-up orders for advanced military equipment from U.S. suppliers, from military forces whose people have been trained by the U.S. in high-tech military strategies.) Poor countries, on the other hand, would be less likely to participate in the training, since they would be unable to take advantage of it when their peacekeeping troops come home. Over time, one result could be the gradual reduction, or even elimination, of troops from the impoverished South as part of UN operations — excluded based on their lack of familiarity with and inability to use U.S.-level advanced computerized military equipment.

Besides the techno-gap, there is also a political distinction. Close allies of the U.S. continue to have virtually unlimited access to the most advanced and comprehensive training methods — whether the training is for the national army itself or for contingents promised to UN operations. On the other hand, contingents from countries less cozy with Washington, especially those from the South and most especially those with a legacy of antagonism to or from the U.S., find themselves out of the technological-training loop both for their own national purposes as well as in preparing for international participation. Even in those exceptional circumstances in which the U.S. welcomed the participation of its erstwhile enemies, such as Washington's wooing of Syria for participation in the Gulf War's anti-Iraq coalition, the terms were drawn exceedingly narrowly. While the U.S. won official Syrian participation, both sides understood that Damascus would send only a token contingent of militarily insignificant troops. The Syrian troops were present — that was the important thing — but they were kept very far from access to operational or tactical information, intelligence material, or anything that might be deemed strategic.

Even the new, post-Cold War allies are kept at arms' length. According to Col. Coffey, in mid-1994 the Army had just carried out a "joint training operation with the Russians. It was especially sensitive since their army was recently the enemy. It was just general training, things like how to set up roadblocks, staffing, things like that. It wasn't based on a specific scenario, just coordination and communications. Later we might do some more sophisticated training."[27] Then again, they might not.

Along with creating U.S.-standard training methods for troops and officer corps of international troops destined for UN or other multinational operations, since the early 1990s the Pentagon has been attempting to bring the non-military non-governmental organizations involved in humanitarian relief work directly under the military's umbrella. Col. Coffey acknowledged that recent military training "has had NGOs involved in peacekeeping exercises. They include InterAction, which coordinates NGO activities including Doctors Without Borders, ICRC [the International Committee of the Red Cross], Oxfam, and others."

Asked whether the NGOs had expressed any concern about losing the appearance of neutrality, if not the real thing, in the often politically fragile environment of UN-run peacekeeping operations, Coffey described the NGO-military relationship as one of mutual value. "The intent for us is to show the NGOs what the military can or cannot provide. The NGOs themselves bring capabilities more appropriate than the military's to some situations. Our goal is not to train them how to do their humanitarian operations, but how to work with military bureaucracy, how to coordinate transportation, water supplies, logistics, etc." It all sounded very rational.

"Lately," Coffey went on, "we have built more robust relationship with the NGOs through the Civilian-Military Operations Center (C-MOC). It functions as a clearinghouse for military and NGO/PVO groups, where they can gather, hash out problems, figure out storage facilities, distribution arrangements, clearance through airports or seaports, whatever. The C-MOC is created at the site of each mission. In Rwanda, for instance, it worked well. The C-MOC was established in Entebbe, to coordinate relief assistance to Goma and Kigali. It included military representatives, State Department representatives, and the NGOs. It provided a coordinating hub for information. I was just talking this morning to someone at Fort Bragg, who's working on a video for NGOs/PVOs to educate them on how C-MOC works."

The bottom line, however, is still one of power. The U.S. military, with unquestionable superiority not only in force projection but in all the myriad of logistical back-up facilities that often make or break a complex relief operation, is in charge. Non-governmental and private agencies are not consulted, they are simply trained by the army in how to do their work under maximized military influence. If in fact the Civilian-Military Operations Center does serve as the hub of a relief campaign, Col. Coffey's proprietary definition of it is instructive. "C-MOC is our organization," he said. "It's run by the military. The others come to us."

In an era of UN operations that increasingly blur the crucial distinction between emergency/humanitarian relief and militarized peacekeeping, the consequences of this military control of relief workers are severe. The already-marginal independence of action, and even more marginal political/strategic influence, of the non-governmental organizations involved in relief activities are being eroded even further.

There is an urgent need to redesign peacekeeping mandates to focus on the economic and social conditions underlying emergency-level conflicts. In the first years of aggressive post-Cold War peacekeeping, the UN largely failed to balance the often-contradictory goals of disarming or militarily suppressing warring factions against the broader economic/social demands of societies in crisis.

It was not that no one in the UN raised such issues. Boutros-Ghali described what he called the qualitative change in UN peacekeeping. "Often," he said, "owing to the scope of the mission involved, these operations go far beyond the sole objective of peacekeeping. They now include electoral assistance, humanitarian aid, administrative management, rehabilitation of infrastructures, clearance of mines from roads and fields, promotion of democracy, and protection of human rights." The secretary-general described the significance of UN actions being more and more in response to conflicts taking place within, rather than between nations: "This has significantly changed traditional peacekeeping concepts, as regards both legal principles and methods of action, especially when it becomes necessary to intervene in situations when national institutions have disintegrated and the State is no longer capable of ensuring the safety of its citizens without outside assistance." Humanitarian intervention again.

But Boutros-Ghali himself admits that "this broadened concept of United Nations peacekeeping has, in practice, revealed its limitations. Without material, financial, logistical, and military means, and at times without the clearly expressed political will of its member states, the United Nations has not always been able to fulfill the hopes that it raised."[28]

REGIONS AND THE WORLD:
THE UN, NATO, AND REGIONAL ORGANIZATIONS

So as the world changed the U.S. and its confederates increasingly looked to the UN as a post-Cold War military peacekeeping instrument. But the organization, whatever hopes it had managed to raise, was still a reflection of, rather than a challenge to, the world balance of power. That meant that UN activism was held hostage to the unity — whether real or imposed — of its most powerful member states.

The U.S. alone could still call the strategic shots. When it chose not to exercise that power, whether because of reluctance to expend the requisite political or financial capital, or because Washington simply did not have a compelling enough strategic interest, tactical differences between the secondary powers could still leave the UN paralyzed.

Inside the UN, a shifting dynamic took shape, involving both collaboration and contention, joining and dividing the U.S. and its most influential allies, especially Britain and France. The result is that decisions about peacekeeping and other invasive operations simultaneously reflect the overall domination of the South by those U.S.-led Northern powers, and their tactical jockeying for influence in segregable parts of the rest of the world. The U.S. remains unchallenged in its strategic reach, but the Northern powers often contend among themselves for tactical predominance in a specific instance; in those situations, if Britain and France (and sometimes, as in Bosnia, Germany) do not agree, and Washington is not clearly willing to impose its own strategic agenda, multilateral paralysis may result.

One aspect of breaking the logjam emerges when the UN's powerful members look to regional organizations to respond to specific crises, instead of relying only on the UN as a whole. The relationship between the United Nations and the variety of regional organizations that have sprung up since the end of World War II is a complicated one. The Charter asserts the UN's authority over the actions, or even discussions, of regional organizations regarding enforcement activities. Article 54 demands that the "Security Council shall at all times be kept fully informed of activities undertaken or in contemplation under regional arrangements or by regional agencies for the maintenance of international peace and security."

A strict reading of the Charter would indicate that it simultaneously relies on and constricts those actions in considering its own involvement. Article 52, section 2 calls on UN members to "make every effort to achieve pacific settlement of local disputes through such regional arrangements or by such regional agencies before referring them to the

Security Council." And in Article 53, the Council is mandated to "where appropriate, utilize such regional arrangements or agencies for enforcement action under its authority." But section 1 (of Article 53) goes on to narrow the power of the regional structures. With a couple of narrow, World War II-based exceptions, it warns that "no enforcement action shall be taken under regional arrangements or by regional agencies without the authorization of the Security Council."

No surprise that the efforts of the Arab League to mediate Iraq's invasion of Kuwait, or the Organization of American States' involvement in the UN intervention against the anti-Aristide Haitian military junta, were so lacking in serious UN backing, and ultimately came to naught.

During the years of the Cold War, the contention between NATO and the Warsaw Pact transformed those ostensibly regional security systems into competitors in a global power struggle. On the regional level, the nature and character of the alliances were quite dissimilar; comparing the (British) Commonwealth, the Commonwealth of Independent States, the Conference (now Organization) on Security and Cooperation in Europe, the European Union, the Islamic Conference, the League of Arab States, NATO, the Organization of African Unity, the Organization of American States, the Western European Union, the Economic Community of West African States, the Association of Southeast Asian Nations, etc., is a difficult prospect. What was common was that the regional security pacts were dominated by the overweening U.S. military presence.

By the time the Cold War ended, the Warsaw Pact had dissolved, and post-Soviet Eastern Europe was clamoring to join the West. Boutros-Ghali explained it in characteristic diplo-speak: "The rigid polarization of the world has disappeared," he said, "causing the demise of certain regional defense organizations and prompting others to rethink their objectives."[29] What the secretary-general was really saying was that, despite the plethora of regional choices, at the strategic level of the post-Cold War world, NATO was the only one that mattered.

At the level of peacekeeping, there was already a much more complex relationship between the UN, NATO, and the remaining regional structures involved in — or kept out of — peacekeeping. The secretary-general acknowledged that "the United Nations alone cannot take charge of all the situations in the world that threaten international peace and security."[30] But there was tremendous ambivalence over how much power should be allowed out of direct UN hands.

Boutros-Ghali, reflecting the essence of Washington's position, claimed he was "convinced" that regional organizations should play a more active role in peaceful settlements of disputes, peacekeeping, and possibly peace-enforcement. But he still maintained that "the primary responsibility for the maintenance of peace rests with the Security Council. This should not be changed."[31] That being said, the SG went on to acknowledge rather grudgingly that some regional involvement might be appropriate, as long as "the activities of regional organizations should be conducted with the permission, under the control, and on the authority of the Security Council."[32]

In the real world, the secretary-general's definition of involving regional forces meant "the need to 'contract out' more operations to regional organizations or multinational forces led by *major powers with special interests* in the disputes — like the French operation in Rwanda or the United States forces in Haiti"[33] (emphasis added). In that context, determining which regional organizations would be recruited, and which excluded, from multinational peace operations remained an unsettled business for the U.S. and its Security Council allies.

The result of keeping the Conference on Security and Cooperation in Europe (CSCE) — later changed to Organization for Security and Cooperation in Europe to symbolize its ostensible new permanence) out of the early negotiations on the former Yugoslavia, relying only on NATO instead, was disastrous. There are no guarantees even for Monday morning quarterbacks. But with its representation of not only Western but Eastern European countries as well as Russia, it is likely the CSCE would have had at least a better chance at early preventive diplomatic efforts to stave off the horrifying Yugoslav collapse.

The involvement of Russia, in particular, with its history of close ties to Serbia and the Serbian population, would have qualitatively transformed the political terrain. It might have been significant enough to have prevented the ultra-nationalist Serb leadership in Belgrade, and later in Pale, from gaining support for their claim that oppression of the Serbian population by non-Serb governments was inevitable. By the decision of the U.S. and its allies in the West to sideline the one global power viewed as an ally of the Serbs, the nationalist claims gained new and damning credence, resulting in escalating new hysteria and support for the worst of the Serb extremists, and seriously restricting the potential for creating an anti-nationalist, multi-ethnic opposition.

The UN was thus forced by the U.S. and its European allies to create a diplomatic and military partnership in the former Yugoslavia with NATO. Politically that made the UN a collaborator with the Western forces of NATO in determining who would be allowed in, who excluded, from the diplomatic process swirling around the former Yugoslavia.

On the ground, one immediate result was a level of confusion between the UN and NATO resulting from the "dual key" arrangement designed to balance the role and responsibilities of the two organizations. Theoretically, the "dual key" idea meant that both NATO and UN leaders had to approve military strikes, essentially airstrikes, in Bosnia. In practice, the constant conflicts and confusion between them made the use of airstrikes a rarity, even in the face of massive Serb violations. Certainly there was very real bureaucratic confusion between the two organizations. The thoroughly military nature of the NATO coalition created one type of command structure, the military-as-ostensible-arm-of-Security-Council-leadership created another.

And there was enormous political and media focus on those "divisions" and "splits" and "disagreements" and "tensions" between the UN and NATO in Bosnia. According to the generally thoughtful *Christian Science Monitor*, for example, there was "a burgeoning power struggle between NATO and the United Nations. The stakes: the soul of international peacekeeping efforts." In Bosnia, the *Monitor* went on, "NATO commanders and [their] UN counterparts have engaged in a number of bitter disputes over the use of force against Bosnian Serbs. NATO thinks of the UN as weak-kneed; the UN sees some NATO attitudes as trigger-happy."[34]

But what's wrong with this picture? In fact, bureaucratic ambiguity and confusion were not even close to the real issue. While the statement about squabbling NATO and UN commanders is certainly accurate, the next sentence shows the fundamental problem: "the UN" is no more weak-kneed than "NATO" has attitudes. Neither organization exists as an independent entity with independent attitudes or an independent agenda. Who are the leading powers in both organizations? And why, with U.S. preeminence backed by France, Britain, and Germany (at least during its 1994-95 Council stint) running both shows, should anyone believe that "the UN" could be of such a different mind than "NATO"?

In the case of the Bosnian airstrikes, the illusion of major strategic disagreements between the UN and NATO masked the reality that none of the Northern powers actually supported serious military intervention; even the use of airstrikes, tolerable in some U.S. circles, had few real backers. But public opinion, especially in the U.S., demanded the appearance of "something being done." The result was essentially a complex international scam. And once again the UN would be one of the key instruments for running it.

The battle would be fought not in the Bosnian skies but on the public relations front. NATO would be used by the U.S. and its allies to call for more muscle, greater military responses, a more aggressive response to Serb outrages. But the "dual key" requirement meant that the UN leadership, specifically the secretary-general's special representative Yasushi Akashi and the UN's military commanders, had to approve the strikes as well. The UN bureaucracy, in the name of protecting its peacekeepers on the ground, would be the instrument of moderation, urging a course away from large-scale military intervention. The result was that NATO generals from France or Britain, despite the danger to their troops on the ground and despite their accountability to political leaderships ultimately opposed (despite much French posturing to the contrary) to military escalation, could yell loudly, demanding a "muscular response," knowing that their colleagues, UN commanders on the ground who just happened to be from those same countries, would refuse and make sure the escalation never took place.

This unofficial collaboration does not mean, of course, that NATO and the UN are mere mirror images of each other. NATO has a military structure and hierarchy far more serious and experienced — far more military, if you will — than that of the Blue Helmets. NATO is more serious not least in its level of collaboration with U.S. military authorities and its access to U.S. intelligence information. As multilateral peacekeeping expanded and the UN began the process of stabilizing and upgrading its military staff apparatus, it immediately ran up against U.S. and NATO opposition. Rooted in the U.S. rejection of an even nominally independent UN force, the Pentagon and NATO from the beginning refused to create anything approaching an equal partnership with the nascent UN military structures.

When the secretary-general asked the question "How can we enable the United Nations to obtain, as soon as possible, information from regional organizations about emerging conflicts or threats of conflict?"[35] NATO had an answer ready: You can't.

NATO drafted a plan aimed at directly insuring that its cooperation with the UN remained limited. The secret NATO document cites the Alliance's specific intention not to share intelligence or other data with UN commanders or UN headquarters. The document, MC-327, deals with "NATO Military Planning for Peace Support Operations." Citing the claim that NATO intelligence information comes largely from its member states, the document states that the intelligence material "cannot be given by NATO to a non-member nation or any international organization containing non-member nations. Whatever different requirements emerge for peace support operations, this fundamental principle must be upheld."[36]

In fact, the secret NATO plan does not include any responsibility of the NATO commanders to report to the UN even during Security Council-mandated operations. It states overtly that NATO intends to rely on "its existing command structure"[37] rather than those of the UN in running the operations, while retaining the right to change or withdraw its involvement at any time.

The Clinton administration has made clear that, whatever its preference for the UN's internationalist credential, NATO remains the U.S. "institution of choice where the U.S. national interest"[38] is involved. Given that long history of favored-instrument status, and NATO's continuity after the end of the Cold War, it is significant that NATO's own view of relations with the UN is that, according to an internal NATO document, "the UN/NATO tandem is not delivering the goods," and that "the fortunes of the global organization will increasingly depend on a NATO prepared to envisage autonomous action."[39]

The appropriate model for NATO-UN collaboration, according to the study, is that of Desert Storm, when "UN solidarity was built around the will of the U.S. and its closest allies ... and not vice versa." In keeping with this U.S. preference for NATO's military power and accountability to Washington, it should not be surprising that the NATO proposal is that "NATO should set the decision-making parameters for the UN and not the other way around."[40]

And given that preference, it was also not surprising to note that the 1,500 pages of NATO Operations Plan 40104, preparing for a U.S.-NATO operation to extricate UN peacekeepers from Serb-besieged Bosnia in mid-1995, included no provisions for refugee relief or support.[41] What was to become of the 40,000 newly created refugees from the overrun "UN safe area" of Srebrenica or the 12,000 new refugees from Zepa, let alone the long tormented populations of Sarajevo and the other mortally dangerous "UN safe areas," the NATO plan didn't say.

In the division of labor imposed on the UN and NATO by the countries commanding them both, it was the UN's task to take care of the civilian population in Bosnia; NATO would provide the military muscle to protect — or extract — the UN peacekeepers if necessary. But with the militarization of the UN operation, necessary for its role in the West's shell game over Bosnia, the civilian populations would inevitably be the losers — every shell they might select would be empty.

Notes

1. Clinton Administration's *Policy on Reforming Multilateral Peace Operations*, May 1994.

2. Mark Sommer, "'Blue Helmets Deserve More U.S. Help," *Christian Science Monitor*, July 19, 1994.

3. Anthony Lake, "The Limits of Peacekeeping," *New York Times*, February 6, 1994.

4. Reuters, October 20, 1994.

5. Ibid.

6. George Moffett, "With Dole Legislation, GOP Seeks to Redefine Use of Troops Abroad," *Christian Science Monitor*, January 12, 1995.

7. Eric Schmitt, "House Votes Bill to Cut UN Funds for Peacekeeping," *New York Times*, February 16, 1995.

8. George Moffett, "GOP Seeks Clearer Foreign Policy Path," *Christian Science Monitor*, April 20, 1995.

9. Elaine Sciolino, "G.O.P. Senators Take Aim at Foreign Policy and UN," *New York Times*, January 27, 1995.

10. Jonathan S. Landay, "GOP Seeks Limits to Peacekeeping," *Christian Science Monitor*, February 13, 1995.

11. Sciolino, "G.O.P. Senators."

12. Rep. Lee H. Hamilton, "G.O.P. Bill Endangers UN Peacekeeping," Letter to the Editor, *New York Times*, February 13, 1995.

13. "When U.S. Troops Fly a UN Flag," *New York Times* editorial, February 1, 1994.

14. Paul Lewis, "The Peacekeeper in Chief Needs More Soldiers," *New York Times*, March 4, 1995.

15. Interview with Lt. Col. Doug Coffey, staff aide to U.S. Army Chief of Staff, November 10, 1994.

16. Ibid.

17. Interview with Major Ray Whitehead, Army Public Affairs Department, February 9, 1995.

18. Interview with Lt. Col. Jim Gleisberg, Fort Leavenworth Public Affairs, March 2, 1995.

19. Ibid.

20. Ibid.

21. Ibid.

22. Ibid.

23. Ibid.

24. Interview with Lt. Col. Coffey.

25. Ibid.

26. Ibid. It is likely that the UN's payment for training serves as a secondary but not insignificant factor in the Pentagon's budget-driven calculations of the costs of peacekeeping to military readiness.

27. Ibid.

28. Secretary-General Boutros Boutros-Ghali, address on receiving honorary doctorate, University of Vienna, February 27, 1995.

29. Boutros Boutros-Ghali, statement to working group on cooperation between the UN and regional organizations, August 1, 1994.

30. Boutros-Ghali, address at University of Vienna.

31. Boutros-Ghali, statement to working group.

32. Ibid.

33. Barbara Crossette, "UN Chief Ponders Future of Peacekeepers," *New York Times*, March 3, 1994.

34. Peter Grier, "UN and NATO Bicker Over Who Will Fill Global Peacekeeping Void," *Christian Science Monitor*, September 14, 1994.

35. Boutros-Ghali, statement to working group.

36. NATO Document MC-327, signed by Lt. General J.K. Dangerfield, Director, International Military Staff, August 5, 1993, Annex D.

37. Ibid.

38. *NATO, Peacekeeping and the United Nations* (London: British-American Security Information Council, September 1994).

39. "With the UN Whenever Possible, Without When Necessary?" internal NATO discussion paper, cited in *NATO, Peacekeeping and the United Nations.*

40. Ibid.

41. Eric Schmitt, "Plans for UN Pullout Paint Bleak Picture Full of Pitfalls," *New York Times,* July 13, 1995.

6

Peacekeeping Goes to War

Since 1990 peacekeeping has increasingly dominated the budget, staff focus, and high-level attention of the UN Secretariat. A few of the resulting operations might be deemed partly or even largely successful; others played the major part in undermining the credibility of the United Nations across the globe.

Some UN operations focused on preparing for and monitoring elections aimed at consolidating fragile ceasefires ending Cold War-driven, often decades-old civil wars. Two of these operations, in Cambodia and Namibia, involved huge contingents of UN military as well as civilian staff, with virtually unlimited mandates equivalent to governing the country. In Namibia, where complex post-Cold War negotiations had set the terms for South Africa's withdrawal and Namibian independence, the immediate UN goals of fostering relatively free and fair elections and preventing a large-scale renewal of civil war were largely met. In Cambodia, the election process was forced onto a reluctant opposition by a half-hearted international pressure campaign. Pol Pot's Khmer Rouge ultimately boycotted the election, and its results did not stop the civil war. During just one week in the spring of 1994, 55,000 Cambodians fled their homes in the western part of the country in response to escalating Khmer Rouge attacks.[1] By mid-July 1994, the coalition government elected in the UN-run election had passed new legislation to outlaw the Khmer Rouge.[2] And by October of 1994, a Carnegie scholar would title his analysis "UN Peace in Cambodia Slips into Chaos."[3]

Other peacekeeping operations that reflected directly the collapse of Cold War-driven rivalries were those in Angola, Western Sahara, Mozambique, and El Salvador. In each, the incentive for accepting UN-sponsored negotiations was rooted in the withdrawal of superpower support for one or both sides in the longstanding wars. In El Salvador the election process resulted in institutionalizing a role for the opposition FMLN forces. While the country has yet to overcome the legacy of massive economic inequality, U.S.-backed right-wing

118

death squads, and extra-judicial murder, a process of national reconciliation does appear to be underway. The promise of a UN-sponsored national referendum in Western Sahara remains unfulfilled, with election plans consistently delayed.

Angola was a UN disaster. The UN moved precipitously to hold elections long before the U.S.-backed UNITA rebels had shown any real willingness to abide by the results. The result was a spectacular failure of UN intervention, as UNITA leader Jonas Savimbi led his forces back into the bush to resume the civil war the day after their sound defeat in the UN-backed elections. The UN remained unable to respond for months, and the brutal civil war continued. There were some signs of reconciliation by the spring of 1995, but the price paid was high and success remained uncertain and fragile. In Mozambique, perhaps having learned the lesson of Angola, elections were postponed more than a year until such time as the brutal Western-backed RENAMO guerrillas ceased their assaults and destabilization campaigns.

In all these cases, the willingness of the UN to intervene, and its capacity to do so with any effect, were thoroughly bound up with the expired U.S.-Soviet competition that once raged within these countries. The legacy of that superpower involvement remained at the root of the violence that continues to ravage some of these Cold War left-overs. In other battles of this category, of course, the major powers essentially agreed to let the parties fight it out. In those cases, the UN was functionally kept out of the loop. One example was the terror bombing of Kabul by one of the U.S.-supported *mujahedin* factions, provided with advanced weapons by the United States. The end of the Cold War had led to Washington's abandonment of its client Afghan contras, and the intra-*mujahedin* war was considered unworthy of UN peacekeeping efforts beyond some minimal assistance to refugees fleeing the assault.

But these battles were all fought largely outside the glare of the U.S. and other Western media. It was from the televised scenes of some of the UN's greatest failures — failures to know, failures to act, failures to act in time, failures to act in ways that could help — that UN peacekeeping lost its burnished glow of popular support. And it was at the site of some of those greatest failures, places like Somalia, Rwanda, Haiti, and Bosnia, that U.S. responsibility for "UN failures" can be seen most clearly.

I. SOMALIA: OPERATION FAMINE STORM

During the years of the Cold War, Somalia had been a key strategic battleground. After winning independence in 1960, the impoverished

Horn of Africa country became a loyal ally first of the Soviet Union, and then, by the late 1970s, shifted to a role as client/proxy for the U.S. Under Mohammad Siad Barre, the police official who overthrew parliament and seized power in 1969, a military dictatorship took shape. Some important gains were made in literacy, public health, and popular mobilization during the early years of the Siad Barre regime, but it quickly took on an overwhelmingly military character.[4]

Weapons, military advisers, and military aid poured in to the strategic country looking over the passageway between the Mediterranean, the Red Sea, and the Indian Ocean. In the 1977-78 shift from Moscow to Washington sponsorship, only the nationality of military officials and the brand names of weapon systems changed — what did not change was the military-strategic significance of the country to its shifting Cold War patrons.

What also remained unchanged internally was the clan-based social identity of the Somali people. Somali society was one of the most homogenous in all of Africa, linking the overwhelming majority of the population by ethnic, linguistic, and religious ties. But the veneer of a "national" state apparatus had been imposed by military force on a people who did not historically view themselves as part of or accountable to a "country" called Somalia. Individual loyalty and social organization were based on a complex system of family ties, sub-clans, clans, and clan federations.

With the end of the Cold War, Somalia lost its strategic position. The U.S. no longer needed it to counter perceived Soviet influence elsewhere in the Horn, and effectively abandoned support for its still impoverished client-state. Only the left-over arms remained. Power struggles among competing clans and sub-clans for increasingly scarce resources escalated. By the end of January 1991, Siad Barre was overthrown. But there was no replacement "national" regime. Instead, the power vacuum was replaced by clan conflict between leaders seizing the advanced weapons dumped and then abandoned by Somalia's Cold War sponsors. The resulting battles seriously eroded Somalia's already-weakened social fabric.

The surgical director for the International Committee of the Red Cross in Somalia described how, by early 1991, "four months of street fighting and shelling destroyed Mogadishu. Social checks and balances disappeared. The traditional authority of clan elders no longer held sway with the warlords or the armed bands of disabused rural dwellers, 'camelboys,' who left their homes and occupied the cities .... The country fragmented, institutions disintegrated, and major parts of the economy ceased to function .... Massacres and looting became commonplace. Drought hit and the cyclical Somali famine became a devastating, catastrophic mass starvation. Humanitarian emergency food aid and the salaries and rentals paid by the aid agencies became the new booty of clan rivalries and warfare."[5]

The ICRC, fearing mass starvation in Somalia, issued an emergency appeal for assistance in December 1991. There was virtually no large-scale international response. Significantly, even aside from the looming humanitarian crisis identified by the Red Cross, there was little serious effort at providing direct political or economic support to end the conflict, such as preventive diplomatic approaches, offers to support regional African or Islamic diplomatic approaches, or conflict resolution resources.

The UN imposed an arms embargo in January 1992, but it represented a serious case of closing the barn door long after the Cold War cows had escaped to proliferate throughout Somalia. The resolution also called for diplomatic initiatives with the Organization of African Unity and the League of Arab States, but little resulted. Another ICRC appeal was issued in March 1992. This time again, the large-scale assistance required was not forthcoming.

By early spring of 1992, reports of the Somali famine had hit the U.S. media. In April the Security Council passed resolution 751, creating UNOSOM, the UN Operation in Somalia, including the deployment of 50 UN observers to monitor a then non-existent ceasefire, and to establish "a United Nations security force to be deployed as soon as possible." The secretary-general named Ambassador Mohammad Sakhnoun, former Algerian foreign minister, as his special representative. Some minimal food aid began flowing from the UN, but it was clear that the Security Council's priority was political-military stability, not humanitarian concerns. Taking care of refugees was being left to others: "Despite the relief plan and the arrival of the first UN relief food, by November 1992 NGOs were still undertaking almost 90% of all relief and rehabilitation work in the country."[6]

But while the Council resolution itself paid little attention to specific approaches for resolving the growing crisis, the SG's special representative quickly crafted an unusual and potentially successful strategy. Ambassador Sakhnoun shaped a plan uniquely suited to the particularities of Somalia's crisis and Somali society. Instead of attempting to reimpose a discredited and collapsed "national" state authority, he began to work to rebuild the clan system that had organized the society since before the collapse of the Cold War-bolstered Somali state.

His plan meant working with, rather than against, clan leaders and grassroots organizations to renew the devastated local economies. But the most innovative, as well as the most controversial, aspect of his plan involved trying to stabilize and professionalize, rather than to forcibly disarm, the local militias as part of the process of rebuilding the shattered nation. Recognizing that the militia members' looting was rooted in the lack of any functioning economy beyond that artificially imported by the aid programs, Sakhnoun proposed to provide salaries and training to the militias, transforming them into locally-based and locally-accountable police forces who could, in time, stabilize the anarchic security crisis. It meant giving up, at least for a while, on the U.S. goal of recreating a national government in Somalia with which Washington could deal to insure stability. (The collapse of the Cold War had ended Washington's support for Somalia as a proxy in the fight against Soviet influence in the Horn of Africa. The country was still close enough to vital Gulf oil regions and to the still unsteady Middle East, however, for Washington to insist that Somalia's security crisis could not be allowed to spread.)

But Sakhnoun's plan was never implemented. Flying in the face of standard peacekeeping methods, and running up against Washington's desire for a national government in Mogadishu with or without the consent of the Somali people, his plan was bitterly opposed in the Security Council, most vociferously by the United States, as well as by the secretary-general. While hundreds of millions of dollars were appropriated for deployments of UN observers and peacekeeping troops, no money was made available for Sakhnoun's effort to rebuild the shattered society from within. In late October 1992, before his plan could be implemented, Ambassador Sakhnoun was forced to resign.

In the meantime, the Security Council's military efforts, based on externally imposed troops rather than transforming the internal security situation, wasn't working very well. UN observers were monitoring a ceasefire that existed largely on paper. The mandate of the 500 Pakistani peacekeepers already deployed by the UN limited them to the edge of the Mogadishu airport, and they were unable to fully protect even that. Other countries refused to send the additional 3,000 troops authorized by the Security Council.

Enter Lawrence Eagleburger, acting secretary of state of the lame duck Bush administration. On November 25, 1992 he visited Secretary-General Boutros Boutros-Ghali to propose that the Security Council approve a unilateral U.S. deployment of up to 30,000 troops to Somalia.

Washington was willing, as no other country had been, to go it alone, ignoring the longstanding UN requirement that combatants must agree to accept UN peacekeepers. The only condition the Bush administration laid out was that the U.S. troops should fight under

U.S. command and control; neither the UN nor any nation participating in a U.S.-led operation would have anything to say in Pentagon command decisions.

Somalia, under the Eagleburger plan, would face a (slightly) kinder, gentler Operation Desert Storm.

Five days later Boutros-Ghali sent his report to the Council, supporting instead an operation "to be carried out under United Nations command and control." He acknowledged that the UN itself "does not at present have the capability to command and control an enforcement operation of the size and urgency required." He suggested that countries provide officers as well as troops, who would all "take their orders from the United Nations and not from their national authorities." But, tacitly accepting the U.S. refusal, he admitted that "some Member States might find [it] difficult to accept" placing their troops under UN command. So Boutros-Ghali's last option proposed the Eagleburger idea: a Desert Storm-style "operation undertaken by a group of Member States authorized to do so by the Security Council."[7]

It was assumed that NATO troops would join a UN-approved coalition under U.S. command. The possibility of the wealthy countries funding and equipping an Arab-African force to secure the Arab-African country was never discussed. The Pentagon estimated that 15-25,000 troops would be needed to secure the relief program in Somalia, with perhaps 10,000 more in back-up roles.

Inside the battered country, some clan leaders tentatively endorsed the U.S. troop proposal. The endorsement seemed to be based less on a concern for famine relief than on an effort to jump on the winning side's bandwagon, preparing already to cut deals with the U.S.

So the Somali operation was taken over by American military officials operating in the name of the UN. On December 3, the UN authorized the U.S. to "use all necessary means to establish as soon as possible a secure environment for humanitarian relief operations in Somalia."[8] UNITAF, the Unified Task Force created, commanded, and controlled by the U.S., was deployed within days. The result was a now-unchallenged militarization of the UN's "humanitarian" operation in Somalia.

Some UN diplomats, even some serving on the Security Council such as Zimbabwe's Ambassador Simbarashe Mumbengegwi, stated their preference for a "multinational force controlled and commanded by the United Nations."[9] But their preferences were quite insignificant in the overall power play. Instead, the military operation and the troops authorized by the UN came overwhelmingly from the U.S. Army, and operated solely under Pentagon command. The Security

Council thus took a large step towards consolidating U.S. military control of the United Nations.

It was especially ironic since the U.S. propaganda machine later began to focus on the dangers faced by U.S. troops "under UN command." Washington's UNITAF had been created because the original UN effort, UNOSOM, had failed. The UN mandate was limited; the small, slow successes of the early efforts of Sakhnoun were undermined; and the small size, lack of training, and poor equipping of the initial contingent of UN troops ensured that the UN mission was absolutely *designed* to miscarry.

UNOSOM's failure guaranteed that its replacement by the officially U.S.-run mission, featuring intense media coverage of the U.S. Marines' assault on Mogadishu's empty beach, would loom high in international public opinion. While many aid workers believed that "the level of looting was exaggerated and the worst of the famine had already passed,"[10] the public image was that of heroic, red-blooded American saviors bailing out the UN's "failed" Pakistani Blue Helmets.

The U.S. troops "took," "secured," and "held" the major population centers of Somalia. The role of the hapless UNOSOM troops was quickly reduced to preparing to hand over control to the new more muscular UN operation authorized for March 1993. With U.S. encouragement, UNOSOM II was approved by the Security Council under the UN Charter's Chapter VII, meaning it authorized the use of military force. UNOSOM II was designed unequivocally as a military mission. It focused sharply on disarming the militias, monitoring factional fighting, and protecting aid workers; on its own terms, it had little to do with restoring civil society.

The plan for UNOSOM II called for 28,000 troops and a civilian support staff of 2,800. The U.S. announced its intention to send a quick reaction force "in support" of UNOSOM II. Its thousands of Rangers, Marines, and others would, of course, remain fully under Pentagon command; the UN commander would have nothing to say about their deployment.

As it happened, it might not have made much difference. The secretary-general appointed a new special representative to oversee the entire new Somalia operation. (The respected Iraqi diplomat, Ismat Kittani, had served in the interim following Sakhnoun's resignation.) Boutros-Ghali's man of the hour turned out to be no other than U.S. Admiral Jonathan T. Howe (ret.). So the U.S.-commanded quick reaction force would be serving as back-up to the UN troops involved in peace enforcement in Somalia — who just happened to be under the overall direction of a U.S. admiral. (A Turkish officer, Lt.-Gen. Cevik

Bir, was appointed Force Commander of UNOSOM II. But the UN's mandate gave overall responsibility to the secretary-general's special representative — Adm. Howe.)

But the magic words of UNOSOM II remained militarization and stabilization. In June UNOSOM II initiated a major air and ground offensive in Mogadishu, seizing control of Radio Mogadishu and attacking numerous militia facilities. The following day UNOSOM II troops fired on a large group of Somali civilians in the city; numerous civilian casualties resulted.

As the "muscular" efforts towards enforcement went forward, there was increasing unease among numerous contingents of the multinational UN force. An Italian unit, for example, stationed in Mogadishu, was ordered to participate in one of the heavily armed raids trying to capture clan leader Mohammad Farah Aideed, the current enemy number one of the U.S. The Italians, who, however ironically given their colonial past, knew far more of Somali culture and society than their U.S. colleagues, refused, recognizing the move as ill-advised. Reacting in a huff, Boutros-Ghali tried to have the Italian general recalled. Eventually, after the UN's own legal office had acknowledged that the secretary-general had no legal basis to demand the recall of a contingent's commander, the issue died down. The Italians stayed in Somalia, although they moved out of Mogadishu to avoid future entanglements in military actions they deemed inappropriate.

Washington's militarization strategy was based on an effort first to criminalize and forcibly attack and kidnap, then later to rehabilitate the "warlord" Mohammad Farah Aideed. That strategy's disastrous failure led to, among other things, the deaths of eighteen American Rangers operating under U.S. command in ostensible "support" of the UN. The strategy had earlier left dozens of Blue Helmet peacekeepers and hundreds of Somalis dead. On June 5, 1993, 24 Pakistani UN soldiers were killed in an ambush. On July 12, UN forces had attacked what they believed to be a command post of Aideed's. Dozens of Somalis were killed, including some elders, but Aideed had apparently not been present. Throughout that summer, operating under unilateral, not UN command, the U.S. Rangers had spent weeks raiding various homes and buildings in Mogadishu in a fruitless effort to capture Aideed.

In an October 3 gunfight, more than 200 Somalis and the eighteen Rangers were killed; horrified television viewers saw one of the dead U.S. soldiers being dragged through the Mogadishu streets. Perhaps more than any other event in the last five years, that single incident, and that one set of U.S. casualties, sent the trajectory of U.S. support for UN peacekeeping into a downward spiral from which it has yet to recover. But the history of that tragic event, and those which preceded it, has been written wrong. Public opinion, as well as U.S. political leaders, seem to have accepted the view that the Somali disaster was the fault of the United Nations. In fact, according to the dean of the School for International Training, "the common assertion that the deaths of 18 American soldiers in Somalia in 1993 were 'due largely to wrongheaded foreign commanders' is false .... The American Ranger attack in which 18 United States soldiers died was ordered by American, not United Nations commanders."[11]

The constant ratcheting up of the U.S.-orchestrated militarization level ultimately undermined the UN's efforts at assisting in social reconstruction in Somalia. It wasn't until August 1993 that the UNOSOM humanitarian coordination office moved out of the UNOSOM II military headquarters specifically to distance itself from the military activities. It is interesting to note that advanced non-lethal crowd control weapons, including stun-guns that fire beanbags, and sticky foam sprays that immobilize rioters without injuries or fatalities, were provided to U.S. troops in Somalia only when they were redeployed there briefly to help escort out the last UN peacekeepers in early 1995.[12] When U.S. troops were themselves sent in as peacekeepers, only M16 rifles and tanks were provided.

Progress towards peace remained stalled. In November 1994 the UN voted to withdraw the last 17,000 peacekeeping troops of the $2 billion operation by March 31, 1995. Even before that deadline, the last Blue Helmets were gone. U.S. and Italian forces escorted the last UN peacekeepers out of Mogadishu on March 3.

Militarization of the peacekeeping strategy remained the primary basis for the UN's failure in Somalia. But the flap between Italy and the U.S. over tactics in Mogadishu provided a clear demonstration of the complexity of Washington's UN strategy. On the one hand, there is an effort to treat the global organization like an arm of the State Department — but often the multilateral (albeit not egalitarian) character of the UN pops up anyway. The U.S. can control a specific operation or the overall direction of the UN only if it goes all out, spending whatever the requisite political capital. If it is not willing to make the investment, the outcome is far less certain.

The Somalia operation reflected a particularly cruel twist. The crisis was one for which international responsibility was high and direct: Somalia had been a key playing field of Cold War rivalries, supported first by Moscow and later by Washington. The result was an extraordinary surfeit of powerful weapons "left over" in the country.

For a few short months after the crisis faded from television screens, analysts and politicians continued to ask what were the "lessons" of Somalia. The *New York Times* described the obvious reality that "no one any longer wants to talk about Somalia as a prototype for post-Cold War military action."[13] The Clinton administration acknowledged that their military policies had been a mistake.

But Somalia raises another question as well — a question not addressed by most analysts: the clear question of who or what is responsible for "UN" failures — not the failures of Boutros-Ghali, or General Bir, or even Admiral Howe, but the failure, in this case, of an entire operation, mandated by the world organization, but in which the U.S. played the determinative role. To ask the question, then, is to provide the answer. The "UN decision" to initiate a direct military confrontation with Aideed was based on a Security Council resolution (837) urged on the Council and largely crafted by Washington.

II. RWANDA: THE HORROR OF GENOCIDE

Throughout the Rwanda crisis, editorials and headlines were blunt, sometimes angry. "Inadequate UN Effort Seen Against Killers in Rwanda," "U.S. Might Have Avoided Rwanda Tragedy," "Genocide in Rwanda: U.S. Complicity By Silence"[14] all reflected what UN peacekeeping director Kofi Annan called "the post-Somalia syndrome."[15]

The genocide against moderate Hutu and the entire Tutsi population left up to 800,000 people dead in 100 days of slaughter. The escalation in massacres did not come as a complete surprise, but still the United Nations was unable to act even to blunt, let alone stop, the attacks. Six months before the Rwandese massacres began, eighteen U.S. soldiers had been killed in Somalia. The Somalia syndrome kicked in with a vengeance, and Rwanda paid the price.

The genocidal attacks began in Rwanda following the shooting down of the president's plane on April 6, 1994 — apparently by members of his own presidential guard, displeased by President Juvenal Habyarimana's official acceptance (though largely cosmetic) of the Arusha Accords guaranteeing some level of democratic pluralism for Hutu and Tutsi alike in Rwandan political life.[16] But those attacks came after four years of fighting between the Rwandese government, dominated by Hutu extremists, and the Tutsi-led opposition, the Rwandese Patriotic Front.

The UN had already been involved: the tiny UN Observer Mission Uganda-Rwanda (UNOMUR) was deployed on the Ugandan side of the border. The Arusha agreement took place largely under the sponsorship of the Organization of African Unity; the UN played a back-up role. But the hopes of Arusha for a ceasefire and normalization of political life in Rwanda were never realized. President Habyarimana had the firm backing of U.S. Ambassador David Rawson, who was posted to Rwanda in December of 1993, only a few months before the genocide began. Rawson's earlier experience had been in Somalia, where he oversaw massive weapons shipments to the Siad Barre dictatorship in 1988. Senior RPF officials told Africa Rights that when they "presented evidence of the planned genocide, the ambassador dismissed them with the charge that they were just looking for a pretext to restart the war."[17]

When the Arusha Accords failed to stop the fighting in Rwanda, the Security Council approved the creation of UNAMIR, the UN's Assistance Mission for Rwanda. U.S. Ambassador Albright lobbied hard to reduce the size of the force to be sent (although the U.S. never intended to send its own troops under any circumstances). As a result, the text of resolution 872 asked the secretary-general "to consider ways of reducing the total maximum strength of UNAMIR ... and requests the secretary-general in planning and executing the phased deployment of UNAMIR to seek economies."[18] The force was established on October 5, 1993, and the first battalion, made up of Belgian and Bangladeshi contingents, was deployed in December. Kigali, the Rwandese capital, was declared a "weapons secure area" on Christmas Eve, but the fighting continued and both the limited UNAMIR mandate and the small size of the force sent (which never went above 2,500) conspired to insure the Blue Helmets were unable to do much to contain it. As the directors of Africa Watch described it, "Once burned [in Somalia], the U.S. acted to constrain the UN's peacekeeping role, thus undermining international efforts ... to prevent the crisis in Rwanda."[19]

UNAMIR's mandate was set to expire on April 5, 1994. Belgium (perhaps acting out of some delayed feeling of post-colonial guilt or responsibility) had sent a large contingent of troops as part of the 2,500 Blue Helmets and had joined Tanzania to lead support for extending UNAMIR's mandate. But the Rwandese government, with strong French support, lobbied hard to end the mandate. The U.S. played little role in the debate and ultimately the mandate was continued.

Soon after the killings began when the president's plane was shot down, Belgium withdrew its peacekeepers unilaterally. Instead of moving quickly to replace them, perhaps by providing funds to transport and equip African troops who could be sent immediately to Rwanda, the UN did just the opposite.

Human Rights Watch described how, on April 21st,

> at U.S. insistence, the UN Security Council voted to reduce its 2,500-man [sic] Rwandan peacekeeping force ... to a skeleton crew of just a few hundred. The decision came at the height of the massacres .... The U.S. justified its opposition to UNAMIR on the grounds that the force should not be maintained in a civil war between Rwandan government forces and the advancing Rwandan Patriotic Front (RPF). Yet that excuse was premised on the false notion that the slaughter of civilians was taking place in the context of a civil war. In reality, the vast numbers of civilians exterminated — estimated at upward of 500,000 victims — died in areas of the country where there was no RPF presence and no civil war. If UNAMIR forces had been quickly dispatched with proper equipment to such areas, their presence would have deterred the militia and the Army, whose only significant armed activity was to slaughter terrified men, women, and children cowering in churches and homes. For the next month, UN Secretary-General Boutros Boutros-Ghali strongly advocated redeployment of UNAMIR, and the U.S. continued to resist.[20]

Africa Rights reported how Rwanda became a "test case for the new presidential policy of caution in all peacekeeping affairs."[21] Security Council debates began again when media coverage of the desperate survivors of the genocide began to take hold. In mid-May Boutros-Ghali recommended that the Council send 5,500 new troops, but the U.S. again scuttled the plan. After Washington made clear its opposition to strengthening UNAMIR, resolution 918 authorized a paper "expansion of the UNAMIR force level up to 5,500 troops" but, consistent with the U.S. reluctance to send the Blue Helmets, specifically mandated only a "first phase" transfer of the military observers then in Nairobi. The result was that only an additional 850 troops, already working in UNAMIR in Kenya, arrived in Kigali. UN efforts to recruit the additional 4,700 failed. (It was during this period that 23 countries had agreed to provide troops or equipment for the UN's stand-by force. Each of those countries, when asked to make good on their pledge for Rwanda, refused to do so.)

It was in this context that Washington backed France's move to send troops to Rwanda unilaterally. In July and August of 1994, the Security Council launched a "summer offensive" designed to transfer responsibility for peacekeeping out of UN hands and back to the control of the major powers. UN staff and diplomats alike were stunned by the rapid escalation of events in four weeks.

The decisions came quickly, as powerful countries among the Perm Five Council members asked for and got UN permission to invade other countries on questionably-defined "humanitarian" grounds. France was only the first. The Security Council authorized Paris (the key backer of the Rwandese government and its related death-wielding militias) to intervene unilaterally in Rwanda, despite the UN's inability to find 5,000 mandated Blue Helmet peacekeepers. "Operation Turquoise" was endorsed by the UN with the understanding that France would have complete unilateral control.

The Rwandese opposition raised strong objections to the French playing such a unilateral role, and many in the South viewed the French goal as a return to old-fashioned spheres-of-influence colonial style politics. Even the *New York Times* acknowledged that "there was plenty of evidence that one of their objectives was to keep the Government, which was then led by the majority Hutu ethnic group, from being defeated at the hands of the Rwandan Patriotic Front.... During the first three years of the civil war, which began when the Rwandan Patriotic Front attacked in October 1990, the French dispatched troops on at least two occasions when it looked like the Tutsi-led forces were on the verge of victory."[22] The French forces, with far greater numbers, better equipped, and with a virtually unlimited mandate, were able to accomplish more than the UN Blue Helmets in bringing some level of stability to the corner of Rwanda where they deployed. But the Security Council's decision to grant France a unilateral mandate, backed by the U.S. as the kind of interventionism Washington demands for itself, further eroded the UN's credibility in Rwanda.

No effort was made to insist — or even to urge — that France send those same soldiers to serve as UN Blue Helmets in the still un-staffed UNAMIR expansion that France's ambassador had voted for in the Council only weeks earlier. It didn't matter that France's troops "carried a heavy load of political baggage along with their usual kits."[23]

France was not the only beneficiary of the Council's largesse. Within days the Council endorsed Russia's separatist-backing soldiers in Georgia as peacekeepers. (Russia was widely viewed as supporting the Abkasian rebels against the Georgian government; Moscow's troops, already in place in Georgia before the Council authorization, were known to be far from uninvolved in the conflict.) In Bosnia, the UN turned over its early initiative to the so-called "Contact Group," made up of the U.S., France, Britain, Russia, and Germany, each with its own self-interests to defend. And on the last day of July the Council gave Washington a green light to use "all necessary means" to invade Haiti in the name of democracy.

In the case of Rwanda, the U.S. involvement centered on finances: not contributing money for the force Washington was so reluctant to endorse, but quite the opposite. When the Canadian commander of the truncated UNAMIR contingent struggling to work in Rwanda appealed in public to the U.S. for armored personnel carriers for his troops, Washington was stuck. Too much public attention was already focused on the Rwanda horrors to simply ignore the plea. So the Pentagon agreed to provide the APCs, but, citing the "new realism" of the Clinton administration's policy guidelines for peacekeeping, military officials raised the rental price for the APCs, and demanded that the UN pay additional money to transport them back to Germany when the mission was finished. It would have cost $15 million.[24] Instead, the haggling over money took so long that before the Ghanaian peacekeepers had finished being trained in their use, before the APCs ever rolled into Rwanda, the war was over. The government in Kigali collapsed, the RPF took power, and one of the largest refugee flights in African history began to stream across the border into Zaire. The APCs had never made it.

The U.S. responsibility for the abject failure of the UN and the international community in Rwanda took the form of rejection and refusal at virtually every level of involvement in the war-torn country at a time it might have made a difference. Washington rejected support for jamming the hate-mongering radio broadcasts through which Hutu extremists mobilized much of their genocidal attacks. Human Rights Watch pointed to Pentagon experts who described how "the Rwandan broadcasts could have been jammed by an aircraft called 'Volent Solo,' which was used to jam radio transmissions during the Gulf war. But the Clinton administration ... never seriously investigated jamming the radios and Volent Solo stayed grounded at a Pennsylvania base."[25] The U.S. also never called for a UN effort to provide alternative radio broadcasts aimed at countering the extremist tribal appeals. (It is interesting to compare the U.S. failure to consider radio as a potentially powerful, though non-violent, instrument of peacemaking in Rwanda, given Washington's preference for Radio Marti as a key weapon against Cuba.)

The U.S. refused to expel the Rwandese ambassador during the massacres, despite his government's liability. Africa Rights reported the effect of the delayed move: "On July 16, the Clinton administration expelled the Rwandese ambassador to Washington. Washington had waited until that regime was militarily defeated and a new RPF-headed government was about to take power. Then, suddenly, the administration was indignant: 'The United States,' said President Clinton, 'cannot allow representatives of a regime that supports genocidal massacres to remain on our soil.' Taken in April, the gesture and the words might have had meaning; in July they reeked of opportunism and hollow moralizing."[26]

In June 1994, just before the end of the war, the UN finally officially identified the slaughter of civilians by the Rwandese army as genocide. The U.S. had resisted identifying the attacks as genocide, because the 1948 Convention Against Genocide required its signatories to act against such actions. That wouldn't have fit with Washington's efforts to stay as far away as possible from real commitment in Rwanda. State Department officials refused to use the term, although Secretary of State Warren Christopher grudgingly acknowledged that "acts of genocide may have occurred." Officials of the RPF government were dismayed that the U.S. ambassador, David Rawson, had urged caution before describing the killing as genocide, weeks after the massacres began.[27]

But once the UN finally set the term, it moved slowly to establish a war crimes tribunal. From the beginning there were problems. The U.S. and its allies, apparently hoping to keep the tribunal marginalized and irrelevant, modeled it after the court established for the former Yugoslavia, and in fact placed it under the jurisdiction of the head prosecutor of the Yugoslav tribunal, South African judge Richard Goldstone.

Although the new Rwandese government wanted international involvement and assistance with war crimes trials, its representatives opposed the Security Council resolution establishing the UN tribunal. On November 9, 1994, Rwandese Ambassador Manzi Bakuramuta described it as ironic that "my government requested a tribunal, but we were the only Council member that opposed the resolution. The reason is my Government didn't accept how the resolution and the drafting was handled."[28] The key problem, he said, was in the dates; the UN resolution specified that only those crimes that took place after January 1, 1994 would be considered for prosecution. "There's no logic to that," the ambassador said. The Rwandese government was concerned that those who planned the genocide would be able to avoid prosecution based on the time frame. Included in those potential defendants were some French people who the RPF claims were "complicit" in the atrocities.

Even more damaging than the insufficient mandate was thoroughly insufficient resources. Only two months after the war ended and the UN human rights mandate was underway, the head of the UN investigating team resigned. Irish lawyer Karen Kenny cited the lack of support from the UN for her team's work. A month later, only 27 UN monitors were working in Rwanda, out of 147 requested by the human rights team.

Requests for specialized investigators to analyze forensic material were ignored. According to the *Christian Science Monitor*, "Language experts are needed to analyze local radio broadcasts that incited Hutus to 'fill the half-empty graves' with dead Tutsis, but Ms. Kenny could not even get funding for 200 blank cassette tapes to record the broadcasts. Oxfam and Save the Children Fund-UK ... deplored the 'lamentably slow' UN response, and gave $150,000 to ease the 'funding crisis' of the UN human rights monitors."[29]

While some of the funding problems appeared to stem from confusion of responsibility between the Geneva-based UN Center for Human Rights and the New York-based High Commissioner for Refugees, a far greater threat came from the reluctance of the Security Council to allocate sufficient funds for a serious investigation. The insistence of the UN on holding the human rights trials far from Rwanda, in the Hague, presents additional problems. The Rwandese government wanted the UN tribunals to include possible death penalties for war crimes; the UN refused. But beyond that, the ambassador said, "We want these tribunals for reconciliation. If the trials are held outside, it will be impossible for local people to see them happen in other countries. We want to bring them back to Rwanda .... The Rwandese community will not benefit if the center of the tribunals is outside."[30]

Ultimately it was a question of money. The U.S. and its allies pledged more than $600 million in aid to Rwanda in 1994-95; according to the *New York Times*, "very little has been delivered so far."[31] Instead, efforts have been concentrated in the military sphere. By the summer of 1995, the Security Council remained focused on convincing the Rwandese government to allow 2,500 troops and military observers to stay in the country. (Once the war had ended, the UN Blue Helmet presence had finally reached the authorized 5,500 person level.)

There was no parallel move by the U.S. or its powerful allies to provide desperately needed money to rebuild the country; only soldiers. A U.S. lawyer visiting Rwanda described the overwhelming challenge facing the collapsed legal system:

> Rwanda has no legal system that can deal with killers now or in the foreseeable future. It is virtually a lawless state: no police or prosecutors function, and there are almost no judges and courtrooms .... There are fewer than 10 judges to try the tens of thousands involved in the massacres .... A legal system must be created that is fair to the Hutus and Tutsis. But the international tribunal being assembled in the Hague is no solution. Its trials are many years away .... The country needs a Jurists Without Borders — a group of lawyers and judges familiar with criminal prosecutions that would try the cases in Rwanda under Rwandan sovereignty .... The international community has sent food, troops, and medical aid to meet Rwanda's emergency needs. Now it must find lawyers and judges to help restore the rule of law.[32]

So far Washington still wants to send (someone else's) troops.

The Rwandese ambassador was even more direct. "Here for once we have a small African country with difficulties who knows what it wants and what it needs to do," he said. "Give us a chance to help ourselves. We need the doctors, the judges, the lawyers, the people who can help us lift the country. We don't need any more military."[33] The U.S. ignored the plea, maintaining its Council position that the emphasis should remain on convincing the government in Kigali to accept more troops.

The U.S., without a strategic commitment to Rwanda, had sat back and allowed the UN to take the heat for failure. "The fact that the world can watch 500,000 people die is a failure for us," a UN official said. "What will be the result of genocide if no action is taken? What credibility will we have? In Rwanda we are in danger of losing our souls."[34]

III. HAITI: IN WASHNGTON'S BACKYARD

On the morning of September 22, 1994, the *New York Times* was filled with articles about the UN: Taiwan's bid for UN membership had been turned down; UN-sponsored negotiations on nuclear power plants were stalled; the UN faced continuing crises in Rwanda, Somalia, Bosnia.

There were also two-and-a-half entire pages devoted to the thousands of U.S. troops occupying Haiti and the pending return of exiled President Aristide, and the words "United Nations" never even appeared.

That night, *Nightline* devoted a full 45-minute show to an hour-by-hour chronology of the Haiti crisis, and the decision-making process that led to the U.S. occupation. In the entire 45 minutes, nowhere did the words "United Nations" appear. Once having granted its before-the-fact approval of anything the U.S. might choose to do, the UN was utterly excluded from Washington's decisions about Haiti's fate.

When Dante Caputo resigned his post as the UN's special envoy to Haiti on September 19, 1993, he committed the unthinkable for a top UN official: he openly criticized the U.S., the organization's most powerful member state. "In effect," he wrote in his letter of resignation, "the total absence of consultation and information from the United States Government makes me believe that this country has in fact made the decision to act unilaterally in the Haitian process."[35]

His resignation marked a key juncture in the UN's involvement in Haiti. The organization had done little during the years that Haiti languished under the U.S.-backed family-military dictatorship of Papa Doc Duvalier and his successor son, Baby Doc. Haiti was understood to be central to Washington's sphere of influence, and the UN had been kept marginalized. Even when mass mobilization finally led to the end of Duvalier rule and the election of the popular priest, Father Jean-Bertrand Aristide early in 1990, the UN also played relatively little role in assisting the fledgling government in dealing with the economic devastation that had for years made Haiti the poorest country in the western hemisphere and a lucrative center for U.S. manufacturing industries eager to exploit Haiti's few cents a day workers.

But when mass uprisings threatened the long-standing industry-friendly stability of Haiti, and brought Father Aristide to power, the U.S. realized its interests now lay in stabilizing the desperately poor country, insuring that U.S. economic interests were unaffected — whoever occupied the presidential palace. So when the Haitian army, many of whose officers had been trained by the Pentagon, overthrew Father Aristide, replacing him with a military junta, the U.S. allowed Aristide to wait out his banishment in Washington D.C.

During his more than two years of exile, Father Aristide became a rallying point for the anti-junta mobilization of the huge expatriate Haitian communities in New York, Miami, and elsewhere in the country. Simultaneously, his months of dispossession taught the populist priest the bitter realities of what his hosts would require to insure his return.

Caputo, a former foreign minister of Argentina, was appointed to represent the United Nations in opening negotiations aimed at ending the military government's rule. He was the key architect of the UN-brokered Governor's Island Accord that achieved the first commitment by the junta leaders to leave the island, in July 1993. But the Haitian military quickly reneged on their agreement to step down.

Further, they expelled the team of human rights monitors operating jointly under United Nations-Organization of American States auspices. While the monitors had been unable to prevent virtually any of the violence that wracked Haiti under the junta's rule, their presence had played an important role in keeping public attention focused on the brutality and human rights violations that continued unabated.

The U.S. role was ambiguous, because while Washington policy-makers officially supported Father Aristide and backed his return to Haiti, the military junta was led by officers with a long history of training by and continued connections to U.S. military and CIA institutions. And the U.S. itself was clear that while the removal of junta leader Raoul Cedras was necessary to restore stability, that however he left the scene, "the United States intends to contain Haiti's popular movement, by force if necessary. The objective, in the words of one U.S. Army Psychological Operations official, is to see to it that Haitians 'don't get the idea that they can do whatever they want.' "[36]

What the U.S. did want was minimal stability, just enough to insure economic viability for Haiti to continue as an offshore factory labor pool for U.S. manufacturers. A World Bank plan was crafted in August 1994, imposing structural adjustment plans on the feeble Haitian economy. Implementing those plans could be most credibly carried out by Father Aristide — although that was not necessarily required. There were no illusions in the Pentagon: one military official asked rhetorically, "Who are we going back to save? .... It's not going to be the slum guy from Cité Soleil .... It'll be the same elites, the bourgeoisie and the five families that run the country."[37]

But while U.S. military officials may have been clear on their goals, the uncertainties of how to mesh those goals with "peacekeeping" realities quickly emerged. Soon the Somalia syndrome came into play once again, as fear of casualties and uncertainty about how much to risk led to a debacle at the harbor of Port-au-Prince. Under the terms of the Governor's Island Accord, a UN embargo against Haiti was to be lifted, in exchange for the creation of a 1,300-person international force to retrain the Haitian police, and the return of Father Aristide at the end of October. On October 11, the amphibious ship U.S.S. *Harlan County* sailed close to Port-au-Prince, carrying the first contingent of UN police trainers.

The navy ship was greeted by a few hundred supporters of the military regime, who fired their guns in the air and threatened a port-side riot. Although the port was largely empty of civilians, other than a small coterie of diplomats led by the U.S. charge d'affaires, no effort was made to challenge the pro-junta thugs. Instead, the Clinton administration immediately decided to turn the ship away from the Port-au-Prince harbor, causing a major UN retreat and ultimately providing Lt. General Cedras and his junta with another year in power.

U.S.-UN relations in Haiti continued to deteriorate. Throughout the crisis, the initial weak and unenforced sanctions allowed massive transit of embargoed goods, especially gasoline, across the porous Dominican border and in sanctions-busting ships that "escaped" the scrutiny of the U.S. fleet sailing off the Haitian coast looking for refugees. Not till late spring of 1994 did the Council tighten the so-far largely cosmetic sanctions. (The impact of the sanctions on the Haitian population was not cosmetic, of course, except for the wealthy elite.) Once the sanctions resolution was ratcheted up, leading to potentially serious consequences for those in power in Haiti, Security Council talk immediately shifted to military options without waiting the year or more estimated for the newly-strengthened sanctions to take their toll.

Eventually, the failure of the Governor's Island agreement led to a U.S. move in the Security Council that capped the "summer offensive" of 1994. On July 31st, U.S. diplomats won UN agreement to send a U.S. invasion force to Haiti to "Uphold Democracy."

It was another in the two-part series of UN-endorsed invasions that year. President Clinton spoke to the General Assembly a few weeks later, claiming that his administration supported "ready, efficient, and capable UN peacekeeping forces."[38] But it was clear the U.S. had little intention of sharing power, resources, or operational decisions with the global organization.

Many Non-Aligned and other small countries retained strong memories of Washington's Gulf War unilateralism, and the Security Council, in unofficial response, crafted resolution 940 to endorse the U.S. invasion with the proviso guarantee of a UN oversight role in what was acknowledged to be a U.S.-controlled military move against Haiti.

New Zealand's Ambassador Colin Keating believed the resolution reflected "the lessons picked up from the Gulf War." Keating, representing his country on the Security Council, had played a key role in the Council's debate, insisting on assurances of more active UN involvement. The day after Clinton told the Council that the U.S. invasion was imminent, Keating described how "the resolution said the member states could use 'all necessary means,' but it also includes UN monitoring. The monitors will be on the ground even in phase one, 80 or so monitors deployed at the same time as phase one, and will stay in Haiti throughout phase two."[39]

But Ambassador Keating's hopes were misplaced. Phase one was understood to be a non-UN military invasion, led by the U.S. but with enough troops from a few countries to provide a plausible cover of "multilateralism." The commitments of 23 countries to provide token troops were announced with great fanfare by Secretaries Perry and Christopher, but a full week into the U.S. occupation of Haiti, not one soldier from Britain, Israel, the Caribbean states, or any of the other back-up contingents had yet set foot on Haitian soil.

As for UN monitors, the first sixteen were only scheduled to arrive in Haiti seven days *after* the U.S. troops landed.

As things worked out, of course, the U.S. invasion was transformed at the last minute into a no-shots-fired, more or less friendly occupation. Eleventh hour negotiations, accompanied by significant concessions, by former President Jimmy Carter convinced the junta to step down (though not requiring them to leave the country) and allow President Aristide to return.

Part of Special Representative Dante Caputo's anger stemmed from the nature of that compromise agreement negotiated with Cedras by the former president. The Carter agreement provided no guarantees that Cedras and the other military leaders would leave the island, did not disarm the military and police, mandated additional weeks in power for the military junta legitimized by "cooperation" with the U.S., and provided no date certain for the return of President Aristide. "It's so weak that the agreement could become a danger," Caputo told the *New York Times*.

If the overall responsibility for the Haitian crisis was truly an international matter, the UN should have responded when President Clinton announced he was about to send U.S. troops to Haiti. Especially since Clinton was justifying the U.S. invasion on the basis of the Security Council's permission, the Security Council should have gone into emergency session and issued a new mandate to Boutros-Ghali. Instead of relying on a former U.S. president of uncertain accountability, any last-minute diplomacy aimed at averting a potentially-bloody invasion should have been in the hands of the UN directly. The organization's highest ranking negotiator should have been sent back to Port-au-Prince with U.S. support. But the negotiator, Dante Caputo, and the UN as a whole, had already been cut out of Washington's loop. The special envoy's resignation also raised a fundamental question of whether the UN has any control of, or even involvement in, the military actions it authorizes.

Phase two of the UN Mission in Haiti (UNMIH), the post-invasion UN peacekeeping effort, was supposed to be carried out by a truly multilateral UN force. But U.S. officials immediately began negotiating with the secretary-general to allow 70% of the troops and the commander of the UN Blue Helmets to come from the U.S. military. Boutros-Ghali was said to be outraged at the idea of such overt U.S. domination of a UN operation, and the eventual compromise allowed about 40% U.S. troops.

As for the commander of the "UN operation" in phase two, Boutros-Ghali announced on November 15, 1994, that he had appointed U.S. Lt. General Daniel Schroeder as the Force Commander of UNMIH. U.S. Ambassador Madeleine Albright issued a press release the same day, "welcoming" the announcement and noting that the secretary-general had appointed Schroeder "at the suggestion of the United States."[40] Three hours before Boutros-Ghali declared his choice of Gen. Schroeder to the UN command, the Pentagon announced the appointment.

Outlining the lessons of Somalia that it was "unfortunately too late" to apply to Haiti, one analyst described existing parallels: "In both cases, the United States long supported despotic regimes and watched passively as they eventually fell. Innocent people suffered and died during and after the transition. The tragedy for the two countries is that humanitarian relief and military reinforcement came so late. Preventive diplomacy was either insufficient or ineffective."[41]

Certainly since the U.S. occupation and the transfer of authority to the "UN force," the rapes, murders, torture, and arbitrary arrests that characterized the junta's military rule in Haiti diminished somewhat, though they did not end. The World Bank's plan for Haiti, what the *Financial Times* in London called "Big Brother's Haiti Blueprint,"[42] has brought the beginning of a return of U.S.-based manufacturing interests to Port-au-Prince.

But Haitians continue to die of preventable diseases, Haitians still lack basic education and health care, Haitians remain economically, if not absolutely politically, disempowered and dispossessed. When President Clinton traveled to Haiti to oversee the transfer of power from the U.S. occupying force to the UN's phase two force led by General Schroeder, the *Washington Post* headlined the stark reality: "To Clinton, Mission Accomplished; to Haitians, Dashed Hopes" it read.[43] For Clinton, the *Post* said, "the Haiti mission was narrowly defined, and a success. The mission was to return Aristide and give Haitians time to begin to rebuild their battered nation .... " But for the Haitians, hope of actual American help in rebuilding that embattled nation did not arrive. "The United States, burned by the Somalia experience, did not view its mission as ... anything else that smacked of 'nation building' .... A primary concern here, American and Haitian officials said, was avoiding U.S. casualties."[44]

It is certainly possible that the concern for avoiding casualties was part of the real reason for the arrest and court-martial of Captain Lawrence P. Rockwood in Haiti. Capt. Rockwood had taken at face value his commander-in-chief's stated concern for "stopping brutal atrocities." While stationed in Haiti during the U.S. occupation, he managed to talk his way into the national prison in Port-au-Prince, finding and documenting the horrifying conditions in which abused political prisoners were living.

Anyone who had heard President Clinton's speeches explaining U.S. interests in Haiti, especially its interests in stopping such events, might have anticipated that a soldier taking such initiative would be praised. (In fact, only a few days after his conviction Capt. Rockwood did receive the 1995 Ralph E. Kharas Award from the New York Civil Liberties Union, citing his commitment to human rights in Haiti.) But to the U.S. Army, such undue interest in human rights in Haiti edged a little too close to the slippery slope of "nation building." And that was not the U.S. goal; Commander-in-Chief Clinton's claimed concerns about human rights violations and related extraneous matters were designed, it appeared, to soften the reality of a strictly military operation designed simply to re-establish stability, get Haiti horror stories off the front pages, and restore the economic status quo sufficiently to allow U.S. business interests to continue their profitable work. The UN was there to provide a multilateral figleaf. And Capt. Rockwood's reward was a court-martial conviction and dismissal from the service.

The plan was that the U.S. forces would stay until the Haitian environment had been made "safe and secure." Then the UN mission would take over. An optimistic headline writer in the UN's October 1994 *Secretariat News* described a "Big UN Role" in Haiti during phase two. But with the World Bank running the economic show, and U.S. General Schroeder commanding UNMIH's Blue Helmets, the secretary-general's special representative for Haiti, Lakhdar Brahimi, was faced with applying his own version of the "lessons of Somalia" to avoid the pitfalls that destroyed the efforts of his counterpart there, Mohammad Sakhnoun.

Key lessons of Somalia had already been ignored. By the time the U.S. allowed serious involvement of the UN in Haiti, it was already too late for preventive diplomacy. The day after Clinton announced that a U.S. invasion was imminent, instead of urgent discussion over how to avoid the looming threat of military occupation, a Fellini-esque scene took over the UN. It might have been a production designed to mirror the hollowness of the UN's Washington-assigned role. Even as Presidents Carter and Clinton began their private political minuet, and U.S. marines packed their parachutes over Haiti, the UN was kept out of the frame.

The invasion of Haiti was imminent. The Security Council was in closed session — on an unrelated matter. But it was staff day at UN headquarters, and clowns, acrobats, and musicians filled the halls to entertain UN employees and their families. As U.S. planes carrying U.S. paratroopers streaked across the Caribbean sky, and as Security Council discussions dragged endlessly on, three cheerful women wandered, confused, virtually into the Council chamber before being stopped. "Isn't this where we can buy greeting cards?" one asked the bemused guard.

IV. BOSNIA: THE NEW WORLD ORDER FAILS THE TEST

From the first inklings of the then-imminent Balkan wars in 1991, the violent disintegration of the former Yugoslavia has stayed at the center of world attention. Horrifying scenes of genocide, the terrorism of "ethnic cleansing," the collapse of a once-cosmopolitan, multi-ethnic society have kept the wars first in Croatia, and then later, and for much longer, in Bosnia, at center stage.

While the ravages of slaughtered Rwandans were on a larger scale, while the generation-slaying famine in Somalia was for a time more urgent, it was Bosnia that seemed to galvanize politics and governments and the institutions of power throughout the North. Part of the reason was that the crisis in Bosnia lasted longer. But beyond that, it was much harder to turn away, for many in the North, for the assault on Vukovar, the Serbs' rape centers and concentration camps and torture of Bosnians, the relentless attacks on Sarajevo were all happening not only before the TV-focused eyes of the Western world, but *in Europe*, not in some poor and distant country in Africa or Asia that could be dismissed as one more tragedy about which "the world" could do nothing. In Bosnia, for the West, the victims — and the perpetrators — were "like us." When Secretary-General Boutros-Ghali excoriated the Security Council, early on, for ignoring the growing crisis in Somalia while paying too much attention to "the war of the rich" in the former Yugoslavia, politically he had a point.

But the real point was not that the UN was doing too much in the Yugoslav crisis. The real point was that in Bosnia, unlike Somalia or Rwanda, the UN was not the major international player, or even the major strategic instrument of the Western powers. The UN's political role in Bosnia, forced on it by Washington and its European allies, could be likened to that of a rodeo clown during the bronco riding events: bouncing around the ring to distract the audience from the near-misses and full-blown tragedies being played out all around them. But however much the rodeo clowns may hold center stage, they are not the ones who hold the power of life or death over the cowboys and the horses, they are not the decision-makers.

When one looks at the U.S.-UN relationship in Bosnia, it looks very different from other arenas of UN crisis-area peacekeeping, because the UN was not the sole multilateral tool of the U.S. and its allies. In Bosnia the UN was used as an instrument of U.S.-European policy, but without being imbued with U.S.-European power. Other actors, such as NATO, the European Union, the "contact group," and others were given more central roles. The UN's assigned purpose was to carry out, to the minimal extent possible in the face of consistent opposition on the ground, the humanitarian tasks required to provide besieged Bosnians with basic survival needs. But in the political arena the UN was largely confined to taking the blame for Western inaction, and to playing "good cop" against NATO's "bad cop" in imposing or withholding military action against the Pale Serbs.

The United Nations, contrary to appearances and widespread public belief, has never been allowed to function as a major player in the Bosnia crisis.

On July 21, 1995, British Foreign Secretary Malcolm Rifkind announced the West's latest policy shift in besieged Bosnia. "The United Nations must not go to war," he said following the NATO ministerial meeting in London, "but needs to support realistic and effective deterrents."

The ambiguity of his statement reflected the disagreements among the Western powers that would ultimately paralyze the much-touted Western "resolve" that followed the high-profile announcement of a "muscular" approach by NATO and the West. The French wanted to send more troops; the U.S. and Britain said no. The U.S. wanted more bombing raids; the French and British said well okay, maybe, but only if the Serbs go after Gorazde. The U.S. wanted NATO and the military to have final say — U.S. State Department spokesperson Nick Burns even told reporters after the meeting that the leaders had "done away with" the dual-key approach that gave both UN and NATO officials a say in initiating the strikes. The British wanted to be sure UN civilian officials would have final say in approving any air strikes, and the French weren't so sure what to do about the UN role. Secretary-General Boutros-Ghali announced he would not give up his hold on one of the two "keys" of power to authorize or forbid bombing raids, although he later acceded to the U.S. position by delegating his decision-making power to the French General Bernard Janvier commanding the UN forces across the former Yugoslavia.

Haris Siladjiz, prime minister of the Bosnian government that was ostensibly the beneficiary of the whole thing, called the decisions "a collective figleaf." Three days after the NATO summit the claimed unity behind an assertive new policy was in shambles.

The bottom line of the Bosnia policy of the Northern powers — of France, Britain, but most especially of the U.S. — was to satisfy domestic political demands and appear to be "doing something" while in fact doing as little as possible and risking even less. The UN, whose strategic involvement was controlled largely by those three countries, would prove useful for both. At the same time the UN would provide a convenient venue for thrashing out tactical skirmishes among the Big Three, as well as the more strategic tensions between the Western powers and Russia over Bosnia policy. What the UN wouldn't become was a substantive instrument for the West's actual Bosnia policy — let alone a major player in its own right.

In the introduction to their powerful collection *Why Bosnia*, Rabia Ali and Lawrence Lifschultz note that

> Their emphatic denials to the contrary notwithstanding, the Western powers had made their position unmistakably transparent: they would not intervene in the war to defend Bosnia; they would not permit Bosnians to defend their country themselves or allow others to join in their defense; and they would compel them to surrender, accept defeat, and accede to the internationally legitimized carve-up of their country ....[45]

The effect of that carve-up, institutionalized most recently in the September 1995 U.S.-orchestrated agreement, was to force Bosnia, and try to force the Bosnians, to accept a post-war reality entirely opposite from the multi-ethnic cosmopolitanism that had shaped the area's reality throughout generations of Bosnian independence, occupation, autonomy, and integration. Before ethnic cleansing, the high degree of inter-penetration between communities made a mockery of the idea of an ethnically-based division within Bosnia; after ethnic cleansing had largely succeeded, it did not seem so impossible.

The UN would provide those Western governments with a crucial instrument to cover their commitment to inaction.

It was clear from the beginning of Yugoslavia's dissolution that the U.S. and its European allies were not prepared to seriously support first those trying to prevent the break-up, and later, when collapse appeared certain, those trying to protect the multi-ethnic character of Bosnia.

In the early months of 1991, it was the Bosnian president and his Macedonian counterpart who attempted, albeit unsuccessfully, to convince Serbia, Croatia, and Slovenia to agree to a compromise arrangement that would have kept the Yugoslav Federation intact and prevented Croatia and Slovenia from seceding. They failed. By March the nationalist leaders of Serbia and Croatia, Slobodan Milosevic and Franjo Tudjman, met and agreed to partition Bosnia-Herzegovina between their two countries.

Three months later, Croatia and Slovenia declared independence, and the Yugoslav army immediately invaded Slovenia. The European Union's first response was to convince the breakaway Yugoslav republics to suspend implementation of the declarations for three months, in return for the Yugoslav army (now led by the Serbian nationalists) withdrawing. The withdrawal from Slovenia did not take the Serbian army back into Serbia, but directly into Croatia and Bosnia.[46]

By August, full-scale war had broken out between Croatia and Serbia (still acting in the name of the Yugoslav Federation). In response, the Security Council imposed an arms embargo on "Yugoslavia." Croatia and Slovenia were not yet UN members, Bosnia had not yet declared its independence. The ambiguity of terminology (later resolutions would speak of "the former Yugoslavia") would come back to haunt those who continued to defend the embargo, years after its lopsided and horrifyingly inequitable impact became clear — it was too arguable that once Yugoslav republics declared independence, certainly once their independence was recognized by the world and their membership as independent states in the United Nations affirmed, an embargo "on Yugoslavia" should no longer apply to them.

But the legal niceties were lost; the UN's assigned role was tactical and propaganda, not defense of international law. Just before New Year's Eve of 1993, long before Bob Dole jumped opportunistically on the lift-the-embargo bandwagon, the General Assembly itself attempted to respond to the inequality. "Reaffirming once again that, as the Republic of Bosnia and Herzegovina is a sovereign, independent State and a Member of the United Nations, it is entitled to all rights provided for in the Charter of the United Nations, including the right to self-defense under Article 51 thereof," the resolution reads, the General Assembly "urges the Security Council to give all due consideration, on an urgent basis, to exempt the Republic of Bosnia and Herzegovina from the arms embargo as imposed on the former Yugoslavia .... "[47] Back in 1993, it would have mattered a great deal if the U.S. Congress had followed the lead of the General Assembly — far more than when the U.S. Congress pretended to debate the issue two years later. But the Assembly vote carried no force of law, and the embargo remained in effect against Bosnia.

Croatia continued its effort to win diplomatic recognition. In December 1991, only after the historic city of Vukovar had been destroyed in a cataclysm of fire televised around the world, Germany broke Europe's earlier unity by recognizing both Croatia and Slovenia. Rumors abounded that Bonn's motives were primarily commercial, that it was looking to establish stronger ties and influence in Croatia. The U.S. opposed recognizing the independent states, claiming to support the maintenance of Yugoslav unity. But the German position won over the rest of the EC, which recognized the two countries by January of 1992. Washington followed in April, by which time Bosnia had also declared independence, which was recognized by both the U.S. and the EC. Rebel Serbs in both Croatia and Bosnia, denying the results of popular referenda, immediately went to war against their governments and were immediately backed and armed by Belgrade.

From the beginning, Germany's position, and later those of the European powers and the U.S., were claimed to be based on a promise of protection. Only having duly recognized the independent states of Croatia or Bosnia, the argument went, could any other country extend any assistance or protection against the ravages of Serb opposition. Otherwise it would involve interference in the internal affairs of a nation-state, and of course the U.S. or France or Germany or Britain couldn't do that.

But the West had lied. Once recognition was extended, the promised aid and, more importantly, protection, never arrived. The UN's role then came to the fore, with the creation of UNPROFOR, the UN Protection Force. Created in the spring of 1992, UNPROFOR's limited mandate translated on the ground only to the protection of aid convoys providing desperately needed food and medical supplies to besieged Croatian and, immediately thereafter, Bosnian communities. (The actual language of the resolution 743 creating UNPROFOR defines it as "an interim arrangement to create the conditions of peace and security required for the negotiation of an overall settlement of the Yugoslav crisis." But that never happened.)

The aid workers of the UN's humanitarian mission in Bosnia faced daunting opposition, mostly from Serb rebels, in their efforts to provide desperately needed food and medical supplies to near-starving civilian populations throughout the war zones. Their work was carried out heroically and with little international recognition. The aid mission's significance paled, ironically, besides that of the UN Blue Helmet troops sent to protect it.

In May 1992 the UN imposed broader economic sanctions on Serbia and Montenegro, all that was then left of the former Yugoslavia. But those sanctions remained only sporadically implemented, and Serbia's borders remained porous. Despite the presence of numerous UN monitors assigned to verify compliance with the sanctions, their violation continued. As late as July 1995, "United Nations monitors watch and record the tens of thousands of liters of fuel being loaded from a Romanian state oil truck [into planes headed to Belgrade]. The monitors say a friendly hello to the Yugoslav pilot, and after he takes off, they hand official reprimands to the Romanian fuel truck driver and the local customs inspectors. These actions have been going on for months, and represent one of the most flagrant violations of international sanctions against the Belgrade Government, American and European sanctions-monitoring officials said."[48]

This particular violation, though, however flagrant, was actually made possible by Security Council action. In the fall of 1994, the Council agreed to partly lift economic sanctions against Serbia, in return for Belgrade's promise to stop aiding the rebel Pale Serbs in Bosnia. Numerous observers have documented that the Belgrade-Pale supply lines remain open and busy, but the U.S.-led insistence of the Western powers that Serbian President Milosevic be viewed as the key to peace in the Balkans meant that bribes were the order of the day. In this instance, the partial lifting included allowing commercial flights by the Yugoslav carrier to and from Belgrade. After the easing of sanctions, the *New York Times* reports, "the airline immediately began to fly virtually empty 727s to Timisoara [Romania] and fill them up." The flight is about 25 minutes long, and uses about 5,000 liters of fuel; the 727s hold 22,000 liters each.[49]

WAR CRIMES

The same month that the UN created UNPROFOR, the Pale Serbs began their campaign of "ethnic cleansing" in Bosnia.

The establishment of the UN's war crimes tribunal for the former Yugoslavia, headed by noted South African jurist Richard Goldstone, raised significant international law challenges, regarding jurisdiction and scope of war crimes and who makes decisions, but its creation seemed to represent a major advance in how seriously the international community treats war crimes and war criminals.

The UN High Commissioner for Refugees estimated that by the end of 1994, 90% of the 1.7 million non-Serbs who once lived in areas of Bosnia then held by the Serb military had been expelled, imprisoned, or murdered.[50] That was before the tens of thousands of new refugees took flight from the newly overrun "safe areas" of Zepa and Srebrenica in the summer of 1995. In 1992 alone, a European Community investigation team calculated that about 20,000 women and girls, some as young as ten, were raped by Bosnian Serb soldiers "as part of a deliberate strategy to terrorize people, drive them from their homes and shatter communities in Bosnia and Herzegovina. Other estimates are much higher."[51]

So the argument for creating a war crimes tribunal was unassailable. And yet the commission remained a stepchild of UN support and funding. It took over a year for the Security Council to select and approve Judge Goldstone. Officials of the tribunal "say a shortage of money and staff has slowed the pace of their work, leaving them waiting for new funds from the United Nations. Piles of evidence already gathered from refugees lie unsifted and untranslated. Richard Goldstone, the chief prosecutor, said his staff of 80 people required at least twice as many interpreters, secretaries, lawyers and investigators."[52]

The failure of the UN's wealthy countries to adequately fund the tribunal, however, is only one means of demonstrating the ambivalence with which it is viewed in powerful capitals. The *Christian Science Monitor* identified the key issue: "Going after the main perpetrators raises a fundamental question of political will: Are the governments that control the UN really intent on prosecuting those leaders they need for making and keeping a Yugoslav peace accord? For international decisionmakers, the dilemma transcends the former Yugoslavia and strikes directly at whether the great powers can deliver a promised 21st century world order based on high moral principles. Or will they remain wedded to Machiavellian expediency that puts the 'national interest' above all else?"[53] The July 1995 indictment of Bosnian Serb leader Radovan Karadzic and military chief Ratko Mladic as war criminals trained a spotlight on exactly that question. UN and NATO officials indicated immediately that despite the indictments they would continue to negotiate with the Serb leaders.

Because ultimately, aside from its humanitarian and refugee protection work, the UN had a vital political role to play in the Bosnia crisis, with much higher stakes in Washington and London and Paris than "merely" feeding people or arresting war criminals. The UN was brought in to be the centerpiece of an elaborate international shell game designed to convince anyone who looked too closely that "someone else," not the powerful policy-makers in those powerful capitals, was responsible for the failure to find peace, and ultimately for the slaughter of war, in the killing fields of Bosnia.

CLINTON'S CHALLENGE: INTERVENTION ON THE CHEAP

When he spoke at the San Francisco celebration of the 50th anniversary of the signing of the UN Charter, President Clinton admitted that "we have too often asked our peacekeepers to work miracles while denying them the military and political support required and the modern command and control systems they need to do their job as safely and effectively as possible."[54]

In the case of Bosnia, that wasn't the half of it.

Noted international lawyer and Princeton University scholar Richard Falk described how "Clinton's challenge is to seem to do something without the risk of doing anything that could backfire. Bombing is a cheap option, but it's a problem because since there are no U.S. ground forces in Bosnia, its forces are not subject to Serb retaliation but its policy would expose the British and French soldiers as hostages."[55] It was an arrangement in which the UN serves as fulcrum for what are purported to be different, even contradictory, positions between U.S. representatives to the NATO military council and U.S. representatives to the UN Security Council, or British and French generals on the NATO council and British and French diplomats at the UN.

Tom Friedman, the *New York Times*' star foreign affairs columnist, known for his close access to U.S. policy-makers, might have been speaking for his State Department and White House friends: "I don't give two cents about Bosnia," he wrote on June 8, 1995. "Not two cents. The people there have brought on their own troubles." Then he added, lest there be any hesitation about his real fidelities, "but I do feel loyalty to the allies who have put their own troops into harm's way to try to limit the human suffering there."[56]

In the Alice in Wonderland world of U.S. Bosnia policy, that actually makes sense. The human suffering in Bosnia doesn't matter; what matters is that "our allies" are there trying to limit the suffering, and we like our allies. That explains a policy in which U.S. ground troops are not only considered but pledged if needed to protect the extraction of British and French peacekeepers, but are still rejected to stop the Serb rape and slaughter of Bosnians.

(Friedman's reference, clearly, was to the British and French peacekeepers; maybe he had the Canadian and Belgian troops in the back of his mind too. But it is an interesting comment on the tenacity of North-South divisions that neither Friedman, nor virtually any other U.S. commentator, pay any attention to or even mention the 1,000+ Bangladeshi peacekeepers then serving in Bihac, or the Pakistani, Argentine, Jordanian, Kenyan, Malaysian, Turkish, or other peacekeeping contingents from the South that continue to serve in Bosnia and elsewhere in the former Yugoslavia.)

The arms embargo initiated by the UN, at European and U.S. insistence, was imposed in the name of "containing" the war, insuring that it didn't spread. The threat of a Balkan conflict moving across Kosovo and Albania, Hungary or Romania, involving not only Greece and Turkey, key though contentious NATO members, but maybe even Russia, pointed the policy issue for the Northern powers in their unswerving direction: protect NATO, defend NATO unity, maintain NATO's primacy. To the degree the UN could provide a broader international figleaf to do that, it would be used; when vital decisions were made, the UN Security Council chamber sat empty as the five-nation "Contact Group" or the NATO military council took up the debate.

But it must not be forgotten that the arms embargo was first imposed with the claimed commitment that the West would take seriously some responsibility for defending Bosnia and Croatia from the ravages of the far better armed Serbs. The only military action that followed was the imposition of the devastatingly lopsided arms embargo.

It was convenient, certainly, to have the UN as a scapegoat. When the U.S. and its European allies couldn't agree on how to implement their claimed "new" response to Serbian aggression against Srebrenica or Zepa, it was useful to claim that Boutros-Ghali had "refused to give up" his half of the dual-key approach. The bottom line was that NATO was already calling the shots militarily; if the Big Three powers had *wanted* the UN secretary-general out of the decision-making process, they could well have ordered his new role in the Security Council. Yes, Russia would have objected; Moscow might even have threatened to veto such a resolution. But at the end of the day the question was still one of power: Russia, in mid-1995, remained too economically dependent on, and politically subservient to, Western dollars and marks and francs to risk alienating its would-be allies on an issue to which the U.S. and its allies were truly committed. But they weren't.

NECESSARY SOLUTIONS AND MORE QUESTIONS

One solution being debated in Europe, proposed by the Green Party in the German Parliament, among others, led away from the UN towards regional organizations. It was based on two crucial assessments. One, that all the international initiatives proposed by the international mediators had so far failed. Two, that the claimed fears of Serb civilians in Bosnia and Croatia had to be dealt with seriously, despite the opportunist and false basis on which they had been fomented. (The exclusion of Russia, viewed by most Serbs as their strongest ally, from the early negotiations had given renewed power and influence to the worst of the xenophobic, ethnic nationalist forces among the Serbian leadership — and helped crush any nascent effort at anti-nationalist, multi-ethnic organizing.)

The idea was for the European Union to emerge as the major diplomatic player, supplanting the fantasy that the UN held the diplomatic cards. The EU would offer coveted full membership to Croatia, Bosnia, Serbia/Montenegro, Slovenia, and Macedonia — but under two conditions. First, the return of all land, homes, and property that were seized since June 1991 by military force or ethnic cleansing, thus providing for the return of all refugees and displaced persons and the rebuilding of a multi-ethnic society in each of the states. The offer of membership should be combined with a "Marshall" plan for the reconstruction of the war-torn regions. Second, the continuation of the war crimes prosecutions through the UN's International Tribunal in the Hague and through national courts.

Serb popular support for such a plan, it was assumed, would be based on severing the link between the war-weary Serbian population (especially inside Serbia, to a lesser degree among Bosnian Serb civilians) and their extremist nationalist leaderships. As citizens of EU member countries, the Serbs living in Croatia and Bosnia would no longer be dependent only on the governments in Zagreb and Sarajevo to protect their rights and settle grievances. They could turn also to the EU institutions, including human rights agencies, in Brussels and Strasbourg to defend their minority rights. Especially because of the virtually non-existent credibility of the United Nations in the Balkans (however wrongly it has been blamed for the Western governments' failures), reliance on human rights agencies linked to regional, rather than international organizations might hold a different appeal. The same would apply to the Albanians in Kosovo or to the ethnic groups in Macedonia. If each of the new mini-countries on the territory of the former Yugoslavia became members of the EU, the borders between Serbia and Bosnia, or Serbia and Croatia, would, it was hoped, become as irrelevant as the borders between Belgium, Holland, and Germany are today. To the people of the economically, politically, and morally bankrupt Serbia, EU membership would offer an alternative that the Milosevic regime could not offer them under any circumstances — not even after a total lifting of UN sanctions. (Despite all of Belgrade's anti-EU propaganda since 1991, many Serb and international observers are convinced that in a referendum 80 percent of the Serbian population would support EU membership.[57])

Whether reliance on the still new, and relatively untested EU human rights institutions would be accepted by the Serb population as sufficient protection is uncertain. Increasing, rather than ending, UN-imposed sanctions against the Milosevic regime in Serbia might force some consideration of this kind of proposal, among Serbia's civil society at least, if not the extreme nationalists in power. But the possibility of making the regional coalition an active partner in crafting a settlement, rather than undermining the UN's credibility by forcing its collaboration in an international shell game, should not be dismissed out of hand. The U.S.-brokered agreement of September 1995 promised only an ethnically divided Bosnia, with a Bosnian Serb state independent in all but name, and the likelihood of its confederation with Serbia despite years of U.S. promises to oppose exactly that ethnically-cleansed outcome.

The right of the refugees to return home (or be guaranteed compensation if they choose not to return) raises a critical question for which the United Nations, specifically the High Commissioner for Refugees, is uniquely suited to take up. The demand on Washington must be to provide generous financial support, including resettlement in the U.S. of some of the victims of "ethnic cleansing" who may choose not to return to their homes. The UN, perhaps in collaboration with religious organizations and other social groupings, must be provided with all the support it needs, political and financial, to take on this humanitarian crisis. If the UN were to implement this kind of refugee protection, such a program would pose a significant challenge to the Security Council to similarly implement the long-ignored and long-violated resolution 194, mandating the right of return or compensation (at the refugees' choice) for Palestinians driven out of their homes in what became Israel in 1947 and 1948.

In the middle of 1992, I wrote an analysis of the then-new, but already escalating Bosnia crisis for the largest of New York's African-American newspapers. It reflected much of the despair and lack of clear solutions that persist to this day. It included the following paragraphs:

International "peacekeeping" efforts are fruitless, in the absence of a real ceasefire. Protection of civilians, even children, remains a bad joke when the stated goal of the Serbian forces is to "cleanse" the coveted land of its non-Serb inhabitants, the Muslims and Croats who have lived there for generations. The reality reeks of central Europe's Nazi occupation and the Holocaust of half a century ago.

Bosnia has emerged as the central challenge for the New World Order, and all that can be certain so far is that old paradigms based on either U.S. military intervention or on let-them-kill-each-other isolationism are not sufficient. There is no clear strategy that will guarantee an end to the war. The U.S. and its allies remain divided on how to respond ....

Ending the arms embargo would certainly help, as only the Muslim-dominated Bosnian defenders face its consequences. (It should not be forgotten that the former Yugoslavia was once a leading arms exporter, and the Serbian forces now control most of its military depots.)

A key U.S. reality is that Bosnia is not Iraq; the stakes for the U.S. are only broad political positions, not control of strategic resources.

One crucial question is that of multi-lateralism. The Bosnia crisis sparked a debate about how far the U.S. should go in sharing international power and responsibility for defending stability. This debate also shapes the differences within the Security Council as to how far the UN should go.

But there is no indication the UN is prepared to end the arms embargo. The ironic result is the world body's authorization of other countries' using force against the Serbs to protect UN relief convoys, while denying the Bosnians the arms they need to protect themselves.[58]

Three years later things hadn't changed much. In August 1995, Croatia launched a new war against the Serb forces occupying its Krajina region; 150,000 Serb civilians fled to Serbia and Serb-held Bosnia. The United Nations, once again, moved its emergency refugee and humanitarian assistance cadres to respond to the latest crisis. But the action significantly shifted the military equation, and soon a new NATO offensive was launched at Serb gunners targeting Sarajevo. The diplomatic result was the U.S.-sponsored agreement to ethnically divide Bosnia, while maintaining the fiction of a unified country. The initiative was led by the U.S.; Washington's allies signed on. But once again in Bosnia, the U.S. was in command and the UN's role was largely sidelined. The UN was allowed nothing to say.

Notes

1. Associated Press, "55,000 Cambodians Flee Homes as Khmer Rouge Increase Raids," *New York Times*, May 4, 1994.

2. *Christian Science Monitor,* July 8, 1994.

3. Lukas Haynes, "UN Peace in Cambodia Slips into Chaos," *New York Newsday* viewpoint, October 12, 1994.

4. Chris Giannou, "Reaping the Whirlwind: Somalia After the Cold War," in Phyllis Bennis and Michel Moushabeck (eds.), *Altered States: A Reader in the New World Order* (New York: Olive Branch Press/Interlink, 1993), p. 352.

5. Giannou, pp. 354-5.

6. Angela Penrose, "UN Humanitarian Machinery," in Erskine Childers (ed.), *Challenges to the United Nations* (London: CIIR, 1994).

7. Boutros-Ghali's Report to Security Council, November 30, 1992.

8. Security Council Resolution 794, December 3, 1992.

9. Interview with author, November 1992.

10. Penrose, "Humanitarian Machinery," p. 123.

11. John G. Sommer, "U.S. Took the Lead in Somalia Action," letter to *New York Times*, February 2, 1995.

12. Eric Schmitt, "Now, to the Shores of Somalia With Beanbag Guns and Goo," *New York Times*, February 14, 1995.

13. "Somalia: An Accounting," *New York Times* editorial, March 26, 1994.

14. Ray Bonner, *New York Times*, September 4, 1994; Holly Burkhalter, *Christian Science Monitor*, August 9, 1994; Rakiyya Omar and Alex de Waal, *Covert Action Quarterly*, Spring 1995.

15. Richard Lyons, "3,000 Troops to Back UN in Rwanda," *New York Times*, July 28, 1994.

16. Rakiyya Omar and Alex de Waal, "Genocide in Rwanda: U.S. Complicity by Silence," *Covert Action Quarterly*, Spring 1995.

17. Omar and de Waal, "Genocide in Rwanda."

18. UN Security Council resolution 872, October 5, 1993, paragraph 9.

19. Omar and de Waal, "Genocide in Rwanda."

20. Holly Burkhalter, Washington director of Human Rights Watch, "U.S. Might Have Avoided Rwanda Tragedy," *Christian Science Monitor*, August 9, 1994.

21. Omar and de Waal, "Genocide in Rwanda."

22. Raymond Bonner, "As French Leave Rwanda, Critics Reverse Position," *New York Times*, August 22, 1994.

23. "The French in Rwanda," editorial, *Christian Science Monitor*, June 30, 1994.

24. Michael R. Gordon, "U.S. to Supply 60 Vehicles for UN Troops in Rwanda," *New York Times*, June 16, 1994.

25. Burkhalter, "Rwanda Tragedy."

26. Omar and de Waal, "Genocide in Rwanda."

27. Raymond Bonner, "Top Rwandan Criticizes U.S. Envoy," *New York Times*, November 8, 1994.

28. Interview with Ambassador Manzi Bakuramuta, United Nations, November 9, 1994.

29. Scott Peterson, "UN Drags Heels on Rwanda Probe," *Christian Science Monitor*, October 7, 1994.

30. Bakuramuta interview.

31. Donatella Lorch, "UN-Rwanda Ties Sour as Mandate Nears End," *New York Times*, May 17, 1995.

32. Martin Garbus, "Jurists Without Borders," *New York Times*, November 7, 1994.

33. Barbara Crossette, "Send the Peacekeepers Home, a Ravaged Rwanda Tells UN," *New York Times*, June 8, 1995.

34. Peterson, "UN Drags Heels."

35. Dante Caputo, letter to Secretary-General Boutros-Ghali, September 19, 1993.

36. Allan Nairn, "The Eagle Is Landing," *The Nation*, October 3, 1994.

37. Ibid.

38. Clinton address to General Assembly, September 26, 1994.

39. Interview with Amb. Colin Keating, September 16, 1994.

40. Madeleine Albright statement, Press Release #178-(94), U.S. Mission to the United Nations, November 15, 1994.

41. John G. Sommer, Refugee Policy Group, "Haiti Offers a Reminder of Lessons From Somalia," *Christian Science Monitor*, November 1994.

42. October 17, 1994.

43. March 30, 1995.

44. Douglas Farah, "To Clinton, Mission Accomplished; to Haitians, Dashed Hopes," *Washington Post*, March 30, 1995.

45. Rabia Ali and Lawrence Lifschultz, *Why Bosnia: Writings on the Balkan War* (Stony Creek, Conn.: Pamphleteers' Press, 1993), pp. xvi-xvii.

46. Ibid., pp. 343-344.

47. General Assembly Resolution A/48/88, December 29, 1993.

48. Jane Perlez, "UN Watches Romania Violate Sanctions," *New York Times*, July 26, 1995.

49. Ibid.

50. "Prosecute Bosnia's War Criminals," *New York Times* editorial, January 4, 1995.

51. Marlise Simons, "Bosnian Rapes Go Untried by the UN," *New York Times*, October 1994.

52. Ibid.

53. Jonathan S. Landay, "Opening the Docket: Trials of a War Tribunal," *Christian Science Monitor*, November 16, 1994.

54. President Bill Clinton, San Francisco, June 25, 1995.

55. Richard Falk, "Behind the News," WBAI Radio, New York, July 24, 1995.

56. Thomas Friedman, "Foreign Affairs," *New York Times*, June 8, 1995.

57. Andreas Zumach, Geneva correspondent, *Tageszeitung* (Berlin), April 1995.

58. Phyllis Bennis, "Bosnia: The New World Order Fails the Test," New York *Amsterdam News*, August 10, 1992.

7

UN Sanctions:
The Not-Quite Warfare

Direct military involvement in the form of peacekeeping or peace enforcement has not, of course, been the only kind of post-Cold War UN interventionism. The imposition of economic sanctions against countries deemed in violation of UN resolutions or international law has emerged since 1990 as an increasingly common form of UN punishment.

Theoretically, sanctions should work as an "in-between" level of pressure, more than mere condemnation but less than outright military force. In the real world, however, the tactic has been less than successful in actually changing the unacceptable behavior of target governments, though their civilian populations pay a heavy price. And once again, it is Washington's will that determines whether sanctions are imposed punishingly (as against Iraq), or cosmetically (as against South Africa or in the first stage of the Haiti sanctions), or not at all (as in the case of Israel).

The use of economic and other forms of sanctions, unlike peacekeeping, was contemplated by the UN's founders, and is discussed in the Charter. In Chapter VII, dealing with "Action in Respect to Threats to the Peace, Breaches of the Peace and Acts of Aggression," Article 41 provides that the Security Council can impose measures falling short of the use of force, but still designed to impose its decisions. Those measures "may include complete or partial interruption of economic relations and of rail, sea, air, postal, telegraphic, radio and other means of communication [this was pre-television, pre-video, pre-cellular phone, pre-Internet 1945, after all], and the severance of diplomatic relations."

It is no accident that the discussion of sanctions is placed before that of the authorization of force. Article 42 of the Charter authorizes the Council to "take such action by air, sea, or land forces as may be necessary to maintain or restore international peace and security. Such ac-

154

tion may include demonstrations, blockade, and other operations by air, sea, or land forces of Members of the United Nations." But it restricts that decision with the proviso that it can only be used if the previously-discussed non-military sanctions "would be inadequate or have proved to be inadequate."

So the framework for sanctions defines them quite broadly, giving the Council a range of economic and communications cut-offs, from partial to complete. But the legitimate use of sanctions must be to respond to what the Council itself must first determine is "the existence of any threat to the peace, breach of the peace, or act of aggression" (Article 39). And the actions taken, whether economic or other sanctions under Article 41 or the more drastic "other operations by air, sea, or land forces" of Article 42, must be designed "to maintain or restore international peace and security" (Article 39).

The significance of that language is evident in what is left out: sanctions are not to be used to punish governments or states for actions deemed merely inappropriate or even unacceptable by the international community as a whole. According to Australia's foreign minister, Gareth Evans, the "record reveals that the impact of sanctions has been patchy at best. They generally require a longer period of time to have any significant impact, are too often porous, and can have effects opposite to those intended .... To be effective, sanctions must have clearly defined and achievable objectives and be implemented rigorously .... Sanctions introduced simply in order for the international community to be seen as doing something — perhaps in a situation where the only action likely to be successful is full-scale military peace enforcement, but where there is insufficient support for this course — may be better not introduced at all."[1]

There are numerous questions about the efficacy of sanctions as a means of forcing a state's compliance with international norms, and those uncertainties take on increased significance when combined with the fact that sanctions raise "serious questions about their compatibility with the human rights of the target state population, particularly where the instrumentalist calculation is that if there is enough domestic suffering the people will rise up against their government."[2]

In other words, the human rights of the population will always suffer if the sanctions are not aimed at forcing the target government to comply with some UN demand, but rather are designed to make daily life so unbearable for the civilian population that they will overthrow their government. In the years since the U.S. seized on UN activism as a main thrust of foreign policy, Washington's primary approach to sanctions (in Iraq, Libya, and Cuba) has been exactly the latter.

Before that time, sanctions were used quite sparingly by the Council: broad economic sanctions were imposed against white-ruled Rhodesia in 1966 and maintained until the 1979 victory of the Zimbabwean liberation forces. In South Africa, they were imposed in 1977 but limited to arms and military technology. However, with the Gulf War build-up, sanctions emerged as a major tool of the Security Council. Between 1990 and 1993 varieties of economic, oil, and military sanctions were imposed by the UN against Iraq, against the former Yugoslavia, Libya, Somalia, Liberia, and Haiti.

In virtually all of those cases, the impact of the sanctions was felt far more by the civilian population than by the government in power — and there is little indication that the pressure served to change those governments' behavior. (The one partial exception was Liberia, where the arms embargo did not result in additional suffering by the population as a whole.)

Despite official rationales and the requirements of the Charter, sanctions are not only designed to force policy changes. If they were, the porous, cosmetic sanctions imposed against the military junta in Haiti in 1991, for example, would swiftly have been tightened. Once tighter sanctions finally were imposed on the wealthy supporters of the military in 1993, they would have been given time for their effect to bite — instead of being replaced almost immediately with military moves.

The use of sanctions to prepare public support for the later use of military force was applied in Iraq as well. Sanctions were imposed against Baghdad within hours of its invasion of Kuwait on August 2, 1990. Article 42 of the UN Charter legitimizes the use of force "should the Security Council consider the measures provided for in Article 41 [sanctions] ... inadequate." But no effort was made to assess the impact of the sanctions. As noted UN analyst Brian Urquhart describes it, "No formal determination as to the inadequacy of sanctions was ever made by the Security Council before Operation Desert Storm was launched. In retrospect, it seems that sanctions, even when rigorously applied, are unlikely, in the short run at any rate, to force a dictatorial and unscrupulous leader to reverse his course."[3] Sometimes, Urquhart goes on, "sanctions have symbolic functions, and are often used as a form of communication of international values .... They may also be used with the rather different purpose of assuaging domestic opinion in states taking part in the sanctions."[4]

In the U.S., the publicity factor continues to play a major role. It has been particularly influential in the former Yugoslavia, where an arms embargo was imposed against all of the then-remaining republics. The advantage, for Washington, was the appearance of impartiality and an image of wanting to tamp down all potentially escalating violence. The downside, however, was rarely addressed: first, once Bosnia, for good or bad, declared its independence, it therefore should no longer have been subject to sanctions aimed at the rump "Yugoslav Republic." Second, and more important, Serbia's (and their allies, the Bosnian Serbs') control of the arms production capability of the former Yugoslav army (at one time the twelfth largest arms producer in the world) insured a thoroughly lopsided playing field, in which the Bosnian army, despite numerical advantage, faced an overwhelmingly superior military force in the Serbian army and among the Belgrade-backed Bosnian Serb army.

U.S. SANCTIONS STRATEGY

A key question emerges when examining when, and against whom, the Security Council imposes sanctions. For the U.S., determining which countries are fair game for sanctions has little to do with a reasoned assessment about whether governments are or are not likely to respond by changing their unwanted behaviors. Thus the determination has little to do with whether or not the sanctions are likely to accomplish the purpose for which they are ostensibly imposed. Instead, the decision has everything to do with the country's broader relationship with the U.S.

First rule: the North is exempt. The use of sanctions to enforce UN-agreed principles in those wealthy industrialized countries, especially involving violations of UN-agreed economic and social rights, is not even considered; those violations are deemed "internal" matters. Further, close political or commercial allies of the United States, regardless of their behavior, are largely immune from sanctions. Thus Indonesia's occupation of East Timor goes unchallenged; Turkey's seizure of half of Cyprus is answered with years of quiet mediation rather than sanctions.

And then there's Israel, considered more fully in chapter 9. There has been a myriad of UN resolutions passed against Tel Aviv, documenting violations of international law ranging from nuclear collaboration with apartheid South Africa to continued occupation of Palestinian and other Arab land to massive violations of human rights by occupation soldiers. But the U.S. has always made sure that no sanctions are imposed, and in fact are not even considered. Washington's efforts usually aim to soften the language of resolutions if passage seems inevitable or if a veto would have other negative consequences for the U.S., and to make sure that nothing in the "enforceable" paragraphs (as opposed to the preamble) is unacceptable to Israel. The U.S. concern is not so much that Israel might be displeased, but because its rejection of the terms of a Security Council resolution might lead to a call for sanctions to be imposed against Tel Aviv to enforce compliance — and that would be unacceptable.

Sanctions are also supposed to be limited by the Charter requirement that they be imposed in order to reverse "any threat to the peace, breach of the peace, or act of aggression." That restriction has often been used as the excuse for not imposing, or at least considering, sanctions to stop human rights violations, even on a massive scale.

No one ever brought to the Security Council the discussion of possible sanctions against Argentina for its "dirty war" against alleged subversives, a war that resulted in tens of thousands of murdered and "disappeared" victims. No one ever imposed UN sanctions against Chile after the brutal U.S.-backed military coup of 1973 and the years of torture, imprisonment, and murder that followed. Egypt has no need to fear UN sanctions to force an end to its persecution of opposition journalists; nor does Saudi Arabia have to worry about a UN response in the form of sanctions to its imposition of religious laws of a breathtakingly misogynist character. Certainly all these countries are protected by their close ties to the U.S.; but beyond that, all their violations are deemed "internal" or "domestic" issues, and therefore stand outside the realm of possible UN involvement.

But do they really stand outside? That assessment, based on the primacy of national sovereignty, in fact reflects the concerns of numerous non-aligned and small countries of the South. The problem with that approach is that it is applied absolutely inconsistently. When the actions of a state or government are deemed of interest to the U.S. or another major power, some rationale is always found to define its internal breaches as a real or potential "threat to international peace and security," thereby laying the foundation for UN intervention. When the state or government involved is of little interest to Washington or its allies, its transgressions remain "internal" matters.

Haiti is a case in point. The military junta that overthrew President Jean-Bertrand Aristide in 1991 was quickly seen as threatening to U.S. interests in the country and in the region. Those interests were primarily to maintain stability in order to maximize U.S. corporations' access to cheap Haitian labor, as discussed in chapter 6. When it became clear that the military government threatened those interests, the assertion was made that the flow of refugees fleeing the junta's brutality represented an international threat. (The tragedy was not deemed enough of a threat to make the U.S. welcome those refugees, of course, but they did provide a convenient justification.) The internal brutality thus became, by U.S. fiat, an international rather than a domestic concern.

In Chile and Argentina, U.S. interests were deemed better served by leaving in place those brutal regimes. In those instances, the "domestic" character of the repression was highlighted, and the arrest, torture, and killing of hundreds of thousands of people never threatened international peace and security.

For Washington, sanctions are appropriately used against countries deemed "rogue," "outlaw," or "anti-U.S." (interchangeably defined as "anti-Western"). These include several Arab and Islamic countries (Iraq, Libya, Iran), sometimes North Korea, and Cuba. While efforts have in all those cases been made to win international support, most often within a UN framework, the U.S. has been fully willing to impose unilateral sanctions. Those unilateral efforts have sometimes included attempts to force other countries to enforce the U.S. sanctions even when the UN has refused to endorse them. In fact, Washington has sometimes imposed its own sanctions, and insisted on other countries' acceptance of them, in direct violation of UN (usually General Assembly) decisions calling for an end to the sanctions, as in the case of Cuba (see below).

It also should not be forgotten that a U.S.-determined "rogue" state, such as North Korea, let alone not-quite-rogues such as China, often find themselves able to negotiate a way out of a U.S. impasse, rather than facing sanctions. Despite its self-righteous posturing about alleged human rights violations in China, the Clinton administration as well as its predecessors have placed the cheap labor and billion-strong market factors far above those concerns. China has little to fear from U.S.-orchestrated sanctions, even in the tricky UN context of its denial of visas to NGOs and activists involved with issues its government rejects, such as Tibetan independence, Taiwan, and lesbian rights, for the 1995 women's summit in Beijing.

CUBA

The U.S. embargo against Cuba — a complete cut-off of all financial or commercial transactions between the two countries — was imposed in 1960, shortly after the Cuban revolution. Since that time, it has cost the island nation about $20 billion in lost trade opportunities.[5]

From the beginning, other countries, including many close allies of the U.S. who themselves were sometimes quite hostile to the Cuban government, refused to participate in the embargo. The Cubans, whose island status and location isolated from any other major economic power made them especially vulnerable, consider the U.S. embargo a blockade; the U.S. enhanced this view of it by attempting to force other countries to abide by the embargo's terms.

One such manifestation of the effort to internationalize the embargo took the form of the 1992 so-called "Cuba Democracy Act," known as the Toricelli Bill, which called for punishment of any ships from any country who called at Cuban ports by denying them access to U.S. ports for up to six months. Further, congressional efforts during the same period tried to directly internationalize the embargo, by threatening U.S. corporations with financial punishments if wholly foreign-owned subsidiaries conducted any trade with Cuba. What that meant was that a British company, for example, owned and operated and incorporated in England, but a subsidiary of a larger U.S. corporation, was forbidden to sell its goods to Cuba, even if that refusal violated British law, on threat of penalties being exacted on their U.S.-based corporate headquarters.

The response in the UN was outrage. General Assembly resolutions were passed in 1992 and again in 1993, by huge margins, condemning the U.S. effort to impose its anti-Cuba sanctions on other countries. The resolution states that:

> The General Assembly, determined to encourage strict compliance with the purposes and principles enshrined in the Charter of the United Nations, ... concerned about the continued promulgation and application by Member States of laws and regulations whose extraterritorial effects affect the sovereignty of other States and the legitimate interests of entities or persons under their jurisdiction, as well as the freedom of trade and navigation, ... having learned that ... further measures of that nature aimed at strengthening and extending the economic, commercial and financial embargo against Cuba have been promulgated and applied, and concerned about the adverse effects of those measures on the Cuban population, ... once again urges States that have such laws or measures to take the necessary steps to repeal or invalidate them as soon as possible.[6]

Over several years, the votes in the Assembly reflected an increasingly strong opposition to the U.S. embargo and the U.S. effort to apply it to other countries. In 1992, there were 59 votes to condemn the embargo (only the U.S., Israel, and Romania opposed the resolution; 71 countries abstained). A year later, the 1993 vote showed 88 countries siding with Cuba against the embargo (Paraguay and Albania joined the usual U.S.-Israel opposition this time, but only 57 countries abstained).

But for the U.S., an unenforceable Assembly resolution remained just that: unenforced. And along with continuing to violate the Assembly resolutions with impunity, the U.S. had no intention of allowing decisions challenging its Cuba policy to go unanswered. Each year, in preparation for the General Assembly session that begins in September, the U.S. Mission to the UN circulates a letter outlining its goals and priorities for the coming year. Washington makes very certain that there is no misunderstanding regarding how seriously it views other countries' votes.

In 1994, UN Ambassador Madeleine Albright's August 8th letter to the Assembly president, disseminated to every member state, ended with a warning. "Finally," the letter reads, "a word on Cuba. We understand that many UN members disagree with our embargo policy.... Nonetheless, it is our view that Havana interprets votes in favor of its annual anti-embargo resolution as vindicating the repressive policies of the current regime there. For this reason, we ask that you withhold support for this resolution."

While the U.S. did not have the veto option available to prevent the Assembly vote, the implicit threat was unmistakable. As in many other UN initiatives, U.S. reactions to each country's vote could come later, perhaps in a completely separate, bilateral forum — such as crucial votes on loan packages in the IMF or the World Bank, for instance. As a result, while the votes in favor of Cuba and against the U.S. embargo grew every year, a number of countries, especially some in Latin America, could not take the risk, and either voted to abstain or simply did not appear for the vote.

WASHINGTON'S MIDDLE EAST "ROGUES"

1. LIBYA

The U.S. campaigns for UN anti-Iraq and anti-Libya activism began during the Bush administration and continued under Clinton. They were aimed largely at the Security Council, where the threat of a U.S. veto hovers over decision-making. And on each occasion from 1990 to 1995, the U.S. succeeded in first imposing, then maintaining Council sanctions against its chosen Arab enemies, despite eventual Libyan and Iraqi acquiescence to the UN's actual demands. Like the Bush administration's brilliant UN tactician Thomas Pickering, Clinton's Ambassador Madeleine Albright showed little reluctance in moving the Middle East goalposts to insure a few extra U.S. points in the game.

Regarding Libya, UN sanctions were first imposed in April 1992, ostensibly to force compliance with the U.S.-UK demand that Tripoli turn over for trial two Libyan nationals accused of taking part in the 1986 Lockerbie bombing that killed 286 people on board a U.S. airplane over Scotland. (While pressure on Libya was certainly part of Washington's motivation, that sanctions effort itself was itself part of a much larger U.S. effort to consolidate UN power in the Council, away from the more democratic components of the UN such as the International Court of Justice. See chapter 3.)

The legal basis for the sanctions was a U.S. interpretation of the 1971 Montreal Convention against violent attacks on aircraft. The Bush administration claimed that the Convention required Libya to turn over its two nationals for trial in either the U.S. or Britain. But the Bush administration was wrong. Cambridge University analyst Marc Weller cited the treaty's requirement that "Libya can either extradite or try individuals in its own courts" who are accused of attacks against civilian aircraft. "If the Qaddafi Government tries the suspects itself and finds them guilty," he went on, "it has to impose 'severe penalties.'"[7] Many UN analysts also believed that international jurisdiction in resolving the dispute between Libya and the U.S. and Britain belonged to the International Court of Justice in The Hague — not in the Security Council. The Council was and remains politically and structurally incapable of playing a legitimate judicial role; it has neither the power, nor (in the Libyan case) the inclination, to subpoena witnesses, examine or analyze evidence, or deliberate on legal issues.

Libya offered to litigate the issue in an international jurisdiction, but the Council's resolution of January 21, 1992 preempted such arrangements to demand that "the Libyan Government immediately ... provide full and effective response to those requests." This effectively sidestepped the international legal mechanism established precisely to resolve this kind of common international dispute over interpretations of extradition obligations in the absence of treaties. The resolution ordered Libya to turn over its citizens essentially by virtue of its opponents' raw power.

The International Court itself, clearly responding to the U.S. insistence on Council primacy, abdicated its responsibilities. The Court answered the Libyan request that the ICJ maintain jurisdiction of the question of interpreting the Montreal Convention, in a brief statement on April 14, 1992, the day before the Council was to decide on sanctions. The Court voted 11 to 5 that "the circumstances of the case are not such as to require the exercise of its power ...." The Court went on to state that "Libya, the United States and the United Kingdom as members of the United Nations are obliged to accept and carry out the decisions of the Security Council .... This obligation extends to the decision contained in the resolution 748 [sanctions] and whereas in accordance with article 103 of the Charter, the obligations of the parties in that respect prevail over their obligations under any other international agreement including the Montreal convention."

In other words, the Court said, the Security Council's decisions were to reign supreme, and neither the Court's rulings nor pre-existing legal covenants should be allowed to contravene them.

Many countries, especially a number of developing nations, expressed serious concern over what appeared to be a Council usurpation of the ICJ's legal responsibilities. The Council simply acted on the assumption that the two Libyans were guilty as charged. Indeed, the sanctions resolution called not only for Libya to turn its citizens over to the U.S. or Britain for trial, but also, completely separate from any future verdict, to pay reparations to the families of the Pan Am 103 victims. In other words the Council presumed not only the individual guilt of the two Libyan nationals, but the direct complicity of their government as well.

It was the staunchly conservative *Economist* in London that challenged the substance beneath the U.S.-British fanfare. "So far," it editorialized, "this article has been written as though the two Libyans for whom arrest warrants have been issued are guilty. The difficulty is that they may not be .... Some legal niceties intrude. Libya has no extradition treaty with the men's accusers. It therefore had a point when it told the World Court that it was under no legal obligation to give them up .... The Gulf War was a misfortune. Another UN-led action against an Arab country, little more than a year later, begins to look like carelessness — or a deliberate policy of Arab-bashing."[8]

However, the U.S. and Britain did not have such an easy time imposing the new anti-Libya sanctions. The campaign was viewed by many Non-Aligned countries as violating Libyan sovereignty. On the Council, India, Zimbabwe, Morocco, China, and, to a lesser degree, Cape Verde were known to have reservations about the sanctions, and were expected to abstain. UN sources indicated that China faced heavy pressure from the U.S. not to use its veto to prevent the sanctions from being imposed. Although the Chinese ambassador denied it, other knowledgeable UN sources confirmed that China had been threatened with the loss of its Most Favored Nation trading status with the U.S. if it used such a veto.[9]

There was also concern from the Non-Aligned about how long the sanctions might be imposed. Venezuela's Ambassador Diego Arria, president of the Council throughout the March 1992 debate that preceded the vote, acknowledged as much when he said that Libya "should ask the Iraqis" just how difficult it is to lift sanctions once they are imposed.[10]

The U.S. at first tried to impose broadly-defined economic sanctions against Tripoli, but the strong opposition from the Non-Aligned members of the Council, combined with a distinct lack of enthusiasm from all Council members other than Britain, scuttled the plan. Instead, without the encouragement of a much larger investment of political (and perhaps financial) capital than Washington was willing to make, the Council imposed somewhat narrower sanctions, limited largely to an arms embargo, limitations on commercial airline flights, and the lowering of Libya's diplomatic relations with some countries. Additionally, the sanctions passed the Council by a much narrower margin than the U.S. hoped. Washington and London could persuade only ten of the 15 Council members to vote in favor of the sanctions at all, only one vote more than the minimum needed to pass a resolution.

In the fall of 1993, the U.S. moved once again to tighten the sanctions against Tripoli. There had been no changes in the investigation of the Lockerbie bombing (numerous reports still placed more responsibility on nationals, perhaps agents, of Syria and Iran than of Libya), but Washington appeared concerned that Libya was being viewed as less of an outlaw state than before.

The primary goal this time was to freeze Tripoli's access to Libya's overseas assets, particularly from foreign investments. Washington had floated the idea of imposing an Iraq-style oil embargo on Libya, but too many European oil companies depended on Libyan crude. "French, Belgian, Italian and other foreign oil companies will be able to maintain the lucrative oil and gas exploration and drilling contracts they have with Libya," said the *New York Times* in describing the limits on the sanctions.[11] Russia, too, was concerned, because of Libya's estimated $1 billion debt to Moscow. Russia had threatened early on to veto any new sanctions bill, but ultimately backed down in the face of U.S. pressure.

The U.S. recognized the lack of support in the Council for harsher sanctions. Ambassador Albright reminded the Council on November 11 of the unilateral measures Washington had already imposed against Libya. She said the U.S. would go further if the new sanctions didn't work, but acknowledged that "we have considered and respected the views of those countries whose economic interests at stake might exceed our own."[12] The existing sanctions remained in place.

In October 1994, the Libyan government made a new offer. Libyan leader Muammar Qaddafi relayed to Turkish Prime Minister Tansu Ciller an offer that "Qaddafi would 'accept' the Middle East peace process and turn over the two Libyans accused of planting the bomb that destroyed Pan American flight 103 over Lockerbie, Scotland, in 1988. In return, he wanted the United States to lift its economic sanctions on Libya and allow the two suspects — both Libyan intelligence agents — to be tried in a neutral country."[13] Just a few days later the Libyan representative told the General Assembly that his country accepted an Arab League proposal to try the two Libyan suspects under Scottish law, by Scottish judges, in a trial held at The Hague, the seat of the International Court of Justice.[14] But for the U.S. and Britain, that was still not enough.

Within a few weeks, the U.S. brought to the Council a move to extend the sanctions. The scheduled December 1 vote on continuing sanctions against Libya was moved back a day to insure the debate would go on during U.S. Ambassador Albright's November presidency of the Council. The extension decision was taken at U.S. urging, despite Tripoli's latest offer, widely viewed as a significant concession, to allow the two suspects to be tried by Scottish judges and laws.

Few believed that the U.S. insistence on maintaining sanctions against Libya — especially since the existing terms of the sanctions had had little impact on the Libyan government and showed no sign of doing so in the future — was actually based on forcing the Libyan government to hand over the suspects for trial. Clearly the sanctions were designed to undermine the government itself.

2. IRAQ*

Sanctions can work in some circumstances, when they are applied in an even-handed, non-porous way, based on real, not imposed, international agreement. Most important, for sanctions to have at least a fighting chance to work, it must be clear exactly what the target country is required to do in order for the sanctions to be lifted — and those imposing the sanctions must be prepared to carry those commitments through.

When sanctions are imposed to insure compliance with multiple requirements, there is a need for clear signposts along the way for lifting them section by section as partial compliance is confirmed. This standard, the only way sanctions might have a chance of accomplishing their supposed goal, stands in sharp contrast to the U.S. interpretation of the anti-Iraq sanctions imposed under Security Council resolution 687, the "mother of all resolutions,"[15] following the Gulf War (see chapter 2). Instead, Washington insured that the UN could not lift any part of the sanctions, because it proceeded to move the political goalposts with each act of partial Iraqi compliance.

---

* Parts of this section were first published in my "Give My Regards to Basra — The Embargo on Iraq: Mixing Oil, Politics, and Hunger," *Covert Action Quarterly*, June 1995.

Each of the Council decisions to renew its punishing oil sanctions against Iraq was taken despite Baghdad's fulfillment of virtually all of the specific relevant requirements imposed by the 1991 ceasefire resolution. The prohibition against Iraq's export of oil in resolution 687 was imposed to enforce six specific conditions, aimed at ending Iraq's nuclear and weapons of mass destruction projects. The requirements include the destruction of chemical, biological, and ballistic weapons systems; acceptance of a UN special commission to monitor their destruction; agreement not to produce or use such weapons; reaffirmation of Iraq's obligations under the nuclear Non-Proliferation Treaty; agreement not to acquire or develop nuclear weapons or material; and the creation of a UN-IAEA (International Atomic Energy Agency) plan to monitor and verify Iraqi compliance with the anti-nuclear provisions. By October 7, 1994, according to the report issued that day by the UN's own Special Commission investigating Iraqi weapons systems (UNSCOM), all those stipulations had been at least minimally met.

However grudging his compliance may have been, the terms of ceasefire resolution 687 did not require Saddam Hussein to change his attitude, only his weaponry. But the UNSCOM report did not result in even a partial lifting of the oil embargo.

Certainly Iraq's own ill-conceived troop movement the same month that the 1994 UNSCOM report was released made the U.S. keep-the-sanctions effort easier. Russia and France, both of whom were owed large sums of money by Baghdad and were looking towards future trade and likely arms deals, wanted to seriously consider lifting the embargo. China also appeared open to lifting the restrictions. But the U.S.-British alliance (under increased pressure because of reports that a resumption of Iraqi oil exports would lead to a 15% drop in world oil prices, to the dismay of the [relatively] depressed Saudi oil economy) proved too powerful.

Both Washington and London were unwilling to budge from their position that Iraqi compliance with the six specific requirements for lifting the oil embargo was now insufficient — instead, as British Ambassador David Hannay described it "there is a very long list of things Iraq has to do to get sanctions lifted, which relate to its policies and practices." [16]

It appeared that the Clinton administration, like its predecessor, had concluded that those "policies and practices" needing to be changed include the presidency, or perhaps even the survival, of Saddam Hussein himself. In fact, even Iraq's subsequent acceptance of the UN-determined border of Kuwait failed to convince the Council to lift the sanctions in the spring of 1995.

In early April 1995 the Security Council announced its latest — and by then routine — refusal to consider lifting oil sanctions against Iraq. It wasn't much of an item in the press; it was simply one more notch on the U.S. sanctions belt. The UN's special observer, Rolf Ekeus, charged that Iraq seemed to have failed to meet the ever-changing requirements for lifting the prohibition on its oil sales; this time, UNSCOM could not account for all of the non-toxic material that *could* be used in the production of biological weapons.

The government in Baghdad appeared secure. But by the middle of the month, it appeared that someone in the Security Council was feeling the heat generated by a growing global unease over the plight of several million Iraqi children growing up without adequate food or medical care, victims of the harsh measures designed by U.S. policymakers to bring Baghdad to its knees. The Council proffered a new version of an earlier offer, which would allow Iraq to sell restricted quantities of oil and use part of the proceeds to purchase limited amounts of food and medicine. Payment for the oil would be made to the UN, which would then dole out enough for Iraq, under strict UN monitoring, to purchase the humanitarian supplies. Thirty percent of the proceeds would be sent directly to Kuwait, as part of UN-mandated reparations. Another chunk was destined for Iraq's Kurdish population, living largely autonomously under U.S.-British protection.

But Iraq refused, claiming that the humiliating terms violated its sovereignty. The Baghdad regime was right, of course — the UN terms would violate Iraq's national rights to control its own resources. But that was certainly nothing new. Ever since Saddam Hussein's defeated government was forced to accept the punishing terms of Security Council end-the-war resolutions 687 and 688, post-Desert Storm Iraq had faced little *but* humiliation and violation from the U.S. and the UN. Saddam Hussein appeared to hope that rejection of the incremental easing might force the Security Council to reconsider lifting all the sanctions; the Council's goal, on the other hand, was simply to insure that the Iraqi government would be blamed for the population's suffering, rather than the UN sanctions. Concern for the country's long-suffering population was not at the top of anyone's agenda.

The announcement of the extension of sanctions did not merit even the short-lived media flurry that accompanied the brief mini-skirmish between Iraq and the U.S. in October 1994, just six months earlier. At that time, Baghdad sent several thousand troops south towards the demilitarized zone along the Kuwaiti border.

The troop movement was an elaborate piece of Iraqi theater, whose target audience was the UN Security Council. With the UNSCOM report just released, the Council members were about to consider, for the first time seriously, the conditions under which oil sanctions against Iraq might be lifted. The troop movement was a clumsy and misguided diplomatic gesture that ended up giving Bill Clinton an unexpected boost, and its impact was precisely the opposite of what Saddam Hussein hoped for. It was a message sent via military bombast because military rulers know no other kind. What it *wasn't* was a serious effort to invade Kuwait.

U.S. officials knew that. It is unlikely anyone in the Pentagon, or anyone else in the Security Council, seriously believed that Kuwait's oil-bloated emirs were actually endangered by Baghdad's maneuvers. After all, however inept Iraq's diplomacy, Baghdad was rarely militarily foolhardy. Especially in his seriously weakened state of late 1994, the chance that Saddam Hussein would risk his few crack troops by sending them across the Kuwaiti border without a shred of air support (the U.S.-imposed no-fly-zone was still being rigorously enforced) was hardly a serious possibility.

But the provocative troop move provided a golden opportunity for the Clinton administration to divert the Council's agenda, and re-establish Iraq-related dominance over France and Russia, then threatening to play havoc with the sanctions regime, a far more serious threat to the U.S. than Baghdad's military posturing. Just as it would six months later, Washington maintained its go-for-broke determination to keep ratcheting up sanctions against Iraq as long as Saddam Hussein remained in power.

For Washington, overall Gulf regional policy in the mid-1990s was shaped by the imperatives of what policy-makers called "dual containment" — a strategy aimed at keeping both of the potential regional "rogue" powers weakened and under U.S. control; Washington could no longer rely on Iran and Iraq fighting each other.

Within that framework, preventing Iraq from exporting oil — not Saddam Hussein's bluster — was the centerpiece of U.S. policy towards Iraq. First, the U.S. was determined to keep Iraq economically crippled and politically besieged. And while preventing any possible resurgence of the regime in Baghdad as a regional power was one goal, Washington was simultaneously reasserting its terms for the post-Desert Storm Middle East.

Those Arab governments that joined the U.S. coalition were to be rewarded; those that refused to climb on board with the desert stormers were to be punished or left to languish in isolation. If the U.S. had its way, Saddam Hussein's government — and the Iraqi people — would face crippling sanctions as long as the Ba'athist leader remained in power.

A second, perhaps even more important reason for U.S. insistence on maintaining sanctions has to do with the petro-interests that under-girded the Gulf War in the first place — specifically, Washington's role as protector of the industrialized world's access to that precious re-source. If Iraq were allowed to resume oil exports, most analysts ex-pected a 15% drop in world oil prices to result. By itself that would not be such a bad thing for the U.S. and its oil-guzzling Northern allies. But it would seriously damage the already depressed Saudi economy (a relative depression, to be sure, based on the oil-inflated standards of Saudi financial privilege). Washington remained determined to defend that economy, largely to safeguard the North's unfettered access to the Saudis' 25% of known world oil reserves. All indications were that the U.S. was prepared to wait for world economic growth to spur enough of an oil demand to offset competitive losses, before allowing the UN to lift the sanctions and allow Iraq to return to oil sales.

But clearly the impact of a slow-down in the oil industry had only the most insignificant impact on the Saudi population. This contrasts sharply with the effect of the oil embargo and the resulting cash crisis in Iraq. Even with escalating Iraqi efforts to smuggle some small amounts of oil onto the international black market — at half-price markdowns — conditions for Iraq's population as a result of the oil sanctions were ruinous. By mid-1995, out-of-control inflation meant that most Iraqis could rely only on the minimal food provided in gov-ernment rations. The World Food Organization estimated that the amounts of food available constituted barely one-third of nutritional requirements. UNICEF reported a 9% rise in infant malnutrition; the spring 1995 ration reduction, according to the Rome-based World In-ternational Food Program, "constitutes a risk for the health of 2.25 million children and 230,000 pregnant women or those breast-feed-ing."[17]

Back at the Security Council, the timing of the 1994 Iraqi military maneuvers could not have been more fortuitous for Washington's de-fend-the-Saudis, keep-the-sanctions-on campaign. The Iraqi troops' journey south began just as the Council was preparing to discuss the report of Rolf Ekeus, head of the UN's Special Commission overseeing the destruction of Iraq's weapons of mass destruction. Ekeus's October 7th report asserted that the complex UN-mandated monitoring system designed to insure future Iraqi compliance "is now provisionally op-erational." His report essentially challenged the CIA's claim that Iraq was still maintaining weapons of mass destruction, especially biologi-cal, chemical, and ballistic weapons, and was working on nuclear weap-ons. Further, Ekeus acknowledged that despite Baghdad's bombastic rhetoric, "if Iraq extends ... the same level of cooperation that it has to date ... there can be cause for optimism."

It seemed clear by October 1994 that the weapons no longer existed (the UN had certified as early as 1992 that some, including major ballistic systems, had already been destroyed) when Ekeus issued his report regarding the monitoring systems. Under ordinary circumstances, Ekeus's report of Iraqi compliance with all the requirements should and probably would have led to an immediate discussion in the Security Council over what timetable should be set for the lifting of sanctions. But these were not ordinary circumstances. The U.S., in defiance of the clear language of the UN resolution, insisted once again that the Baghdad regime's compliance with the requirements of 687 was deficient.

Moving the goalposts of the diplomatic game reflected the consistent U.S. position that Saddam Hussein must be ousted before sanctions could be lifted. On October 16, 1994, Warren Christopher was asked whether the U.S. refusal to lift sanctions was in fact aimed at getting rid of the Iraqi president. The secretary of state did not deny the charge, admitting that "we want compliance with all the UN resolutions. And I don't believe he can do that and stay in office."[18]

Washington succeeded by using the provocation of Iraq's troop movements to delay for an indefinite period the Council's mandated discussion of sanctions-lifting. France and Russia may not have shared all the U.S. concerns regarding Saudi oil income (since they had been largely locked out of the lucrative contracts), but the tactical divisions among the Council's permanent members were patched over with a broad acceptance of the U.S. position. According to the Council statement issued after the sanctions were continued, it was troop movements, not sanctions, that were the only issue.

A high-visibility Russian diplomatic initiative a few weeks later, sending Foreign Minister Andrei Kosyrev to Baghdad, led to Iraqi acceptance of a key U.S. demand, recognition of Kuwait's UN-mandated borders. In return, Russia promised Iraq it would place the sanctions issue back on the Council's agenda. But Washington succeeded in keeping the two issues separate, allowing only a brief reference to diplomatic efforts in the final resolution condemning the troop movements, and making no commitments or even references to the sanctions.

Other Council resistance, particularly from France and Brazil, focused on the U.S. demand to create a military exclusion zone in southern Iraq, as well as on the proposed British requirement that Baghdad notify the secretary-general two weeks before any troop movements.

Paris and Brasilia raised concerns regarding the dangerous precedent set by the further UN undermining of Iraq's already-weakened sovereignty.

Other countries, including New Zealand, China, Spain, and Pakistan, opposed the proposed exclusion zone and notification requirements as unworkable. Ultimately, whatever economic or other national interests may have motivated the expressed concerns of Council members (especially France and Russia, both of which had billion dollar interests in Iraq), it was clear that the U.S.-imposed "consensus" that characterized much of Gulf War decision-making in the Council had become, by late 1994, at least somewhat shaky.

By the end of the discussion, once Washington and London had backed down from their new demands for a military no-go zone, the U.S.-orchestrated resolution condemning Iraq's troop movements passed in a unanimous Council vote. A month later, on November 14, within two hours of the arrival in New York of Iraqi Deputy Foreign Minister Tariq Aziz, the Council voted to continue the oil sanctions without modification. The vote followed a closed-door Council briefing by U.S. Ambassador Madeleine Albright using spy-satellite photographs to "prove" that Saddam Hussein was building lavish palaces while the Iraqi population lacked basic food and medicine. However likely the truth of those claims, their assertion by the U.S. provided a stark contrast to Washington's permanent silence on the issue of the billions siphoned off from Saudi oil revenues for the private and personal enjoyment of the Saudi king and princes. (King Fahd's personal wealth in 1995 exceeded $12 billion, and included a dozen palaces in Europe and in the kingdom, a $60 million yacht, and a private Boeing 747.[19])

Clinton administration officials through the mid-1990s continued to assert that the newest military requirements imposed on Baghdad by the United States somehow had become actual UN positions. These false claims tended to go unchallenged by journalists, UN officials, and even other members of the Security Council. The phenomenon reflected similar success stories in previous years, in which Washington managed to convince not only the American people but much of the diplomatic world that, for example, the "no-fly-zones" established in northern and southern Iraq were UN operations. In fact, neither was mandated in any UN resolution, and both zones were patrolled without UN oversight by the U.S. and its Gulf War allies.

A few months after the November extension of sanctions, in January 1995, although some procurement information was still missing, Ekeus certified that monitoring was well under way. Once again the U.S. opposed lifting sanctions. This time Albright's complaint was that Iraq had not yet returned or paid for all of the Kuwaiti weapons it had supposedly captured. Once again the U.S. led the charge, and once again the U.S. succeeded in preventing the Council from allowing any relaxation of sanctions.

According to article 22 of Security Council resolution 687, when Iraq "has completed all actions contemplated" in the specific paragraphs mentioned above, the UN oil sanctions "shall have no further force or effect." The significance here is that the requirements for ending the oil embargo were very specific. Add-on demands for Iraqi recognition of Kuwait's border, return of Kuwaiti property, information regarding Kuwaiti nationals missing in the war, all identified by U.S. officials at various times as reasons the oil sanctions must remain in place, were included in completely separate parts of the ten-page resolution, and were not among the listed prerequisites for lifting oil sanctions.

Ironically, even Iraq's 1995 diplomatic effort to answer Washington's demands, by recognizing Kuwait's sovereignty and accepting the long-disputed border, was spurned by the U.S. as insufficient to allow the sanctions to be lifted — even though it already went beyond the actual requirements of 687. Concerns over human rights abuses, however legitimate, were never included in resolution 687 at all, but were raised in separate, subsequent resolutions that also had nothing to do with the oil sanctions.

Throughout the mid-1990s, the last word on anti-Iraq sanctions remained that of Warren Christopher. Even considering lifting sanctions, he said, regardless of Iraq's compliance with the UN's actual requirements, was "dangerously misguided."[20] If Washington had any concern for validating UN resolutions as they were written, not as Washington would like to interpret them, such concern remained unspoken.

Iraq, Libya, and Cuba, despite their enormous diversity, share a crucial feature: dubbed "rogue" or "outlaw" states by Washington, whether for occasional (however rhetorical) anti-U.S. mobilization or for domestic political goals (such as Cuban-American votes), the three countries remain pressed under relentless U.S. embargoes. For Iraq and Libya, the U.S. engineered UN acquiescence; for Cuba, it imposes, and attempts to internationalize, its blockade without regard for overwhelming UN opposition. But in each case, the choice of crippling sanctions is rooted in the U.S. effort to go head-to-head, but not quite to war, with governments Washington would like nothing more than to see overthrown.

Sanctions remain, according to international law, an act of war. By relying on harsh sanctions almost solely against governments it dubs opponents, and by ignoring the humanitarian toll on the civilian population, Washington can intervene powerfully, without having to answer for a more direct act of aggression. When it forces the UN to its will, it has an even more potent protective shield against public outrage or opposition.

Notes

1. Gareth Evans, *Cooperating for Peace: The Global Agenda for the 1990s and Beyond* (St. Leonards, Australia: Allen & Unwin, 1993), pp. 138-139.

2. Adam Roberts and Benedict Kingsbury, "Introduction: The UN's Role in International Society Since 1945," in Roberts and Kingsbury (eds.), *United Nations, Divided World* (New York: Oxford University Press, 1993), pp. 33-34.

3. Brian Urquhart, "The UN and International Security After the Cold War," in Roberts and Kingsbury, *United Nations*, p. 84.

4. Ibid.

5. *Cuba Info Newsletter*, May 18, 1992, cited in Medea Benjamin, "On Its Own: Cuba in the Post-Cold War Era," in Phyllis Bennis and Michel Moushabeck (eds.), *Altered States: A Reader in the New World Order* (New York: Olive Branch Press/ Interlink, 1993), p. 419.

6. General Assembly resolution A/48/L.14/Rev.1, "Necessity of Ending the Economic, Commercial and Financial Embargo Imposed by the United States of America Against Cuba."

7. Marc Weller, "Libyan Terrorism, American Swagger," *New York Times*, February 15, 1992.

8. *Economist*, London, April 17, 1992.

9. Interviews with UN official, March 1992.

10. Interview with Ambassador Diego Arria, March 1992.

11. Paul Lewis, "UN Tightens Sanctions Against Libya," *New York Times*, November 12, 1993.

12. Ibid.

13. George Moffett, "Strain of Isolation Compels Qaddafi to Approach U.S.," *Christian Science Monitor*, November 9, 1994.

14. Speech by Omar Mustafa Muntasser, Secretary of the General People's Committee for Foreign Liaison and International Cooperation of Libya, General Assembly, October 7, 1994.

15. Urquhart, "The UN and International Security," p. 85.

16. British Ambassador Sir David Hannay, outside Council chambers, November 11, 1994.

17. *New York Times*, October 25, 1994.

18. *MacNeil-Lehrer Newshour*, PBS, October 16, 1994.

19. Dilip Ganguly, "Saudis Facing New Challenges," Associated Press, February 18, 1995.

20. *MacNeil-Lehrer*, op. cit.

8

To the World's Attention

U.S. political and financial hegemony at the UN is not yet complete. While real economic policy decisions, and certainly the power to enforce decisions, have largely been taken out of its hands, the General Assembly continues to discuss and debate issues of North-South disparities, global concerns regarding social and environmental problems, and other wide-ranging topics.

Since 1990, the Assembly has mandated and coordinated a series of high-profile global conferences, designed to spotlight particular areas of concern, and to heighten the pressure on powerful governments in the North to respond to increasing desperation in the South. From the vantage point of the U.S., the conferences were perfectly acceptable: they served to compartmentalize potentially explosive hot-button issues by funneling inordinate resources into the planning and execution of these high-visibility (not to mention high cost) extravaganzas.

The conferences began in 1990, with the World Summit for Children (transformed by U.S. diplomats into the World Summit for Desert Storm). The series continued with the 1992 Rio Earth Summit, the 1993 Vienna Human Rights Conference, the 1994 Cairo Population Conference, the 1995 Copenhagen Social Development Summit, culminating with the September 1995 Fourth World Conference on Women in Beijing. The UN-sponsored international conference in the spring of 1995, designed to (ostensibly) evaluate and (definitely) extend the treaty on nuclear non-proliferation (NPT), shared many of the features of the Assembly-sponsored events.

Overall, the conferences were helpful in attracting vast amounts of previously-unavailable media attention, especially in the North. However perceptive or obtuse the coverage, it could only be useful for people in the U.S., Japan, Europe, as well as in the South, to be inundated, at least for a few weeks, with articles and radio and television reports documenting the urgency of environmental crises or the need to chal-

lenge traditional planning approaches that leave women out of the social development equation.

The catch, in analyzing the media's utility from the vantage point of
making real changes, was that the conferences lasted only two weeks.
And, to no one's surprise, much of the media attention focused on the
presence (or absence, in the case of the U.S.) of heads of state using the
conferences, in many cases, to shore up their own political credibility.
It also meant that longstanding and urgent chronic problems of the
South were, through the "prepare it/convene it/forget it" dynamic of
the conferences, relegated to the status of sudden or short-term crises
to be answered only with short-term and woefully insufficient solutions.

The conference series, what the *New York Times* called "the traveling
United Nations global road show" is based on the same formula each
time: "incremental agreements, offering something more than plati-
tudes but something less than action."[1]

In defending the necessity of the UN taking its show on the road, at
such high costs, Secretary-General Boutros-Ghali described the inability of the UN to get the U.S. to pay attention to much of its work. "Between New York and Washington, we are passing through a terrible
crisis of credibility of the United Nations. In all the United States you
have ... a kind of negative indifference. But outside the United States
we are able to obtain the presence of 120 countries for a subject which
is quite complicated .... It means support for the United Nations. It
means that they believe in the United Nations, they trust the United
Nations."[2]

Maybe. But that trust means little without the support of the UN's
most powerful member states to implement even broadly agreed-on decisions. The high level of press and public attention paid to the conferences is seen by many diplomats and policy-makers, especially those
from the South, as a substitute for the disempowerment of the General
Assembly, and, more broadly, the marginalization of economic and social development issues in the United Nations relative to the Security
Council and its concentration on peacekeeping.

It is important to note here, that despite the uncertain value of the
conferences as a means of implementing substantive change in North-
South relations or in solving crisis-level social problems engulfing
much of the world, there are two areas in which the meetings have
played an undisputably positive role.

One is in the emergence of the NGO movement as a vibrant and dynamic component of United Nations life. The NGOs, or non-governmental organizations, created parallel conferences, beginning with the

Earth Summit, to mobilize often-unheard constituencies and lobby strenuously for voices outside of governmental and policy elites to have a say in strategic discussions. Some of these groups represented large, wealthy, and professionally-staffed organizations based in the U.S. or Europe, with deep pockets and the capacity to send teams of people to Brazil or Austria or Egypt or Denmark or China equipped with cellular phones, mobile fax machines, computers, and copiers. Others were tiny groups of grassroots activists from impoverished African villages or remote endangered rain forests, who had to continue small-scale fundraising at the conference itself (often by selling handcrafted artifacts from home) just to pay for their transportation. The NGOs also served as undaunted lobbyists of their own governments' official delegations, demanding that the needs of poor people, of dispossessed indigenous populations, of women, of people of color in largely white societies, of gays and lesbians in virtually all societies be taken seriously. When combined with the massive media presence, the role of the NGOs, especially in their preparation and follow-up work in their own countries, made it much more likely that the crucial issues framed by the UN's limited conference structure would make it, however briefly, onto the world's stage.

The other major gain was in the new articulation, as a shared international understanding, of the need for women's empowerment as a necessary component of all efforts towards economic growth, population control, fighting environmental degradation, human rights, etc. Again the NGOs played the major role, although their success in reformulating the language of resolutions, beginning in Rio, bore more fruit than the more difficult battles of implementation. While tensions between women from North and South remained, there was unusual North-South dialogue and cooperation, as well as some genuine efforts by important women's organizations and leaders from the North to insure that women from the South were included in decision-making and caucusing at every level. The creation of the Women's Caucus in Rio, convened initially by the U.S.-based Women's Environment and Development Organization (WEDO), set a precedent for future conferences. In each, the caucus would meet early each morning, to analyze the planned agenda and develop, to whatever degree possible in that extraordinary diversity of opinion, a common set of goals for influencing the delegates.

That pattern was followed at subsequent conferences. In Vienna, violence against women, and particularly the inclusion of rape in the international legal definitions of war crimes, emerged as major concerns. In Cairo, the women's caucus succeeded in winning broad understanding that issues of population cannot be separated from questions of women's empowerment. At the social development summit in Copenhagen, women fought for special attention to be paid to the needs of disenfranchised women living on the economic fringes of the least developed countries. By the time the September 1995 Fourth Global Conference on Women took place in Beijing, women's NGOs and women activists from around the world had gained crucial experience, confidence, and strategic clarity that would stand them in good stead in challenging the harrassment and restrictions imposed by the Chinese authorities.

But the Beijing conference was the last in a series that had begun several years earlier. On the "UN road show" circuit, they began in Rio.

THE UN CONFERENCE ON THE ENVIRONMENT AND DEVELOPMENT: THE EARTH SUMMIT

The Rio Earth Summit of 1992 (officially the UN Conference on the Environment and Development, or UNCED) brought about important symbolic results in putting environmental concerns on the international agenda, but the lack of U.S. seriousness meant there was no thoroughgoing shift in priorities and potential implementation. Nevertheless, Rio did reflect a growing, relatively more serious UN response to the new international concern with environmental issues.

But with its timing, in the midst of Desert Storm-generated boosterism, the Earth Summit also provided a new showcase for the White House to demonstrate its domination of multilateral diplomacy in the post-Cold War world.

In what the *Los Angeles Times* called a "tactical tour de force," the Bush administration beat back the environmental concerns of Europe and the developing countries alike. "Thanks to the Bush administration," the *Times* wrote even before the conference began, "government leaders will sign a global warming treaty that has none of the teeth sought by U.S. allies and trading partners in the industrialized world."[3] Even aside from the needs of the South, Washington asserted and held the line on its sharply limited commitment to environmental goals, and in doing so, reasserted U.S. hegemony over global environmental action.

Just three days before the conference opened, on May 30, 1992, Bush administration officials made public their long-anticipated refusal to sign the treaty on bio-diversity and habitat protection scheduled to be finalized in Rio. The move followed by less than a month Bush's success in forcing the Europeans to abandon their own crucial and hard-fought commitment to set timetables for the industrialized countries to roll back global warming-causing emissions to 1990 levels by the year 2000. Taken together, the two positions provided a far clearer picture of the administration's actual environmental policy than did the grandstanding that heralded Bush's announcement that he would join other world leaders in attending the Earth Summit.

James Speth, who chaired the President's Council on Environmental Quality during the Carter administration, and later became director of UNDP, said grudgingly, "It is a treaty worth having. But because of the United States, what could have been a giant step has become only a baby step forward."[4]

The Bush administration took more than usual pains to make sure the world knew that it had no intention of knuckling under to an environmentalist agenda. A large part of the vitriol in President Bush's own position came from his electoral concerns: the Earth Summit was convened just five months before the election he would lose to Bill Clinton. At the time of the summit, Bush was under additional pressure stemming from heated allegations that, as vice-president, he had conspired with Ronald Reagan in 1980 to delay the release of U.S. hostages held in Iran to insure the defeat of Jimmy Carter. Presumably out of election-time fear of alienating his core right-wing constituency, Bush himself did not play a strong visible role in the conference. One observer characterized Bush's position in Rio as a "defensive crouch."[5]

But that does not mean U.S. influence was missing. According to the *New York Times*, "Blandness can sometimes prove a surprisingly effective bludgeon. The parcel of treaties signed here have been portrayed by disappointed advocates as pitiful gutless creatures with no bite." And Singapore's foreign minister Tommy Koh, who chaired the main conference session, remarked, "This will teach the United Nations not to hold a conference in an American election year."[6]

Along with Washington's heavy-handed diplomatic pressure, the U.S. role in Rio reflected the dominant influence of major corporations in setting Bush administration environmental policy — the same corporations that represent the greatest disdain for ecological concerns. The corporations themselves banded together for lobbying strength in Rio. They created new alliances with such eco-friendly names as the "Global Climate Coalition," which grouped 25 major corporations and eighteen large trade associations with the U.S. Chamber of Commerce, the Edison Electric Institute, representing electrical utility companies, and the National Coal Association. Their goal was to prevent Washington from signing the treaties, or at least to ensure their lack of enforceability. According to Tia Armstrong, an "environmental specialist" for the U.S. Chamber of Commerce, "Every time we see timetables and targets, we go berserk."[7] As it happened, the corporate eco-spindoctors had no cause for even mild irritation, let alone "going berserk." Their will prevailed.

The broader U.S. agenda for the UN played a role too, beyond the corporations' own intervention. One of the last projects of the UN's Center on Transnational Corporations (CTC) before it was dismantled in February 1992 was a plan to be introduced in Rio for monitoring corporate adherence to Earth Summit resolutions. But instead, as early as three months before delegates gathered in Rio, it was clear that

> the biggest gap in the official UNCED documents being negotiated for signing by world leaders in Rio in June is the absence of proposals for the international regulation or control of big businesses and transnational corporations to ensure that they reduce or stop activities that are harmful to the natural environment, human health and development. The Agenda 21 document being negotiated now does have a section on "strengthening the role of business and industry," but locates it in a section on how the rights of major groups (such as women, youth, indigenous people and non-governmental organizations) can be strengthened. Thus, industry and TNCs are being treated as entities whose roles or rights can be strengthened, rather than as entities whose activities should be regulated.[8]

The fact that the Center on Transnational Corporations was about to be shut down was far from irrelevant. The promotion by some U.S. (and UN) officials of the corporate-backed Business Council for Sustainable Development as a legitimte force in the UN's environmental work, without the oversight potential the Center would have made possible, reflected an extraordinary cynicism in the claimed "good world citizenship" of powerful transnational corporations.

The five years of preparatory work for the Rio summit often brought the U.S. head to head against its erstwhile allies in the European Community, and more fundamentally against the interests of the South. The European position, reluctantly or not, acknowledged the responsibility of the industrialized countries to scale back the production of environmentally catastrophic emissions, especially those linked to global warming. The position reflected the increasing influence of Green movements and increasingly, Green parliamentarians, in European politics. The U.S. admitted no such thing.

Ultimately the European support for binding commitments to stabilize emissions by 2000 survived only until Bush threatened not to attend the summit if they persisted. The U.S. came to the final preparatory meeting a month before the Rio conference alone among its allies in refusing to support a commitment to stabilize greenhouse emissions. "But concerned that President Bush would stay away from the Earth Summit and thereby turn the massively publicized conference into a fiasco, European governments acceded to U.S. demands to abandon a binding reduction target and a firm deadline."[9]

A key factor in the U.S. position in Rio focused on the question of transfer of resources — in a word, efforts towards balancing out the tremendous disparity of income between North and South. Specifically, the South called for a binding commitment from countries in the North to provide 0.7% of their economic output in assistance to the South, by the year 2000. The wealthy countries (with one notable exception) had accepted the goal of 0.7% twenty years earlier. It had been voted at the UN's first Conference on the Human Environment held in Stockholm in 1972. On average, most countries in the North actually paid about 0.45%, and the South was eager to implement the earlier commitment. While no binding language was included, a stronger statement of intent by some of the Northern powers to set 0.7% as a "target" to be reached "as soon as possible" was included in the final statement.

But for the U.S., none of that debate mattered — in 1972 the U.S. had refused to endorse the original 0.7% goal. Twenty years later, that much hadn't changed. The percentage of U.S. GNP spent on foreign assistance (of all kinds, not just development aid to the poorest countries) remained at the bottom of the list of countries in the North. In June 1995 UNICEF reported that U.S. aid was down to 0.15% of GNP, the lowest of the 21 industrial countries surveyed. (The Scandinavian countries and the Netherlands led the way, averaging above 0.8%, well above the target set at the Stockholm conference.)[10]

As it happened, the U.S. position was more clearly reflected in a World Bank statement drafted six months before the Earth Summit began. The Bank's U.S.-backed chief economist, Lawrence Summers, wrote a memo, dated December 12, 1991, to the Bank's senior staff. In it, he suggested that the answer to pollution in the industrialized world was to export pollution-causing industries to the South. "Just between you and me," the memo asks, "shouldn't the World Bank be encouraging more migration of the dirty industries to the LDCs [least developed countries]?"

Summers went on to explain that since wages were low, the costs to industry of increased illness and/or death among workers would be lowest in the Third World: "The economic logic behind dumping a load of toxic waste in the lowest wage country is impeccable, and we should face up to that," he wrote. It shouldn't be a problem, Summers asserted: "I've always thought that under-populated countries in Africa are vastly under-polluted."

Ultimately, Summers justified his arguments on the grounds that poor people don't really mind pollution and environmental degradation. After all, he writes, "the concern over an agent that causes a one-in-a-million change in the odds of prostate cancer is obviously going to be much higher in a country where people survive to *get* prostate cancer than in a country where under-five mortality is 200 per thousand."[11]

In the end, the Bank apologized for its top official's embarrassing lapse in committing to paper what many in top leadership positions presumably believe. Thus it should have surprised no one that a key demand of the South's diplomats in Rio was that new environmental aid in the future not be disbursed under the control of the World Bank. It also should have surprised no one that the demand was quietly shelved early on in the debate — and that the U.S. press mentioned it not at all.

For the countries of the South, the issue was even more dire. Pressure had been mounting on those nations, from the IMF, the World Bank, and from Washington directly, to create environmentally-correct strategies for economic development. But those countries, facing endemic poverty and the legacy of centuries of colonial domination by the North, were reluctant to accept the consequences of the way the U.S. defined ecological acceptability: the abandonment of efforts to improve the living standards of their impoverished populations. Instead, the South redefined environmental requirements for developing countries, demanding economic compensation and the large-scale transfer of environmentally-friendly technology to improve, rather than abandon, their commitment to development. The cost would run to billions of dollars — and logic and the UN's Earth Summit organizers called for the costs to be paid by the North.

The U.S., with about one-twentieth of the world's population, was (and remains) responsible for about a quarter of the global emissions of carbon monoxide. Concerns that U.S. businesses might be forced to reduce their exorbitant profit levels to clean up some areas of environmentally disastrous technology meant that Washington had no intention of signing a treaty with anything approaching real teeth.

A key contradiction was reflected in the degree to which the governments and corporations of the North were far more concerned with protecting the pristine beauty of Brazil's rain forests in isolation than in providing the technology, money, and jobs necessary to allow Brazil simultaneously to protect its own forests, while bringing the lives of its people up to the standards of the twenty-first century.

Everyone agreed that the costs would be enormous. The secretary-general of the Organization of American States reminded everyone that, "The cost of sustainable development is very high indeed. Mr. Maurice Strong, Secretary-General of UNCED, has said that a global environmental agenda would require transfers of $125 billion annually from developed to developing countries. Developing countries need large amounts of additional financial and technological resources if they are going to be able to contribute to global environmental goals and at the same time persist in their urgent struggle to develop, which does not admit any delays."[12] Writing in a similar vein in the weeks before Rio, Hilary French, a leading environmental analyst, remarked, "Though nobody expects UNCED to generate this kind of money, some new financing is likely. The question, then: Through what institution should the money flow?"[13]

Unfortunately, Hilary French's optimism was misplaced. The new financing that did result from the Earth Summit was in such tiny increments that the flow-chart problem of how to channel it never came up. None came from the U.S.

Through it all, the General Assembly, having issued the call and approved the UN Secretariat's organizing and financing the conference, was largely unable to push the summit towards higher levels of accountability and enforceability than those accepted by Washington. As one New Delhi scientist described the wealthy countries that control the international funding for environmental projects, "They are the environmental crooks, and they have all the levers of power."[14]

WHOSE HUMAN RIGHTS?

When Paul Lewis wrote his background feature piece on the World Conference on Human Rights, ten days before it convened in Vienna on June 14, 1993, he started out with an undeniable assertion: "Deep divisions between developing and industrialized nations threaten the success of a conference this month on strengthening human rights."[15] No question about it.

Lewis's next sentence might have been something like: "At issue is the contention by the U.S. and other industrialized countries that international protocols identifying the right to development as an inalienable right can be ignored, and that political rights involving multiple parties and a free press are much more important than the economic rights to sufficient food, a job, health care, and education."

But it wasn't. Instead, Lewis wrote: "At issue is a contention by many Third World nations that Western standards of practice and fairness do not necessarily apply to other cultures."[16] That the UN correspondent for the *New York Times* should broadly reflect Washington's vantage point of a multinational event or issue is not surprising. The problem was that Paul Lewis was wrong.

Certainly there were a few countries who claimed that political rights, such as freedom of speech to criticize governments, freedom of assembly, etc., were "not appropriate" in their political culture, asserting that outsiders' concern with those rights represented unacceptable interference. But those countries were in fact very few, and, overwhelmingly, most of those repressive governments had long been among Washington's close friends, allies, arms customers, or trading partners: China, Indonesia, Malaysia, and Singapore were among them.

There was continuing criticism for what many perceived as hypocrisy in the Clinton administration's human rights policy, which "hawk[s] trade and investment deals while relegating human rights to the ineffectual realm of private diplomacy."[17] With regards to Indonesia, for example, during the November 1994 summit of the Asia Pacific Economic Cooperation (APEC) conference, U.S. Commerce Secretary Ron Brown deflected any discussion of Indonesian human rights violations and workplace abuses.[18]

For the majority of countries of the South, the issue at Vienna was not whether political human rights matter, but rather the claim that they are meaningless (not to mention impossible to guarantee) without the parallel economic and social rights, including the right to development, called for in the UN's own human rights conventions. As one knowledgeable Non-Aligned diplomat stated heatedly, "You can't protect [political] human rights if 70% of your population is illiterate. The priorities must be growth and development, and within that context, inside of that process, must be the expansion of democracy."[19]

There was also significant unease among the South that behind Washington's claimed commitment to human rights lay a cold calculation that in the post-Cold War world "defending human rights" provided a much easier justification for the U.S. to intervene in other countries. While multilateral, UN-endorsed intervention might be the official cover, there was little doubt in many capitals of the South that Washington would be calling the shots in determining which human rights violations — real or fabricated — constituted a legitimate rationale for intervention or invasion.

The secretary-general added to the fear. During his speech welcoming the delegates to the Vienna conference, Boutros-Ghali acknowledged that "human rights, by their very nature, do away with the distinction traditionally drawn between the internal order and the international order. Human rights give rise to a new legal permeability. They should thus not be considered either from the viewpoint of absolute sovereignty, or from the viewpoint of political intervention."[20]

UN human rights work is shaped by two primary international conventions, both adopted in 1966: the International Covenant on Civil and Political Rights (ICCPR) and the International Covenant on Economic, Social and Cultural Rights (ICESCR). While the Universal Declaration of Human Rights was created as far back as 1948, its implementation — or lack thereof — was largely ignored by the UN until specific conventions could be framed that would satisfy governments' concerns. The fact that the two sets of human rights were separated at all goes back to the Cold War legacy that shaped everything the UN attempted:

> The Western countries, led by the U.S.A., argued for the supremacy of civil and political rights, which often amounted to denying that economic and social rights were, or could become, human rights. The Soviet-led communist and/or socialist bloc argued that economic and social rights should take precedence over civil and political rights, which often resulted in the denial of civil rights and political liberties .... This protracted process lasted until 1966, when the two Covenants were adopted, and it took ten additional years for them to come into force — it was neither easy nor fast.[21]

The U.S. only ratified the covenant on economic, social, and cultural rights in 1992, and, when it did, included "reservations" limiting its effect. Most significant among those conditions was the declaration that unlike other ratified treaties, it would not automatically become domestic law. The result is that the requirements of the treaty cannot be cited in U.S. courts. According to the director of Human Rights Watch, the conditions mean that U.S. adherence to the treaty "is purely cosmetic and has no practical value for Americans."[22]

And the U.S. focus solely on political rights found few allies. A key, often unstated, reality was that the position of the "Soviet bloc," identifying economic and social rights as equal or even greater priorities than political rights, was supported by a vast array of poor countries, most with little claim to a socialist orientation. Whether repressive or laissez-faire governments, they were concerned that the West's — and especially Washington's — fixation on political rights was giving the wealthy countries a new dodge to avoid economic development assistance.

Even the *New York Times'* key correspondent in Vienna was forced to acknowledge at least some legitimacy in the South's concerns. "Perhaps the greatest weakness in the West's case," Alan Riding wrote, "is that it has traditionally emphasized political over economic rights. 'It's hard for people who have never faced hunger or illiteracy to understand how crucial they are to a majority of mankind,' Reed Brody of the International Human Rights Law Group said. 'Ask an American about human rights and he'll [sic] say: freedom of speech. Ask an African woman about human rights and she'll say: the right to feed her children.' "[23]

With the collapse of the socialist bloc, the South was left alone to fight against the Western effort to bifurcate human rights. It was, and remains, a difficult battle. The Western press overwhelmingly accepted the U.S. claim that it was the Western view of human rights that was truly "universal," and that it was the South's efforts to stop threats of holding development assistance or debt relief hostage to outside assessments of political rights that were examples of "cultural relativism." Concerns of governments in the South about their inability to guarantee the internationally-targeted human right to housing or medical care because of insufficient funds were marginalized. Even the concerns of NGOs from the South, whose own focus was indeed political and civil rights and who targeted their own government, were rarely taken seriously, possibly because their criticism of and demands on their own governments, however harsh, still took into account the overriding need for development.

In examining states' human rights records, for example, it is interesting to compare the voting records of North and South on a critical convention. The International Covenant on Civil and Political Rights, the one so central to Washington's definition of what the UN's human rights work should be about, deals primarily with the responsibilities of states and governments. But there is an "Optional Protocol" to the ICCPR, in which signatory governments state their willingness to allow individual people, not just governments, to seek redress from the UN's Human Rights Committee if domestic remedies should prove inadequate. Fully two-thirds of the countries now party to that Optional Protocol are from the South (47). Of the 23 from the North, the U.S. is conspicuously absent.

The 1993 Vienna human rights summit was the culmination of a three-year debate within the UN on just those questions of what the nature of the organization's mandate should be in defending human rights. From the start, there were different definitions, different understandings of the role and goals of the UN's human rights work in general and the planned international conference in particular, and from the beginning the debate split the member states along North-South lines.

At its essence, the U.S. demanded that the overriding focus of the conference be limited to targeting solely political rights: political prisoners, legalizing multi-party political systems, etc. Washington wanted an aggressive, interventionist approach by the UN, reflecting the new Clinton administration's professed commitment to human rights as a key component of U.S. foreign policy.

Countries in the South had a very different view. While those governments were widely divergent, from broadly if chaotically democratic to military-controlled and repressive, there was a widespread fear of creating a highly interventionist UN mandate in a world in which the U.S. and its allies remain unchallenged within the UN.

For some governments in the South, the unease was patently defensive. Indonesia, however legitimate its concerns about national sovereignty and the legacies of colonialism, was far more worried about a possible UN investigation of its treatment of Timorese civilians living under Jakarta's military occupation of East Timor. Malaysia, despite its sometimes leading role as a voice for non-alignment, did not look forward to the United Nations scrutinizing its brutal treatment of criminal, let alone political, prisoners.

China was in a whole different category. Sought after by the U.S. and most of the North for its skyrocketing economy and enormous billions-strong market potential, neither the Clinton administration or any other Northern governments were eager to shine too bright a spotlight on China's political repression, denial of workers' rights, or prison labor. Beijing itself was simultaneously confident and uneasy about the possible consequences of too-close UN scrutiny. One of its first acts in Vienna was to demand, successfully, the expulsion of non-governmental human rights organizations, already accredited by the UN to attend, from the meetings of the drafting committee. It set the stage for the boldness Beijing would show two years later, in attempting to isolate the NGO mobilization from the global women's conference there in September 1995.

But for most of the South, unease with the UN's human rights focus was shaped by the knowledge that the scarce resources of the UN's human rights institutions were unlikely to be used to enforce the human right to development — to a job, to food, to education. Jimmy Carter called the UN mechanisms for dealing with human rights "incredibly weak."[24] The UN's human rights staff had actually been reduced in the decade between 1982 and 1992, from a ridiculously insufficient 81 professional-level staff to the completely preposterous 79; all human rights work combined, including the Human Rights Committee of the General Assembly, and its Geneva-based secretariat, the Center for Human Rights, along with its field staffs, accounted for only 0.8% of UN funds in 1994.[25] Given those limitations, there were no illusions that UN human rights work would reflect the interests of the South, rather than be used for selective intervention by the North.

Boutros Boutros-Ghali, speaking at the Vienna conference, argued for the right of "the international community" to intervene if governments "become tormentors" of their people. "In these circumstances," he said, "the international community must take over from the states that fail to fulfill their obligations." He did not define "torment" as failing to provide sufficient food or medical care, nor did he identify which obligations' failure would merit international intervention within a state. To the South, keeping in mind the infinitesimal resources available to UN human rights work overall, the SG's position was anything but encouraging.

A key U.S. goal in Vienna was to reaffirm its claim that the South denied the legitimacy of political human rights. To bolster its own position, the Clinton administration floated the possibility that it was moving towards acceptance of development as a human right (ignoring the fact that a UN resolution in 1986 had stated exactly that). It signaled that it would in the future ask the Senate to ratify the original 1966 International Convention on Economic, Social and Cultural Rights, which it had never signed.[26]

But no one was fooled. U.S. officials had already made clear that the Clinton administration's acceptance was solely tactical, designed, in the words of State Department officials, to avoid "a sterile debate at Vienna." There was no intention to implement any responsibilities inherent in that convention. Even though the U.S. delegation in Vienna ultimately did accept language identifying an "inalienable right" to development, it was far more significant that officials at the State Department had already said that the civil and political rights Washington had long considered primary would have to be observed immediately, while the economic, social, and cultural rights could wait, to be achieved only "incrementally, in step with development."[27]

The mood in Vienna was also influenced by a strong consciousness among countries of the South regarding Washington's political double standard in using UN mechanisms to condemn alleged human rights violations. Especially cynical in this regard was the persistent U.S. efforts to target Cuba as a major violator of human rights.

The view that Washington's obsession with Cuba's human rights transgressions had little to do with human rights, but was rather a cynical ploy rooted in domestic U.S. politics, was reinforced by the report of the UN's High Commissioner for Human Rights who visited

Cuba in 1994. Havana had opposed his visit, and agreed to it only reluctantly. But even with that hesitation, Jose Ayala Lasso's critique of Cuba's human rights performance was relatively mild.

In response to the report, the Assembly called on Cuba to "recognize the right of political parties and non-governmental organizations to function legally in the country, allow for freedom of expression, information and assembly and the freedom to demonstrate peacefully, and that it review sentences for crimes of a political nature."[28] Lasso's criticisms hardly seemed to compare with the horrifying litany of "ethnic cleansing" in Bosnia, Khmer Rouge massacres in Cambodia, airplane attacks on civilians in the Sudan, denial of access to food and medical aid, creation of internal refugees and exiles, torture of prisoners, and mass executions and disappearances throughout the world.

(Certainly there have been problems in Cuba's adherence to certain international human rights norms — primarily regarding the prohibition against forming contending political parties and, in some instances, jailing political opponents. But it should be noted that even Cuba's longstanding rejection of a multi-party system has changed dramatically. For a generation resistance to party pluralism had been unequivocal, and ideologically justified. By 1992 the position of most Cuban leaders had shifted to a far more pragmatic approach — stating that as long as Cuba remained under attack by U.S. efforts to destroy its government, multiple parties were a luxury they could not afford. There was the understanding that Cuba, domestically, could never compete with the money and propaganda Washington would shower on opposition parties, and that not only Cuban socialism but Cuban sovereignty would be destroyed. The clear implication, of course, is that once U.S. anti-Cuban attacks cease, the possibility of multiple parties would be on the agenda.[29])

Further underscoring Washington's tactical view of the UN's legitimacy, the U.S. had fought vigorously against 1993 and 1994 General Assembly votes calling for an end to the U.S. embargo against Cuba. On both occasions, Washington's defense of the embargo lost by strong margins with only Israel and one or two other countries supporting the U.S. position. But in response, the U.S. simply ignored the result. And being General Assembly, rather than Security Council decisions, the resolutions had no enforcement power.

Washington's attack on Cuba's human rights record was also measured against the violations of the U.S.-backed Salvadoran government throughout the 1980s, which the U.S. never brought to UN attention. Only six months after the Vienna conference, new documentation was declassified proving what had long been denied, that the Reagan administration had supported right-wing backers of the Salvadoran death squads responsible for numerous murders of priests, nuns, opposition political figures, and other civilians. The Salvadoran rightists backing the killers were identified in a March 1993 UN report as those long supported by the U.S. Reagan and Bush had knowingly continued to provide economic and military support to the Salvadoran military, despite U.S. laws forbidding such aid to human rights violators.

One of the few areas of partial North-South rapprochement in Vienna, it should be noted, was on the question of including attacks against women as violations of human rights. The language of the final declaration reflected that understanding, including both "equal status" and "human rights" of women. The reference was made possible largely because of the activism and lobbying power of the women's caucus. But, as Laura Flanders has pointed out, "The conference had an easier time with women's human rights than it did with equal status. Of the recommendations from the Women's Caucus, those that addressed violence mostly got accepted. Those that dealt with poverty and development did not. The Women's Caucus asked for the appointment of a special rapporteur to investigate 'violence and its causes'; the world conference recommended one on 'violence'...."[30]

The women's caucus was not without its own North-South divide, however. The well-known U.S. anti-pornography campaigner Catherine MacKinnon showed up in Vienna to speak about the evidence of "Serbian tanks plastered with pornography .... Some massacres in villages as well as rapes and/or executions in camps are being videotaped as they are happening." She called the systematic rape of women in Bosnia "a violation of women's humanity of unprecedented visibility and priority." According to Flanders:

> Those who attended her presentation appeared to concur. The Bangladeshi women didn't stir even when she [MacKinnon] said that rape for forced pregnancy and detention camps for pregnant Bosnian women were "unprecedented" in world history. Yet Pakistani men raped Bangladeshi women in the early 1970s and forced their pregnancies, holding them in detention camps to give birth to "true Muslims" .... Roughly 500 people turned up to hear her [MacKinnon] take on the violation of women's human rights in Bosnia and Herzegovina. When she left, so did her mostly U.S. and European audience. No one from MacKinnon's crowd stayed on afterward to listen to the women from southern Sudan, whose workshop followed. "Please stay," the two African speakers pleaded from the platform. "We have a story of rape too." But as they started their presentation, only a handful of Sudanese supporters remained behind .... The world conference delegates talked of human rights and saving lives as they passed TV

monitors broadcasting footage of the U.S. airstrike on Mogadishu. The irony barely surfaced as teatime talk.[31]

OUR BODIES, OURSELVES?

The International Conference on Population and Development, held in Cairo in 1994, made some gains in acknowledging and shaping the debate within North-South terms. While the U.S., unlike in Rio, was not the main problem in Cairo (that honor was assigned unhesitatingly to the Vatican), the broad parameters of the North's assumptions about population still hold sway over the South's efforts to redefine the debate.

On a global scale, few disagreed with the UN's estimate that the world's 1994 population of 5.6 billion would, if left unchecked, reach 8.5 billion by the year 2025, and, if rates of increase continue to decline, would reach 10 billion only 25 years later. If rates of increase start back up again, the projection reaches a possible 12.5 billion population by the year 2050.[32]

With increased awareness of environmental challenges and a widening North-South divide between those with and those without access to even basic resources, there was little disagreement about the need to lower the level of population growth. The bottom line disagreement lay in the unacknowledged (by the North) but overwhelming influence of money in defining and judging solutions for the "problem" of overpopulation.

While many of the UN documents included references to the much larger amount of resources consumed by smaller populations in the North, at the broadest level, including among the most influential governments, the "problem" of "overpopulation" means a problem of too many poor, darker-skinned people. A classic example of this problem is seen in the selection of which countries are frequently identified as examples of "overpopulation." According to Ramon Sanchez Medal, of the Mexican Commission for Human Rights, "No one talks about a small country like Japan being a threat because it has 100 million people, but a Mexico with 120 million people in the next century is considered a menace to the rich."[33]

It is true that Mexico's rate of population growth is higher than that of Japan, but that statistical fact does not account for the distinct way in which the two countries are viewed: one is wealthy, powerful, and "crowded," the other has an emerging economy, is still poor, subordinate to the U.S., and "overpopulated." The effect of this set of assumptions — and they were dominant in Cairo — was that "the burden of

limiting population still falls on the poor, while the richer industrialized nations are a greater danger to the earth and its environment because of their disproportionate consumption of natural resources and
contribution to pollution."[34]

With that broadly-defined North-South divide shaping the political
terrain for the discussion, the differences within both North and South
emerged far more visibly and volubly. Representatives of both were
able to agree on language that defined the primacy of women's education, health, and empowerment (both political and social) as key to answering the population challenge. But immediately abortion emerged
as a target of right-wing forces in both North and South. Some Catho-
lic-dominated countries in the South, especially in Latin America, and
some conservative Muslim governments, joined the Vatican in launching a major challenge not only to the call for full abortion rights but to
other program concepts, especially broadening access to contraception,
whose effect, if implemented, would be to dramatically cut back on the
number of necessary abortions. In that fight, the U.S. played a relatively positive role, with Vice-President Al Gore leading the North's
"moderates" against Vatican efforts to keep abortion rights off the
agenda entirely.

The result was a significant watering down of the language in the
conference's final document, in which no mention is made of a right to
abortion. Instead, there is an action call (paragraph 7.6) for countries
"to make accessible through the primary health-care system, reproductive health [not reproductive rights] including ... abortion as specified
in Paragraph 8.25." That paragraph begins with the assertion that, "In
no case should abortion be promoted as a method of family planning."
The obscure language calls on governments "and relevant intergovernmental and non-governmental organizations" to "deal with the health
impact of unsafe abortion as a major public health concern and to reduce the recourse to abortion through expanded and improved family
planning services." In a footnote, "unsafe" abortion is defined as a
"procedure for terminating an unwanted pregnancy either by persons
lacking necessary skills or in an environment lacking the minimal
medical standards or both."[35]

Thus there is no clear statement that women have a right to a safe
and legal abortion. The pope's language police accepted the final formulation, but ultimately the Vatican refused to sign the entire document anyway.

The U.S. position was more equivocal. Certainly the Clinton administration's general, if sometimes reluctant, support for abortion
rights was a world away from the Reagan administration's alliance with

the Vatican at the 1984 Mexico City conference on population, which prevented any reference to abortion with the exception of a statement identifying it an an impermissible form of family planning. But the Clinton administration was hardly willing to take on the Vatican with full force. That was left to Norwegian Prime Minister Gro Harlem Brundtland, who called opponents hypocritical, and called for the full legalization of abortion. Clearly directing her remarks to the Vatican, she stated, "Morality becomes hypocrisy if it means accepting mothers' suffering of dying in connection with unwanted pregnancies and illegal abortions and unwanted children."[36]

The U.S. role in Cairo was to conciliate the Vatican's demands as much as it felt it could get away with without alienating core supporters. The *New York Times* reported that, "Before the gathering, for instance, the United States had raised objections to the inclusion in the text of what, for the Vatican, was a key term: that abortion could never be used as a form of family planning. But when the conference ended, that language had been revived as the first sentence on a crucial paragraph on safe abortion .... The notion of legal abortion was diluted .... As a result, a senior Vatican official said, the whole [pre-Cairo] thrust of the conclusions about abortion was changed. 'It doesn't say abortion should be legal .... Whereas the text says that even where it's legal, it's not safe.' "[37]

The Clinton administration had, to a large degree, caved in.

In some ways, the Vatican's real success was in turning the Cairo conference overall into a referendum on abortion, which many participants believed to be a necessary, but ultimately overplayed, side story. As with many other UN documents coming out of General Assembly initiatives, the Action Program from Cairo has much soaring language and much uncertainty about implementation. Numerous press articles identified money as the "hidden issue" of the conference; for most of them, however, the issue was insuring access to funds for direct population control measures. The U.S. has long been the largest donor to international population programs, with about $595 million earmarked for the 1995 fiscal year. The future assessment of the U.S. role in implementing the UN's new vision of population control as a function of women's own empowerment and access to health care will have to be judged on the basis of how (and, in the late 1995 era of congressional UN-bashing and budget-slashing, whether) that money is spent. If business stays as usual, $60 million of that money will go to purchase American-manufactured contraceptives for distribution in international programs, about $50 million for UN population programs, and $250 million in direct government-to-government assistance. Whether

U.S. pressure will be brought to bear on the UN or governments' own selection of "population" programs broader than just passing out condoms remains uncertain.

THE POOR GET ON TOP OF THE WORLD'S AGENDA — BUT STAY POOR

In many ways the World Conference on Social Development in Copenhagen in March 1995 brought the sequence of UN conferences full circle. The focus this time was unmistakable, not just a hidden and often-ignored subtext: poverty. Not surprisingly, that brought Washington into direct conflict with the interests of much of the South.

And, not surprisingly, the summit itself was widely deemed a failure, variously identified in the Western press as "blurry," "ineffectual," a "flop," and a "charade."

The failure was not a function of a lack of need for such a gathering, or for increased attention paid to social development. According to leading UN researchers, "From the perspective of social advance, the 1980s have been labeled the Lost Decade. In many regions of the world, notably Africa, Eastern Europe and Latin America, economies stagnated, poverty levels increased, the social fabric weakened and environmental degradation further eroded the livelihood of the urban and rural poor. International policy concerns shifted away from such issues as 'basic needs' and 'food security' to economic adjustment, privatization and democratization."[38]

The UN's preparation for the social development conference was rooted in delegates' growing concerns that social progress, the improvement of the lives of real people in the real world, was not accompanying the broadly-defined economic growth in many countries. Throughout the 1980s and into the 90s it had become increasingly clear, even in the insular halls of diplomacy, that the poor in all countries, but especially in the South, were getting poorer, and that access to basic services such as education, clean water, or health care were sliding out of reach of larger and larger numbers of people.

According to Juan Somavia, Chile's ambassador to the UN and prime mover of the conference, "If you have growth that doesn't take social development into account, you end up with polarization. The profit drive in a society is extremely important in terms of creating wealth, but nonprofit values are essential to a balanced society .... We need to reestablish the balance.' "[39]

The conference emerged in a period characterized by widening, not narrowing, gaps between haves and have-nots, both in wealthy coun-

194 Calling the Shots

tries in the North, and, most dramatically in poorer nations of the South facing "emerging" — and rapidly expanding — economies.

The U.S. had hoped that it could limit its support of the social development summit to rhetorical flourishes, while keeping its usual approach of rejecting any binding promise to increase spending or international assistance. And with the summit scheduled at the height of the Clinton administration's conflict with the anti-foreign aid, anti-UN, and anti-Third World Gingrich-led Congress, the interest in making new pledges was as low as it gets.

The particular problem Washington faced in Copenhagen, though, was the specificity of the UN conference's acknowledged goal: to get clear commitments from governments to back programs designed to eradicate "profound social problems" by 2010. The core problems identified were poverty, unemployment, and social exclusion. Of particular concern to Washington, early on, was the inclusion in the final draft declaration, prepared a month before the summit convened, of an acknowledgment that, among other factors, "these major problems represent a manifestation of ineffectiveness in the functioning of markets, and ... the need to intervene to prevent or counteract market failure."[40]

The North was asked to commit new funds, the South to commit to decrease their arms purchases in favor of social development and employment measures.

Some countries in the North did make specific commitments. Denmark, host of the summit, announced its cancelation of about $200 million in debts from six poor countries: Angola, Egypt, Ghana, Zimbabwe, Bolivia, and Nicaragua.[41] Austria wrote off $100 million in debts from the poorest nations.[42]

This one would be more difficult for Washington to circumvent. So instead of Bush's Rio-style seize-control-and-stare-them-down approach, the Clinton administration opted to downplay the conference as much as possible. The White House made clear early on that President Clinton had no intention of showing up at the conference; speculation would only heighten interest in the conference's work, after all. (That was complicated by the fact that the Copenhagen conference was billed as a "world summit." The 120 heads of state and government who showed up made it the largest such gathering in years.) The U.S. also announced ahead of time its rejection of any increased commitment of funds.

The U.S. effort at the conference focused on Washington's so-called "20/20 plan." It would require donor countries to earmark 20% of development aid for social and educational programs, and demand that poor countries make 20% of their national budgets available for those programs. Those figures would require tripling the North's current spending on those programs; but the summit said nothing of how such a recommendation might be imposed. Poor countries would have to double their spending; there was also no discussion of where such additional funds might come from.

And the high-visibility effort to cut arms purchases in the South, as part of the 20/20 plan, highlighted Washington's double standard on military spending. For example, a UNDP staff member described the difference in how arms trafficking and drug trafficking are viewed in the West. In examining arms trafficking, the U.S. looks at consumers, the Third World, and aims its attack there. Washington condemns governments in the South for purchasing arms, even though it is itself the largest supplier of arms throughout the world. Regarding drug trafficking, the U.S. targets the producers, not the consumers, who are largely within the U.S. itself, and aims its attack that way — so again it is the countries of the South that pay the price. Who benefits, and who gets hurt, remain constant.

Ultimately the 20/20 plan emerged as a clear example of Washington's approach to rectifying the North-South poverty gap: come up with clever slogans, and make sure there's nothing that comes close to a binding commitment for more aid or even debt relief. The usually compassionate Tim Wirth, Clinton's under secretary of state for global affairs, came up, perhaps unintentionally, with a classic "blame the poor for their poverty" argument: "They [the debtor nations] have to understand that their debt is causing a problem and they have to think about this," he said.[43]

Overall, the social development summit must be rated a failure. After the failure of implementation in Rio, and the failure of balance in Vienna, realistic expectations were already low for Copenhagen. But even those minimal hopes were unmet. "According to critics, $30 million [the cost of putting on the conference] has been wasted on yet another UN global extravaganza that produced far more pabulum than specific commitments to eradicate poverty. 'We are not satisfied. We hoped that the industrial countries would give us more …. I'm disappointed,' says Haman Adama, a delegate from Cameroon."[44]

The language of the final declaration included a call for major reforms not only in the UN itself, but in the IMF and World Bank. But, as at earlier UN conferences, the U.S. insured there was no binding language. The conference agreed on the necessity that structural adjustment programs, already wreaking such havoc on the South's social and economic life, be made "socially responsible." But there was no agreement, and no binding decision, on what that term meant or on how to impose such a requirement on the wealthy institutions imposing those programs on the South. There were some specific timetables agreed to, such as the goal of having 80% of children throughout the world completing primary school by the year 2000 — but no implementation mechanism and no decision as to where the funds might come from to make such an effort possible.

UN officials and development agencies seeking positive assessments were reduced to expressing gratitude that the final document did not specifically erase any hard-fought earlier gains. As for the U.S., the vice-president's speech tried to portray the Clinton administration's emphasis on privatizing international aid as a major gain for social development. Gore's speech asserted that they had "begun to abandon the old strategies to eradicate poverty with massive government bureaucracies. We cannot succeed if the poor are passive recipients."[45] Taking a lesson whole cloth from his Republican opponents' welfare "reform" plans for the U.S., Gore then spelled out U.S. intentions to privatize at least 40% of U.S. aid.

Tim Wirth, Clinton's man for global affairs, told an interviewer he was surprised that the talks didn't break down into "a North-South battle about new and additional resources."[46] If it didn't, it was only because the South knew the battle had already been lost before their diplomats ever arrived in Copenhagen.

ON TO BEIJING

The participation of NGOs emerged early as a major battle in the run-up to the 1995 Fourth Global Women's Conference in Beijing. Five months before the September conference, the All-China Women's Federation, official host of the conference, announced it was moving the site of the parallel NGO conference to a small town more than 30 miles from the official conference venue in Beijing, thus effectively insuring inadequate and uneven communication between the NGO activists and the official delegations across town. The move paralleled a further effort to exclude certain NGOs deemed unacceptable by the Chinese authorities. Visas and credentials were thus denied (or "inexplicably" though permanently delayed) to Tibetan NGOs, Taiwanese women's groups, and many lesbian organizations. China also made a blatant move to divide the NGO movement even further, by separating those accredited by the UN to attend the official conference from those limited to the NGO forum alone. The effect would be that, aside from only certain NGOs having direct access to the delegates and meetings themselves, those "official" NGOs would be physically based in a different location from the smaller, less influential, less privileged NGOs watching the proceedings on television 30 miles away. A key result would be a significant lack of input from those NGOs, overwhelmingly from the South, without access to the more privileged location.

In an effort to defend the decision, China's NGO coordinator claimed that "China welcomes and respects all NGOs and individuals who come to attend the Conference and the Forum. According to the provision of the United Nations, accredited NGOs will be able to enter the Conference. Therefore it is for their convenience that the Chinese side offers them activity site and accommodations which are located near the Conference site. Likewise, it is also for the convenience of the majority of NGOs that the accommodations for them are arranged in Huairou [the alternative site]."[47]

When the NGO Forum finally convened, over 10,000 would-be participants were missing, denied or delayed visas, hotel reservations, or credentials by the Chinese authorities. Thousands did attend the Forum's workshops and discussions, including some on the supposedly-resolved issues from the 1994 Population Conference such as abortion rights, the link between women's education and women's empowerment, and sexual freedom. There was as well the over-arching debate, and some level of tension, between women from the South wanting to emphasize development, ending structural adjustment-imposed poverty, and criticizing the IMF, and women from the North whose agenda in some cases was more limited to individual freedoms and male-female equality.

But to the world watching events in Beijing, virtually all of the substantive work was sidelined by the conflicts posed by Chinese government restrictions on the speech, participation, and work of the conference activists. Televised scenes of Chinese police pushing and shoving participants in workshops on Tibet or lesbian activism were broadcast around the world. Speeches by U.S. and other delegates to the parallel official conference in Beijing criticized the Chinese practices.

But despite the clear violation of UN regulations (among others, that the NGO conference site was to be considered "UN territory" with its requisite openness of thought and debate) Secretary-General Boutros Boutros-Ghali suddenly canceled his scheduled participation in the opening of the conference. His spokesman said he was ill with the flu. Many UN-watchers believed Boutros-Ghali's flu might have been caused (or at least exacerbated) by his ongoing campaign to be appointed for a second five-year term as secretary-general. China, as a permanent member of the Security Council, would of course be in a position to veto his candidacy if Beijing were unhappy with Boutros-Ghali. No other permanent members, not the French, or the British, certainly not the U.S., were known to have urged the secretary-general to come to Beijing to help solve the burgeoning crisis.

PROLIFERATING NON-PROLIFERATION

Although it was not part of the General Assembly-initiated global conference series, the April-May 1995 UN-sponsored conference of signatories to the 1970 Nuclear Non-Proliferation Treaty, or NPT, bore four major similarities to the earlier events. First, it brought new and heightened levels of media and public attention to an important, yet often ignored, issue of international policy. Second, the key political division split largely along North-South lines. Third, non-governmental lobbying was a visible feature. And fourth, the end result was crafted and imposed by the U.S., with all the available variety of diplomatic bribes and threats, on a reluctant majority.

Like the Assembly conferences, if assessed from the vantage point of the interests of the have-nots of the world, the NPT conference was a U.S.-orchestrated failure. For Washington, it was a high-investment success story.

The conference convened in 1995 to consider an earlier decision made a quarter-century earlier. In 1970, when the NPT was signed, the drafters left for the next meeting, scheduled 25 years in the future, to determine whether the terms of the treaty would thereafter be indefinitely and unconditionally extended, or whether finite terms and specific conditions would have to be met by various parties to insure its continuity. The decision was to be grounded in a full-blown international assessment of how well the treaty had met its original goals; if everyone agreed the purposes of the NPT had been met during the first 25 years, there would be no reason not to move towards indefinite and unconditional extension.

The evaluation of the NPT's success was supposed to have been based on the Report of the Main Committee to the 1995 Review and Extension Conference of the Parties to the Treaty on the Non-Proliferation of Nuclear Weapons. But it surprised few observers in New York that the Report was hardly examined (and then only after the final vote) and was in fact never adopted. There were too many "bracketed" sections left in the final draft, meaning too many statements on which agreement, usually between nuclear and non-nuclear powers, could not be reached. Of the several versions assessing the "general and complete disarmament" section in the review, all references to nuclear weapons were completely bracketed.

For the U.S. and most of its nuclear allies, the question was easy. Non-proliferation was defined as preventing nuclear have-nots from becoming nuclear haves, and it had largely been achieved. There were some complications, but they could be easily dealt with: Iraq's nuclear potential would be militarily wiped out. Of the nuclear powers or wannabes who were not signatories to the NPT, North Korea's nuclear ambitions would be negotiated away, India's and Pakistan's would largely cancel each other out, and Israel's would be embraced. No problem.

But the non-nuclear countries didn't see it that way. The Non-Proliferation Treaty of 1970 was not only about preventing new nuclear states. Article VI also mandated the existing nuclear powers to move towards the "objective of complete prohibition and thorough destruction of nuclear weapons as an ultimate objective." Unease, resentment, and outright resistance to an indefinite extension of the NPT stemmed largely from the understanding by non-nuclear states that the Big Five nuclear powers (conveniently identical to the permanent members of the Security Council) had done little since 1970 to move towards that goal.

According to Mexico's Ambassador Miguel Marin Bosch, 1994 Chairman of the NPT Committee of the UN's Conference on Disarmament and leader of Mexico's delegation in New York the following year, in the years since the NPT was signed, "what has occurred is an incredible accumulation of nuclear arms in five countries, especially the U.S. and the former USSR .... Why are NWS [nuclear weapons states] so reluctant to begin a process of genuine nuclear disarmament? .... In part it is also because of the fear of losing their status, a status they would deny others .... But why are their so-called national security needs more important than those of others? Why do they insist, as adults to children, that the rest of the world 'do as I say, not as I do'?"[48]

U.S. officials were far more direct. Thomas Graham, Special Representative of the President for Arms Control and Disarmament, was Clinton's point man in the run-up to the conference and in the New York negotiations themselves. "To say that we have to have a timetable for a nuclear-free world is disingenuous; it is nothing short of ridiculous," he said. Even planning "a serious negotiation about getting to a nuclear-free world ... is not possible under any foreseeable circumstances .... No one [among nuclear weapons states] is willing to give up the necessary degree of sovereignty to accomplish it."[49]

But the U.S. refusal to even consider its own responsibilities under the NPT — that is, its responsibility to eliminate nuclear weapons —

did not mean a parallel softening of Washington's view of other countries' responsibilities under the treaty. The Clinton administration had invested a great deal of domestic and international capital in reaching, if not unanimity, at least an overwhelming show of support for unconditional indefinite extension of the NPT. That meant avoiding distracting debate about whether the nuclear powers had implemented or undermined Article VI, and there was to be no rhetorical posturing from the South about the inherent inequities in a treaty that had "allowed a small number of countries to have a monopoly over nuclear arms and that these nations were not providing nuclear technology for peaceful uses"[50] as required, to the non-nuclear states.

By the time the conference opened at the UN in April 1995, Graham had been on the road for over a year, cajoling, bribing, and threatening one capital after another that the U.S. expected support for its position, and that everybody better toe the line. It was a diplomatic investment not seen since Bush's success at forcing a "consensus" to support Washington's war against Iraq.

According to the head of Venezuela's negotiating team in New York, Adolfo Taylhardat, "We used to play in the stadium of the Cold War. Now we play in yanqui stadium." Ambassador Taylhardat resigned his position in protest at his government's sudden reversal of policy at the conference, from backing a limited and conditional extension to becoming a sponsor of the U.S. proposal. "Many countries have been submitted to these pressures," he said. "If all the conference countries had the opportunity to express their views, the indefinite extension would never have won."[51]

By the time the conference was about to start, it was clear the U.S. was far from a majority in support of its position, for unconditional and indefinite extension. Much work was needed, because a simple majority would have been an insufficient show of international backing for Washington. The opposition, led by governments in Mexico, Venezuela, Egypt, Nigeria, Indonesia, Malaysia, and others in the South, called for what were known as "rolling extensions." That method would have required sequential meetings, every five or ten years, or in later incarnations as much as 25 years apart, to reassess implementation of the treaty and decide again about the terms of renewal. Further, the South demanded greater compliance by the nuclear states with the NPT's requirement that they share nuclear energy technology with non-nuclear countries, and, most important, that the Big Five make a demonstrable commitment to disarmament for themselves, not just for the rest of the world.

But, once the U.S. pressure on the South mounted, various countries' willingness to stand against Washington faltered. The treaty conference began April 17, and was scheduled to last until May 12. Two weeks into the session, the Non-Aligned Movement held a summit meeting in Bandung, Indonesia. Already the South's unity was fraying.

The most serious blow to the opposition came from South Africa, who early on crafted a "compromise" position that ultimately set the stage for the U.S. victory. Under apartheid, South Africa had been an outlaw nuclear power; it had refused to sign the NPT, and had collaborated with fellow non-signer Israel in the building and testing of a nuclear device. Under President Nelson Mandela, post-apartheid South Africa signed the NPT (in 1992) and became a leading advocate of nuclear disarmament.

But its role in the run-up to the NPT extension conference would be very different. According to the respected London *Guardian*, during the NPT conference, "U.S. tactics succeeded in dividing the non-aligned movement. It was finished by South Africa."[52]

South Africa brought to the other countries of the South a proposal for indefinite extension, but with a package of what were essentially confidence-building measures designed to soften the South's capitulation. Nothing in South Africa's proposed assurances imposed any binding commitment on any nuclear weapons states; nothing in the assurances gave the South any power to hold the U.S. or its nuclear allies accountable to the feel-good representations they made.

Before the NPT conference had convened, the U.S. had invited South Africa to become a member of an elite Missile Control Technology Group. Its self-described mandate is to monitor export controls on plutonium and nuclear technology in a setting outside the more public fora of the UN's own non-proliferation mechanisms, or the International Atomic Energy Agency. According to NGO disarmament analysts, any member of the Group, whose members beside the U.S. are primarily European, has the "inalienable right to nuclear power for peaceful use," with controls outside the requirements of the NPT. Moving thus behind the scenes, the U.S. was able to offer South Africa access to an arena in which Pretoria could buy or sell sophisticated nuclear power technology from or to a select group of countries in the North. The admission of South Africa would, of course, give the struggling new African democracy an economic head start in maximizing its nuclear energy trade. Participation in this group would also provide South Africa with a much-needed means of disposing of its highly enriched uranium that was the legacy of apartheid's nuclear efforts. The U.S., viewing the stockpile similarly to that in Ukraine, would then be in a powerful position to gain influence and possibly control over it: whether taking custody of it for destruction, or controlling it while it remained in South African hands, the U.S. gained either way.

South Africa was offered membership in this elite club before the serious campaign for NPT negotiations was under way. But the U.S. was taking no chances on the sufficiency of a South African understanding of the inherent *quid pro quo*. U.S. officials, as the New York conference got closer, targeted a number of countries viewed as having particular regional influence or credibility, including South Africa, for special pressure. A month before the conference began, the U.S. ambassador to South Africa delivered a diplomatic letter stating that a vote against the U.S. position would undermine "mutual interests," and would change Washington's view of South Africa's "non-proliferation credentials." The letter reminded South Africa that Washington's sponsorship of Pretoria in the Nuclear Suppliers Group was "because we felt confident about South Africa's commitment" to a permanent NPT extension and that failure to achieve this goal "would constrain the ability of the nuclear supplier states to engage in peaceful nuclear cooperation."[53]

According to NGO observers, some of South Africa's delegates admitted they had never felt pressure like that, that it was unlike anything they had ever experienced. During the January 1995 preparatory meeting, the delegation had recommended to their government, and they believed the South African government agreed to, a proposal for a fifteen-year extension, with conditions on the nuclear weapons states. That appeared to be South Africa's position until about two weeks before the conference, when they began to shift. Only two days into the NPT conference, South Africa announced its support for indefinite extension.

Having taken that position, South Africa campaigned strongly among countries of the South to win their support. At the Non-Aligned summit in Bandung, two weeks into the NPT conference, South Africa, backed by Benin, Lesotho, and Swaziland, virtually blocked what might have become a Non-Aligned consensus against indefinite extension. Lesotho and Swaziland's following of South Africa was hardly surprising; the two tiny countries have been completely dependent on Pretoria since before apartheid. But Benin was a surprise. Not often known for leadership within either the OAU or the Non-Aligned movement, it soon became clear that Benin had succumbed to intense economic pressure from France, its major trading partner and one-time colonial ruler.

The particular intensity of U.S. pressure on South Africa was the result of the confluence of that country's prestige and influence, both from the heroism of the anti-apartheid struggle, but as well for abjuring its own nuclear weapons capacity. Not unrelated were U.S. fears that South Africa intended to lead the Non-Aligned demand for pressuring the nuclear weapons states towards disarmament. An earlier South African diplomatic note spoke of the need "to find some mechanism for continuing pressure on the nuclear weapons states to meet their NPT disarmament commitment; leverage ... that would be lost if the NPT is extended indefinitely."[54] Both South Africa and the U.S. claimed that its membership in the Nuclear Suppliers Group, membership that began one week before the NPT conference convened, was not related to its vote.

South Africa was not, of course, the only country subject to U.S. pressure. Mexico, a leader in the campaign for conditioned and limited extension, abruptly changed its position too as the conference neared. Mexico had played a leading role not only in mobilizing against unconditional and permanent extension but in supporting two key procedural issues. One was to demand a secret ballot in the voting on extension, to insure that countries would not feel pressured by the threat of economic or political sanctions by the U.S. or the other major nuclear weapons powers. The second was the call to wait until after the evaluation of the review of the NPT's first 25 years, scheduled towards the end of the four-week conference, before declaring positions on extension.

Prior to the convening of the conference, many Non-Aligned countries were following Mexico's lead. But Mexico's own position was already weakening under a barrage of U.S. threats. Still reeling from the devastation of the peso collapse, Mexico was virtually in thrall to its economic savior. And Washington had no intention of bailing out its Southern NAFTA neighbor scot-free. Among other demands on Mexico, as payment for the peso bail-out, Washington demanded that Mexico pull back from its close diplomatic and economic ties to Cuba, and that it soften its opposition to the U.S. line on NPT extension.

Mexico's official line, as stated by the deputy leader of its delegation, Ambassador Miguel Marin-Bosch, was that "Mexico changed our position when the U.S. achieved a majority to favor indefinite extension .... [It] would have been political suicide to oppose it."[55] Differing from his Venezuelan colleague only in timing, Marin-Bosch resigned following the NPT conference as well, followed by persistent reports that his ouster had been demanded by Washington.

One of the key diplomatic tactics the U.S. used was to project a more visible role for non-nuclear states in the North closely tied to U.S. policies but without Washington's nuclear credibility problems. Canada played an especially active role doing, as one NGO analyst described it, "Washington's dirty work." Canada as well as Australia were actively involved in the pressure campaign against South Africa; some reports indicated that Canadian diplomats, with the blessing of the U.S. Arms Control and Disarmament Agency (ACDA), had a hand in drafting the "compromise" South African position.

One reason for understanding the unusual visibility of Canada's role in backing the U.S. position may have come in a meeting held in Geneva about two weeks after the NPT conference ended. According to disarmament experts, Canadian representatives discussed with their U.S. counterparts the new ban on fissile materials that applies to both weapons and civilian materials. Canada was eager to obtain U.S. weapons material, including plutonium, for use in its CANDU (Canadian Deterium-Uranium) reactor, which can use plutonium fuels. Canadian interest in getting access to that U.S. plutonium may provide at least a partial explanation for the sudden emergence of Ottawa as a major pro-U.S. player at the NPT.

Coming out of the January preparatory meeting in Geneva, Washington wasn't sure it would have the necessary votes in New York. The 68 actual votes counted in Geneva remained static for weeks. But the U.S. determination to win a near-consensus required some white-lie style sleight of hand: by declaring that an "overwhelming majority" was already in place, Washington's diplomats significantly ratcheted up the pressure on not-yet-declared countries. One of the key diplomatic tools involved the NGO movement — although in this case the nomenclature was itself part of Washington disingenuousness.

The Campaign for the NPT had emerged as the most visible and most quoted NGO in the U.S. Based in Washington, it coordinated the publication of an NPT newsletter beginning before and continuing on a daily basis right through the New York conference itself. The newsletter asserted, early on, that the "indefinite extension was virtually sewed up," dealing what one NGO analyst called "a death blow to the heart" of opposition to the extension. It caused NGOs and, more significantly, governments (especially those poorer governments without the resources to send large teams able to monitor constantly changing events on their own) to reassess the changing balance of forces, ultimately increasing the influence of the U.S. position and demoralizing countries standing against the pro-U.S. tide.

If anyone wondered who the "Campaign for the NPT" really was, there was evidence aplenty. On a provisional UN list of accredited *nongovernmental* organization participants, Thomas Graham was listed under the Campaign for NPT, the most influential NGO. The same Thomas Graham was President Clinton's Special Representative for Arms Control and Disarmament.

As the conference came closer, U.S. pressure on the South toughened. One Non-Aligned diplomat told an NGO observer that "the U.S. has stopped twisting arms, now they're taking out baseball bats and are breaking knees." By the last two days before the conference was to vote, Clinton himself personally took up the cudgel, writing "tough messages" to Egypt and Mexico. According to one U.S. official, "There were no threats implied, but ... it was made clear that the United States would find it hard to understand why friendly nations that had received help from Washington would not be more cooperative."[56]

Early on in the pre-conference jockeying, a new wrinkle threatened to scuttle Clinton's plan for a near-unanimous claim of NPT victory. In early January, Egypt, one of those countries that had "received help" from Washington, announced that it would refuse to endorse indefinite expansion as long as Israel remained the sole nuclear power in the Middle East and refused to sign the NPT. "If we are to sign an agreement, we must all sign," said Egyptian President Hosni Mubarak.[57] Israel, which refuses to acknowledge but does not deny that it has at least 200 high-density nuclear warheads in its Dimona plant in the Negev desert, refused to make any even incremental moves towards signing the NPT.

Worse than Egypt's own resistance, from Washington's vantage point, Cairo managed to reclaim its traditional leadership of the Arab world, bringing most Arab capitals on board a no-indefinite-extension-with-Israeli-nukes-on-our-borders train. In mid-February, "even though Israel has refused to sign the worldwide treaty limiting nuclear arms, the Administration is largely ignoring Israel's position and is pressing Egypt to vote for an indefinite extension of the treaty."[58]

By March, U.S. officials were irritated with Egypt's stance. When U.S. Secretary of State Warren Christopher began a week of Middle East shuttle diplomacy, a senior U.S. official said in Cairo that "we're in a posture where we're talking to them about the issue." The Egyptians claimed the U.S. "are not pressuring us, but they are not pressuring the Israelis either." But Egyptian Foreign Minister Amr Moussa went on to explain that "the secretary [Christopher] said it is a policy priority to work for an indefinite extension of the treaty, that it is in their best interests and the best interests of the international community. Fine, but we can't accept that with Israel's nuclear program anonymous, vague and in doubt."[59]

U.S. diplomats used the meetings at the Copenhagen social development summit to lobby Egypt further. By April Clinton himself weighed in, stating his support for efforts to establish a nuclear-free zone in the Middle East only after peace is established — reflecting Israel's long-standing terms for signing the NPT.

Finally it was the "fine" part of Amr Moussa's answer that turned out to be the best indicator of Egypt's position. The second-largest recipient of U.S. aid (about $2 billion a year, second only to Israel's almost $4 billion), Egypt is thoroughly dependent on U.S. economic assistance and has been, since the signing of the Camp David accords in 1977 broke Egypt's link to the Non-Aligned Movement and most of the Arab world, completely accountable to Washington's agenda in the region. While Egypt's official opening speech (April 20) at the NPT conference formally announced its refusal to support indefinite extension, by the end U.S. pressure proved irresistible. Forty-eight hours before the vote Egypt received a message personally from President Clinton. Overnight Cairo changed its vote.

Giving up its rejection of Washington's unlimited extension position, Egypt joined other Arab countries in a U.S.-approved compromise. Submitting a separate resolution calling on Israel to "accede without delay" to the terms of the NPT, fourteen Arab capitals agreed that they would sign if the resolution also became part of a consensus decision by the conference.

But there was one problem left: the U.S. still was not quite sure of just how big its margin of victory would be. For most countries of the South, a key to resisting U.S. pressure had lain with the right to a secret ballot — in which Washington would not be able to identify the countries refusing to toe its indefinite extension line. The pressure was fierce, and like the substantive resistance to the U.S. position itself, the South's insistence on secret voting ultimately collapsed. By the time the final votes came, after a day or two delay wrangling over the language of the Arab resolution, the U.S. demand for open declared balloting had carried the day.

But instead of actually holding the vote, Washington engineered an arrangement with conference president Jayantha Dhanapala of Sri Lanka. To avoid any potential media embarrassment, the announcement was made that the vote would be taken "by acclamation," but without an actual call even for a voice vote. That way, no one could spoil Clinton's moment with an uncalled-for "no" from the back of the hall.

A number of Non-Aligned countries did make statements after the vote, criticizing the results and the heavy-handed campaign that had achieved it. Malaysia's representative, Hasmy bin Agam, said the NPT extension provided a carte blanche to the nuclear weapons states and that the agreement could be interpreted as "justifying nuclear weapons states for eternity."[60]

Once the non-vote vote was over, and the U.S. could claim victory, efforts shifted to how to use the loose terms of the NPT to justify continued nuclear weapons involvement. When French President Jacques Chirac announced his intention to continue limited testing, President Clinton expressed only mild disagreement.

Perhaps more indicative of Washington's true intentions were the on-going post-NPT discussions with China. Beijing had gone along with Washington's insistence on an indefinite extension, although early on it had expressed some sympathy for the Non-Aligned position of rolling extensions with conditions for the nuclear weapons states.

Shortly before Chirac's visit, and knowing the French president was adamant about continuing small-scale nuclear tests, a secret meeting was held in Nebraska between the U.S. Department of Defense, the Department of Energy, and a number of laboratories involved in nuclear strategy. While part of the agenda was the French resumption of testing, the Secretary of Defense apparently tried to convince others to agree to provide China with U.S. virtual-reality computer simulation technology that obviates the need for direct nuclear testing. Framed as an effort to convince the Chinese to eschew further testing, Secretary Perry's plan would provide them with the technology to make the tests unnecessary — so instead of Beijing having to reinvent the latest nuclear wheel, Washington would simply sell it the wheel.

Ultimately, the U.S. role at the NPT conference also insured that the final report of compliance since 1970 was never adopted. The U.S. team disputed virtually every major acknowledgment of the treaty's failure to have moved towards the elimination of nuclear weapons. By the time of the 1995 extension conference, there were substantially more nuclear arms in the world than when the treaty was signed 25 years before, and the signing process took place without any agreed-on review of the performance of the nuclear weapons powers.

The mayor of Hiroshima, Takashi Hiraoka, who was not among those invited to the NPT conference, said that he opposed extending the Non-Proliferation Treaty because it does not aim at eliminating all nuclear weapons. "I will keep saying that use of nuclear arms violates international law and constitutes a crime against humans."[61]

It was perhaps emblematic of the hollowness of the U.S. claims of indefinite NPT extension representing a great victory for peace, that within days of the conference's forced conclusion, first France announced plans for its new nuclear tests in the South Pacific, and then the NPT-cheerleading Clinton administration admitted it was "discussing" a similar resumption.[62] Any such testing would be in clear violation not only of the Comprehensive Test Ban Treaty, but certainly of the claims and promises of renewed commitment to disarmament made by the nuclear weapons states in New York. According to one close NPT observer, "If they do it, it will mean the end of the treaty. The non-nuclear countries won't put up with it — that's for sure."[63]

In fact, in early September 1995 when the French tests on the Muroroa atoll were actually launched, protests erupted throughout the world, especially in the South Pacific, Australia, and New Zealand. The Tahitian capital was lacerated with severe rioting, forcing the French government to send in additional military reinforcements. And French products faced growing boycotts, especially in the once-lucrative markets of Australia.

Washington expressed general unhappiness with the French resumption of tests, but did little of substance to respond — despite the fact that the French position was justified largely through the claimed legitimacy of a "European" nuclear umbrella that would not have to depend on the U.S. But at the end of the day, regardless of massive opposition in the South or quiet unease in the North, the tests went on. The NPT's hard-won extension still only extended the limits the treaty imposed on non-nuclear states. The domination of the nuclear powers remained unchecked. Whether the countries of the South *wanted* to "put up with" the blatant violation of the goals of the NPT inherent in the French nuclear testing, international power realities insured they could do little to stop it.

THE WORLD SPEAKS, BUT WHO LISTENS?

The renewal of nuclear testing within a few months of the NPT's extension was emblematic, perhaps, of the limits inherent in the entire series of UN-sponsored international conferences. On those few occasions when the great powers choose to implement a decision taken by these gatherings, its significance is anointed with the credibility of a global consensus. When, far more frequently, the U.S. or one or another of its allies choose to ignore the results, the conferences are denigrated as merely "advisory," and the non-binding nature of commitments reached mean they could — and would — be violated with impunity.

Notes

1. Barbara Crossette, "Why the UN Became the World's Fair," *New York Times*, March 12, 1995.
2. Ibid.
3. Rudy Abramson, "U.S. Flexes Its Muscle Before Earth Summit," *Los Angeles Times*, May 30, 1992.
4. Ibid.

5. William K. Stevens, "Lessons of Rio," *New York Times*, June 14, 1992.

6. Ibid.

7. Marlise Simons, "North-South Divide is Marring Environmental Talks," *New York Times*, March 17, 1992.

8. Martin Khor Kok Peng, "Regulating TNCs Is Biggest Gap in UNCED," *Third World Resurgence* (Kuala Lumpur, Malaysia) no. 20, March 1992, p. 21.

9. Abramson, "U.S. Flexes Its Muscle."

10. "UNICEF Report on International Aid," UNICEF, New York, June 9, 1995.

11. Memo cited in Vendana Shiva, "The New Environmental Order," *Third World Resurgence* (Kuala Lumpur, Malaysia), no. 20, March 1992, p. 2.

12. Keynote address by Ambassador Joao Clemente Baena Soares, Secretary-General of the Organization of American States, at the Conference on Environmental Challenges and the Global South: UNCED and Beyond, Center for the Global South, American University, Washington, D.C., April 14, 1992.

13. Hilary F. French, "From Discord to Accord," *World Watch*, May-June 1992.

14. William A. Ryan, "Media Warms to Earth Summit Coverage," *Lies of Our Times*, July-August 1992.

15. Paul Lewis, "Differing Views on Human Rights Threaten Forum," *New York Times*, June 6, 1993.

16. Ibid.

17. Human Rights Watch World Report 1995, December 9, 1994, cited in Barbara Crossette, "Human Rights Organization Urges Stronger Action by the UN," *New York Times*, December 11, 1994.

18. Ibid.

19. UN diplomat interview, May 1995.

20. Speech by Boutros Boutros-Ghali, June 14, 1993, Vienna.

21. Katarina Tomasevski, "Human Rights: Fundamental Freedom for All," in Erskine Childers (ed.), *Challenges to the United Nations* (London: CIIR, 1994), p. 84.

22. Julia Preston, "U.S. Rebuts UN Critics of Human Rights Record," *Washington Post*, March 29, 1995.

23. Alan Riding, "Human Rights: The West Gets Some Tough Questions," *New York Times*, June 20, 1993.

24. Jimmy Carter, "Get Tough on Rights," *New York Times*, September 21, 1993.

25. Ibid.

26. Alan Riding, "A Rights Meeting, but Don't Mention the Wronged," *New York Times*, June 13, 1993.

27. Lewis, "Differing Views on Human Rights."

28. Draft Resolution V, paragraph 5, Report of the Third Committee (Part IV), on Human Rights Questions: Human Rights Situations and Reports of Special Rapporteurs and Representatives; UN General Assembly, A/49/610/Add.3, December 16, 1994.

29. Medea Benjamin, "On Its Own: Cuba in the Post-Cold War Era," in Phyllis Bennis and Michel Moushabeck (eds.), *Altered States: A Reader in the New World* Order (New York: Olive Branch Press/Interlink, 1993), p. 425.

30. Laura Flanders, "C. MacKinnon in The City of Freud," *The Nation*, August 9-16, 1993.

31. Ibid.

32. UN Population Fund, *The State of World Population 1994* (New York, 1994).

33. Howard LaFranchi, "Southern Nations Buck the Blame for Problems Tied to Population," *Christian Science Monitor*, September 7, 1994.

34. Barbara Crossette, "Population Debate: The Premises Are Changes," *New York Times*, September 14, 1994.

35. "Programme of Action of the United Nations Conference on Population and Development," issued in Cairo, 1994.

36. Barbara Crossette, "Population Meeting Opens With Challenge to the Right," *New York Times,* September 6, 1994.

37. Alan Cowell, "How Vatican Views Cairo," *New York Times,* September 18, 1994.

38. UN Research Institute for Social Development, "The Importance of Social Development Research" (Geneva, 1992).

39. Lucia Mouat,"Future UN Social Summit Hopes to Measure Progress By Human Scale, Not GNP," *Christian Science Monitor,* August 31, 1994.

40. UN Press Release, Information Service, UN Office at Geneva, February 24, 1995.

41. Barbara Crossette, "UN Parley Puts Focus on Africa," *New York Times,* March 9, 1995.

42. Barbara Crossette, "As World Leaders Confer on Poverty, Mitterrand Urges New Tax," *New York Times,* March 12, 1995.

43. Barbara Crossette, "Talks in Denmark Redefine 'Foreign' Aid in Post-Cold War Era," *New York Times,* March 10, 1995.

44. David Rohde, "Poverty Summit Falters in Giving a Map of Future," *Christian Science Monitor,* March 13, 1995.

45. Ibid.

46. Crossette, "Talks in Denmark."

47. May 22, 1995 letter to the coordinator of the NGO Forum, Khunying Supatra Masdit, from the Director of the NGO Forum Committee of the China Organizing Committee, Huang Qizao.

48. Statement at opening of Conference on Disarmament, Geneva, January 31, 1995.

49. "Ambassador Graham on U.S. Policy and the Non-Proliferation Treaty," interviewed by Dan Plesch and Stephen Young, *BASIC Reports,* British-American Security Information Council, April 14, 1995.

50. Barbara Crossette, "Treaty Aimed at Halting Spread of Nuclear Weapons Extended," *New York Times,* May 12, 1995.

51. Jonathan Steele and Ian Black, "Return of the Nuclear Nightmare," *The Guardian,* London, June 10, 1995.

52. Ibid.

53. R. Jeffrey Smith, "Some Nonaligned Nations Bristle at Nuclear Treaty; Many Don't Want Public Vote on Extension," *Washington Post,* April 17, 1995.

54. Ibid.

55. Steele and Black, "Return of the Nuclear Nightmare."

56. Crossette, "Treaty Aimed at Halting ...."

57. John Battersby, "U.S. Hunts for Pledge to Ban Nuclear Arms in the Middle East," *Christian Science Monitor,* January 19, 1995.

58. Steven Greenhouse, "A-Arms in the Mideast: U.S. Tailors Its Appeals," *New York Times,* February 15, 1995.

59. Elaine Sciolino, "Christopher Plunges Into Israel-Egypt Nuclear Dispute," *New York Times,* March 9, 1995.

60. Crossette, "Treaty Aimed at Halting ...."

61. C. Douglas Lummis, "Time to Watch the Watchers," *The Nation,* September 26, 1994.

62. Unnamed Clinton administration officials, National Public Radio News, June 17, 1995.

63. Andreas Zumach, Geneva correspondent for *Die Tageszeitung,* Berlin, June 14, 1995.

9

The Exception:
The Middle East and Palestine

Most of the time, U.S. influence on (and often control of) the UN comes in the form of coercing the organization to take one or another position, or to reject some other position, or pressuring a country or countries to vote a certain way in the General Assembly or the Security Council or another UN agency. That may mean bribing Colombia with a new arms deal, offering China its much-desired diplomatic rehabilitation after the horrors of Tienanmen Square, or punishing impoverished Yemen by withdrawing all foreign aid in response to its rejection of a U.S. demand.

Most of the time, Washington's goal is to engage the UN, involving it, forcefully or otherwise, in a U.S.-orchestrated initiative. Most of the time it works, and the U.S. gets its way. But once in a while the U.S. gets its way using a slightly different, though no less effective, technique: by using the same hard-ball pressure tactics ordinarily used to force the UN to a specific action, it denies the UN a place at the diplomatic table in those arenas that Washington is determined to keep under its own tight control.

Of them all, no issue has been more consistently targeted for this approach than the Middle East. Despite a myriad of resolutions over the years (those that were not vetoed outright in the Council), the U.S. has managed quite successfully to keep the UN out of the decision-making side of Middle East diplomacy.

At various points in its history the UN has been a major player in the Middle East — for good or bad, it was responsible for the partitioning of Palestine through General Assembly resolution 181, creating the state of Israel, while endorsing a Palestinian state and international status for Jerusalem, neither of which were ever allowed to come into existence. After the 1967 war, the Security Council passed resolution 242, which first called for the exchange of (Israeli-occupied Palestinian) land for (presumably Palestinian-disrupting Israeli) peace. Then in the early 1970s the UN played a key role in establishing the legitimacy and recognition of the Palestine Liberation Organization, highlighted by Chairman Yasir Arafat's speech to the General Assembly in 1974. But since that time, the UN has been largely excluded, not allowed to function as a significant player in Middle East diplomacy as a whole, and especially not on the question of Palestine.

It is not a coincidence that the end of UN activism around the Middle East after 1974 matched, more or less, the beginning of the period in which the U.S. wielded its veto much more often, both in actual frequency and relative to vetoes cast by the Soviet Union (or any other Council members). As noted in chapter 3, Washington's vetoes exploded exponentially by the mid-1970s, and a very large percentage of them were used to block the Council from responding to Israel's occupation.

There is a particular irony to this reality. It was only after the 1967 war that support for Israel became an article of faith for a large portion of the U.S. population. There are a number of reasons for this phenomenal rise in Israel's acceptance and fashionableness in the U.S. (having far more to do with changes in Washington's foreign policy imperatives than with the efforts of the Jewish community or the pro-Israel lobby), but the significance to this study is the correlation in time to the growing mass opposition to Israel's occupation that emerged in most of the rest of the world — and in the UN.

While in the U.S. public support for Israel grew, in many other countries, and in the United Nations as a multilateral whole, efforts took shape to demand an end to Israel's continuing military occupation and the resulting violations of human rights, and to affirm support for Palestinian national rights.

It is true, as Palestine's representative to the UN has pointed out, that it was difficult even in those years to forge a full consensus on the Palestine issue, even in the General Assembly.[1] But this was no straight-down-the-middle international divide. There was a consistent near-consensus overwhelmingly reflecting support for an international peace conference under the auspices of the UN to resolve the conflict; for all parties including Israel and the PLO taking part in those talks; and for an end to Israel's occupation of Palestinian (or Lebanese) land. The votes always reflected the kind of near-consensus in which the whole Assembly voted for (sometimes with some rather abashed abstentions), while only two countries voted against — the U.S. and Israel. (Once in a while El Salvador or Costa Rica or Romania would vote with Israel and the U.S. against the rest of the Assembly.)

These resolutions reflected a clear UN consensus on the way forward towards solving what had been for so long an intractable regional crisis with clear global implications — a broadly representative international peace conference, sponsored by the UN or some component of it (the permanent members of the Council were often proposed as guarantors), with every interested party present at the table.

It was the kind of approach that would, as the Cold War wound down, prove at least relatively successful in crisis zones across the world — bringing together opposing parties to talk. But Israel, from 1967 on, absolutely rejected UN involvement. It viewed the UN as implacably antagonistic to Israeli interests, and approached the post-decolonization General Assembly, with its demographic dominance of the South, as hostile territory. (It was not forgotten in the Assembly that Israel's own colonial settlement project, once the theological justifications had been stripped away, had itself come to fruition and UN-backed legality in 1948 — just when decolonization was coming to the top of the agenda in the rest of Africa, Asia, and the Middle East.)

Tel Aviv on its own would have been unable to stand against those initiatives. It might have refused to participate, but its refusal would have brought it universal opprobrium and the likelihood of serious sanctions.

But unilateral U.S. interest in creating and bolstering a reliably pro-U.S. ally in the sometimes volatile and always (both economically and geographically) strategic Middle East meant that Washington agreed to back Tel Aviv's rejectionism as far as it wished to go. Further, the shift away from Security Council intervention (such as resolution 242 in 1967 and resolution 338, mandating implementation of the earlier resolution, in 1973) ended by the mid-1970s, in tandem with the U.S. marginalization of the UN as a whole. Instead, as decolonization transformed the once-compliant Assembly into a more critical voice of the global South, the UN's involvement with the Middle East shifted there.

Given the realities of UN democracy and power divisions, this meant that the General Assembly was largely free to pass resolutions condemning and demanding an end to Israel's occupation of the West Bank, the Gaza Strip, and Arab East Jerusalem. There were serious exceptions (including Washington's refusal to grant Yasir Arafat a visa to address the Assembly in 1988, and the high-profile pressure campaign in 1991 to force the Assembly to revoke its 1975 "Zionism is a form of racism" resolution — see pp. 57-58). Every year Assembly sessions featured a consistent effort to pressure Israel.

But while the language may have been tough, the resolutions lacked any means of exacting compliance. The pressure was limited to publicity and public opinion, neither of which was taken very seriously by Israel. Without access to any enforcement mechanism, Assembly resolutions were routinely passed, routinely excoriated by Tel Aviv and Washington as evidence of UN "bias," and routinely ignored.

The U.S. strategy did not, of course, mean excluding the UN from playing a role in the occupied territories. For decades the UN continued to play the key role in humanitarian work and some development in the territories. The UN's Refugee Works Agency (UNRWA), one of the earliest large-scale humanitarian projects, continued its work, and in many cases, especially in the impoverished Gaza Strip and most especially in periods of long Israeli-imposed curfews and closures, helped assure basic survival of the Palestinians living in refugee camps. The UN Development Program has been involved for many years, and is likely to play an even larger role in the period of so-called "self-rule" mandated by the Washington-backed Oslo Accords between Israel and the PLO. Other UN humanitarian agencies, including the UN High Commissioner for Refugees (UNHCR), UNICEF, and others also continue their work.

But overall U.S. concern in the Middle East, and especially regarding the Israel-Palestine conflict, is strategic, not humanitarian. Washington has an interest in insuring that some modicum of social stability exists, and is perfectly willing for the UN to take the lead in providing basic survival support networks (thus substantially lowering what the U.S. alone might have to pay for). What it is not willing to do is have the UN involved in the political decision-making of the Middle East.

Throughout the last weeks leading up to the November 29, 1990 vote authorizing war in the Gulf, for example, Israel's occupation and its anti-UN intransigence proved significant stumbling blocks in Washington's effort to co-opt Arab partners to its anti-Iraq coalition. The U.S. and Israeli rejection of the longstanding global consensus supporting an international peace conference under the auspices of the United Nations brought the issue of U.S. double standards to the front of the agenda — of the UN and the international community in general, but especially of the South. But the U.S. was willing to take the risks inherent in the double standard accusation rather than pressure Israel towards greater accommodation at that time.

Even in the immediate post-Gulf War period of Washington's sudden and enthusiastic embrace of the UN, a key exception remained regarding Palestine. U.S. power in the political arena of the Middle East, unlike in humanitarian and economic areas, takes the form of *preventing*, rather than *imposing*, a significant UN role. That rejection by the

U.S. exists despite Washington's search for stability and an end to conflict. (Ending conflict does not necessarily translate as an end to Israel's occupation, since that is not of strategic concern to the U.S. But social and political tranquility is.)

A much earlier example of the significance of the Palestine issue in Washington's UN strategy came in the period of intense U.S. efforts to undermine the UN in the 1970s, largely because the process of decolonization had led to the dominance of the South in the General Assembly. A key target of the U.S. campaign was an extended attack on UNESCO.

The UN Educational, Scientific and Cultural Organization had become a key arena of South-South cooperation, and was especially active in coordinating scientific research and providing assistance to countries in the South who found this support invaluable in their challenge to the North's hold on intellectual resources. The U.S. attack on UNESCO included relentless criticism of the agency's finances, management, and leadership. Coming in for special condemnation was UNESCO's longstanding Senegalese director-general, Amadou Mahtar M'Bow.

The U.S. critique was wide-ranging, but the essential accusation was that UNESCO had been "politicized," meaning it had begun to reflect more overtly the partisan nature of an agency whose brief at least partly was to democratize the world's distribution of resources. By the early 1980s the Reagan administration had almost ceased paying its dues to UNESCO. But then the agency committed the final sin. It invited the PLO, since 1974 already an official observer organization of the UN, to join UNESCO on a similar basis, to participate in its educational/cultural activities. For the U.S., and especially for President Reagan's UN-bashing Ambassador Jeane Kirkpatrick, such legitimation of the PLO was too much.

In 1984 the U.S. withdrew its membership from UNESCO and stopped payment on all its assessments.

PULLING IN THE WELCOME MAT

In 1974, the General Assembly had invited Yasir Arafat to visit the United Nations. As required by the Host Country Agreement signed between the U.S. and the UN, a limited visa was issued to the PLO chairman restricting his movements to a 25-mile radius from UN headquarters. The international attention generated by his famous "freedom fighter's gun and olive branch" speech played a key role in winning UN recognition of the PLO as the "sole legitimate representative" of the Palestinian people, as well as observer status within the UN itself. It also helped to gain broad international recognition, including full diplomatic relations with numerous countries, for the organization. Since that time, the PLO diplomatic team at the UN has participated as a full, albeit unofficial, member of the Arab Group, and has actively sought a voice in Council as well as Assembly and other debates touching on the question of Israeli occupation or Palestinian rights.

Washington knew that much of the PLO's credibility, especially in the 1980s when its armed actions had significantly dwindled, could be traced to Arafat's UN appearance. As a result, when the Assembly again invited the PLO leader to address the body, in December 1988, Washington was in a quandary. It was a delicate moment. Only a month earlier, the PLO's parliament-in-exile, the Palestine National Council, meeting in Algiers on November 15, had declared an independent Palestinian state in the West Bank, the Gaza Strip, and East Jerusalem. The intifada, the uprising characterized by mass popular resistance in the occupied territories and Palestinian children throwing stones at Israeli soldiers, was at its height.

What Washington and its Israeli junior partners didn't need just then was a new boost to the PLO's credibility — it was bad enough that leading Palestinian voices inside the occupied territories continually asserted that anyone who wanted to negotiate an end to the intifada could find their representatives at PLO headquarters in Tunis. A parallel international campaign further legitimating the PLO and crediting it with the largely non-violent intifada would mean a disaster for Tel Aviv, and a public relations nightmare in Washington.

So the U.S. decided the best way out would be to use its power as Host Country simply to deny a visa to Arafat, barring him from the U.S., thus refusing outright to allow the UN to hear him speak. While the Host Country Agreement allows certain narrowly construed circumstances under which the U.S. might legally deny a visa to someone invited for an official UN function, nobody was fooled. The claim that Arafat's brief visit to New York somehow represented a "security threat" to the U.S. was nonsense; the State Department did little to try to justify it.

The result was almost comic. The entire General Assembly, including Secretariat officials, translators, clerks, security guards, public information people, and more, packed up and decamped from New York to Switzerland. The cost, for a single two-hour meeting and a couple of press conferences in Geneva's Palais des Nations, was astronomical, at a time when Washington was already complaining about the UN's profligate standards and inappropriate use of funds. The question of double standards re-emerged.

(The later irony, of course, was that any potential PLO propaganda bonanza that might have resulted from Arafat speaking to the UN in Geneva was immediately overshadowed by Washington's own use of the occasion to announce its new official recognition of the PLO and a bilateral diplomatic initiative. Compared with the long-denied high-level official meetings with the U.S., an invitation to join a few more UN agencies or even a prized Arafat appearance on U.S. television would mean little. Except for the UN's enormous costs in overtime pay, plane fares, taxis, hotel accommodations, meals, and other expenses for the New York-based staff, little had changed.)

DESERT STORM CLOUDS OVER PALESTINE

During the last weeks leading up to the November 29, 1990 passage of resolution 678 in the Security Council, authorizing the use of force against Iraq, the U.S. diplomatic team was focused on preventing the Council from discussing a proposed resolution aimed at protecting Palestinians living under occupation.

The resolution had been proposed in response to the October killing of at least 22 Palestinians by Israeli military authorities on the steps of the Haram al-Sharif, or the Temple Mount. The attack, and the international outrage it generated, had called into question the smooth running of the UN front of Washington's Gulf build-up.

Within hours of the killings, the seven Non-Aligned members of the Security Council introduced a resolution backed by the PLO. It won immediate support, albeit with varying degrees of enthusiasm, from fourteen of the fifteen Council members, even including Britain, whose ambassador, Sir David Hannay, was that month's president of the Council. The U.S. was the one hold-out.

The resolution initially did not use the word "condemn" in reference to the attack. It "deplored" the killings, a lower level of criticism in diplomatic parlance. But far more significantly, it called on the Council to send its own mission to Jerusalem to investigate the killings and to return with recommendations for how Palestinians living under occupation could be protected.

The debate was sharp, with speaker after speaker expressing their nation's outrage at the carnage in Al-Aqsa Mosque. The Malaysian ambassador, despite his government's close ties to the U.S., was among the strongest voices. He called Israel's policy "truly a bloody one." He cautioned that Israel and its friends "must not be allowed to ... masquerade behind what the Israeli representative described as 'the international coalition mustered against Iraqi aggression.' " He spoke of possible sanctions against Israel, stating that "the Council could not ignore those serious Israeli violations in the light of recent developments in the region. To do so would mean that the Council was allowing double standards to prevail over justice and moral considerations." The French, supporting the call for a Council-sponsored mission, spoke of the necessity of the Security Council receiving "on the spot information" directly in order to move forward.

U.S. diplomats forced a delay in the vote. By the next afternoon, Washington had submitted its own resolution, which became, for the U.S. press, the only one under discussion. The U.S. draft used the stronger word "condemn" for the first time. But PLO diplomats, and the Non-Aligned members of the Council supporting them, made clear that they were not concerned about issues of language. The real sticking point was the nature of the investigation team to be sent to Jerusalem. Washington's proposal left the Security Council out of the picture, calling instead for the secretary-general to send his own representative. While SG missions had traveled to Jerusalem and the rest of the occupied territories before, they had never had any impact on persistent Israeli violations of international law and human rights. The special representatives would go, look, and return, without the influence, prestige, and ultimately enforcement power of the Security Council, the UN's highest body.

Palestine's Permanent Observer to the UN at the time, Ambassador Zehdi Labib Terzi, made clear his delegation's priorities. Outside the Council chamber, speaking at 1:00 a.m. on October 9, he said, "We are not interested in semantics; what we want is for the Council to take action. The U.S. draft does not call on the Council to do anything."[2]

The immutable U.S. rejection of a Council role was rooted partly in U.S. support for Israel's longstanding rejection of any internationally-mandated ombudsman position monitoring its adherence to or violation of international human rights conventions. But it also reflected the U.S. recognition that such a resolution would finally place the Council in a position of assuming responsibility for the Palestinians living under Israeli occupation. That, for the U.S., represented the first step down the slippery slope towards a UN-sponsored international peace conference. U.S. backing for Israeli rejection of such a conference remained a cornerstone of the U.S.-Israeli alliance, and not even the new set of commitments to new Arab allies would change Washington's position.

What was different this time around was the potentially fateful consequences of a U.S. veto. In past incidents of Israeli atrocities, a routine

U.S. veto on the grounds that a resolution was "one-sided," or that it "did not advance the peace process," would be roundly condemned, but then set aside. This time, Washington's carefully constructed Arab legitimacy for its military build-up in the Gulf could not afford the political fall-out of a U.S. veto of a Council resolution condemning Israel's bloodbath at the doors of one of Islam's holiest shrines.

The governments of Saudi Arabia and Egypt, in particular, as well as Syria, were uneasy about the consequences of a U.S. veto. They stood to lose even more popular support if they continued backing U.S. troops against Saddam Hussein in the face of Washington's veto of Palestinian rights. Non-Aligned diplomatic sources indicated that Saudi and Egyptian pressure on the PLO to give the U.S. a compromise way out was "fierce."

A Soviet diplomat indicated in the early morning hours of October 10 that his government would not back down "unless the Palestinians agreed." Palestine's diplomats did not agree, however, hoping that the commitments of other Council members to support a Council mission would remain strong. The French and the Canadians refused early U.S. efforts to persuade them to abandon the Non-Aligned resolution.

By the night of October 10, the British had engineered a compromise, calling for the secretary-general to send a representative, but asking that he report back to the Council. The observer's mandate abandoned earlier language calling on the Council to find ways to protect the Palestinians living under occupation.

Throughout the days and nights of October 11 and 12, the U.S. rope tightened. Washington cajoled its Western allies, alternately pressuring and threatening the Non-Aligned members of the Council. Late on the night of October 12 the vote was taken, and resolution 672, calling for only a representative of the secretary-general to investigate, was unanimously accepted.

Unanimity had been preserved — or imposed. But the U.S. refusal brought the question of Washington's double standards to center stage. U.S. credibility among the developing countries, and among some of its Western allies, plummeted.

As it happened, the U.S. battle may have been unnecessary. Israel responded to the resolution by immediately announcing its refusal to accept any UN mission, including that of the secretary-general. In response, the Council passed resolution 673 on October 24, reaffirming Israel's obligations as a member of the UN to accept Council resolutions and urging Tel Aviv to "reconsider its decision ... and to permit the mission of the secretary-general to proceed."

The SG's special representative ultimately made a brief trip and reported to the Council. A resolution was drafted in response to that report, aimed at broadening UN involvement in protecting Palestinians living under occupation. But over the next two months, from mid-October until December 17, while the military build-up in the Gulf continued at breakneck speed, the U.S. continued its efforts to delay the vote and to strip the proposed resolution of anything likely to offend Israel.

The original language of the resolution called on the Security Council to deploy troops from UNTSO (the UN Treaty Supervision Organization, deployed on Israel's borders with Syria, Lebanon, Jordan, and Egypt since 1949) to monitor the treatment of Palestinians living under occupation. It condemned Israel's policy of expelling, or deporting, Palestinians, and demanded that the practice cease and that those expelled be allowed to return. And, for the first time, it would have placed the Council on record supporting an international peace conference long called for by the General Assembly, to solve the crises of the Middle East.

The next draft dropped the reference to UNTSO, and called for a commissioner representing the secretary-general, not the Council, to be sent to the occupied territories. The third draft dismissed that idea, and simply called for an SG representative to monitor the situation.

U.S.-backed versions also replaced the earlier language that "condemned" Israel's expulsions of Palestinians with a softer criticism that "deplored" the practice. Washington also deleted calls for Israel to stop expelling people or to allow those already expelled to return.

When Washington forced the first delay in the vote, it was a long enough break to convince its European allies to weaken the terms of the original resolution. Then another delay was imposed, and another. On December 1st, Yemen's Ambassador Abdullah al-Ashtal took over the presidency of the Council. Discussion of the resolution resumed on December 5th.

In all, the Council prepared and was ready to vote seven times. But seven times, U.S. diplomats managed to orchestrate delay, each time draining more power from the proposed resolution.

The final drafts acceded to the longstanding U.S.-Israeli rejection of an international peace conference by removing the reference to it from the operative paragraphs, and relegating that reference to a separate statement issued by then-Council president, Yemen's Ambassador al-Ashtal. (Presidential statements, while reflecting Council unanimity, do not have even the pretense of enforceability.)

The U.S. was determined that the enforceable sections of the resolution exclude anything the Israelis would be likely to reject (which included virtually all of the proposals for protection of Palestinians). The White House was quietly nervous that some Non-Aligned Council members might actually propose sanctions against Tel Aviv to force its compliance with the Council decisions — using Washington's own anti-Iraq sanctions as precedent.

Some time after midnight the night of December 17, the U.S. once again forced a delay, this time pressuring the Council to call a halt until the morning of December 19. By that time there were so many drafts circulating that neither the exhausted Council diplomats nor the punch-drunk UN press corps could keep track.

Forty-eight hours later, the Council voted unanimously to accept resolution 681 in a form that bore little resemblance to the original version introduced seven weeks before. In fact, it was virtually unrecognizable. It had been stripped of the call for the Council to deploy UN troops to protect Palestinians, lost the condemnation of Israel's expelling Palestinians, and the demand that it stop the practice and allow those expelled to return home. It had even lost the renewed call for an international peace conference, a longstanding UN principal despite vehement opposition to it by Washington and Tel Aviv, and seen it replaced with a non-binding suggestion by the Security Council president.

The breathtaking double standard of Washington's UN responses to Iraq's occupation of Kuwait and Israel's occupation of Palestine did not receive much attention in the mainstream U.S. media. In an especially cynical example, an article by *New York Times* reporter Paul Lewis, describing Washington's effort at gutting the already-enfeebled fourth draft resolution, was headlined "U.S. Backs UN Bid Criticizing Israel." Implying U.S. leadership in the anti-Israel effort, Lewis asserted that the "United States has agreed to sponsor a new United Nations Security Council resolution critical of Israel to avoid a rupture in the Arab coalition it has assembled against Iraq for its invasion of Kuwait."[3]

TALKS IN THE HALLWAYS

U.S. reliance on the UN for credibility in the Gulf War did not extend to its post-Gulf political initiative. Once the military part of Desert Storm had ended and the U.S. had declared a yellow ribbon victory over the bodies of somewhere between one and three hundred thousand Iraqis, the political component of the Gulf War, the Madrid process, began. It was crafted to simultaneously implement and reflect the newly unchallenged system of U.S. domination of the vital Middle East. Only within that new political environment in the region, in which Arab unity had been shattered by the U.S. anti-Iraq coalition and the U.S. itself emerged the sole superpower, would Israel agree to sit face to face, for the first time, with its Arab opponents — themselves now uniformly dependent on, and to an unprecedented degree accountable to, Washington.

The Madrid "peace process" set the terms for four separate sets of negotiations — between Israel and Syria, Lebanon, Jordan, and the Palestinians. (The talks would not, officially, be with the PLO, and Tel Aviv's U.S.-backed legal fiction insisted that the restricted Palestinian diplomatic team, made up only of Palestinians from inside the occupied territories not including Jerusalem, be officially considered a subset of the Jordanian contingent.)

But despite the multi-party participation, the presence of high-level diplomatic teams not only from the U.S. and Soviet co-sponsors but from the European Union and numerous countries in the region, there was to be no illusion that this was the long-sought "international" peace conference on the Middle East. Israel had agreed to participate only if the high-profile opening formalities, in Madrid's glittering Crystal Palace, were designed only as the prelude to separate bilateral talks with each of the Arab parties; the terms of reference even specified that the multi-party conference would only be reconvened if all sides agreed — giving Israel a veto over even any appearance of real multilateral negotiations. As for the United Nations, its single representative was ordered humiliatingly silent by the joint agreement of Washington and Tel Aviv.

The terms for an Israeli agreement with Syria were set, in fact if not on paper, when Damascus agreed to join Washington's anti-Iraq coalition. The payback would come after Desert Storm had functionally leveled Syrian president Hafez al-Assad's longstanding Ba'ath Party rival in Baghdad. The Israel-Syria conflict engendered the bitterest level of acrimony of any of the Middle East disputes, but in fact the basis for an agreement was long known. What would comprise the final terms was clear long before the opening speeches, filled with vitriolic posturing on both the Israeli and Syrian sides, were made in Madrid.

Syria would get at least official, if not complete on the ground, Israeli withdrawal from the once-strategic (though questionably so in the era of advanced missile technology) Golan Heights, and Israeli acknowledgment of formal Syrian sovereignty. In return, it would provide Tel Aviv with continued guaranteed access to Golani water sources (a key reason for Israel's concern about giving up the Heights — far more important than security); family reunification for the 15,000 Syrians living under Israeli occupation would be arranged; the demilitarization of not only the Heights, but a major chunk of Syrian territory below the Heights would be guaranteed by international (U.S.-led, and definitely not UN) troops; and Israel would get something called peace and relative normalization with its longstanding enemy. All would be arranged and imposed under stringent U.S. guarantees, with financial and political rewards for compliance (more cash for Israel, removal from the list of "terrorist states" for Syria); and threats of punishment for (at least Syrian) resistance. After the bombast, what was actually left to negotiate were exact details, and a timetable.

Once the Syrian-Israeli agreement was set, Israeli-Lebanese talks could be expected to fall into place. Israel would be expected to withdraw from at least part of the Lebanese territory it had occupied since 1978, in return for Syrian guarantees that no Palestinian forces would be allowed to launch attacks from the area. As for Jordan, its real battle with Israel had been over for years; its official state of belligerence was simply derivative of Jordan's unwitting geographical and historic involvement in the Israel-Palestine conflict, and actual Jordanian-Israeli relations had been cordial and cooperative for a generation. Making it official, with the signing of the Israel-Jordan accord in the spring of 1994, was clearly a reflection of motion on the more significant Israel-Palestine front.

In none of these negotiations was the UN called on — or allowed — to play a role beyond that of cheerleader.

PALESTINE

But Palestine was much more complicated. Five months of shuttle diplomacy by Secretary of State James Baker following the defeat of Saddam Hussein led to the agreement of Israel and the Palestinians to join the Madrid talks.

The terms of participation of Israel and the Arab parties was guaranteed through Letters of Assurance agreed to between the U.S. (with the Soviet Union haplessly following along) and each government. Preparation of the Letters, whose final text was never made public, was based on Memoranda of Understanding (MOUs) drafted jointly by the U.S. and each country.

While none of the MOUs called for UN involvement, the U.S.-Israel MOU spelled out a stunningly explicit exclusion of the world organization. In paragraph 7 the U.S. assured Israel that the "UN representative will have no authority. He [it was assumed to be a he] may hold talks only in the hallways, note down the content of the talks, and report to the secretary general."

An addendum to paragraph 10 went on to assert that the "United States is also required to make a commitment that the UN Security Council will not convene to discuss the [Middle East] conflict during negotiations .... "[4] And in one leaked version of the final U.S.-Israel Letter of Assurance, Washington agreed to "take steps to ... have UN Resolution 3379 equating Zionism and racism annulled."[5]

Later that same year, the U.S. rammed through the General Assembly the revocation of the Zionism is racism resolution (see pp. 57-58). The effort was partly a simple fulfillment of the U.S. commitment to the Israeli government. But it was also designed to eliminate one more arena in which a UN role in the Middle East could be seen. It was engineered by the U.S. in such a way as to deny any discussion of whether the original assessment of Zionism had been wrong, or whether the practitioners of political Zionism had in some profound way changed their direction so that the racialized character no longer existed, or anything else. It was simply imposed, almost by fiat, on a compliant and beaten-down General Assembly.

Early in 1994, when an Israeli settler-soldier murdered 29 and wounded scores of Palestinians inside the ancient Al-Ibrahimi Mosque in Hebron, there was a new effort to get the Security Council on board, not only in condemning the massacre but in trying to do something to prevent such occurrences in the future.

Once again the resolution was delayed by the U.S., ostensibly because of its references to Jerusalem as part of the occupied territories, but also because it authorized a "temporary international presence" to be sent as observers in Hebron, something Israel had long opposed. But significantly, the resolution even specified they were not to be UN peacekeeping troops, but rather "international observers" not under UN Blue Helmet command. The secretary-general volunteered to send observers, but the U.S. condemned his offer as not being "particularly helpful or useful." The debate raged for over three weeks, and in the final agreement the U.S. demanded a separate vote on each paragraph of the resolution.

The U.S. objected to two paragraphs. One, in the preamble, described the Security Council as "gravely concerned by the consequent Palestinian casualties in the occupied Palestinian territory as a result of the massacre, which underlines the need to provide protection and security for the Palestinian people." The other objection was to the Council "reaffirming its relevant resolutions, which affirmed the applicability of the Fourth Geneva Convention of 12 August 1949 to the territories occupied by Israel in June 1967, including Jerusalem, and the Israeli responsibilities thereunder .... "

In the final vote, Washington abstained rather than vetoing the references to Jerusalem. U.S. Ambassador Madeleine Albright said she didn't veto the resolution because the offending references were "only" in the preambular paragraphs, not in the operative language; presumably, therefore, the U.S. could ignore them with impunity. The final decision sent 160 observers, mostly Norwegian and a few Italian, to Hebron, only 60 of them actually working in the field. They were not Blue Helmet soldiers or observers; most of them had been involved in various NGO-related work. They had no means of insuring even their own protection.

Perhaps inevitably, the observers were immediately dubbed the "ice cream soldiers," not only because of their white uniforms but because at the first sign of trouble, they melted. (It should be noted that this assessment had nothing to do with any lack of personal courage; the observers were well-motivated, brave, and many of them worked very hard.) But their mandate severely limited their activities. They were ordered only to observe the actions of Israeli soldiers and settlers. If abuses were seen, they had no authority to intervene, but could only report to UN officials who would relay the information to someone in New York. The last anyone heard of them was in May 1994, when Israeli soldiers ordered them out of a part of Hebron where Israeli settlers and reportedly soldiers were firing on unarmed Palestinians.

But in the meantime diplomacy went on, not only through the faltering and (we now know) irrelevant Madrid talks, but through the back-door Israel-PLO channel sponsored by the Norwegians. And after the signing ceremony of the Oslo Accord in Washington in September 1993, Yasir Arafat came back to the UN, to New York again this time. After his meeting with the secretary-general, I asked Arafat whether he had discussed with Boutros-Ghali any plans for an active UN role in guaranteeing or maintaining the future peace. The PLO chairman could say only that they had discussed better and higher-level coordination of the UN institutions already working in the occupied territories. That meant the economic and humanitarian agencies alone — once again the UN was out of the political loop.

As for real UN peacekeeping operations, despite their expansion and redefinition, there is a continuing campaign in the U.S. government and press aimed at keeping UN Blue Helmets out of the region. It emerged strongly around the issue of observers for an Israel-Syria agreement on the Golan Heights. It is understood and accepted by all sides that the anticipated international peacekeeping force monitoring Israel's withdrawal from and Syria's commitment to demilitarization on the Golan Heights will not involve UN Blue Helmets. Rather, a

U.S.-based "multinational force" will monitor the withdrawal lines, reflecting Israel's traditional rejectionist posture towards the UN, as well as Syria's apparent lack of concern with bolstering the international organization's credibility and power.

Some point to the need of both Israel and Syria for an international force that cannot be dislodged by either side withdrawing permission for its presence as the reason for going around the UN. But this denies the reality that if both sides agreed to accept a UN deployment under Chapter VII (for which the consent of the parties is not required), the UN would be well-positioned to carry out the responsibility of guarding a Golani peace.

Lee Hamilton, an influential member of the House Foreign Affairs Committee, wrote that his preferred model of a "successful" peacekeeping operation is the Multi-National Force and Observers (MFO) in the Sinai, the observer body mandated by the Israeli-Egyptian Camp David Accords. Hamilton defines the MFO as successful precisely because it is *not* a UN operation. The MFO "holds valuable lessons," he writes, "particularly in the Middle East. ... Because it operates outside the UN system, it has been innovative in important ways that UN peacekeeping should emulate .... The MFO can hire its own staff, and has hired top-notch people, without concerns about UN-style nationality quotas .... "[6] The implication is that "top-notch people" will only be found outside the UN. Ironically, unlike the informal arrangements in certain Secretariat personnel categories, there are no "nationality quotas" in UN peacekeeping operations; troops are not recruited as individuals at all, but are deployed and led by their own governments who agree to participate.

As it stands now, instead of strengthening a truly multilateral presence in the Middle East, the arrangement will consolidate even further Washington's unchallenged post-Gulf War regional domination.

CLINTON CLONES BUSH

While the Clinton presidency has differed from that of Bush in a number of respects, the overall pattern of how the UN should and should not be involved in Washington's Middle East strategy has remained largely unchanged. The most explicit articulation of the Clinton administration's Middle East goals for the UN emerged in the August 8, 1994 letter sent by Ambassador Albright to the incoming president of the Assembly, outlining U.S. priorities for the coming term.

The Middle East section, first of the "Key Issues" identified in the letter, focused solely on developments in the peace process, especially on the Israeli-Palestinian track. It was here that the Clinton administration's more-Catholic-than-the-pope position towards Israel at the UN became clear, especially if one compared Albright's letter to the statement of Israel's Ambassador Gad Yaacobi made just about a month later.

Yaacobi's statement was a relatively modest one. He welcomed moves already taken by the UN, such as increasing the role of UNDP, UNRWA, and other agencies in providing economic and development aid in the region; embracing the Madrid process and its progeny; repealing the Zionism is a form of racism resolution, and thereby, he claimed, showing that the General Assembly had "taken to heart ... the dangers of abusing this forum of peace"; as well as "the removal of contentious language and issues from other resolutions on the Middle East, and the elimination of obsolete resolutions that were contrary to the new reality."[7] The only new thing Yaacobi called for was for Tel Aviv's admission into one of the regional groups (which determine rotating Security Council seats and participation in other geographically chosen positions; in the past Israel had been excluded).

Albright's pro-Israeli agenda was much more ambitious. Her unmistakable goal was to completely remove the issues of Arab-Israeli relations, and especially the question of Palestine, from the UN's political agenda. Albright's approach was to make the claim that the bilateral Israeli-Palestinian negotiations of the Madrid/Oslo processes had rendered *"caduc"* any role or responsibility for the UN beyond economic and development assistance. (*"Caduc"* is the French word for lapsed, or out of date; Arafat used it with great fanfare in describing the Palestinian Covenant's anti-Israel language.)

Albright began her letter with what sounded like a threat: "Adopting a positive resolution welcoming progress in the peace process, as we did in 1993," she asserted, "will test the UN's new realistic approach." She did not articulate the possible consequence if the General Assembly failed to define as "progress" the expansion of settlements, failure to redeploy troops out of Palestinian population centers and delays in holding elections, and continuing killings on both sides that characterized Israel's post-Oslo occupation of Palestine.

She went on to make specific demands. "Contentious resolutions that accentuate political differences without promoting solutions should be consolidated (the various UNRWA resolutions), improved (the Golan resolution) *or eliminated* (the Israeli nuclear armament resolution and the self-determination resolution)" (emphasis added). Given Israel's consistent failure to even consider signing the Non-Proliferation Treaty in the face of world knowledge of its 200+ high-density nuclear bombs in the Dimona plant, this was a stunning proposal.

The *pièce de résistance* of the U.S. 1994 plan for the General Assembly was the demand that "resolution language referring to 'final status' issues should be dropped, *since these issues are now under negotiations by the parties* themselves. These include refugees, settlements, territorial sovereignty and the status of Jerusalem"[8] (emphasis added).

In response, Palestine's Ambassador al-Kidwe conveyed to Albright his "shock" concerning her letter's claim that references to "final status issues should be dropped." He reminded Albright of the not insignificant reality that the final status issues to which she referred in fact "are not yet under negotiation." The Oslo Agreement defers those issues, mandating discussions to begin within three years. Further, al-Kidwe stated, their "deferral does not, and should not, entail any compromise or undermining of the positions held by the international community and the General Assembly in accordance with international law on these issues. Dropping such positions at this stage would be tantamount to forsaking international law and international legitimacy and effectively allowing the illegal, de facto situation created by Israel, the Occupying Power, to prevail when the time for negotiation arrives."[9]

The Assembly in 1994 did vote a ringing endorsement of the peace process, though on the specifics of most of the other resolutions mentioned in Albright's letter, the U.S. did not completely succeed. Ambassador al-Kidwe called the Israeli and U.S. efforts "a big mistake .... It seems their effort backfired because their claim of 'UN hands off' was hard to swallow by anybody at the UN."[10]

If analyzed only by looking separately at each specific demand, he was right. The Assembly did pass a resolution calling for the application of the Geneva Conventions to all occupied territories including Jerusalem; it was opposed only by the U.S., Israel, and Gambia. The vote on Israeli practices in the occupied territories was opposed only by the U.S. and Israel; and even the vote on the work of the Special Committee to Investigate Israeli Practices, targeted for dismemberment by Washington, saw only the U.S. and Israel voting against. And in a series of technical status changes, the emergence of "Palestine" at the UN as a non-member observer, with status parallel to other non-member states, rather than that of a non-member organization, took hold. These included enhanced levels of consultation in planning for the 1995 UN 50th anniversary celebrations, and the lifting of travel restrictions on the Palestinian diplomatic team. Additionally, the secretary-general appointed a special coordinator for the occupied territories. (Although it must be noted that his mandate is narrowly drawn to include only issues of economic and development aid to the new Palestinian Authority, not political questions.)

But the results of unenforceable Assembly resolutions and symbolic gains within the UN bureaucracy cannot be the only basis for assessing U.S. goals. More broadly, Washington's efforts by the middle of the Clinton administration's term had succeeded at keeping the UN out of the political trajectory in the Middle East.

There was a certain irony in the Clinton administration's extreme activism supporting Israel at the UN, especially its position regarding Jerusalem and the other issues deferred by the Oslo agreement. Early in his campaign, Clinton had staked out a position calling for Washington to move its embassy to Jerusalem; by the spring of 1995 he faced a new and now embarrassing campaign by Republicans in Congress for this very move, as the GOP tried to reposition itself with Jewish voters in the U.S. as the "real" defender of Israel. With even the Labor-led Israeli government less than enthusiastic about the proposal, understanding its threat to the already-stumbling peace process, the administration was caught. While the need at least to appear even-handed on this explosive issue, as the co-sponsor of the peace process, did not seem high on Clinton's list of Middle East priorities, Oslo had changed some realities. After Oslo, U.S. recognition of Jerusalem as the capital of Israel, in contradiction to longstanding UN resolutions going back to the 1947 UN partition of Palestine, would mean a shocking abandonment of already frayed U.S. claims of being an honest broker.

On the other hand, a public reversal of his campaign commitment was not an appealing choice either. By the summer of 1995, Clinton's avoid-the-issue tendency seemed rooted in some hope that by the time of serious election pressures, some factor outside his own position might have changed.

MAJOR-MINOR

Palestine's Ambassador al-Kidwe described his belief, in early 1995, that the U.S. would ensure that "the UN will be playing some role, but will not be allowed to be a major player — major events in Middle East diplomacy will not be played on UN ground."

If anyone wonders whether anything has changed in political circumstances after the end of the Cold War, and the U.S. dominance of the post-Desert Storm Middle East, all she would have to do is look once again at U.S. veto patterns. The last pre-Gulf War veto was cast on May 31, 1990. The U.S. used its power to prevent the Security Council from passing a resolution condemning Israel's latest violation of Palestinian rights.

After that, the "new" UN of the post-Cold War era was said to be the post-veto era as well, a period of Security Council harmony and growing mutuality of interests. More or less that has proved true, as Russia's desperation to maintain aid and support from the West, and China's trading policy of abstaining from or supporting U.S. initiatives in return for economic or diplomatic perks, led to a virtual abandonment of the veto as part of normal Security Council life.

Until Palestine. In May 1995, the Israeli government, in clear defiance of the Oslo Agreement's plan to defer discussion of the status of Jerusalem, and its commitment to do nothing that would preempt those negotiations, announced new plans to confiscate 53 hectares of Palestinian-owned land for massive settlement building in occupied East Jerusalem. The plan called for the creation of about 3,300 new apartment units, virtually all of them in Jews-only settlements in the Arab side of the city. There was immediate international outrage.

In the UN, the Security Council began to debate the issue on May 12. Ambassador al-Kidwe, Palestine's Permanent Observer, described the Israeli plan. He said that,"Israel must also understand that it cannot achieve peace while continuing to hold the land, that it is not possible to maintain its grip on Jerusalem while demanding normal relations with its neighbors and their friends. Finally, Israel must choose: either there is agreement with the Palestinian side or there is no agreement, because the status of half-agreement is unacceptable and absolutely untenable."[11]

The Israeli answer was simply to claim that "the issue has been taken out of context and blown out of proportion." From Israeli Ambassador Yaacobi's vantage point, the only problems were semantic. "The recent decision," he told the Council, "to expropriate, not to confiscate, land for construction in Jerusalem — not for settlements as was said here — is based on our longstanding policy ...."[12]

As for the U.S., Middle East specialist Tom Gnehm told the Council that "it is difficult to see how such actions [as Israel's land seizures] promote the peace process." But, he went on, "having said that, we do not believe that this [the UN] is the appropriate forum for dealing with this issue."[13] The U.S. would not deviate from its assurance to Tel Aviv that it would "show due consideration for Israel's positions in the peace process."[14]

Ambassador al-Kidwe reminded the Council of the special role of the U.S. "The American co-sponsors [of the peace process] carry a larger responsibility in this regard because of their special relationship with Israel and because of the letters of assurance they provided to the parties participating in the process, including the letter of assurance to the Palestinian side, which was an integral component of the basis for Palestinian participation in the whole process. The letter of assurance, dated 24 October 1991, states the following about the issue of Jerusalem:

> The United States is opposed to the Israeli annexation of East Jerusalem and the extension of Israeli law on it and the extension of Jerusalem's municipal boundaries. We encourage all sides to avoid unilateral acts that would exacerbate local tensions or make negotiations more difficult or preempt their outcome.

We are now witnessing precisely such actions, and we hope that the United States will take a clear position in keeping with its assurances in this regard."[15]

The U.S. position remained clear; its assurances to Israel remained preeminent. After four days of debate, the Council voted on a resolution condemning Israel's land seizure and calling for it to be reversed. The vote was 14 to 1. The U.S. voted no. The veto was cast, the first since the end of the Cold War.

It is likely not a coincidence that the 1994 edition of the UN's annual report on "The United Nations and the Question of Palestine,"[16] unlike all earlier editions, left out the official maps featured before: the map of the UN's 1947 Partition Plan and UN Armistice Lines of 1949, showing the large area designated for an internationally-supervised Jerusalem[17]; the map of territories occupied by Israel since June 1967, showing half of Jerusalem as occupied[18]; and the map showing the proliferation of Israeli settlements throughout the occupied territories.[19]

The photographs, in the slick and larger-sized 1994 edition, are missing too; maybe it was only financial considerations that led to the decision to drop the maps. But maybe not. With the UN kept so starkly out of the political loop on the question of Palestine, in contrast to U.S.-orchestrated UN activism in so many other conflicts, and with the charges of U.S. double standards hovering over the issue, the political symbolism of missing maps is impossible to ignore.

Notes

1. Ambassador Nasser al-Kidwe, speech to annual symposium of North American Coordinating Committee of NGOs on the Question of Palestine, Toronto, June 1994.

2. Interview, October 9, 1990.

3. Paul Lewis, "U.S. Backs UN Bid Criticizing Israel," *New York Times*, December 17, 1990.

4. *Maariv*, Israel, August 4, 1991, Draft U.S.-Israeli Memorandum of Understanding of 2 August 1991, reprinted in "Documents and Source Material," *Journal of Palestine Studies* #81, Autumn 1991, p. 182.

5. *Jerusalem Post*, October 16, 1991, reprinted in "Documents and Source Material," *Journal of Palestine Studies* #83, Spring 1992, p. 114.

6. Lee H. Hamilton, "Peacekeeping That Works," *Christian Science Monitor*, June 30, 1994.

7. Ambassador Gad Yaacobi, statement on Commemoration of 50th Anniversary of the UN, November 9, 1994.

8. Ambassador Madeleine Albright, letter to president of General Assembly, August 8, 1994.

9. Ambassador Nasser al-Kidwe, letter to Madeleine Albright, September 13, 1994.

10. Interview with Ambassador al-Kidwe, January 25, 1995.

11. Ambassador Nasser al-Kidwe, Security Council speech, May 12, 1995.

12. Ambassador Gad Yaacobi, Security Council speech, May 12, 1995.

13. Tom Gnehm, U.S. representative, Security Council speech, May 12, 1995.

14. U.S. Letter of Assurance to Israel, *Jerusalem Post*, October 16, 1991.

15. Ambassador al-Kidwe, letter to Madeleine Albright.

16. "The UN and the Question of Palestine," DPI/1481- 94-93324, October 1994, published by UN Department of Public Information.

17. "The United Nations and the Question of Palestine," DPI/861-41360, November 1985, published by UN Department of Public Information, p. 8.

18. Ibid., p. 17.

19. Ibid., p. 25.

10

Democratizing the UN

In many ways the conclusion of this book is contained in its title. There can be little doubt that at all levels the U.S. dominates, and when it chooses to exercise its power controls, the workings, the actions and inactions, the successes and the failures of the United Nations. Despite that reality, however, at the end of the day we have little choice but to defend the UN — there is nothing else that holds even the possibility of representing the broad diversity of the world's nations.

But that assertion alone is inadequate. "Defending the UN" must itself be redefined to mean defending the organization *against* its most powerful member, the commanding force within it. Defense of the UN means opposing much of what the UN is today. It means defending UN democracy, defending whatever voice can speak for the disenfranchised global South, defending the use of UN resources in the interests of the weakest of nations and the poorest of peoples — and yes, opposing the U.S. claim that "when the United States leads, the United Nations will follow. When it suits our interest to do so, we will do so. When it does not suit our interests, we will not."[1]

In 1995, 50 years after the UN's founding, that statement remains true. Reform of the UN, if serious, must result in overturning that reality and defending the internationalist integrity of the global organization. As the UN celebrated its fiftieth year, a process of public rethinking and reassessment of the organization's goals, functions, successes, and failures spread across the globe.

In the U.S., much of the public rethinking in the media and the various academic and policy-oriented journals was limited to various levels of criticism and blame for the variety of what were called the "UN's failures" around the world. Some focused on financial mismanagement or inefficiency in relief activities, on charges of corruption or

233

the ever-popular "bloated bureaucracy" argument. Other than the last, most of those problems are real, and deserving of serious considera-tion. The problem is, they're not the fundamental problems facing the UN, and solving them will not, ultimately, answer the key question of what role the UN should be playing in a uni-polar post-Cold War world.

That key UN problem, so consistently missing from those pages of print and flashes of sound-bite analysis, is the question of power. Vir-tually no one has been prepared to state directly that the UN does what it does, that it succeeds in vaccinating children or fails in bringing peace to Somalia, because the U.S. and its allies, the wealthy and pow-erful of the UN, want it that way.

Among the American people as a whole, attention paid to the fifti-eth anniversary of the UN reflected the usual level of attention paid to the global organization: that is, it wasn't on top of anyone's agenda. The UN at fifty remained a convenient scapegoat in Bosnia for those who follow the headlines, its headquarters continued to be popular with tourists, perhaps its children's fund was still a source of holiday cards for the more socially conscious. Beyond that, few were interested.

Efforts by powerful UN-bashers in Washington largely failed, it should be noted, to win a majority of Americans to active opposition to the UN (black helicopter sightings aside). Polls consistently showed support for the UN at levels far above those shown for most U.S. gov-ernment institutions. But still, it was a passive expression of support, articulated only in the context of answering a survey question. The constituency of UN activism remained dormant.

But in one respect Americans' view of the UN had unalterably changed. The rethinking of the organization, as short-lived as it may have been, emerged in the political context of the Gulf War. And what-ever those Americans might think about the UN, Desert Storm, the "UN's war," was usually wrapped up somewhere in their memory.

The result has been a newly popular set of assumptions regarding the UN's role as an important tool of U.S. foreign policy. At least part of George Bush's decision to seize control of the UN to legitimize De-sert Storm was based on his effort to recast the UN's identity as an in-strument of Washington's will. And to that extent, at least, George Bush succeeded.

A contradiction, however, is built into the transformation: to maxi-mize the value of the UN as a legitimating agent for its own unilateral actions, Washington must protect at least the appearance of the UN's own credibility. But the U.S. is now the only superpower, unassailably the most powerful member state of the organization. It can't "use" the

UN with impunity and expect it to maintain its legitimacy as a multilateral organization.

A conference in Washington in early 1994 held a debate on the question of "should we strengthen the United Nations to strengthen U.S. national security." The title itself provided a clear example of the distortion of power in the global organization. The United States was left after the Gulf War as the uncontested superpower, a superpower without a sparring partner. Unlike the countries of the global South, the U.S. does not need the United Nations to worry about its national security. There is no other country in the world today that could ask the question "should we strengthen the United Nations as a means of strengthening our own national security," and know that it is possible to use the United Nations to do just that. Only the United States has that capacity.

If we start from the vantage point of strengthening U.S. security as the key UN goal, or even as the key reason for Americans to support the UN, we have already lost the battle for UN democracy.

If the UN is to be taken seriously as an organization dedicated to the protection of all countries, large and small, it cannot be judged a success by the standard of strengthening U.S. foreign policy. Rather, the United Nations should be strengthened precisely to provide some level of international balance in this extraordinarily unbalanced and asymmetrical world that we are living in.

So far, that has not been the case. So far, in the years that began with the forced Security Council endorsement of the U.S. war in the Gulf, the reality has been very different. That reality shows that the U.S., when it chooses to invest the requisite political and/or financial capital, can and does call the shots in United Nations decision-making. Washington brings to bear an overwhelming, but not absolute, level of control of the United Nations. It can't control all decisions, all the time, because the political costs and financial investment aren't always practical in the trenches of U.S. domestic political considerations.

But if the U.S. can pick and choose when, how often, and how intensely to manipulate the UN's role in the world, the rest of the world has no such choices. There is little question that the large majority of countries of the South, as well as some in the North, would like the UN — a reconfigured UN — to play a large part in the collective defense against Washington's effort to impose a global version of its own neoliberal economic and political system — complete with UN-endorsed spheres of influence. But few diplomats will say so out loud.

The bottom line, once again, is that of power. The U.S. has a wide range of methods for influencing other countries outside the UN framework — the South does not. And the UN, therefore, exists squarely within, not outside of, the power relationships of its member states.

So what is the consequence? And what is the call for progressives and democrats and civil society — most especially U.S. civil society whose government remains the key world power? However flawed the UN of the mid-1990s may be, the U.S. should be pressed to support it, financially and politically — not by reneging on billions in dues, or by dropping out of and destroying agencies that criticize or even diverge from the U.S. position. The call from civil society should be one of championing the global organization — for the stark reason that there is nothing else to provide a multilateral voice for the majority of the world's countries — and sometimes, albeit rarely, of the world's peoples.

A 1995 Ford Foundation/Yale University study recognized that the UN's "members have frequently expressed their disappointment at the Organization's performance, usually with little regard for the fact that it can only be as effective as governments allow it to be. The Organization has deficiencies, but it has too often been a useful scapegoat for the mistakes or failings of Member States, or a fig leaf for their unfulfilled promises or intentions."[2]

But support for the UN cannot be reduced either to cheerleading or dismissing the possibility of any reform because it won't be enough. It is true that none of the reforms that seem conceivable today would lead to real, fundamental democratization of the UN — the organization remains a reflection of a U.S.-dominated uni-polar world in which the South remains voiceless. But some changes are possible, and the most significant among those changes would make a real difference in the UN's capacity to protect the South.

Those serious reforms in the organization must aim at creating a level of international democracy rarely seen in multilateral decision-making. UN democracy means re-empowering the General Assembly, fighting for broader representation in the Security Council and less power for its veto-wielding permanent members. It means demanding that the UN reclaim its right to oversee — and overturn — the decisions of the Bretton Woods organizations, so that global macro-economic policy is not set by the wealthy countries alone.

The U.S., as the UN's most powerful member, should be pressured to redirect its UN resources and attention away from the current militarization of UN programs, to support instead the UN's work in humanitarian and development areas. And UN peacekeeping should be seen in that context: as a pro-active process aimed at identifying potential crises early enough to not only identify but begin to rectify the root causes of instability so often based on economic dislocation and political disempowerment.

This should not be translated, however, to mean an increased pattern of UN endorsement of unilateral military interventions by its major powers. If the U.S. is to storm across the desert, or colonial France is to re-occupy part of Rwanda, or the U.S. is to invade Haiti, whether or not the actions are carried out in the name of "restoring democracy" or "providing hope" they should do so without asking for a UN imprimatur, and inevitable UN collaboration.

There are no magic solutions. But the result of these changes would mean at least the beginning of UN democratization.

UN REFORM

Pressures and counter-pressures at the United Nations oscillate between the often contradictory impulses of democracy and power. The most democratic sectors of the UN, including the General Assembly, in which every nation has one vote regardless of number of nuclear warheads or size of national treasury, have become the least powerful.

But ironically, the movement towards UN reform has not emerged in response to that threat to UN democracy. It has another trajectory altogether. Cynically enough, Washington's Gulf crisis embrace of the UN included an early jump onto the reform bandwagon. For the U.S., the "problems" of the UN in need of reform were those of structural and financial inefficiency and a perceived lack of accountability to the agendas of the U.S. and the other powerful countries. Issues of non-representation of the South in an increasing North-South divide, lack of democracy within UN institutions, and the perennial problem of U.S. refusal to pay its regular and peacekeeping dues on time did not figure into the Bush and later Clinton administrations' concerns.

While the run-up to the UN's fiftieth anniversary launched numerous new initiatives and discussions of what UN reform might look like, Washington largely succeeded in confining the terms of debate to two issues: adding Germany and Japan to the Security Council, and downsizing, "streamlining," and cost-cutting in the Secretariat.

A serious definition of UN reform, one which acknowledges how deep are the changes required to create the kind of UN the world demands, must go far beyond changes in structure: it must remold the vision of what the United Nations is and can be.

Redefining "human security" may begin the right approach to that debate. The 1995 Ford-Yale study discussed how the UN "must pursue the goal of international security in the coming years. In this pursuit, security must be seen as encompassing the political, the economic and the social conditions within which people and nations exist. No state is now an island unto itself, able to provide, in isolation, this broad security for its people."[3]

That means moving out of the narrow definition of "security" as a military question. To provide that broadly-defined kind of security, or at least to be part of the process of providing it, the UN's humanitarian and development programs must be protected from having to compete with peacekeeping agencies for money and resources, both by governments and within the UN Secretariat. The 1994 situation, in which the United Nations spent $3.6 billion on peacekeeping, more than the aggregate sum spent by all countries on all the development projects that year, must be reversed.

During the two years or so culminating in the 1995 fiftieth anniversary celebrations, the issue of Council reform moved higher on the UN's official agenda. The U.S. response was to wage — and at least among the U.S. population largely win — a battle of definitions. UN reform, by Washington's standards, would be defined simply as the addition of Germany and Japan to the Council, accompanied by some variant of financial and managerial rearrangements. The plan was justified in Washington as being appropriate both to reward past and encourage future contributions of Bonn and Tokyo to UN fundraising and peacekeeping.

COUNCIL COMPOSITION

The U.S. has never wavered in its support for adding both Germany and Japan to the Council, and few analysts are willing to admit that Germany and Japan as permanent members will not enhance either the Council's work or UN democracy. In Tokyo and Bonn, decades-old constitutional bans on fielding troops abroad have recently come under attack; Germany's Supreme Court ruled in July 1994 that there is no constitutional ban on its troops participating in peacekeeping or other mobilizations abroad, including direct combat involvement: one year later, German Tornado pilots were preparing for NATO enforcement missions in Bosnia. Few have noted that participation in military peacekeeping has never been a prerequisite for permanent Council membership; the U.S. itself, it should be remembered, only grudgingly sent a tiny contingent to join the UN "tripwire" observer force in Macedonia, preferring, in virtually all other UN operations, to maintain Pentagon command of its own troops.

There were, from other quarters, a variety of proposals submitted to challenge the North-South disparity. While the Group of 77 has yet to agree on a proposed formula for Non-Aligned participation in a reconfigured Council, insuring permanent representation of the South remains indispensable to rebuilding the Council's credibility and protecting UN democracy. It is difficult to formulate exactly how that would best work, since the countries of the South share longstanding national antagonisms as well as regional and global interests. The often-suggested triad of India, Brazil, and Nigeria as permanent members, for example, thought to represent the most powerful countries of the South, has some supporters. But the idea ignores the regional particularities of the South: certainly neither Pakistan nor Argentina, the regional competitors, would accept this formulation, and Nigeria at the moment remains thoroughly destabilized by a repressive military junta. Ultimately the Non-Aligned countries themselves will have to forge a more creative solution than any that have yet been proposed.

South-oriented proposals for Council reform tend to be quite far-reaching. At their broadest, those proposals look towards (1) ending permanent Council membership altogether; (2) adding new permanent members from the South to at least partly balance the North's domination; and (3) ending the veto power. But it is widely understood that any proposal that seriously challenges the power of Washington and its allies would almost inevitably be derailed by the North.

There have been some proposals with somewhat wider support that call for a broader expansion of Council membership. Those ideas have come both from some powerful countries of the South and particularly the more neutral "UN activist" states (fluid combinations of the Scandinavian countries, Australia, New Zealand, Canada, and others). One of the more innovative proposals for dealing with the veto came from the Ford Foundation-Yale University working group (whose members were almost evenly divided between North and South). Their proposal envisions both enlarging the number of permanent (though non-veto) members in the Council, while restricting use of the veto by the Perm Five "only to peacekeeping and enforcement measures .... A change in the use of the veto could be arranged by agreement among the Permanent Members and without Charter amendment, and would be in order even if no alteration is made in the Council's membership."[4] If that proposal was viewed as a first, short-term step towards eventual complete elimination of the veto, it would pose an interesting possibility.

The report falls into the U.S. assumption, however, that criteria for selecting new permanent members of the Council should include "their ability and will to contribute, according to their capabilities, to peacekeeping and enforcement operations," and the panel's optimistic belief that the Perm Five would voluntarily cooperate on an agreement to limit their use of the veto only to enforcement resolutions is naive at best. But yet, implementation of the proposals *would* result in some incremental steps to diminish, however slightly, the power of the U.S. and its allies. And even in the absence of compliance, raising such possibilities helps to document the inequities that currently shape Security Council power.

THE COUNCIL'S MANDATE

Serious UN reform means remaking the entire decision-making process of the organization. Security Council reform means not only changing composition and veto use, but revamping the whole question of what is and is not considered to be in the sole purview of Council jurisdiction. U.S. strategy at the UN, in tandem with its exercise of control within the Security Council, includes increasing the overall power of the Council by claiming virtually all decisions to be within its sole mandate.

That shift significantly undermined the potential power and credibility of the most democratic components of the UN. The General Assembly must reforge the global influence that characterized it during the era of decolonization, in the 1950s and 60s, when the Assembly was the repository of UN power and at least some levels of authority, despite — or perhaps because of — the Cold War paralysis of the Security Council.

The Yale-Ford report's proposition for separate Economic and Social Councils, functioning in those arenas much as the Security Council does but without permanent members or veto rights, may help in broadening involvement in key economic and social strategy questions.

The problem with that commission's proposals, however, comes back to the issue of power. The new Social Council would be "responsible for supervision and integration of all UN agencies and international institutions, programs and offices involved with all social issues, including social development, humanitarian questions, human rights and restoration of states under stress."[5] The operative word here is "supervision," implying, at best, influence. The Economic Council, similarly, "would focus on coordinating monetary, financial and trade policies at the global level, as well as addressing the economic aspects of sustainable development .... "[6] Operative words on the economic front: "coordinating" and "addressing." Later descriptions speak of "receiving periodic reports," "request[ing] special reports," and "invit[ing] representatives to meet with it." The effect, of course, is to leave existing power relations unchanged. Specifically, leaving the IMF/World Bank domination over global economic programs intact and unimpeded means that economic democracy remains off the UN's agenda.

There is also the danger that a plan to create new smaller bodies, however representative, responsible for economic and social issues, would have the effect of undermining the role of a re-empowered General Assembly in the UN system overall.

As the only one-country/one-vote agency in the entire UN system, the Assembly remains the ultimate repository of UN democracy — though not, given the non-binding nature of its resolutions, of UN power. While the U.S. does not have an official veto in the Assembly, its outside-the-UN-walls political and economic stranglehold on most countries, especially of the South, gives it vast clout for imposing its will. With the collapse of the Soviet Union, and the resulting dislocation and broad political and strategic disunity within the South, a strategy for re-empowering the Assembly remains unarticulated. Without such a move, the potential for shifting the UN's center of gravity away from the Council and towards the General Assembly will remain impossible.

FIGHTING THE MILITARIZATION OF THE UN

Crucially, a broad-side challenge in the war of definitions must be waged against the tendency over the last several years to interpret the UN's work solely in terms of peacekeeping, and to define peacekeeping solely in military terms. Those definitions represent a grave threat to the UN's future role, credibility, and success as a peace-supporting organization.

Australia's foreign minister, Gareth Evans, speaking at the September 1993 meeting of the General Assembly, reflected his concern with how even the peaceful language of the UN's militarized peacekeeping threatened to marginalize the non-military aspects of the search for peace. "If we use, as many people still do, the expression 'peacemaking' to describe military enforcement action," he said, "then — simply because this is such an innocuous and constructive sounding expression — there is a danger that we may over time become a little more relaxed than we should be about taking such 'action.' It is much better, I suggest, to confine 'peacemaking' to diplomatic-type activity to resolve conflict; reserving the expression 'peace enforcement' to describe the always dangerous and messy — and what should be last-resort — activity of applying military force."[7]

With the end of the Cold War, a fundamental goal for any UN reform effort must remain transforming the current militarized nature of UN "peacekeeping" responses to the political-economic-social crises emerging within (more than between) countries around the world, and replacing those methods with social and political solutions.

A further problem that must be addressed is the increasing tendency of the Security Council to endorse unilateral operations by individual countries (with or without figleaf "coalitions") rather than initiating UN actions. For example, during the 1994 "July offensive," the Council franchised France's "Operation Turquoise" in Rwanda, credentialed Russian "peacekeepers" in Georgia, and gave the U.S. a green light to invade Haiti.

On one level, this may reflect a longer-range tendency towards lowering the level of direct UN military intervention in crisis zones in the South, thus signaling a relatively positive move away from UN military intervention and back towards peaceful solution-finding. But it is also true that these endorsements serve to give unwarranted international credibility to thoroughly unilateral actions by the U.S. and its allies, while simultaneously eroding the UN's own credibility as a collective voice for the world's people against such unilateral moves.

The ambiguity is a broader reflection of the conflict faced in Bosnia: if the UN abjures direct participation in military enforcement activities, one consequence is the tacit endorsement of other powers' use of military force. Of course the further step of granting official UN authorization for unilateral military events that remain outside any UN accountability erodes UN credibility even more seriously.

A host of questions remain unanswered regarding UN peacekeeping activities. If indeed the UN were the democratic global organization its boosters like to tout, a UN decision, reluctant or not, to use military force to enforce international law or roll back aggression would be understood around the world to reflect a single-standard, humanitarian move — not completely egalitarian, maybe, but certainly reflective of the overwhelming majority of the world's nations.

But the UN is not that democratic organization. In the mid-1990s, and for the foreseeable future, "UN decisions" are those approved by, orchestrated by, and taken in defense of the interests of Washington, with or without its allies. With that reality as a backdrop, it remains uncertain whether there can be any legitimacy to UN decisions at any level that lead to military intervention.

When Washington decides it does not have enough strategic interest to invest fully in the military or political requirements of a multilateral response to a regional crisis, as in Bosnia, strategic paralysis overlaid with a cosmetic fig leaf effort to influence public opinion is likely to result. Will UN reform efforts change the power dynamics at the UN to insure a potential role for the global South as full actor/decision-maker in UN peacekeeping strategy, or will the countries of the South remain only as the objects of those interventions?

How legitimate and/or sufficient are the current criteria for UN decision-making in determining appropriate venues for multilateral intervention, especially in the South? That is, does a particular crisis really represent a "threat to regional or international peace" as specified in the UN Charter, and whose definition of "international peace" obtains? It is interesting that the brutality of the military junta in Haiti threatened "international peace" only in the context of potential refugee flows of Haitians *to the U.S.* But the enormity of refugee floods of Afghans into Pakistan, or between a number of crisis-riven African states whose refugees remain on the "lost continent," on the other hand, don't seem to qualify.

WHOSE AGENDA?

The problem remains that serious UN reform, beyond retooling the structure of the Secretariat or changing the number or duties of the deputy under-secretaries and assistant deputy secretaries, does not seem to be very high on the organization's priority list — especially in those sectors and member states where the power to actually implement changes may be found. One knowledgeable UN staffer, asked about the status of the various reform proposals, replied, "Is that still on anyone's agenda?" Whether those countries that have staked out a political position demanding reform will continue their quest, especially if the U.S. and its allies remain firm on limiting reform to financial restructuring and adding Germany and Japan to the Council, remains uncertain.

For any measures aimed at creating even a modicum of UN democracy, there is a desperate need for increasing the role of civil society. All non-governmental organizations concerned with preserving and expanding the potential of the UN as a repository of internationalism, working to resolve the North-South conflict, or finding some kind of global check on U.S. power run rampant, have a responsibility not only to support the continued existence of the UN, but to fight for and defend the independence, reform, and democratization of the United Nations.

President Clinton himself, ironically enough, recognized the real problem facing the UN in the post-Cold War era. "We must all remember," he told the celebrants of the fiftieth anniversary of the signing of the UN Charter, "that the United Nations is a reflection of the world it represents. Therefore, it will remain far from perfect."[8]

Clinton's vision of an imperfect world is something very different. What remains true is that the world today is "far from perfect" precisely because it remains largely under the thumb of a strategically-unchallenged United States. At the end of the day, that overarching reality shapes, limits, and constrains any effort at reforming global institutions. The UN was first created to enforce, not to contest, that reality. Fifty years later, that much has not changed.

But again, the UN remains all we have. Abandonment of it, whatever its limitations, is still unacceptable. We have to challenge the terms of the debate, so that supporting the UN is not justified from the vantage point of strengthening "our own" U.S. security. The national security of the wealthiest and most strategically powerful country in the world today is not in danger. We don't need the United Nations to protect that power.

But we do need it to at least try to provide some level of internationalism, some level of protection of the South, some level of what the founders claimed they were interested in. That commitment was to end the scourge of war — not to increase the might of the world's sole superpower.

Notes

1. John Bolton, former Under Secretary of State for International Organizations, speech at Global Structures Convocation, Washington D.C., February 1994.

2. Independent Working Group on the Future of the United Nations, "The Challenges to Humanity at Century's End," *The United Nations in Its Second Half-Century* (New York: Ford Foundation, 1995), p. 5.

3. Ibid., p. 4.

4. Ibid., p. 16.

5. Ibid., p. 27.

6. Ibid.. p. 27.

7. Foreign Minister Gareth Evans, address to 48th General Assembly, United Nations, September 27, 1993.

8. President Bill Clinton, UN 50th anniversary celebration, San Francisco, California, June 25, 1995.

11

The Laws of Empire and the UN's New Internationalism

Throughout the 1990s, U.S. relations with the United Nations remained emblematic of the changing nature of Washington's post-Cold War foreign policy. However cynically the UN was used, despite the bribes, threats and punishments needed to enforce the UN's false "consensus" legitimating Washington's Gulf War, the 1990–1991 period saw the U.S. projecting the UN as a necessary, if subservient, partner. But throughout the decade, the significance, symbolic as well as real, of the UN in U.S. policymaking dramatically declined. At the decade's mid-point, then-Ambassador to the UN Madeleine Albright declared frankly that "the UN is a tool of American foreign policy."[1] By the end of the decade, when the festering Kosovo crisis loomed, Washington openly bypassed the UN altogether, anointing NATO instead as simultaneous legitimator and implementor of war against Yugoslavia.

The "assertive multilateralism" of the Clinton administration's early years was gone. Beginning with the spring 1999 Kosovo crisis, and peaking with the U.S. Senate rejection of the Comprehensive Test Ban Treaty (CTBT) later that year, the new mood in Washington was extensively analyzed, but consistently misinterpreted. Following the CTBT's defeat in October 1999, the perceived wisdom was that the "new isolationism" in the right-wing of the Republican Party had won the day.

The perceived wisdom, however, was wrong. The right-wing congressional opposition was not retreating from global involvement. Real "isolationists" would have been busy removing nuclear warheads from bases scattered across the world, withdrawing far-flung troops from international deployments and restationing them on the U.S. borders—not just rejecting a particular arms control treaty. They would be pulling back corporate interests from the U.S.-centered trade webs criss-crossing the globe—not simply trying to limit U.S. contributions to the International Monetary Fund.

It was not isolationism, but a thoroughly interventionist unilateralism that was the driving force behind the CTBT's defeat.

Interventionism itself remained a unifying point between the Republicans in the Congress—hard-core rightists and the "moderate" center-right alike—and the centrist "Third Way" Democrats in the White House. It was clear that the Clinton administration had paid little attention to mobilizing support for CTBT ratification, either in Congress or among the American public as a whole. The same was true for the longstanding U.S. debt to the UN—Clinton claimed to want to repay the back dues, but did little in Congress and virtually nothing at the bully pulpit level of his presidency to move the public towards making that possible.

Washington's unpaid UN dues remained a foreign policy irritant. The impact on the UN was devastating, but the severity of the arrears-driven UN crisis was taken far less seriously in Washington than in other capitals, and was largely unknown by the American people. Instead, it was the CTBT's ignominious defeat in the Senate that signaled the degree to which multilateralism itself—and including especially the United Nations as the ultimate symbol of multilateralism—had become the fall guy in Washington's newest blame game.

Given the rapid rise of unilateralist sentiment among some of Washington's most powerful, the scapegoating of the UN was eminently predictable.

Only a few weeks after NATO's spring 1999 bombing campaign, U.S. officials were already blaming the United Nations for their own and their allies' failure to restore anything resembling peace in Kosovo and the rest of Yugoslavia. The Kosovo crisis had not been unforeseen or sudden. Rather, its escalation had been tacitly predicted during the late 1995 U.S.-brokered negotiations in Dayton, Ohio for the agreement that imposed an uneasy cease-fire in most of Bosnia. Tensions had already been escalating in the Serbian province of Kosovo, where the 90 percent ethnic Albanian Kosovars faced increasing repression and the rescinding of their longstanding cultural and regional autonomy by the Milosevic-led government in Belgrade. Richard Holbrooke, then the U.S. special envoy to the Balkans and later to become U.S. ambassador to the UN, orchestrated negotiations involving the Bosnian parties as well as Milosevic. One condition of the fragile Bosnia settlement was that the "Kosovo question" was left unaddressed.

Kosovo

In early 1998 tensions mounted in the province. Repression by the Serbian government increased and Albanian Kosovars were increasingly disenfranchised from political and economic power. A longstanding non-violent nationalist movement, which had given rise to a semi-clandestine "parallel government" for the Kosovars was largely marginalized by the rapid rise of the Kosovo Liberation Army, an underground militant movement that soon began attacks on police officers and other Serbian targets. The Serb government response was brutal and largely undifferentiated—the Kosovar population as a whole was targeted for retaliation. Expulsions, attacks, and killing of Kosovar civilians increased.

By the middle of 1998 the situation was widely known in the U.S. and elsewhere. The U.S. and its European allies ensured that the UN remained largely silent, but in July the Organization for Security and Cooperation in Europe (OSCE) agreed to send unarmed observers into Kosovo. They documented the deteriorating humanitarian situation, and in some instances provided an important buffer, but the OSCE's mandate was limited, and the observers could do little to protect the population of the province, still a legal part of what remained of the truncated Yugoslav Federation (now only Serbia and Montenegro). Media reports describing "a new spate of ethnic killing by Serbs" indicated that "the irregular fighting in Kosovo comes just as the international community has begun to press for a cease-fire."[2] But a Kosovo cease-fire was not really on the agenda. The U.S. and its allies did not allow the OSCE to expand its mandate to include armed protection of civilians, and did not allow the UN to consider more serious efforts at preventive diplomacy.

The repression continued, and the "CNN Factor" came into play. Scenes of desperate refugees fleeing burning homes and villages, horrifying reports of brutal attacks and even murder, filled the television screens of the U.S. and western Europe. And those fleeing refugees were white and European. It was too close to home. But still the U.S. and Europe refused to move to protect the refugees or the rest of Kosovo's embattled civilian population. Numerous possibilities were proposed. One idea was to expand the OSCE's mission to include armed protection of civilians. The UN Charter speaks of looking first for regional solutions to regional problems, and certainly the OSCE, which includes eastern Europe and Russia as well as the western European powers, was a far better example of a regional diplomatic actor than the U.S.-dominated NATO military alliance. Other ideas included imposing an interim UN Trusteeship Council mandate over the province, or creating a UN Preventive Diplomacy team for Kosovo. All these ideas and others were proposed by outside analysts. Some were whispered by a few government officials, but none were considered seriously by those in power.

The UN was kept completely out of the loop. What might a broader UN role have looked like? Under the precedent set by the Korean War-era Uniting for Peace resolution, the General Assembly can, when the Council is judged to be deadlocked or otherwise unable to work, meet in special session to make decisions regarding war and peace, issues generally left to the providence of the Council. Once the NATO attacks had actually begun the Russians proposed just such an Assembly meeting. Its first task at that time would have been to call for a halt both to NATO's bombing and the Serb expulsions, release of all detainees, and massive refugee assistance.

Further, the Assembly could have not only called for a resumption of serious multilateral diplomacy, but might, as the most democratic part of the UN, have chosen its own representatives to carry out such negotiations on behalf of the international community. Such an effort might have been delegated, for example, to Nelson Mandela and Kofi Annan, two African statesmen without personal or national vested interests in the regional conflict—a diplomatic "dream team" combining the international institutional legitimacy of the UN with the unsurpassed global credibility of the South African leader.

But that was not to be. Serious diplomacy—by UN dream teams or others—was not on the U.S. agenda. Why? U.S. goals in Kosovo were far broader and more strategic than the protection of Kosovar civilians. They included the assertion of U.S. indispensability and indeed domination within Europe's "security" framework. Since U.S. power vis-à-vis Europe is strongest in the military realm, that goal would be achievable largely through militarizing the "solutions" chosen for essentially political security problems. It would also mean asserting the primacy of NATO, in which U.S. military might remains indisputably preeminent. NATO was to be the global enforcer, authorized simultaneously to implement international interventions and grant them credibility. The effect would be to replace the singular legitimacy of the UN with a new, broader role for NATO as the Cold War's paramount military alliance moved into its second fifty years.

The threat remained, as president of the Cuban parliament and Havana's former Ambassador to the UN Ricardo Alarcon described it, that "after the Balkan war, the rubble of the United Nations will be among the debris that will have to be swept up."[3]

By the autumn of 1998 the security situation in Kosovo had further deteriorated. Stories continued to pour out of Kosovo about Serb government terror against civilians. While some casualty figures were exaggerated, there was little doubt that human rights—political and economic—and overall conditions of life in Kosovo were in a dangerously precarious state.

When the CNN factor became irresistible and events threatened to spill over into other parts of the already-unstable region, the Clinton administration finally moved. While a militarized response would be favorable for U.S. goals in Europe, a political response was a necessary preparatory step. The U.S. organized a diplomatic process bringing Milosevic's government and the Albanian Kosovars together. After a failed meeting in Paris in late autumn, a new round of talks was convened in Rambouillet, France in early 1999. But the U.S.-brokered "negotiations" were hardly an example of serious give-and-take, diplomatic exchanges, and a shared commitment to ending hostilities and a just and peaceful future. Keeping its strategic European goals in mind, the U.S. viewed the Rambouillet talks as an opportunity to ensure Serbia's rejection of Washington's predetermined "sign it or face the consequences" settlement. The talks would thus provide a pretext for Washington's preference for a military, rather than diplomatic, solution.

The agreement proposed to the parties at Rambouillet included a number of onerous provisions; neither side, as U.S. diplomats unfailingly claimed, was offered "everything" it wanted. But it was clear that Rambouillet was not about the two sides sharing some pain for a peaceful gain; it was designed to ensure Serb, not Kosovar, rejection. It was designed to provide a justification for war.

The Rambouillet text called for an end to violence and repression in Kosovo, and creation of an international protection force based on NATO. It envisioned a NATO force under NATO command and control, with no UN oversight beyond the Security Council being "invited to pass a resolution under Chapter VII of the Charter endorsing and adopting the arrangements" made by NATO to establish the NATO force. It made NATO responsible for the right of return of all refugees and displaced Kosovars, while claiming to recognize the territorial integrity of Yugoslavia. For the future, it called for interim autonomy in Kosovo, to be followed by a public referendum on independence in three years. The text did not explicitly mention the KLA, but allowed at least 2,500 Serb military personnel to remain in Kosovo during an interim period.

At the economic level, the U.S. proposal would have imposed on Kosovo's largely government-controlled economy, an arrangement in which "the economy of Kosovo shall function in accordance with free market principles" (Article I, Section 1). It demanded privatization of all significant government-owned resources in Kosovo, ensuring that "the Parties agree to reallocate ownership and resources...in the following areas: (a) government-owned assets (including educational institutions, hospitals, natural resources, and production facilities)" (Article II, Section 1).

But even more serious was the military annex to the Rambouillet text. Initially kept secret by U.S. and allied diplomats, the existence of "Appendix B" was first broken by Andreas Zumach in the Berlin daily *die Tageszeitung* on April 6, 1999. It demonstrated just how the Rambouillet process was designed to ensure Yugoslavia's rejection, revealing that the agreement called for what would have amounted to a complete NATO occupation not just of Kosovo, but of all of Yugoslavia. In Washington's proposed text at Rambouillet, NATO personnel were to be granted "free and unrestricted passage *and unimpeded access throughout the Federal Republic of Yugoslavia.*" (Emphasis added.) This was not a negotiation process; this was, by design, a prelude to war.

The Kosovars, under U.S. pressure and with tacit promises of a significant role for the KLA, agreed to sign. But, surprising no one, Milosevic's representatives refused. By March 23rd, NATO bombers were on their way to begin the air assault on Yugoslavia.

The UN had been excluded from the beginning. Suggestions for non-military UN-mandated interventions during the deterioration of conditions in Kosovo during late 1997 and throughout 1998 had gone nowhere. When Washington finally decided some kind of response was necessary, it made clear that NATO was to be the international instrument of choice—not the UN. France proposed a Security Council discussion of the crisis, but the U.S. refused to consider it, insisting on going directly to NATO. And in making such a choice, Washington stood in stark violation of the requirements of the UN Charter.

The Charter is unambiguous that only the UN Security Council is empowered to "determine the existence of any threat to the peace, breach of the peace, or act of aggression and shall make recommendations, or decide what measures shall be taken in accordance with Articles 41 and 42, to maintain or restore international peace and security" (Article 39 of Chapter VII, the so-called "Use of Force" chapter).

In the Kosovo crisis, the Security Council did not discuss or pass a resolution identifying the existence or nature of the threat to peace, let alone "decide what measures shall be taken" before NATO, at Washington's insistence, made its own decision to launch air strikes across Yugoslavia. U.S. diplomats claimed that they bypassed the Council because Russia and perhaps China would have vetoed any use of force against Serbia (by this time of course the use of force was the only choice on the table), and therefore a Council decision should not even be sought. Instead, NATO's North Atlantic Council alone would serve as the decision-making agency.

Ironically enough, it is not at all clear that a Russian and/or Chinese veto would in fact have been exercised to prevent the Council from acting against growing state aggression within Kosovo. With Chechnya and Tibet in mind, certainly both Moscow and Beijing were uneasy about precedents regarding interference in other countries' internal human rights and security crises. But both remained aware that their privileged status as part of the Perm Five club of veto-wielding states, ensured dependable self-protection against future unwanted UN involvements. Russia's economic crisis at the end of the 1990s, and its fundamental dependence on western, and especially U.S., good will in ensuring its economic survival, provided a strong incentive against going "head to head" with Washington over Kosovo. In the months preceding the NATO military actions, including the Rambouillet negotiations, Moscow was not yet certain of its access to a highly-coveted new IMF loan, and so the claim of an "inevitable" veto by Russia in the Security Council was at least premature, and was in fact a highly unlikely proposition. China, too, was far more concerned with its own economic and trade relations with the west and particularly with the U.S., especially with the delicate negotiations underway to orchestrate Beijing's long-sought entry to the World Trade Organization. China might well have abstained in a Council vote, but its economy-focused leadership would been extraordinarily cautious about expending so much political capital to protest military action in a region far from its own zone of influence.

In any case, regardless of the accuracy or legal sufficiency of the claimed threat of a Russian and/or Chinese veto, at the end of the day the Council was not allowed to take up the Kosovo issue. In that circumstance, the General Assembly could have legitimately placed the item on its own agenda. In dividing up functions between the Council and the General Assembly, Article 12 of the Charter states that "While the Security Council is exercising in respect of any dispute or situations the functions assigned to it in the present Charter [including issues of peace and security], the General Assembly shall not make any recommendation with regard to that dispute or situation unless the Security Council so requests." But in the Kosovo crisis, the Council was *not* exercising its authority on the issue, and therefore the Assembly was free to act.

Certainly a pre-airstrike referral to the Assembly might have allowed for responses no longer viable once military attacks had begun. But even during the military action an Assembly resolution might have included a call for an end to NATO bombing; an internationally-unified call on the Yugoslav authorities to stop the expulsions, destruction and killing in Kosovo; creation of a joint UN-OSCE armed protection force to create and hold corridors and safe havens throughout Kosovo to enable the safe return of refugees; assertion of the primacy of the UN High Commissioner for Refugees as the highest authority to coordinate international response to the refugee crisis rather than NATO maintaining authority; authorization of the all-but-defunct UN Trusteeship Council to create an oversight mechanism to secure governance within Kosovo as an intermediate position between independence and full control by the Serbian government. But none of that happened. Instead of bolstering the OSCE monitors' numbers and capacity, for example, the U.S. and its allies withdrew the monitors altogether forty-eight hours before the bombing began.

In April, as the withering NATO bombing campaign continued across Yugoslavia, the European Union issued its own proposal for a temporary European administration of Kosovo if Serbia withdrew its forces and allowed refugees to return. Germany floated a separate proposal calling for Kosovo to be placed under a UN administration. While neither proposal held much chance of success, they were linked to growing European calls for greater roles in the Kosovo crisis for Europe itself, for Russia, and significantly, for the United Nations.

But the bombing continued, disregarding the Geneva Conventions and other international requirements of "proportionality" of military attacks, avoiding civilian targets and protecting civilians. Roads, bridges, and electrical generating plants were destroyed. Market shoppers, trains, even a convoy of Kosovar refugees and, infamously, the Chinese embassy in Belgrade all were hit by NATO bombers. The attacks were matched by the immediate escalation in Serb government and militia attacks on Kosovar civilians under cover of the NATO strikes. As the bombs fell, the refugee stream of displaced Kosovars turned into a raging river of humanity; the two thousands or so murdered in the conflict throughout 1998 expanded; the number of villages razed to the ground grew exponentially. NATO had not started the ethnic cleansing campaign in Kosovo—but the NATO bombing campaign fueled its intensity and accelerated its pace.

In May, while the bombing continued, Milosevic was indicted for war crimes and crimes against humanity by the International Criminal Tribunal for the Former Yugoslavia, the first sitting head of state to face such charges. The allegations were limited to his responsibility for actions in Kosovo; the U.S. and its allies continued to withhold from the Tribunal the vast array of intelligence material in their possession that could be used to prove Milosevic's role in the chain of command for earlier, far larger scale, atrocities outside Serbia's borders in Bosnia and Croatia. And no serious effort was made at effecting the arrest of Milosevic. Like Radovan Karadzic and Ratko Mladic, the political and military leaders of the Bosnian Serbs who continued living openly in and around Pale and later in Serbia for years after their indictments, Milosevic remained at large.

In the middle of NATO's bombing campaign, the Alliance held a birthday party. NATO turned fifty, and the long-planned summit celebration in Washington was transformed from a lively party to the somber, martial affair deemed appropriate to a military bloc at war for the first time.

But if a few of the more festive concerts and fireworks displays were canceled, the streets of Washington were still shut down for the limousine-choked occasion, and the substantive theme of the mid-April summit remained unchanged. That was the approval of a new "strategic concept" for what was created to be the Cold War's military alliance. Recognizing that its original raison d'être, facing down its Warsaw Pact counterpart, had disappeared with the collapse of the Soviet Union and the end of the Cold War, NATO reformulated a new set of justifications for its continued existence, its continued centrality in intra-European and U.S.-European relations, and its continuity of arms production, acquisition and expansion in the name of "inter-operability."

NATO's new Strategic Concept paid lip service to the fact that "the United Nations Security Council has the primary responsibility for the maintenance of international peace and security." But that claim was far outweighed by a new emphasis on "out of area" operations. The new strategic concept paper noted that *beyond* "any armed attack on the territory of the Allies," NATO's traditional rationale, "Alliance security must also take account of the global context. Alliance security interests can be affected by other risks of a wider nature...." What does that mean? According to Article 52, it means deploying NATO troops "to conduct crisis response operations, sometimes at short notice, distant from their home stations, including beyond the Allies' territory." Article 53e calls on NATO countries to make troops available ready "to sustain prolonged operations, whether within *or beyond* Alliance territory." And Articles 56 and 59 take for granted that "NATO forces may be called upon to operate beyond NATO's borders"; the only significant caution is the "special logistical challenges" such deployment might require.

What it does not seem to mean is that the UN's "primary responsibility" for peace and security might mean that only the UN is legally empowered to authorize the use of force.

If the original NATO goals for Europe were to keep the Americans in, the Germans down, and the Russians out, perhaps the 1999–2000 version could be summarized as keeping the Germans in, the Russians still out, and the Americans on top. The problem, of course, was that the new strategic concept, like the process of NATO expansion it paralleled, was guaranteed to antagonize Russia and simultaneously to create new fault lines not only within Europe but between Europe and other parts of the world.

It should not have been a surprise when Russia's newly revised military guidelines, released only months later in January 2000, announced broader scenarios for the possible use of nuclear weapons, referred to NATO's new strategic doctrine as part of the rationale for the dangerous change. Moscow's Concept on National Security noted specifically that NATO's self-declared right to take military action outside of its own territory and without UN approval "is fraught with the threat of destabilization of the whole strategic situation in the world."[4] And, perhaps most ominously, NATO's much-heralded new Strategic Concept set the stage for a U.S. campaign to replace UN primacy with the easier-to-achieve unanimity of NATO in order to provide a multilateral imprimatur for essentially unilateral acts of international intervention.

After the bombing of Yugoslavia had continued for some weeks, it became clear that Washington and other analysts were wrong in assessing that Milosevic would collapse after just a few days of airstrikes. Public opposition to the bombing in the U.S. and even more in Europe was increasing as well, and efforts escalated to find a diplomatic way out. With the Rambouillet charade over, terms for a new NATO-Yugoslavia agreement were still being set by the U.S. and its NATO allies, but a broader diplomatic team was required. Washington tacitly acknowledged that the U.S. and NATO alone could not negotiate their way out of the political mess their bombing had created. They needed the UN on board. So with the UN finally allowed into the game, initially behind the scenes, a new international team was fielded, negotiating officially on behalf of the European Union and Russia. They were represented by Finnish President Martti Ahtisaari and Moscow's special envoy Victor Chernomyrdin. Their settlement would be finalized in the form of a UN Security Council resolution.

The June 3rd Ahtisaari-Chernomyrdin agreement with Yugoslavia included many of the same provisions as the failed Rambouillet text. But the new agreement eliminated those parts of Rambouillet that had been clearly designed to ensure Rambouillet's failure. The final agreement placed the international peacekeeping force "under UN auspices" to act "according to Chapter VII of the UN Charter," rather than solely under NATO's control; the force would be deployed only within Kosovo rather than throughout all of Yugoslavia, and the interim administration of Kosovo and guarantee of the refugees' return would be in the hands of the UN, not NATO (although the UN was provided with precious few resources for this monumental task). Those nuanced differences, in the context of an overall similar result (including deployment of an international force, international authority over refugee return, etc.) demonstrated the fundamental disinguousness of the Rambouillet process. The Serb parliament itself, in rejecting the Rambouillet terms, had stated that it was prepared to accept a UN-controlled peacekeeping force in Kosovo.

So the fundamental similarities between the Rambouillet proposals and the final agreement make clear that if the earlier U.S. diplomatic process had been serious, an internationally acceptable agreement might have been achievable months before, *without the devastation of Yugoslavia and the escalation of the anti-Albanian "ethnic cleansing" in Kosovo wrought by NATO's bombing campaign.* If essentially the same agreement *could* have been achieved without the war, the illegality and immorality of NATO's military assault become even more clear.

Only after the months of NATO bombing had failed to stop the ethnic cleansing and expulsions in Kosovo, and instead had devastated Yugoslavia and shored up support for Milosevic, did Washington grudgingly allow a role for the once-excluded UN. The U.S. strategy was to reject UN decisionmaking, deny the UN adequate resources, personnel, and authority, and then set it up to take the blame for the messy and violent aftermath of the U.S.-NATO war.

Chairman of the U.S. Joint Chiefs of Staff Gen. Henry Shelton, and Secretary of Defense William Cohen, testifying before the Senate Armed Services Committee only weeks after the war, sharply condemned the United Nations. "We need to put as much pressure as possible on the UN to do more," threatened Cohen. The Committee's chair, Senator John W. Warner, berated the UN because it "moves very slowly to assume its responsibilities."[5]

The U.S. officials bemoaned the fact that at that time, only 150 police officers were on the ground in Kosovo out of the 3,110 member force mandated by the UN.[6] One could almost see the shaking heads of disapproval at "the UN's" failure. But the real problem was that the entire international volunteer force of more than 3,000 had to be individually recruited and sent to Kosovo by separate governments around the world. Why? Because the U.S. had long prevented the creation of a standing UN rapid reaction or international police force that could, under the direction of the Secretary General, be deployed swiftly and pro-actively to crisis zones.

The Clinton administration reasserted its refusal to help rebuild Serbia's bomb-devastated infrastructure so long as Milosevic remained in power, and it pressured other NATO members to do the same. Albright said Washington would only provide humanitarian aid, and diplomats quoted her as saying that aid was limited to food and medicine. The secretary-general, perhaps mindful of the results of a similar U.S.-driven policy in Iraq under sanctions, responded that humanitarian needs should be defined as broadly as possible, including repair of the electrical and water systems badly damaged during NATO's 11-week bombing campaign. "It is pointless to take in loads and loads of medicine if people are going to drink dirty water and fall sick," Annan said.[7]

But U.S. sluggishness in funding reconstruction efforts did not apply to politically popular immediate refugee assistance. And even the serious disparity between aid to Albanian Kosovars and reconstruction of the rest of NATO-battered Serbia, paled before the chasm that divided the refugee aid available to the Balkans and that obtainable for the far more numerous African refugees. Within weeks of the end of the NATO war in Yugoslavia, the outpouring of aid to Albanian Kosovars "stunned humanitarian groups which continuously fight for dollars for refugees in Africa." Some of the distinctions in refugee care were based on aid agencies' assessments of the differing requirements to maintain what aid officials call the refugees' sense of dignity—so maybe the cost of each day's 2,100 calories of chicken pate, fresh oranges, milk, cheese and fruit tarts available in many Balkan camps was not directly responsible for the decision to provide Somali and Eritrean refugees with that same number of calories worth of uncooked wheat or sorghum.[8]

Maybe. But the basic discrepancy, in such things as the ratio of one doctor per 100,000 refugees in Africa against the one doctor per 700 in Macedonia (better than in many U.S. inner-city and rural areas), came down to money. In May 1999, the UN's High Commissioner for Refugees was spending about 11 cents a day per refugee in Africa; in the Balkan refugee camps, it was $1.23 per person per day. And money, or lack of it, came down largely to race. According to Andrew Ross, a refugee worker who came from Africa to work in the Balkans in April 1999, the Macedonian camps were "far superior" to those in Africa. "What's the difference? There's white people here."[9]

The victims of the institutional racism that continues to make the U.S. and other wealthy governments so much more generous for white European refugees than for black Africans driven from their homes, are the UN humanitarian and emergency programs, and through them, the refugees themselves. In May 1999 the *Los Angeles Times* reported "the World Food Program has a fundraising goal this year of $98.5 million for the area around Africa's Great Lakes—Rwanda, Burundi, Tanzania, Uganda— where long-simmering, though often ignored conflicts have created hundreds of thousands of refugees. So far, the food agency has received 22 percent of that amount. In Liberia, the situation is even worse. The agency made an appeal for $71.6 million. It received $500,000. That compares with the situation around Kosovo, for which the agency has requested $97.4 million and received more than 70 percent of that amount already, with a 'large number of commitments' now under negotiation."[10]

Back in the Balkans, at the end of the day what remained was the stark reality that the Albanian Kosovars would soon receive millions in reconstruction money, while the rest of the Serbian population got nothing. With ethnic tensions thus exacerbated, the UN's reconstruction tasks remained even more daunting, and Washington's position made the UN's failure more likely. Similar inadequacies soon loomed over the UN's ambitious $1 billion-plus peacekeeping and nation-building effort in the even more devastated East Timor.

EAST TIMOR

The vast destruction of much of East Timor's cities, towns, and villages by Indonesian military and militia forces that followed the August 30, 1999 referendum on independence provided another wrenching example of what happens when UN involvement is allowed only after direct U.S. orchestration has failed. The UN was allowed in only to provide some humanitarian assistance in the aftermath of chaos. But it was hardly the UN's first connection to East Timor.

During Indonesia's 1975 invasion of the territory when Portugal ended its 300-year colonial occupation, 200,000 East Timorese civilians, about one quarter of the population, were killed. From 1976 on, a series of UN resolutions condemned Indonesia's occupation and deemed it illegal; only Australia officially recognized Jakarta's "right" to rule East Timor. The U.S., eager to continue exploiting Indonesia's huge population and emerging economic clout, did not officially acknowledge the occupation but continued close military and political ties with Jakarta, as if Indonesian rule in East Timor were an unchallenged fact of life. In the first years after the invasion, Washington's ambassador to the UN, Daniel Patrick Moynihan, played a major role in keeping a tight rein on the growing international opposition to the occupation. In January 1976 Moynihan sent a secret cable to his boss, then-Secretary of State Henry Kissinger, bragging that "the Department of State desired that the United Nations prove utterly ineffective in whatever measures it undertook [to challenge Indonesia's occupation]. This task was given to me, and I carried it forward with no inconsiderable success."[11]

By the mid-1990s, international public, and eventually some diplomatic, support for East Timorese independence was on the rise. The 1998 Nobel Prize for Peace was awarded to the pro-independence Bishop Carlos Belo and exiled independence leader Jose Ramos-Horta. In mid-1999, after a year of internal instability and the overthrow of the longstanding U.S.-supported dictator Suharto,

Indonesia agreed in UN-brokered negotiations with Portugal to allow a referendum in East Timor to choose between autonomy within Indonesia and independence. The Security Council voted to accept UN responsibility for organizing the elections. Knowledgeable observers inside and outside the UN immediately warned of the serious threat of violence by Indonesian forces following the vote. The UN draft called for disarming the anti-independence militias and confining the military itself to barracks. But Jakarta rejected those terms, and the U.S. did nothing to press its ally.[12] Nor did Washington allow the Security Council's election mandate to include any serious UN protection for the population following the voting itself.

The UN-organized poll was held under international supervision in August 1999. The vote, as expected, was overwhelming, with almost 80 percent of the population supporting independence. And, also as expected, as the international monitors packed to leave, Indonesian militia forces backed by the military itself moved in, and began the slaughter that left the capital city of Dili and much of the rest of East Timor virtually burned to the ground. Many hundreds, perhaps thousands, were killed, and more than three-quarters of the population was driven into hiding in the East Timor hills or across the border into Indonesian West Timor.

Still the U.S. held back, refusing to allow a UN protection force to be sent to stop the Indonesian violence until the government in Jakarta agreed. It hesitated as much as if East Timor was a legitimate province of Indonesia, rather than a territory languishing under a military occupation long deemed illegal by the Security Council itself.

Washington had been Jakarta's key protector, arms provider, and economic sponsor since the bloody U.S.-backed military coup in 1965 overthrew the Sukarno regime and installed Washington loyalist Suharto. Ties between the Pentagon and the Indonesian army remained close, as did Indonesian reliance on U.S. sponsorship for access to IMF and World Bank loans. In the past, Jakarta had been one of the four top recipients of World Bank assistance.[13]

There was never any doubt that U.S. pressure would bring results. It is virtually certain that a serious pre-election warning to Jakarta's military and political leadership, "reminding" them of their reliance on U.S. support, and explicitly linking the future of that support to protection of the East Timorese, could have prevented the onslaught of violence. But that warning never came. Only after the Indonesian military-backed anti-independence militias had savaged East Timor for days, burning, looting, killing, driving hundreds of thousands into terrified exile, did Clinton move—and then, it was with undisguised deference to Jakarta's illegal occupation.

On September 8th, more than a week into the post-election brutality, the *New York Times* front-page headline read "With Other Goals in Indonesia, U.S. Moves Gently on East Timor; Administration Avoiding a Threat of Sanctions." That same day, Clinton's national security adviser Sandy Berger effectively rejected any U.S. responsibility for protecting East Timor's civilians still under assault by Washington's long-time ally, insulting the victims and dismissing the U.S. obligation with an off-handed "you know my daughter has a very messy apartment up in college. Maybe I shouldn't intervene to have that cleaned up."[14]

A full day later, Clinton finally said the Indonesian government "must invite" an international force if it did not end the violence on its own. The IMF suspended its multi-billion dollar loans to Indonesia, and the World Bank implied future new conditionalities on Indonesia's access to funds. But nowhere did Clinton acknowledge that Jakarta's very presence in East Timor was illegitimate. And "the President did not threaten an immediate cutoff of economic assistance to Indonesia, as some lawmakers and human rights groups had wanted. Nor did he cut off commercial arms sales to Indonesia, which are expected to total about $16 million over the next year."[15]

As it would have been months earlier, Clinton's demand for an "invitation" was enough. On September 12th, Suharto's replacement, President B.J. Habibie, bowed to what the *New York Times* called "world opinion" in allowing international peacekeepers into East Timor. The "world," through the United Nations, had long called for ending Indonesia's illegal occupation; the opinion that mattered in this case was that of the U.S.

And that opinion had not been offered early enough. The negotiations leading to Indonesia's agreement to hold the referendum on Timorese independence did not officially include the U.S., but the tripartite talks (Indonesia, Portugal and the UN) were hardly secret. A senior U.S. official claimed the "Clinton administration was appalled that the agreement excluded UN peacekeepers and provided for just 300 civilian police and 50 unarmed UN military liaison officers." But nowhere is there any indication that the Clinton administration made any effort to pressure its client in Jakarta to allow real international protection—the kind of U.S. pressure neither the UN nor Portugal could hope to bring to bear. In fact, as soon as the May 5, 1999 agreement to hold the referendum was signed, the U.S. joined talks with the UN, Britain, Australia, New Zealand, and Japan to plan an international peacekeeping operation to follow the anticipated Indonesian withdrawal. Vice-Chairman of the Joint Chiefs, Gen. Joseph Ralston, reportedly spoke sternly to his Indonesian counterpart Gen. Wiranto.[16] But if the pressure on Indonesia was to work, it had to come publicly, from the president himself, and had to be linked to the possibility of serious consequences. Requesting that the Indonesian general please maintain order obviously was not enough. If the Clinton administration understood the likelihood of Indonesian violence enough to be "appalled" at the exclusion of peacekeepers and to order a top U.S. general to hold talks with his Indonesian counterpart, and was involved enough already to be planning a post-election peacekeeping operation, there is no justification for Washington's failure to have pressed its ultimately compliant ally much earlier—before the devastation of East Timor.

During the first week of October, Secretary-General Kofi Annan outlined an ambitious plan for the UN to take over responsibility for both maintaining security (unlike Kosovo, where NATO kept that role) and creating a civil administration during the rebuilding of East Timor. The plan, approved by the Security Council on October 25th, established the UN Transitional Administration in East Timor (UNTAET) that included a 9,000-strong international peacekeeping force.

UNTAET was anticipated to cost about $1 billion over a two-to-three year period. The U.S., according to longstanding General Assembly decisions regarding the financing of peacekeeping operations, was responsible for 31 percent of the total. But the UN was already stretched thin. The U.S. Congress had unilaterally announced its decision to pay no more than 25 percent of any peacekeeping assessment, despite the existing 31 percent responsibility. And as of October 1999, Washington had still not paid any of the $27.9 million it owed the UN just for the initial start-up costs of the Kosovo mission.[17]

The UN children's agency was particularly critical of Western nations for breaking promises they made to provide humanitarian aid. "They came here to pledge aid to the East Timorese refugees," said UNICEF's Stephen Woodhouse. "They said they would provide aid, but they did not."[18]

THE LAWS OF EMPIRE
The Clinton administration played lip service to supporting the UN.

Once in a while it called for, but consistently failed to mobilize support for, paying long overdue UN dues. Instead, it separated the UN from its operative foreign policy, relying instead largely on the projection of unilateral power. Only rarely did the administration show the "assertive multilateralism" that was briefly the official hallmark of early Clintonian diplomacy; now the partnership was with NATO, its premiere military alliance.

In turning to NATO to approve its air war against Yugoslavia instead of placing the issue before the United Nations, the U.S. explicitly violated the UN Charter's requirement that only the Security Council can authorize the use of force. In refusing to allow the UN to send peacekeepers to Dili until its Indonesian ally reluctantly agreed, Washington followed its longstanding pattern of ignoring UN resolutions deeming Jakarta's occupation of East Timor completely illegal. As in the Kosovo case, in East Timor Washington used the very real human rights atrocities as a cover to win international backing for unilateral decisions *not* based primarily on human rights concerns at all.

In today's world it is clear there may be times when widespread human rights violations, such as those that occurred in East Timor or Kosovo, may indeed necessitate at least the consideration of international intervention within a sovereign state or in a territory illegally occupied by another sovereign state. But only the UN is entitled to make such grave determinations. Fear (exaggerated or real) of a possible veto by other Security Council members does not give the U.S., with or without tag-along Britain, the right to conduct an end run around UN primacy in matters of international peace and security. By acting alone, the U.S. trumpets its contempt for other nations.

So what was going on here? Why was the U.S.—including the once relatively multilateralist Clinton administration—leading the charge to discredit and undermine the UN and international law even further, once NATO's unauthorized war in Yugoslavia was over and the difficult work of rebuilding a shattered East Timor was only beginning?

It's an old story, really. It's the story of a strategically unchallenged dominion, at the apogee of its power and influence, rewriting the global rules for how to manage its empire. Two thousand years ago Thucydides described how Mylos, the island the Greeks conquered to ensure stability for their Empire's golden age, was invaded and occupied according to laws wholly different from those governing democratic (if slavery-dependent) Athens. The Roman empire followed suit, creating one set of laws for Rome's own citizens, imposing another on its far-flung possessions. In the last couple hundred years the sun-never-sets-on-us British empire did much the same thing. And then, at the end of the twentieth century, having achieved once unimaginable heights of military, economic, and political power, it was Washington's turn.

This American-style *fin de 20th siecle* law of empire took the form of the U.S. exempting itself from UN-brokered treaties and other international agreements that it demanded others accept. It was evident in Washington's rejection of the International Criminal Court in 1998, its refusal to sign the 1997 Convention against anti-personnel land mines, its failures on the Convention on the Rights of the Child, the Law of the Sea, the Comprehensive Test Ban Treaty and more. It was also sharply apparent in the dramatic abandonment throughout the decade of Washington's Gulf War-era assertion (however cynical or tactical) of the need for United Nations endorsement to confer legitimacy on fundamentally unilateral interventions.

U.S. Victims in Iraq: Civilians, Disarmament, and the UN

Throughout the second half of the 1990s, Iraq remained the poster child for those unilateral U.S. interventions legitimized only through coerced UN decisions. Overthrowing Saddam Hussein remained the claimed U.S. goal, but "regime change" failed, and Saddam Hussein remained in power, outlasting both George Bush and Bill Clinton. The real victims of Washington's Iraq policy were the civilian population of Iraq, the potential for real disarmament, and ultimately, the United Nations itself.

After the 1991 war, the U.S. had orchestrated a regime of severe economic sanctions to be imposed on Iraq, ostensibly designed to push Baghdad to identify and eliminate its weapons of mass destruction (WMD) programs—chemical, biological, and nuclear weapons and the missiles to deliver them. (See Chapter Two.) The international economic sanctions imposed in the name of the UN were the broadest, most comprehensive, and most tightly implemented sanctions ever created. Throughout the 1990s the U.S. continued its practice of "moving the goalposts," a diplomatic maneuver designed to assert U.S. primacy, and having the effect of undermining the UN's own decisions and legitimacy. Regarding Iraq, this meant periodic announcements by U.S. officials that despite the specific terms set by

UN Resolution 687 for lifting sanctions (eliminating weapons of mass destruction programs), the sanctions would remain in place until some other later point.

In the first weeks after the 1991 war, then-Secretary of State James Baker said "we are not interested in seeking a relaxation of sanctions as long as Saddam Hussein is in power." In early 1997 then-Ambassador Bill Richardson announced that "sanctions may stay on in perpetuity."[19] And in November of that same year President Clinton boasted that economic sanctions would remain in place until "the end of time or as long as he [Saddam Hussein] lasts."[20] The effect, of course, was a kind of negative incentive—it told the Iraqi regime that despite their level of compliance with UN requirements, sanctions would remain in place. So why should they comply at all?

The problem was exacerbated in September 1996. Only a few months after Madeleine Albright's acknowledgment that she viewed the UN as "a tool of American foreign policy," the U.S. responded unilaterally to an Iraqi military move into northern Iraq with a massive bombing campaign of unrelated targets in the south and center of the country. The Iraqi regime's move was aimed at shoring up one of two feuding Kurdish factions and reestablishing its position in the northern "no fly zone" which had become a U.S.-British protectorate. A key Iraqi goal was to eliminate the CIA-sponsored resistance beginning to take shape there; following Baghdad's incursion, over 6,000 Iraqis, most linked to CIA-backed organizations, were evacuated to the U.S.

At that point Washington said it no longer needed new UN resolutions to justify the assaults. The U.S., with British support (France had been involved at the beginning, but had withdrawn its support early on), had established, on their own, the "no fly zones" in northern and southern Iraq. President Clinton claimed that the reason for continual bombing and airstrikes on the zones was that "enforcing the no-fly zone [is what] we're still bound to do under the United Nations resolution."[21] But no such zones, and certainly no such "enforcement," had ever been authorized or even mentioned in any UN resolutions. The U.S.-British bombing of Iraq remained outside UN decisionmaking. The bombings seriously undermined the legal requirement of Security Council consultations included in the final language of each UN resolution on Iraq: "the Security Council remains seized of the issue." In UN diplo-speak, "remains seized" means the issue remains on the agenda of and under the authority of, the Security Council—not the Pentagon or the White House.

In the meantime, economic sanctions continued to wreak havoc on the Iraqi population. With the complete prohibition on the sale of Iraqi oil, the basis for 90 percent of Iraq's foreign exchange, food and medical stocks soon ran perilously low, and the bomb-damaged infrastructure (electrical generation, water and sewage treatment, etc.) deteriorated even further. In 1994–95, discussions began between the UN and Iraq to allow a limited oil sale, with the money to be spent on food, medicine and humanitarian supplies. Baghdad outlined a proposal to implement the idea, but Security Council negotiators, led by the U.S., refused, claiming the mechanism allowed Iraq too much independence. Negotiations continued, and by 1996 plans for an "oil for food" deal were finalized. The first food deliveries began in May/June 1997.

Under the arrangement, Iraq would be allowed to sell a limited amount of oil over six-month periods. The oil money would not be paid to Iraq, but instead would be deposited in a UN-controlled escrow account. Iraq would then contract with suppliers around the world for food, medicine, and other humanitarian goods who would be paid out of the UN account. The problems were legion: every contract had to be approved by the Sanctions Committee, made up of all Security Council countries and with veto power for the five permanent members. Contracts were routinely held up, often on the grounds of "dual use"—where one country, most often the U.S. and occasionally Britain, would decide that some proposed import could be used for potential military, rather than humanitarian purposes. A classic example was that of chlorine. With Iraq's water treatment system destroyed in the 1991 bombing, hundreds of thousands died throughout the decade from water-borne diseases once wiped out in pre-Gulf War and pre-sanctions Iraq. Without functioning treatment plants, massive infusions of chlorine were needed to at least partly purify the water. But the U.S., claiming that chlorine could also be used for military purposes, withheld contracts for chlorine for years. Not until late 1998 were contracts for large-scale purchases of chlorine consistently approved.

But the most important, and intractable, problem was simply the lack of money. Even with the oil-for-food program in place, Baghdad could not produce and export enough oil to adequately feed and care for a population of almost 23 million Iraqis. Its oil producing infrastructure was simply in too bad shape following the 1991 bombing and years of poverty-driven neglect, and under oil-for-food restrictions the investment funds Iraq needed to rebuild the oil equipment were denied. And even the oil-for-food money that did trickle in was not all available to meet Iraq's civilian needs. Thirty percent of oil-for-food funds was deducted immediately off the top to pay reparations, much of it to wealthy Kuwaiti royals and U.S. and other western oil companies, for their losses during Iraq's invasion of Kuwait. The rationed "food basket" distributed to all Iraqis each month from the remaining oil-for-food money was quantitatively and qualitatively inadequate for proper diet and especially for growing children: made up largely of flour, rice, sugar, cooking oil, tea, and some beans or lentils, it lacked vitamins, protein, and most nutritional requirements. Powdered milk was added almost a year into the program, but fruit, vegetables, eggs, meat, chicken, fish—all remained absent.

The UN staff in Baghdad found itself gripped by a fundamental contradiction: humanitarian workers monitoring the oil-for-food program or assisting in pest eradication programs represented the same organization in whose name the crippling economic sanctions were being imposed in the first place. Work in Baghdad was extraordinarily difficult as a result. And the U.S.-led demonization of Saddam Hussein and, by extension, all Iraqis, affected even some in the UN secretariat.

Dr. Anupama Rao Singh, UNICEF's director in Iraq, described two serious problems. A physician with 30 years of UNICEF field experience, she told a group of congressional staff aides in 1999 of the distrust by some in the international community in what UN agencies and staff based in Baghdad say. She described spending about 20 percent of her time demonstrating UNICEF's objectivity to those in headquarters and various capitals. "This is time that should be spent on substantive work, not proving my case," she said, "and this is a new problem, one I never faced before in any other post."[22] It remained an unresolved problem.

The inability of the oil-for-food program to solve the human crisis in Iraq quickly became clear to its first director. Assistant Secretary General Denis Halliday, an Irishman with more than 30 years UN experience, went to Baghdad in August 1997 at Kofi Annan's request to become the UN Humanitarian Coordinator in Iraq. He made a number of efforts to improve the oil-for-food program, but soon realized that, limited by its Security Council-imposed goal of stabilizing rather than improving the humanitarian disaster, the program would never provide enough. The numbers of vulnerable people dying—especially children and the elderly—might remain constant rather than increasing; the shredding of Iraq's social fabric might continue at the same rather than a faster pace. But the sanctions imposed in the name of the United Nations would continue to ravage 23 million Iraqis.

Just over a year after arriving in Baghdad, Denis Halliday quit his position in Iraq and resigned from the United Nations in order to raise more comprehensively his critique of the economic sanctions. As an international civil servant, Halliday recognized the limits beyond which he could not raise serious criticisms of the Council's sanctions policy and of the member states, especially the U.S. and Britain, responsible for it. His became an internationally high-profile resignation. Immediately after he quit, Halliday flew directly to Washington to testify in Congress about the impact of the U.S. sanctions policy on Iraqi civilians, and then began working full-time travelling, speaking and organizing across the United States, throughout Europe and elsewhere against the economic sanctions. From 1997 on, scaffolded by wide-scale public opposition to the escalating U.S. bombing of Iraq, a newly visible anti-sanctions movement emerged across the U.S., Europe and elsewhere in the world.

In 1998 a crisis resulted from the public admission that UNSCOM, the UN's special commission charged with finding and eliminating Iraq's weapons of mass destruction, was riddled with operatives working without UN approval on behalf of U.S. and Israeli intelligence agencies. UNSCOM had been carrying out a policy of invasive inspections, attempting entry to locations Baghdad deemed the most privileged "presidential sites." Iraq continued trying to obstruct the inspectors' access. Despite those efforts, UNSCOM had, by the mid- to late 1990s, found and eliminated the overwhelming majority of Iraq's prohibited weapons systems. In early 1998, UNSCOM chief Richard Butler said that his team was satisfied there was no longer any nuclear or long-range missile capability in Iraq, and that UNSCOM was "very close" to completing the chemical and biological phases.[23]

The partial stand-off continued throughout 1998, with Iraq attempting to claim at least a symbolic defense to the tattered remains of its sovereignty, and UNSCOM determined to bring every square inch of the country under its looking glass. Tensions rose, and U.S. threats to resume full-scale war increased. In March, Kofi Annan went to Baghdad and negotiated a new agreement with Baghdad on UNSCOM inspections with special arrangements for the contested "presidential sites." It came out later that at the same time Annan was negotiating in Baghdad, UNSCOM inspectors were installing what the *New York Times* called "an American eavesdropping system so secret that only a handful of Americans, British, Australians and New Zealanders had full access to it. This, understandably, led to tensions, notably between the Americans on one side and the Russians, the Chinese and the French on the other."[24]

Only that summer did the story surface of this latest example of U.S. disrespect for the UN. Information emerged in the press that UNSCOM had been sharing, with Washington and Tel Aviv, intelligence material including the whereabouts of Saddam Hussein and his Republican Guards, aimed not at eliminating Iraq's prohibited weapons but at overthrowing the Iraqi government. Such unilateral appropriation and unauthorized use of UNSCOM material, of course, violated UNSCOM's own mandate and UN resolutions, none of which permitted efforts to crush any government or assassinate any leader, however unpopular or undemocratic. The equivalent would have been if UN teams, legally and openly inspecting American nuclear sites under international agreements, secretly wiretapped classified communications among Secret Service agents responsible for the President's safety, and provided that information to a country publicly committed to overthrowing the U.S. government. Further, the inspectors, supposedly accountable to the Security Council as a whole, provided information that clearly helped Washington refine the target planning for its continuing unilateral air strikes. In so doing, UNSCOM and its U.S. backers undermined the legitimacy and credibility of the United Nations itself.

When Annan returned from Baghdad after negotiating a stand-down to the February crisis and the threat of renewed U.S. bombing, the Security Council met to sign off on the new UN-Iraq agreement. U.S. Ambassador Bill Richardson demanded that the resolution call for "severest consequences" if Iraq should violate the agreement in the future; under pressure, the Council agreed.

But there had been serious discussion of just what that meant. The Russian ambassador had even coined a new phrase—"automaticity"—to describe what severest consequences did *not* mean. "Severest consequences," the Council had decided, did not mean any state had the right to move on its own against Iraq. The Council, again, "remained seized" of the issue. After the resolution passed, a parade of ambassadors came out of the Council chamber to warn explicitly that their resolution did *not* grant unilateral military authorization to any country. But when Richardson followed his colleagues out of the room, he blithely shrugged when informed of his predecessors' concerns, and told the press, "we think it does."[25] Months later, Desert Fox's four days of bombs and cruise missiles devastated Iraq.

DESERT FOX

Washington's intensive four-day bombing campaign of December 1998 followed another episode in the ongoing conflict between UNSCOM's demand for absolute access and Iraq's effort to keep some sovereign privileges. The immediate pretext was the issuance of UNSCOM's late November report on its progress.

UNSCOM director Richard Butler's report was deliberately ambiguous. He described several discrete instances of Iraqi non-compliance with UNSCOM. And, since Iraq's February 1998 agreement with Kofi Annan had promised "unconditional and unrestricted" access, those instances did represent at least a technical violation of the agreement. However, Butler's own language placed those specific instances of defiance in a broader context of overall Iraqi compliance.

The report states that "the majority of the inspections of facilities and sites under the ongoing monitoring system were carried out with Iraq's cooperation." The accompanying International Atomic Energy Agency (IAEA) report was even less ambiguous. It stated unequivocally that Iraq "has provided the necessary level of cooperation to enable the above-enumerated activities to be completed efficiently and effectively."

But Butler's conclusions did not match those facts as stated in his own account. He ended his report in a crisis mode, stating that "the Commission is not able to conduct the substantive disarmament work mandated to it by the Security Council." There was no mention in the conclusion of the inconvenient fact that his own report admitted that UNSCOM *had* been able to conduct "the majority" of its inspections.

(This is aside from the actual significance of the reported violations. One dispute described in the report, for example, focused on UNSCOM's effort to enter the Baghdad headquarters of the ruling Ba'ath Party. While technically legal under the terms of the UN-Iraq agreement, if UNSCOM's goal was a serious search for weapons material rather than political provocation, it was hardly an appropriate venue.)

The U.S. response was immediate. Washington ratcheted up the crisis rhetoric, repeating the apocalyptic tone of Butler's conclusions, while ignoring the actual facts of his report. And U.S. officials completely ignored the IAEA's unequivocal statement of Iraqi cooperation. The IAEA report on Iraq's nuclear program was particularly significant, since it followed a year-long assessment by the IAEA that, although they could not prove a negative (the complete absence of such a program), they had found no evidence that Baghdad had any viable nuclear weapons program.

So Butler's conclusion that the inspectors could not function became the basis for the U.S. launching of a four-day bombing campaign against Iraq of unprecedented intensity. The UN was again kept out of the decision-making loop.

The UNSCOM report was used unilaterally to justify a military escalation in Iraq, a goal held by the U.S. and Britain alone, not by other member states or the UN itself. Clinton administration officials admitted they had advance knowledge of the contents of the report even before Butler provided it to his ostensible boss, the Security Council. Senator Joseph Biden met with Butler at length in the U.S. mission to the UN, two days before the report was issued. And the report's tone and its ominous conclusion that deviated so thoroughly from its own facts, reflected a clear intent to justify a military response.

The U.S. had advised Butler to withdraw his inspection team from Iraq before the Security Council had even discussed the report. On the morning of December 16th Kofi Annan told reporters that "I got a call from [Acting U.S.] Ambassador Burleigh saying they are asking U.S. personnel in the region to leave. And they had also advised Butler to withdraw UNSCOM." Butler also confirmed he withdrew his inspectors, as well as those of the IAEA (which depended on UNSCOM for logistical support) at the suggestion of the U.S. He said his only concern was for the safety of his inspectors. He did not, however, show the same concern for the safety of the UN's vulnerable humanitarian workers, whom he did not evacuate or even notify about the U.S. advice. About 300 international and 850 local staff of the UN's humanitarian agencies remained in Iraq when the U.S. bombing began. Most of them spent the first days of the bombing campaign huddled in a windowless hallway in the basement of UN headquarters.

Just as was the case on January 16th 1991 when the U.S. air strikes launched Operation Desert Storm over Baghdad, the 1998 Desert Fox air strikes began while the Security Council was in session. This time the Council was actually discussing Butler's report when the strikes, allegedly based on that report's conclusions, began. It was not surprising that Kofi Annan was furious. In an unusually harsh though subtle criticism of the U.S., he stated that his thoughts "are with the people of Iraq and the UN's humanitarian workers."

Butler's report of discrete instances of non-compliance within the broader environment of Iraqi cooperation should have been answered with a Security Council discussion of appropriate options, not with unauthorized U.S.-British military action. Certainly diplomatic rather than military, and international rather than unilateral approaches, should have been the starting point. Three new approaches might have been considered:

1) The Council should have allowed UNSCOM to go public with records found in Iraq documenting the source of Baghdad's weapons programs (from its creation, UNSCOM remained specifically prohibited from making such disclosures). This would have facilitated shutting down extant versions of smuggling and/or legal weapons trade routes. Most weapons flooding the Middle East region were coming from the U.S.

2) The Council should have broadened its efforts regarding Iraqi disarmament by requesting involvement of other agencies, to bring new thinking to the debate. These might have included the Disarmament Committee of the General Assembly, the good offices of the Secretary General, regional organizations (the Arab League and/or the Organization of the Islamic Conference), UN agencies such as the Conference on Disarmament or the Disarmament Commission, or multi-lateral fora such as the Conference of States parties to the Biological Weapons Convention in which Iraq might actually have participated.

3) The Council should have begun the process called for in Resolution 687 to carry out disarmament in Iraq in the context of regional disarmament. It should have convened a high-level conference to discuss how to implement 687's calls for establishment of a Nuclear Weapons Free Zone and Weapons of Mass Destruction-Free Zone throughout the Middle East.

The 1998 Desert Fox bombing strikes were a violation of international law. *No* UN resolution called for, allowed, justified, or accepted unilateral attacks by a member state against Iraq in retaliation for real or alleged violations. U.S. officials relied on two UN resolutions to try to justify military strikes. But both claims were false.

a) Security Council Resolution 678, passed November 29, 1990, originally authorized the use of force against Iraq. (See Chapter Two.)

This was the U.S.-initiated resolution providing a UN cover for Washington's decision to launch a military response to Iraq's illegal invasion of Kuwait. It was taken under Chapter VII of the UN Charter (the only way use of force can be authorized) and called for "all necessary means" to make Iraq "withdraw immediately and unconditionally all its forces" from Kuwait. But that resolution's authority inherently expired with the expulsion of Iraqi troops from Kuwait. There were no Iraqi troops in Kuwait in 1998; one could not rely on a resolution designed to expel Iraqi troops from Kuwait, to justify bombing Iraq for a completely different reason eight years later.

b) Council Resolution 1154 passed on March 2nd, 1998. This was the Council's endorsement of Kofi Annan's negotiated settlement that Baghdad, that included the threat of "severest consequences" in case of future violations. It stated that the Council itself, not any individual government acting on its own, had the authority to "ensure implementation of this resolution and peace and security in the area." But despite that, then-U.S. Ambassador to the UN Bill Richardson declared that the resolution "did not preclude the unilateral use of force."[26] State Department spokesman James Rubin insisted "We don't see the need to return to the Security Council if there is a violation of the agreement."[27] And President Clinton asserted, despite the Security Council's actual language, that the resolution "provides authority to act" if the U.S. is not satisfied with the level of Iraq's compliance.[28]

Their sham reliance on irrelevant UN resolutions to validate Washington's unilateral military attack only demonstrated the U.S. policymakers' lack of a legitimate legal basis for the assault.

Following the bombing campaign, UNSCOM inspectors remained outside of Iraq, no weapons monitoring proceeded, and only the crippling economic sanctions remained. The longer-term goals identified in Resolution 687, including efforts towards a weapons of mass destruction-free zone throughout the Middle East, regional disarmament, and a Middle East nuclear weapons-free zone, were still ignored.

And throughout post-Desert Fox 1999, bombing attacks in both the northern and southern U.S. "no fly zones" escalated, to an average of three or more attacks per week. By the end of the year more than 1,500 attacks had been launched. They received little attention in the U.S. press, and any mention was limned by the claim that these were "self-defense" strikes against the Iraqi military, either a radar beam "painting" a U.S. or British bomber in the skies, or Iraqi planes darting into the "no fly" zones to provoke the Western air patrols. Soon after Desert Fox, the Pentagon broadened its rules of engagement. "Self-defense attacks" were redefined to include strikes hours or even days after an alleged Iraqi infraction, against any of a long list of pre-determined targets, many military but some explicitly (and thus illegally) economic, located almost anywhere in the U.S.-imposed "no fly" zones.

In August 1999, the first group of U.S. congressional aides traveled to Iraq on a fact-finding delegation investigating the impact of economic sanctions. That September, the U.S. Air Force commander of "Operation Southern Watch" Lt. General Hal M. Hornburg, responsible for the Saudi-based bombing raids in the southern "no fly" zone, said that he agreed that the brief congressional staffers' stay in Iraq would, if nothing else, provide the Iraqi population with a five-day respite from U.S. bombing. It had been widely assumed that no bombing would be conducted during the aides' stay, for fear of injuring a congressional staffer who might wander too close to a chosen U.S. target in southern Iraq. When asked how he could square such a political assessment with the Pentagon's usual claim that self-defense "required" the continuing U.S. assaults, General Hornburg simply laughed, shrugged, and held out his hands in the universal gesture of an amused "what can I do?"[29]

As the millennium drew to a close, the Security Council got bogged down in what seemed an intractable debate over Iraq policy. The U.S., Britain and the Netherlands continued to insist on a virtually unchanged approach, raising the limits of oil-for-food oil sales, but maintaining the system's existing limits, plus reverting to an UNSCOM-style monitoring system designed to continue the fruitless quest for finding every remaining shred of chemical or biological material. France and Russia took the lead in demanding a new approach, in which a future-oriented monitoring agency would work on the ground to insure no *re*-armament occurred, but ending the intrusive, provocative approach of UNSCOM and, most important, ending the murderous civilian-targeted economic sanctions. In late November, facing its own international opprobrium caused by its brutal suppression of separatist movements in the restive province of Chechnya, Russia offered the U.S. a deal in which it would back away from its effort to change the Iraqi sanctions policy, in return for Washington's easing the pressure on Moscow.

Eventually, by early December 1999, the Security Council passed Resolution 1284, calling for a new UN inspection and monitoring team to be sent to Iraq and holding out the possibility of temporary suspensions of the economic sanctions after almost a year of Iraqi compliance. Baghdad had made clear long before the vote that it would not accept any new monitoring unless it was imposed simultaneously with the first steps towards actually *lifting*, not simply temporarily suspending, the crippling economic sanctions. Without steps towards permanent lifting, it would be impossible to get the large-scale investments its depleted oil infrastructure needed to rebuild its oil producing capacity. With only a series of temporary suspensions possible, no oil company worth its shareholders would be likely to risk major funding commitments. Without at least the potential for permanent lifting, it was no surprise that Iraqi officials announced an initial rejection of the plan only days after the vote.

What was perhaps more surprising was the count in the Council. While there were of course no vetoes cast, only the U.S. and Britain of the five permanent members voted for the resolution. France, Russia and China (along with non-permanent member Malaysia) all abstained, sending a clear message of dissent and disunity among the world powers.

By the end of 1999, with economic sanctions continuing to devastate Iraqi civilians, even the *New York Times* admitted that what it called the "fireworks" of the Desert Fox assault represented "the final retreat of the Clinton administration from a policy of making the United Nations the focal point of policy on Iraq."[30] Certainly one might quibble whether that retreat had in fact occurred even before December 1998. But what became clear over the almost decade-long U.S. obsession with Iraq as its post-Cold War enemy *du décade* and poster-child of why U.S. power should lead the world, was that Washington had indeed abandoned the UN as the necessary instrument of its Iraq policy, replacing it with an unapologetic unilateralism.

ENDING THE CULTURAL IMPUNITY

Throughout the 1990s, the UN documented 103 major armed conflicts that killed two million children, forced 50 million people to flee their homes, sent about 100 million spinning in a cycle of unimaginable war, hunger, and despair. Ninety percent of those killed in these wars were civilians.[31] The horror of the 1990s wars, especially their impact on civilians, opened a new debate among both governments and international social movements, on the need to create a new global institution to bring to justice those responsible. The tribunals created by the Security Council to try accused war criminals from the Bosnian and

Rwandan conflicts, while providing an important precedent, were narrow in scope and limited by their political accountability to the Perm Five.

The International Criminal Court (ICC) was envisioned by both its state and non-governmental backers with a much broader mandate: linked to but largely independent of the Council, it would hold individuals, of whatever political or military position, accountable for war crimes and genocide. Throughout 1997 and 1998 the Clinton administration, through David Scheffer, U.S. Ambassador for War Crimes Issues, reaffirmed official U.S. support for the creation of such a court. Scheffer was thus reiterating a position Washington first claimed at the end of the Second World War at Nuremberg, when the U.S. fought for individuals to be held personally accountable for war crimes, genocide, crimes against humanity and crimes against peace.

While the UN was central to organizing the diplomatic groundwork for the ICC, the new court was conceptualized with an independent structure connected to but not controlled by existing UN agencies. One of the biggest issues to settle was the scope of jurisdiction: would an international court be able to prosecute war crimes carried out by soldiers or ordered by political leaders of the most powerful countries?

The U.S. had backed the creation of the Bosnian and Rwanda tribunals, and even claimed it supported a permanent court. When the Clinton administration's then-UN Ambassador Bill Richardson addressed the opening session of the ICC negotiations in Rome, he called the Court's creation "an important piece of unfinished business... It is time that we make real the aspirations of the past fifty years: the establishment of a Court to ensure that the perpetrators of the worst criminal assaults on humankind...do not escape from justice."

But when serious discussions began, Washington's resistance became clear. By the time the conference turned from speeches to real negotiating, Washington was playing hardball, demanding a weak court with no independence of action. The U.S. fielded a huge diplomatic team in Rome, with 200 operatives able to cover every committee, every sub-committee, and still have time to corner individual delegates to keep the pressure on. Poor countries were threatened with serious economic consequences if they voted contrary to U.S. interests. Even Germany, Washington's powerful European ally, was threatened, however implausibly, with a large-scale pull-out of U.S. troops from NATO deployments in Europe.

Still the U.S. claimed it wanted a permanent court. That was probably true: it wanted a court for all *other* people in the world except

Americans. It demanded and expected full immunity for war crimes that might be committed by American troops, American generals, American policymakers. Scheffer proudly asserted that "We constantly have troops serving abroad on humanitarian missions, rescue operations or missions to destroy weapons of mass destruction. Someone out there isn't going to like it, but we are the ones who do it."[32] And Richardson reminded negotiators that American "soldiers deployed far from home need to do their jobs without the exposure to politicized proceedings."[33]

(Ironically, Richardson based U.S. opposition to the Court's independent jurisdiction on the claim that "because of the Security Council's legal responsibilities for maintaining international peace and security, the United States believes that the Council must play an important role in the work of a permanent Court, including the Court's trigger mechanism. The Council must be able to pursue the aims of peace."[34] One assumes he forgot the UN Security Council's "importance" and "legal responsibility" when Washington made its unilateral decision to bomb Iraq, against explicit Council decisions, almost exactly six months later.)

Rhetoric aside, even before the Rome negotiations began the U.S. had no intention of signing on to a treaty that just might someday hold U.S. political or military officials accountable to an international tribunal. Scheffer made clear from the beginning "that it would be politically unacceptable here to expose U.S. troops worldwide to prosecution outside the U.S. justice system. Senate Foreign Relations Committee Chairman Jesse Helms (R-N.C.) made clear that he would never approve any agreement that did so."[35]

At the end of a rigorous six-week negotiating session in Rome, the new Court was approved in July 1998. Cheers erupted throughout the conference center looking out over the Roman coliseum. Exhausted delegates burst into tears. "Since Nuremberg," international legal scholar Diane F. Orentlicher wrote, "international law has affirmed that serious war crimes, genocide and other crimes against humanity are subject to universal jurisdiction."[36] Now, after half a century, it was finally possible to contemplate that authority being enforced. The vote, at the end, was overwhelming: 120 countries voted to create the Court, only 7 against. Now, finally, the nations of the world had created an international criminal court that could, if the unthinkable happened again, hold responsible individuals personally accountable for charges of genocide, crimes against humanity, war crimes, and aggression.

But when the vote was tallied, while the South Africans and Germans and Brazilians and all the others cheered, the U.S. delegation sat silent, stony-faced. Washington's "no" vote had led the small, isolated rejection front of Israel, Libya, China, Iraq, Qatar and Sudan. Because, as Scheffer said later, "The court places at risk those who shoulder the responsibility for international peace and security."[37]

In fact, hoping for U.S. backing, the statute creating the new International Criminal Court was actually crafted with giant loopholes through which a future war criminal might avoid the court's jurisdiction. It delayed defining the crime of aggression, what former Nuremberg prosecutor and leading ICC supporter Ben Ferencz called the "supreme crime." It did not specify the use of nuclear weapons as a war crime, and allowed the Security Council to halt an ongoing prosecution for a full year. Most of the weaknesses reflected efforts by the broad coalition of nations supporting the Court, the so-called "Like-Minded Group," to win U.S. acquiescence by weakening the Court's jurisdiction, limiting its independence, and constraining its power.

But despite Washington's refusal to join it, the very creation of the Court represented a major global accomplishment. Its existence stood as a challenge to U.S. efforts to dominate the UN and control broader international initiatives. UN Secretary General Kofi Annan, welcoming the success of the Rome conference, called the Court's birth a victory for the "new diplomacy" at work in the world. That concept, of diplomacy linking the work of non-state actors, civil society organizations and transnational social movements with more traditional governmental negotiations, reflected the reality of the late 1990s when states alone were unwilling and often unable to respond to growing crises. It was a new concept of diplomacy made desperately urgent by the outbreaks of bitter wars, often within countries but sometimes through invasions or occupations, and the human horror that accompanied them: genocide in Rwanda, "ethnic cleansing" and mass rape in Bosnia, a scorched earth policy in East Timor among the most horrific examples.

The ad hoc Council-established courts to try war criminals from the Rwanda and former Yugoslavia wars remained constrained by political expedience as defined by the U.S. and its allies—so consistency and the rule of law remained out of reach. The Council had never, for example, created a war crimes tribunal to investigate the Indonesian generals and government officials responsible for the slaughter of 200,000 Timorese civilians during Jakarta's illegal occupation of East

Timor; it had never held the U.S.-backed Argentine military junta accountable for the tens of thousands of murdered, tortured, and "disappeared" citizens during Latin America's dirty war of the 1970s. Creation of the ICC reflected larger international initiatives underway at the end of the 1990s that were already challenging the culture of impunity that had long provided former dictators and war criminals with safe havens and comfortable retirement.

A key element in this global trajectory was the October 1998 arrest in London of General Augusto Pinochet, who had declared himself president of Chile in his blood-soaked 1973 coup against the elected government of President Salvador Allende. Pinochet's rule had been characterized by the murder and disappearance of over 3,000 people, and the arrest and torture of thousands more. Pinochet, on a visit to London, was arrested under a Spanish warrant asking that he be extradited to Madrid to stand trial under terms of the UN's Convention Against Torture, which authorizes any signatory state to try violators. Held under guard in a London suburb throughout more than a year of extradition hearings, the Chilean dictator's arrest transformed the international human rights movement. It gave rise to a new verb: "to Pinochet," (or sometimes "to be Pinocheted") meaning to hold someone or to be held accountable for such international crimes. Made necessary by the Chilean government's own 1990 grant of absolute immunity to the former dictator, three additional European countries filed extradition papers against Pinochet, forming a queue of waiting tribunals if London should reject the Spanish request.

(By early 2000, however, the U.S. had still failed either to state its support for putting Pinochet on trial, or to provide full disclosure of its own extensive intelligence files to the Spanish courts, or to join the line of countries requesting extradition of Pinochet after the Spanish proceedings. It had not even attempted a U.S. indictment of Pinochet for the 1976 carbomb murders in Washington DC of the exiled former Chilean ambassador to the U.S., Orlando Letelier, then a Fellow of the Institute for Policy Studies, and his young IPS colleague, Ronni Karpen Moffitt. Three top Chilean military officers were convicted and jailed for the murder; their connection to Chilean Commander in Chief Pinochet has long been known. But more than 23 years later, Washington claimed it was "still investigating" the possibility of going after Pinochet.)

Ultimately Washington's bribes and threats proved insufficient to completely undermine the Court. While jurisdiction was weakened, and implementation remained some years off, the momentum towards a court was finally underway, opening a new era in global accountability and ending the culture of international impunity.

LAND MINES, CHILDREN, & THE "NEW DIPLOMACY"

While the United Nations provided coordination, sometimes a venue for initial political debates, and international credibility and legitimacy, many of these campaigns (the land mines convention, the ICC and others) took shape parallel to, but separate from full UN control, while remaining comfortably inside the broadly defined framework of the UN system as a whole. Final agreements, once created through these "new diplomacy" campaigns, were treated as United Nations documents, with the UN presiding over signature and ratification processes and serving as guarantor of the treaties' coming into force.

But U.S. power remained. The law of empire was again clear in the U.S. refusal to sign the 1997 convention prohibiting the use of anti-personnel land mines. The Convention represented the culmination of a years-long effort to mobilize international opinion, and ultimately international law, against these weapons that had been responsible for far more civilian than military deaths. The campaign's momentum was rooted in the vast suffering of civilians, most often children, in places where low-tech, high-casualty wars were taking place, often outside CNN's camera range, like Afghanistan, Angola, Sudan, or the Ethiopia-Eritrea border. The impact of the anti-personnel landmines was perhaps even more dramatically seen in places like Cambodia or Bosnia—where the wars were at least tentatively over, but where hidden mines continued to kill children, adults, and livestock on a daily basis.

Led by transnational social movements, an international campaign began to ban landmines. The mines—cheap, accessible, easy to distribute and lethal—were as often manufactured in wealthy Northern countries for sale in the global South, as they were made in primitive workshops in developing countries themselves. The mines quickly became a popular target for the efforts by International Committee of the Red Cross and peace activists around the world. U.S. officials waxed poetic in expressions of support for banning the anti-personnel mines.

But early efforts to bring the issue to the UN's Convention on Disarmament foundered. The U.S. and others succeeded at bottling up the issue in bureaucratic delays and in committees, ensuring that the UN would never be allowed to impose a serious international ban.

The international activists working to ban the landmines, frustrated with the slow pace of the U.S.-hindered UN effort, moved to a new venue. In collaboration with a number of supportive governments, and with Canada's Foreign Minister Lloyd Axworthy in the lead, the International Campaign to Ban Landmines moved to create an independent forum for negotiations towards a ban. The Ottawa process was born, leading to the birth of the International Convention Against Landmines created in the Ottawa Treaty of 1997.

The international citizens campaign was awarded the Nobel Prize for Peace in 1997. U.S. officials cheered it on, bemoaning the deaths caused by mines left behind by irresponsible nations. But during the Ottawa negotiations (to which it came as a reluctant participant), Washington still demanded that the U.S. be exempt from any such ban. We are a more "responsible" nation, U.S. officials claimed, and we make better and more reliable mines that will self-destruct after set periods, or that won't respond to the lighter weight of a child's step. Therefore, they argued, while the rest of the world should indeed ban all kinds of anti-personnel land mines for all time and in all places, the Pentagon should be allowed to continue using land mines in Korea's demilitarized zone and around the U.S. naval base at Guantanamo Bay in Cuba. Why? Because Pentagon planners say they need them, and that should be good enough. Of course at some point in the future when we concoct a new weapon as efficient and useful as landmines we will be glad to sign on to the Convention. But for now, everyone else should sign on and ban the mines. The United States is a more responsible nation, we take more responsibility around the world, and therefore we should be the exception.

By January 2000, the U.S. had still not signed the Convention. Anti-personnel land mines are only one of the ways that children are particularly victimized in times of war. By the end of the 1990s, new attention to the 1994 Convention on the Rights of the Child reflected growing international concern about children in war, with a particular focus on the use of children—through kidnapping, coercion, and lack of economic alternatives—as soldiers or other military workers, porters, or sex slaves. An optional protocol to the Convention would outlaw all military recruitment of children under the age of 18. The U.S. led the campaign to derail that protocol—because the Pentagon finds it convenient to continue to recruit 17-year-olds into the U.S. military forces. In 1999 the U.S. military included only 2,500 under-18 GIs past their basic training. But it was the principle of being able to recruit whoever they wished seemed more important than any military significance.

In January 2000, the Pentagon finally agreed to let U.S. diplomats in Geneva "compromise" on the deployment of children protocol. Faced with the alternative of a continued U.S. rejection, the other countries accepted softened language allowing the U.S. military to continue recruiting and training 17-year-olds, as long as it takes "all feasible measures" to keep them out of combat until they turn 18. Given the lack of implementation guidelines or even the pretense of enforcement, deciding what is "feasible" rests with the Joint Chiefs of Staff. According to one U.S. defense official, "the chiefs weren't crazy about it, but we felt we could live with it with that kind of construction."[38]

The Clinton administration hinted that it might consider bringing the protocol to the Senate for ratification. Clinton had signed the Convention in 1995, but refused even to try to mobilize support for Senate ratification. Senator Jesse Helms and the Republican right-wing claimed the Convention somehow violated the sanctity of parents' rights. And the administration was not willing to challenge them. So whatever the result of the specific protocol, the U.S. remained, at the beginning of the 21st century, one of only two countries that still refused to ratify the main text of the Convention on the Rights of the Child. The other was war-ravaged, child-militia filled Somalia.

The U.S. lack of concern for international guarantees of children's rights reemerged in late 1999, in Washington's refusal for months to return six-year-old Elián González to his father in Cuba. The child's mother and stepfather had taken Elián on an illegal and ill-fated leaky boat journey to Florida. When the boat sank, most of the adults on board, including his mother and stepfather, drowned; the child survived, and was found clinging to an inner tube off the Florida Keys. After hospital treatment, when U.S. officials were obligated, under all existing child welfare and custody laws as well as a 1994 immigration agreement with Cuba, to send the child home immediately, they instead turned Elián over to distant relatives in Miami, whom the child had never met.

The case was immediately seized by the ideologically-driven and powerful anti-Castro Cuban American National Foundation, and its supporters in Congress, who demanded that the boy be kept in the U.S. Given the claimed primacy that Jesse Helms, the Cuban-American congressional caucus and their Miami backers allegedly place on the sanctity of the nuclear family, this stance was particularly ironic. Instead of going home to his father to be allowed to grieve for his mother, Elián became a poster child for the "better life" that toys, cell phones, and trips to Disney World could provide as substitute for his father and grandparents in Cuba. UNICEF's representative in Cuba, Alfred Missair, deemed the U.S. refusal to send the child home a violation of Article 9 of the Convention on the Rights of the Child, which states that children should not be separated from their parents.[39] Few in Washington paid attention, perhaps because they knew the U.S. had never ratified the Convention in the first place.

PEACEKEEPING: NARROWER MANDATES, A TIGHTER LEASH

The downturn in the number of UN peacekeeping operations (PKOs) continued throughout the late 1990s, although by the end of 1999 the trajectory had turned up again. By December 1999, the total number of UN peacekeepers stood at 14,545 blue helmets in seventeen separate operations. Continuing blue helmet operations in crisis zones such as the Western Sahara and Cyprus faced shifts in mandate, size, authority, and the constant threat of decreasing funding and personnel.

In fact the decrease in PKOs throughout the late 1990s seriously exacerbated the UN's overall financial crisis. Earlier in the decade, as both the number and size of blue helmet operations increased, the peacekeeping assessments provided a cushion for UN bean counters to shift funds back and forth, borrowing from peacekeeping revenues to pay for organizational accounts in the red because of the escalating arrears in U.S. dues payments. One serious effect was frequent delays in payments due to countries (often poor nations of the South— Bangladesh, Fiji, India, others) that provided peacekeeping troops. In fact the destabilizing military coup d'etat in Cote d'Ivoire just before Christmas of 1999 was partly caused by the U.S.-driven UN financial crisis. While provoked generally by the overall economic collapse caused by low and diminishing commodity prices for coffee and cocoa, much of the immediate spark for the coup leaders in Abidjan stemmed from their anger at not being paid overdue wages for peacekeeping duties in the UN's blue helmet mission in the Central African Republic.

Earlier access to peacekeeping funds had at least meant the organization could be protected from complete financial collapse. With peacekeeping operations decreasing, peacekeeping funds and the relative flexibility they once provided declined as well, threatening the very survival of some UN programs. As the Atlanta *Journal-*

Constitution noted in the fall of 1999, "never before has the UN's peacekeeping unit faced so many demands and had fewer resources to meet them."[40]

Of the seventeen peacekeeping operations underway at the beginning of 2000, five were new missions established since 1998: MINURCA in the Central African Republic (established April 1998), UNMIK in Kosovo (June 1999), UNAMSIL in Sierra Leone (October 1999), UNTAET in East Timor (October 1999), and MONUC in the Democratic Republic of the Congo (November 1999). Each faced severe discrepancies between the number of troops authorized in their original mandates, and the troops actually made available in time to implement the Security Council commitment. To cope with the devastation wrought by Indonesia's military and militias, for example, 89,050 troops, 200 military observers and 1,640 civilian police were authorized in early October; by December, UNTAET could field a total of only 391 blue helmets in East Timor. The Council had authorized 500 military observers for MONUC in the Congo; by December only 60 were available. Sierra Leone was a little better, but it still took almost three months before at least two-thirds of the 6,000 troops authorized began to deploy in the country.

What had not changed was the continuing price paid for by the refusal of Washington and other powerful capitals to allow the UN to create the kind of rapidly deployable international peacekeeping, protection, or police force in which individual people would serve under UN authority. Instead, every peacekeeping mandate required painstaking and lengthy delays to convince governments to provide troops or units or equipment required—often with deadly results

There were, however, two new patterns of UN peacekeeping assignments emerging by the turn of the century: take-over peacekeeping and reconstruction/nation-building.

In persistent regional conflicts, where emergency crises had been brought under some level of usually tenuous control by regional forces, UN operations were authorized to take over responsibility from those original peacekeepers. This was the case in Sierra Leone, for example, where a horrifying guerrilla war, characterized by the torture and slaughter of civilians largely by rebel militias, had raged for several years, broken by occasional short-lived lulls. The latest cease-fire was signed between President Ahmad Tejan Kabbah and rebel leader Foday Sankoh in July 1999. There were particularly difficult conditions involved in the peace talks. Sankoh's forces had been noted for brutal attacks on civilians—their trademark was hacked-off limbs. Sankoh himself was found, imprisoned and sentenced to death for his involvement. But he was later freed, in order to participate in talks in Togo, largely orchestrated by the U.S. Those talks led to the new 1999 cease-fire. But the terms outraged many UN and other observers: the rebels would not only be granted amnesty, but Sankoh and his top lieutenants were guaranteed seats in the new government. UN officials from the pre-UNAMSIL observer team as well as secretariat officials at headquarters agreed to witness the agreement, but only with the public announcement that Sierra Leone's internal amnesty would not bar war crimes prosecutions by international war crimes jurisdictions.

Once the cease-fire was signed, the largely Nigerian regional peacekeeping team in Sierra Leone began to withdraw, to be replaced by UN blue helmets. Under the terms set by the October Security Council resolution, a key responsibility for UNAMSIL was to be overseeing the disarming and demobilization of the 45,000 rebel forces, as well as protection of civilians against further threats of violence. The 6,000 authorized peacekeepers made UNAMSIL the largest peace mission so far approved by the UN since 1996, though it was dwarfed by the authorization of the much larger (11,000 strong) UNTAET in East Timor only days later—a deployment made urgent by the Security Council's own failure to take serious pro-active steps to protect civilians from the time the independence referendum was first announced. But in fact, months after their highly publicized creation, both UNAMSIL and UNTAET remained severely under-staffed and stretched thin in still-tense Sierra Leone and East Timor.

In crises like those in East Timor and Kosovo, the new UN operations were granted wide mandates for nation-building tasks and at least temporary governance, after military carnage (in Kosovo, caused by all sides) had been brought under at least partial control. The optimistic model was perhaps more Cambodia than Somalia, but in both regions the UN faced new challenges. In both cases the UN was given the assignment of cleaning up after horrifying (as well as thoroughly preventable) humanitarian crises that left the physical, social and human infrastructure in tatters. In both cases the UN was denied the requisite military, financial, and human resources to meet the enormous challenges. And in both cases, the U.S. sought not to praise but first to blame the UN and then, perhaps, to bury it.

Of the twelve PKOs that pre-dated 1996, some dated back to the earliest UN operations, such as the 1948-to-present UN Treaty

Supervision Organization (UNTSO) between Israel and Syria. (Given Israel's long-standing and U.S.-backed hostility to the UN, neither UNTSO nor even UNDOF, the UN Disengagement Observer Force established on the Golan Heights in June 1974, were likely to have much of a role to play in the 1999–2000 negotiations between Israel and Syria aimed at ending Israeli occupation of the Golan and creating a peace treaty.) Similarly, the UN Military Observer Group in India and Pakistan (UNMOGIP), also in place since 1949, had not been empowered to prevent or even respond to the 1998 nuclear tests in both country, nor the 1999 Kargil crisis over Kashmir that brought the two countries close to a new war.

The mandate and sometimes even the name of other ongoing missions had changed, including the newly reformulated and much more limited UN Civilian Police Mission in Haiti that replaced the earlier UN Mission in Haiti in 1997. As for UNIKOM (the Iraq-Kuwait Observation Mission established shortly after the Gulf War in April 1991), its border demarcation tasks ended when the boundary it had established was accepted by Iraq in the late 1990s, but its border monitoring work continued.

Other conflict-riven areas of the world, especially in Africa, remained largely outside the purview of UN peacekeeping operations. Not unrelated was the fact that most of them remained outside the view of CNN cameras. In Angola, UN efforts at demobilization after short-lived cease-fires in 1991 and 1994 left the anti-government UNITA rebels' military capacity largely untouched. Just before Christmas of 1998, UNITA resumed shelling of Cuito, the city in the central highlands that had become home to 70,000 internal refugees. Half a million Angolans depended on World Food Program assistance by early 1999,[41] but the Security Council withdrew the peacekeeping operation altogether in early 1999 when it became clear to the UN's PKO Department that governments had refused to send enough troops to carry out the badly understaffed mission.

In the Balkans, UNMOP, the UN Mission of Observers in Prevlaka, had remained in Croatia since January 1996. The Mission in Bosnia and Herzegovina (UNMIBH) established at the end of 1995 remained in place. But its role was hardly that of peacekeeping. Following the December Dayton peace agreement that year, NATO's Stabilization Force (SFOR) took over peacekeeping duties in an ethnically divided Bosnia with the U.S., Britain, and France each maintaining responsibility for specific sectors. Their mandate included a call to arrest suspects indicted by the war crimes tribunal in the Hague if they came across them in the course of "ordinary" activities (meaning no search-and-arrest missions were required of NATO), but although British troops did make several arrests, there was widespread reluctance to implement even that responsibility. For years after their indictment, many of the alleged war criminals, including Bosnian Serb military and political leaders Ratko Mladic and Radovan Karadzic, lived openly in and around Pale in the French sector, and often traveled between sectors controlled by the U.S. and others. None of the occupying contingents took seriously the need to arrest indictees; by early 2000 both Mladic and Karadzic remained at large, believed to have moved to Serbia.

LESSONS LEARNED: RWANDA AND SREBRENICA

When President Clinton traveled to Africa in 1998, he "apologized" to the people of Rwanda for the international community's failure to stop the genocide four years earlier. But while significant simply because such a phenomenon had never happened before, the apology was general and failed to take real responsibility for what the U.S. government itself had done: resisted, delayed, and rejected creation of a UN peacekeeping operation capable of protecting Rwanda's civilian victims from a genocide known to be imminent.

Clinton's real understanding was likely more accurately represented at the General Assembly in October 1993, as the Rwanda crisis was escalating and warnings of the genocide to come were known. At that time, still smarting from the U.S. debacle in Somalia, he lectured the assembled world leaders on the dangers of international peace operations: "If the American people are to say yes to peacekeeping," he reprimanded, "the UN must know when to say no."[42]

U.S. insistence on the UN saying no, as it turned out, led to disaster. In December 1999 the UN issued its "Report of the Independent Inquiry into the Actions of the United Nations During the 1994 Genocide in Rwanda." In clear contrast to President Clinton's superficial camera-driven apology, it was both comprehensive and painfully self-critical. The UN's Report focused with much greater specificity on the internal role of the UN— decisions of the peacekeeping department of the secretariat and actions of the UN blue helmets on the ground—than on the decisions and actions prevented by the Security Council and its most powerful members. Certainly, for the Togolese, Ghanaian, Belgian and other

UN soldiers whose Council mandate was officially limited to implementing a non-existent peace process, there were few options. Indeed, General Dallaire, the Canadian commander of the peacekeepers, stated that shortly after the killing of the ten Belgian soldiers early in the genocide, "he did not believe that there was a military option to intervene."[43] Some of the peacekeepers made bad judgments and decisions that proved fatal to Rwandan civilians under their protection. And it is without question that officials in the Department of Peacekeeping Operations (DPKO) failed at key moments either to understand or, if they understood, failed to act on specific information, including a crucial fax from General Dallaire, that warned of the coming genocide.

At the very least, DPKO officials and ultimately the secretary-general should have seen their obligation to go public with the information in their hands. Even if the Council still refused to respond, a high-profile public announcement that mass slaughter, a holocaust, a genocide, was about to occur, might have spurred international public or governmental pressure sufficient to force the reluctant Western powers' hands. However inappropriate or impolitic such action by the secretary-general may have seemed to some in Washington or Paris, or even at the UN itself, it was needed to save lives—and UN officials failed in that overriding obligation.

But the fundamental responsibility for the international failure to stop genocide in Rwanda lay not with the DPKO or the secretary-general, but with the Security Council, where the U.S. and France staked out (for somewhat different reasons) unswerving opposition to serious protection for Rwanda's beleaguered Tutsi and moderate Hutu civilians. (See Chapter Five.) The UN's unsparing Report describes how "the statement by the President of the Council to the press on 15 April [1994] is telling of the atmosphere in the Council at the time. The statement makes no mention of the ongoing massacres. It states that the 'immediate priority in Rwanda is the establishment of a cease-fire between the Government forces and the RPF.'"

The Council's goal was to reduce the number of peacekeeping troops, and narrow their mandate. According to the Report, "Dallaire painted the following picture of the dilemma facing the UN under the scenarios being discussed: "The consequences of a withdrawal by UNAMIR will definitely have an adverse affect [sic] on the morale of the civil population, especially the refugees, who will feel that we are deserting them."

The report continued, "On 21 April, the Council voted unanimously to reduce UNAMIR to about 270 and to change the mission's mandate. The resolution stated that the Council was 'appalled at the ensuing large-scale violence in Rwanda, which has resulted in the deaths of thousands of innocent civilians, including women and children.'" But nonetheless Resolution 912 provided nothing to stop the attacks. A week later, Boutros-Ghali sent a letter to the Council that "provided an important shift in emphasis—from viewing the role of the United Nations as that of neutral mediator in a civil war to recognising the need to bring to an end the massacres against civilians, which had by then been going on for three weeks and were estimated to have killed some 200,000 people. The Secretary-General stated that the mandate contained in Resolution 912 (1994) did not give UNAMIR the power to take effective action to halt the massacres.... The Council was asked to reconsider its previous decisions and to consider 'what action, including forceful action, it could take, or could authorize Member States to take in order to restore law and order.' In a biting final remark, the Secretary-General wrote that he was aware 'that such action would require a commitment of human and material resources on a scale which Member States have so far proved reluctant to contemplate.'"

Two weeks later, "the Secretary-General formalized his recommendations in a report to the Security Council, which outlined the phased deployment of UNAMIR II up to a strength of 5,500, emphasizing the need for haste in getting the troops into the field. ...[But] the United States proposals contained ... an explicit reference to the need for the parties' consent, the postponement of later phases of deployment pending further decisions in the Council and requirement that the Secretary-General return to the Council with a refined concept of operations, including among other elements the consent of the parties and available resources.... By 25 July, over two months after Resolution 918 (1994) was adopted, UNAMIR still only had 550 troops, a tenth of the authorized strength. Thus the lack of political will to react firmly against the genocide when it began was compounded by a lack of commitment by the broader membership of the United Nations to provide the necessary troops in order to permit the United Nations to try to stop the killing."

The UN Report documented an early account, prepared by a special mission to the region during the genocide period and presented to the Council May 31, 1994, that described a "frenzy of massacres" and estimated that between 250,000 and 500,000 people had already been killed. It said there was "little doubt" that what happened constituted genocide. The 1999 Investigation goes on, "The [1994] report's final observations were bitter: 'The delay in reaction by the international community to the genocide in Rwanda has demonstrated graphically its extreme inadequacy to respond urgently with prompt and decisive action to humanitarian crises entwined with armed conflict. Having quickly reduced UNAMIR to a minimum presence on the ground, since its original mandate did not allow it to take action when the carnage started, the international community appears paralyzed in reacting almost two months later even to the revised mandate established by the Security Council. We must all realize that, in this respect, we have failed in our response to the agony of Rwanda, and thus have acquiesced in the continued loss of human lives.'"

The self-critical approach was unmistakable. Washington, which never conducted a public investigation into its own responsibilities for the genocide, appeared satisfied when President Clinton felt the pain of Rwanda's devastated survivors.

Like the Rwandan genocide, the 1995 massacre of at least 7,414 Muslim men and boys in the Bosnian town of Srebrenica came to symbolize the inability of the United Nations to protect civilians under threat. Like Rwanda, the failure to prevent the catastrophe continued to be blamed on "the UN," rather than the Security Council and its most powerful member states.

Acting pursuant to a November 1998 General Assembly resolution, the UN secretary-general commissioned a report entitled simply "The Fall of Srebrenica." Quoting from the International Tribunal for the Former Yugoslavia's indictment of Bosnian Serb leaders Radovan Karadzic and Ratko Mladic for the massacre, the Report describes how "After Srebrenica fell to besieging Serbian forces in July 1995, a truly terrible massacre of the Muslim population appears to have taken place. The evidence tendered by the prosecutor describes scenes of unimaginable savagery: thousands of men executed and buried in mass graves, hundreds of men buried alive, men and women mutilated and slaughtered, children killed before their mothers' eyes, a grandfather forced to eat the liver of his own grandson. These are truly scenes from hell, written on the darkest pages of human history."[44]

Srebrenica had been the first of the Security Council's so-called "safe areas." The Council's goal was to appear to be protecting civilians from rapidly escalating Serb assaults, while maintaining the claim to UN "neutrality" in the war. The result was that only 450 lightly armed Dutch peacekeepers were sent to "protect" tens of thousands of local inhabitants against a three-year siege by the far better armed Bosnian Serb forces. In July 1995, the siege ended with the Serb forces, under the direct (and later televised) command of Ratko Mladic, taking numerous peacekeepers hostage, then forcibly separating woman and children from men and teenage boys, expelling the women and systematically and brutally slaughtering the mostly unarmed men and boys. The 7,417 figure is based on the almost 2,500 bodies later found unburied or in mass graves,[45] and on the missing men who were never accounted for. The butchery was the worst war crime in Europe since the Holocaust. The Dutch peacekeepers stood by and watched the separation of men and women, and the expulsion of the women. They did not prevent the men from being rounded up and carried off to what was known to be their deaths.

As the Report notes, "many observers have been quick to point to the soldiers of the UNPROFOR Netherlands battalion as the most immediate culprits. They blame them for not attempting to stop the Serb attack, and they blame them for not protecting the thousands of people who sought refuge in their compound."[46]

There is no question that the out-gunned Dutch blue helmets requested air support, and did not get it. There is no question that the effort suffered from what the Report called "the command-and-control problems from which UNPROFOR suffered throughout its history." And there is no question that the Dutch peacekeepers did not behave as heroes. It is a very legitimate, but ultimately unanswerable question whether the Dutch battalion could have prevented any Bosnian Muslim deaths had they stood their ground, sacrificed their hostage counterparts, and militarily attacked the surrounding Serb forces.

What is not unanswerable is the question of why they would have been in direct violation of their UN mandate had they done so. The answer there lies in the decisions of the Security Council, whose most powerful members consistently denied to UNPROFOR's blue helmets either the permission or the means to do what they were ostensibly deployed to do: protect civilians facing deadly peril. The Report notes that "We were fully aware that...the lightly armed forces in the enclaves would be no match for (and were not intended to resist) a Serb attack supported by infantry and armor...We believed there was no choice under the Security Council resolutions but to deploy more and more peacekeepers into harm's way."[47]

The Report recognizes that the arms embargo, humanitarian aid and peacekeepers "were poor substitutes for more decisive and forceful action to prevent the unfolding horror... None of the conditions for the deployment of peacekeepers had been met: there was no peace agreement—not even a functioning cease-fire—there was no clear will to peace and there was no clear consent by the belligerents. Nevertheless, *faute de mieux,* the Security Council decided that a United Nations peacekeeping force would be deployed. Lightly armed, highly visible in their white vehicles, scattered across the country in numerous indefensible observation posts, they were able to confirm the obvious: there was no peace to keep."

By the time the Report was issued, in November 1999, the crises in East Timor and, closer to the area under discussion, Kosovo, had exploded in brutal force. The Security Council, led by the U.S. had failed to allow "the UN" to do its job of protecting people. Its most powerful members were willing to provide the beleaguered civilians of Srebrenica with the illusion of international support and protection, but not the reality.

The UN itself took seriously the need for self-critical reflection, recognizing that "the United Nations experience in Bosnia was one of the most difficult and painful in our history....The tragedy of Srebrenica will haunt our history forever."[48] It called on member states "to engage in a process of reflection and analysis, focused on the key challenges the narrative uncovers." Canadian, Belgian and Dutch efforts, evaluating their roles in Rwanda and Bosnia, have begun to do just that, at least on the part of the military participants in the blue helmet and UN-authorized (see Chapter Five) operations. There has been no indication yet from the Pentagon—let alone from the State Department or the White House, where the fundamental decisions leading to the fall of Srebrenica and the slaughter of its citizens ultimately were made—that such a review was ever thought necessary.

But if Washington's positions vis-à-vis Sierra Leone, East Timor, Angola or Kosovo are any guide, the real lessons—the need for pro-active, diplomatic action first and then, if need be, real international protection under truly multi-national political control, the potential for a UN-deployable protection force—have never even been considered.

ISRAEL & PALESTINE: DÉJA VU ALL OVER AGAIN

The second half of the 1990s saw consistent motion, if not progress, in Israeli-Palestinian diplomacy. But the U.S. continued to assert the prerogatives of "sponsor," imposing on the Oslo peace process its own narrow redefinition of international law and exclusion of the United Nations. The U.S. proclaimed by fiat that the only relevant UN resolutions were 242 and 338, calling for the exchange of territory for peace. Thus erased with a wave of Washington's hand were resolutions codifying decades-old international understandings on issues such as the right of Palestinians to return (Resolution 194) and even the original 1947 partition resolution (181) on which Israel's own international legitimacy rested. Only the U.S. claimed the power to dictate the relevance or irrelevance of existing international laws and UN resolutions.

In the context of Israel-Palestine, as others, Washington's law of empire sometimes took the form of undermining the purpose, if not the official form, of international laws. The U.S. was a signatory to the 1949 Fourth Geneva Conventions, but in the Middle East it played the role of spoiler, undermining the potential of the Conventions to do exactly what they were supposed to do: protect people. The Conventions were designed to shield unarmed civilians from the ravages of war, siege, or occupation. In the UN, everybody—except Israel itself—agreed that the Conventions apply to Israel in the occupied Palestinian territories. That much wasn't controversial— even the U.S. admitted that much, and over the years the U.S. accepted 24 other Security Council resolutions saying so.

Those resolutions were supposed to be binding. But in April 1999 the U.S. vetoed two Council resolutions calling for an end to Israel's provocative settlement practices, long condemned by the UN as violating both Security Council and Assembly resolutions, as well as the Geneva Conventions. To override the U.S.-driven impasse, members of the European Union and other countries brought the question to the General Assembly where the U.S. had no veto power. The GA voted overwhelmingly to convene a meeting of the 188 signatories to the Conventions, to discuss Israeli practices in the occupied territories. The U.S. voted against the Assembly resolution—but much more disturbing was the U.S. announcement that it was going to, in Vice-President Al Gore's words "work diligently to halt the meeting of the Fourth Geneva Convention.... America will boycott it, and we will urge others to do the same."[49] Given the overwhelming might of U.S. diplomatic, economic and strategic power to coerce other nations, such a threat represented a grave assault on the legitimacy of international law.

The original goal for the conference was to go beyond the UN's already on-the-record and uncontested (except by Israel itself) finding of applicability of the Geneva Convention, and investigate specific Israeli violations, particularly regarding issues of settlements. The possibility of enforcement was remote, but certainly under consideration: setting a timetable for the Israeli government to demonstrate compliance, or even imposing multilateral economic or diplomatic penalties against Israel for its violations. The decision to hold the meeting was shaped by the understanding that the obligations of international law and compliance with international agreements do not disappear when bilateral negotiations are underway. Specifically, the Palestinian position, backed by the Non-Aligned and somewhat more cautiously by the Europeans, was that international law provides the foundation for ending Israeli occupation of Palestinian land, regardless of what bilateral arrangements may be underway.

But when the meeting was finally held in Switzerland on July 15, everything had changed. The meeting did convene, officially, but as a result of the U.S. pressure it was adjourned after only 10 minutes. The operative goal was not the reassertion of the primacy of international law and UN resolutions, but as the *New York Times* described it, an "effort to avert friction with Israel's new government."[50]

Two leading Palestinian human rights organizations, LAW and the Palestine Human Rights Center issued an immediate response from Geneva: "we deeply regret that the High Contracting Parties meeting here have not fulfilled and appeared to have repudiated the mandate they took upon themselves when they voted for the General Assembly resolution calling for this conference. By failing to hold a substantive conference to address pressing questions of enforcement of the Convention, the Parties have undermined and politicized the application of international humanitarian law, not only with regard to this conflict but other and future conflicts as well."

Given U.S. disdain for the UN and international law in Middle East diplomacy, such a failure was no surprise.

DISARMAMENT AND ITS DISCONTENTS

For anyone who believes the U.S. Senate's 1999 rejection of the Comprehensive Test Ban Treaty (CTBT) to be an aberration, it is necessary to keep in mind the example of the 1968 Non-Proliferation Treaty (NPT) and its 1995 permanent extension. (See Chapter Eight.)

The U.S. signed and ratified the NPT, trumpeting to domestic and international public opinion how the Treaty prohibited any country beyond the existing "Nuke Five" from obtaining nuclear weapons capacity. Twenty-five years later Washington took the lead in orchestrating, through a complex web of bribes and threats, the campaign to permanently extend the Treaty's life. The American betrayal of the NPT came in Washington's blatant refusal to take seriously the NPT's requirement that the five "official" nuclear powers, the U.S., Russia, Britain, France, and China (conveniently the same countries as the permanent members of the Security Council), move seriously towards the "complete prohibition and thorough destruction of nuclear weapons."

Only such a commitment to complete nuclear disarmament could have convinced the rest of the world to accept the NPT's requirement that they forgo nuclear weapons altogether. The terms of the NPT bind the U.S. to exactly that commitment to full nuclear disarmament. Yet U.S. diplomats during the 1995 NPT-extension conference said it was "ridiculous" to call for serious consideration of getting rid of U.S. nuclear weapons.

Small wonder that India, despite having led much of the Non-Aligned Movement's fight against the permanent extension of the NPT, now found a ready, if superficial, excuse for its right-wing Hindu fundamentalist government's own 1998 decision to test a new nuclear weapon at Pokharan. The Indian test, and the Pakistani tests at Chagai that followed in response, derailed the 25-year-old UN Conference on Disarmament regime that, despite its limited "non-proliferation" focus, had provided at least a modicum of nuclear weapons control. Now all bets were off.

Once the NPT was indefinitely extended, and absent a U.S.-Soviet nuclear stand-off, the main nuclear threat for Washington seemed to come from the "loose nukes" finding their market-driven way to unsanctioned purchasers in unapproved nations. National proliferation problems (except those needed to justify U.S.-British war hysteria against Iraq) lost their high-profile position. But the emergence of two new full-fledged and open nuclear weapons states in India and Pakistan in 1998 put the question of proliferation squarely back at center stage. The move threatened escalations in the nuclear arms race between earlier and stronger nuclear powers and these new, unauthorized second-generation nuclear states. There was a threat of efforts to create new kinds of nuclear weapons specifically designed by the U.S. and its allies to oppose the newer, perhaps less sophisticated weapons of the newest nuclear states.

Under U.S. leadership, the Nuke Five refused to concede the reality that India and Pakistan (along with Israel, whose military forces had conducted one or more joint nuclear tests with apartheid South Africa in 1979) were now nuclear-weapons states. The Nuke Five insisted that acknowledgment of the reality of nuclear capacity somehow represented a reward that should be denied the newly-declared nuclear states. Certainly the Indian and Pakistani tests (as well as Israel's almost twenty years ago) represented the failure of the NPT's earlier have/have-nots scheme for nuclear non-proliferation.

In July 1996 the International Court of Justice provided an Advisory Opinion at the request of the General Assembly. The GA had asked the Court to answer the question "is the threat or use of nuclear weapons in any circumstance permitted under international law?" The court's answer (in an unprecedented set of fourteen separate opinions by the fourteen individual judges) was that "the threat or use of nuclear weapons would generally be contrary to the rules of international law applicable in armed conflict, and in particular the principles and rules of humanitarian law."

In point of fact, neither India's nor Pakistan's nuclear weapons test was in direct response to the hypocrisy and power imbalance imposed by the Nuke Five. India's far-right Hindu nationalist ruling party, the BJP, was motivated by far narrower, indeed chauvinist, motivations of its own. And Pakistan's tests were thoroughly reactive to India's. But recognition of the West's double standard, especially in India, played a key role in the widespread (though shallow) popular support that first greeted the tests. And outside of South Asia, opposition to these newest expressions of nuclear prowess was rooted in a simultaneous understanding of, and opposition to, the quarter-century old and now clearly discredited "two-tier" system of nuclear weapons.

There was a particular danger posed by the wide international coverage (however misleading) of the initially euphoric public reactions in both India and Pakistan. The tests demonstrated the urgency to do exactly what Secretary of State Madeleine Albright told the Nuke Five meeting in Geneva shortly after the tests that they would never do: rewrite the terms of the Non-Proliferation Treaty, so that new nuclear states were held to the same standards as the old Nuke Five, and that all of them were forced to move towards serious nuclear disarmament.

The conclusion of the World Court's Advisory Opinion declared that "there exists an obligation to pursue in good faith and bring to a conclusion negotiations leading to nuclear disarmament in all its aspects under strict and effect international control." Even the American judge on the Court signed on. But so far Washington has shown no sign of allowing the UN's Conference on Disarmament to initiate such a negotiating process. The U.S. continues to keep the UN out of the nuclear loop, and even discussing implementation of the NPT's Article VI disarmament requirement remains forbidden.

MADELEINE IN THE RING: WASHINGTON GOES AFTER BOUTROS-GALI

By the middle of 1996, as President Clinton's second election campaign was in full partisan swing, the administration known for its domestic priorities suddenly turned on the United Nations. There was no illusion that the high-profile attention had anything to do with a return to multi-lateralism, or even a new interest in creating a foreign policy that could overcome the disasters of Somalia, Bosnia, Rwanda, and more.

No, the anti-UN spotlight was trained on the 38th floor—the secretary-general's office, and its target was Boutros Boutros-Ghali, the pro-Western Egyptian whom even the staunchly reactionary *Washington Times* admitted "has done nearly all the U.S. wanted— even if he squawked about it."[51] Madeleine Albright, then ambassador to the UN, announced that she intended to veto Boutros-Ghali's expected second term in office.

It wasn't really about Boutros-Ghali, of course. Washington did not suddenly begin condemning the UN and halting UN dues payments in 1996 because they didn't like Boutros-Ghali—it was the Reagan administration, back in 1985, that first refused to pay up. (See Chapter 3.) Boutros-Ghali was merely a convenient scapegoat for an anti-UN crusade thoroughly driven by domestic politics. Three separate campaigns were involved: Bill Clinton's run for president against Bob Dole, Madeleine Albright's drive to become secretary of state in a second Clinton administration, and an administration effort to use Boutros-Ghali's ouster as a sweetener to convince Congress to pay at least part of Washington's back dues. The first two succeeded; the last was a dismal failure.

The main parameters of the administration's campaign were set quietly by State Department officials in early 1996. Public attacks on the secretary-general were already underway by the Dole campaign, whose candidate loved the cheap but consistent applause generated by his specious pledge that President Dole would never allow U.S. troops to serve under Boutros-Ghali—as if they ever had! It was made worse by the blatant appeal to anti-Arab racism behind the slogan, as Dole made fun of the secretary-general's name, stretching out "Boooo-trous Boooo-trous" to the accompanying cheers of the crowd. Quickly the Democrats began to compete with the Republicans to see who could be more hostile to the UN. The State Department team quietly offered Boutros-Ghali a "deal" of one more year; he turned it down, but counter-offered with a bargain of his own: he would accept a two-and-a-half year "half term." Washington refused, and the battle was joined.

An issue involving the contentious UN-Israel relationship further shored up U.S. determination to get rid of the SG. Israel's August 1996 air assault in south Lebanon had targeted, among other things, a UN peacekeeping center at Qana, a small Lebanese village. Hundreds of refugees had taken shelter there from the bombardment. The Israeli attack killed more than 100 Lebanese civilians, and wounded several Fijian peacekeepers serving with UNIFIL. The UN's report, issued some months later, included information documenting the presence of an Israeli drone surveillance plane in the immediate area during the airstrikes, thus rebutting the Israeli claim that the Qana attack was an unfortunate accident. U.S. diplomats worked hard to prevent the information from being released, but eventually Boutros-Ghali allowed the UN report, carefully edited but unmistakably damning to Israeli claims, to be made public. U.S. officials were furious, and their anger at the secretary-general seemed to consolidate Albright's already intense anti-Boutros-Ghali campaign.

Albright had correctly recognized that no one ever lost points inside the beltway by being too antagonistic towards the UN. Her position as ambassador to the institution Washington loves to hate placed her in the best position to target Boutros-Ghali as responsible for every fault Washington found with the UN, orchestrate his downfall, claim credit for it, and reap her just reward—in this case appointment by a victorious Bill Clinton as secretary-general in his second administration.

As it happened, Albright's campaign worked, setting the stage for her aggressively interventionist persona as secretary of state. There was wide international belief that the U.S. anti-Boutros-Ghali campaign was, as French President Jacques Chirac put it, a "campaign ploy that would soften after the November elections." As a result, it was not taken seriously at the UN during the first months of the public ousting effort. Boutros-Ghali had at least official endorsement from virtually every country at the UN, except for Israel and the U.S. And African diplomats, believing the administration wouldn't dare challenge Africa's right to a second term for its first secretary-general, refused to respond until after the election.

The November 4 election came and went, and it turned out they were all wrong. Clinton had won the election, but Albright had not yet been appointed secretary of state, and the anti-Boutros-Ghali campaign continued. On November 19, when the first Security Council tally was held on extending Boutros-Ghali's term for five more years, the count was 14 to 1. The U.S. veto was the sole "no" vote.

Ironically, Boutros-Ghali had been a problem at the UN, but hardly for Washington. Despite Washington's complaints about the prickly secretary-general's often arrogant posture, the five years of his tenure had been characterized by implementation of most major U.S. demands at the UN. Boutros-Ghali's besieged staff faced not only the elimination of 1,000 jobs; the UN's first "no-growth" budget; devastating cuts in vital UN development, social and humanitarian programs; U.S. financial abandonment, and U.S. media and government opprobrium, but as well had had to contend with a secretary-general with little evident respect for, and even less willingness to consult or collaborate with, his hard-working colleagues.

There was a rich irony in the Clinton administration's election-driven crusade against the secretary-general. Prior to the U.S. effort to oust him, Boutros-Ghali was hardly popular with most African countries. The wealthy, Paris-educated Egyptian was widely viewed, despite his occasional rhetorical defenses of the developing countries, as being far more accountable to rich Northern capitals than to the impoverished global South. Washington could have done far worse, in defending its own narrowly-defined interests, than a second Boutros-Ghali term.

But, at the end of the day, it was still Africa's turn for a second five-year term. There was a brief moment when some African countries turned to their long-time favorite also-ran, the Tanzanian Salim Ahmad Salim. Then head of the Organization of African Unity, Salim was widely respected for his leadership and defense of African independence and the non-aligned movement, as well as for a fearsome intellect and quick wit. Salim had orchestrated China's entry to the UN in the early 1970s, and outraged U.S. officials with a celebratory dance in the Assembly hall when Beijing took its seat. In past elections, he was always removed from Africa's short list because of U.S. opposition. But this time, desperate to keep African states on board despite its anti-Boutros-Ghali effort, Washington was stuck. At one point during the deliberations, cornered by a reporter's question probing her claim that the U.S. would accept "any" African candidate other than Boutros-Ghali, Madeleine Albright had to state that yes, this time Washington would accept even Salim Salim.

But by this time, U.S. power was too firmly in control for the divided, war-ravaged, aid-dependent African group at the UN to seriously challenge Washington's preference. That was widely known to lie with Kofi Annan, the Ghanaian then heading the UN's peacekeeping department.

There is little question that U.S. backing brought Kofi Annan to power. But despite the internationally poisonous label of being "Washington's man," Annan proved to be not only an innovative but a surprisingly independent secretary-general—far less in thrall to the U.S. than Washington had assumed. It should not have been so surprising—Annan won Washington's enthusiastic embrace less for himself than simply because he *wasn't* Boutros-Ghali. The UN staff was largely delighted with their new chief. Staff morale soared. Annan, the first black African secretary-general, had risen to the top UN position from within secretariat ranks, and was widely appreciated not only for his political acumen, but for his respect for and willingness to work collaboratively with his colleagues, and defend them against spurious attack. And internationally Annan soon found widespread support, as he moved to reassert UN centrality in crises across the globe. In Iraq, he defied U.S. efforts to prevent him from travelling to Baghdad in February 1998 to broker a diplomatic end to the U.S.-Iraq crisis then on the verge of an imminent unilateral U.S. air assault.

Annan faced a formidable challenge. He had little choice but to continue to implement extreme cuts in staff, resources and budgets in UN programs—faced with a U.S. arrears-driven budget crisis, there was little alternative. And he had to do so without any guarantee that Washington, even in the face of a dramatically "reformed" UN, would cough up even part of the $1.6 billion or so it owed the UN. Certainly the courtly and diplomatic Annan found a more pleasant personal reception in Congress when he came to Washington in 1998 to plead the UN's case. But the dues remained unpaid.

And Annan remained under attack in Washington. In March 1998 during a debate on paying the billion dollar-plus back dues, Rep. Gerald Solomon (R-NY) took the floor, repeating his longstanding condemnation of the UN. (The conservative Republican had co-sponsored the first legislation to prevent the U.S. from paying its UN dues, back in 1985.) Then, in an astonishing display of racism and chauvinism, he announced that Kofi Annan "should be horsewhipped."

One month later, announcing his resignation after twenty years in the House of Representatives, Solomon declared "I just don't believe in hiding your feelings...If you believe somebody ought to be horsewhipped, you should say it." Congressman Donald Payne (D-NJ), former chair of the Congressional Black Caucus and a member of the House Subcommittee on Africa, noted that "for the descendants of slaves to be told by a U.S. congressman that an African man should be 'horsewhipped' is outrageous."

Solomon's statement came only days before Clinton's first African visit, during which the president critically reflected on U.S. Cold War-era complicity in thwarting African development and democracy. One of Clinton's most euphoric moments was his triumphant welcome in Accra, capital of Kofi Annan's home country.

But whatever the personal abilities of Kofi Annan, whatever the claimed gratitude of the Republican right-wing and the Clintonites that the demonized Boutros-Ghali was out of the picture, the U.S. continued its refusal to pay its back dues. In fact, for more than eighteen months beginning in the middle of 1998, Washington moved seemingly inexorably towards losing its vote in the General Assembly. That result would come when the U.S. arrears totaled twice Washington's annual dues, anticipated for the December 31, 1999 deadline.

Not surprisingly, in the last two weeks of 1999, Washington paid $151 million of its arrears, enough to keep its Assembly vote.[52] But the U.S. remained in arrears—still more than $1.5 billion. The Clinton administration and Congress had battled throughout 1999 over paying the UN, although the administration never made it a public issue aimed at garnering popular support or pressure on congress. But the much-heralded final compromise reached that autumn was negotiated between the White House and Congress—the UN was out of the loop. The result was a settlement between the feuding wings of the U.S. government, but one still in substantial violation of UN requirements. The agreement required, before the back dues were paid, a commitment by the UN to accept a unilaterally imposed reduction of Washington's assigned share of the budget from 25 percent to 22 and eventually 20 percent. It mandated a host of U.S.-defined "reforms," of the old slash-and-burn staff and budget cut variety. And, perhaps most indicative of the scorn with which the UN was viewed by all sides of the Washington policy divide, it required the UN to accept *as payment in full* the two-thirds or so of the long-withheld back dues that Washington was prepared to even consider paying. Without that official acceptance by the UN, the "compromise" would be scrapped, and none of the U.S. arrears would be paid.

In January 2000, UN-bashing Senator Jesse Helms visited the Security Council at the invitation of Ambassador Richard Holbrooke, that month's Council president. He lectured the Council members on the inappropriateness of countries' voting against the U.S. in the General Assembly, and claimed that far from owing the UN money, the U.S. should be paid over $10 billion by the UN for costs of Washington's own unilateral military actions in places like Iraq, Somalia or elsewhere. He bragged about the unilateralism of the Reagan Doctrine, in which "we have provided weaponry, training and intelligence. And in other cases, the United States has intervened directly.... In none of those cases, however, did the United States ask for, or receive, the approval of the United Nations to 'legitimize' its actions." Namibia's Ambassador, Martin Andjaba, was outraged, given the Reagan doctrine's denial of independence to Namibia, support to apartheid South Africa and the UNITA rebels in Angola. The Doctrine "contributed to a lot of suffering in Africa," he said. "Some of us in SWAPO who were a legitimate and genuine national liberation movement were called other names: terrorists. And those that caused death and destruction in Africa were called liberators—and they were supported. That page has passed, but we have it fresh in our memories."[53]

Helms threatened a U.S. withdrawal from the UN if the global organization did not serve as an "effective instrument" of the "sovereign rights of the American people." And he claimed that he spoke for the American people in his anti-UN assault. But he was wrong. The irony was that throughout the years of official U.S. non-cooperation with the UN, popular support for the international organization remained high.

A whopping 87 percent of voters wanted the U.S. to retain its UN membership. Poll after poll showed that Americans held the UN in higher esteem (at 72 percent) than Jesse Helms' own Congress (at only 54 percent).[54] A poll in mid-1997 by the University of Maryland revealed the wide gap between policymakers' perception of what people believed about the UN, and what the public actually believes. For example, foreign policy experts in congress, the White House, media figures and other Washington insiders believed that only 14 percent of Americans support a stronger UN. In fact, the same poll showed that 83 percent of Americans believe that strengthening the UN should be a U.S. foreign policy goal. On the question of unpaid U.S. dues, the policymakers thought 11 percent of Americans support paying off the arrears; the true figure turned out to be 58 percent of the public.[55] Even stronger support came from young Americans, aged 18 to 29, of whom 74 percent believe the U.S. should pay its dues, even when the question included reference to the staggering $1.5 billion figure.[56]

A year later, a July 1999 study showed 80 percent of voters believing that "honoring our commitment" is a good reason the U.S. should pay its back dues; 66 percent disapprove of withholding UN dues. And interestingly, the poll indicated widespread understanding that "the U.S. has the clout to make sure no UN action violates our country's right to defend its interests around the world"—78 percent agreed with that statement. By November 1999, almost two-thirds of Americans said the world even needs an international army—they understand, as Washington insiders apparently do not, that an enhanced Pentagon is the not answer.[57]

PERILOUS PARTNERSHIPS & PRIVATIZATIONS

The problem remained that popular support for the UN was wide, but not deep. Most Americans support the UN, but too few had been mobilized to do anything about its financial and political crisis. The Clinton administration, even during its early "assertive multilateralism" stage, did nothing to mobilize the population to defend the UN against the ravages brought about by U.S. withholding of funds and political attack.

As a result, it was understandable when the secretary-general, desperate to find alternate sources of funding, turned to the private sector to try to develop new "partnerships" between the UN and global corporations.

The potential for such partnerships became clear in September 1997, when billionaire Ted Turner donated a billion dollars, the largest such gift in history, to UN programs dealing with children's health, the environment, girls' education and some other specific issues. It was a generous gift from one of the world's wealthiest individuals, and was likely motivated by genuinely internationalist sentiments. But whatever the motivations, Turner's gift set the stage for a dangerous privatization of United Nations decision-making, reducing it from an instrument of potentially powerful global multilateralism, to a vehicle for channeling private individual or, even more perilous, corporate funds.

Turner and his wife Jane Fonda stated that they had "no intention" of interfering with UN decision-making or to dictate the UN's agenda. But by establishing an independent foundation that would make the final decisions regarding which UN programs should benefit, they created precisely what they wanted to avoid: a group of outside individuals, accountable only to their donors and themselves, suddenly playing a major role in determining the strength and viability of UN programs and priorities.

Given the depth of the UN financial crisis, it was not surprising UN officials were thrilled with Turner's announcement. But there were risks. If funding for the humanitarian programs already among the UN's most popular, was no longer in danger, the overall UN financial crisis would appear less urgent. The role of the U.S. in fomenting that crisis by refusing to pay $1.5 billion in overdue general and peacekeeping assessments, would appear less outrageous. Encouraging individual donations and corporate funding, seemingly logical in this era of world-wide privatization, undermined the responsibility of UN member states, most especially the U.S., the biggest deadbeat nation at the UN, to remain accountable *as nations* and as governments to the global organization as a key organ of diplomacy.

If governments' obligations to pay for the most popular of the UN agencies, such as the Children's Fund or the World Health Organization, were subsumed by private donors allowed to pick and choose their own favorite programs, there remained great danger that governments could soon be held responsible only for funding the UN secretariat itself. And with mean-spirited unilateralism dominating Washington decision-making on the United Nations, what hope would remain for U.S. funding of the UN's overall structure? When the organization continued (however inaccurately) to be attacked as a "bloated bureaucracy," who in congress would vote funds to sustain the prosaic UN headquarters and its staff, regardless of their role in scaffolding the more cuddly and photogenic childhood vaccination or education programs?

The message of privatization was being heard. President Clinton, in his September 22, 1997 address to the General Assembly just a few days after the Turner announcement, called on the UN to "focus even more on shifting resources from hand-outs to hand-ups." It was not so difficult to see his application of that kind of Washington-style welfare reform to the world organization: the U.S. would not pay the hundreds of millions of dollars it owes the UN, but it will applaud private sector donations instead. The United Nations "no longer need go it alone," Clinton said. Turner's donation "highlights the potential for partnership between the UN and the private sector.... And I hope more will follow his lead."

Ted Turner said that "everyone who's rich in the world can expect a call from me" asking for money for the UN. But neither Turner nor his supporters raised the question of a similar appeal for the richest *nations* in the world to consider, instead of more private or corporate charity, imposing a specially designated UN-support tax on global financial transactions, through which most of the wealth of today's super-rich is generated. Even a tiny 0.1 percent tax on those cross-border capital flows, collected and disbursed to the UN by governments (especially the U.S. government, where the vast majority of those cross-border profits are made) would generate enough to cover the UN's $1 billion-plus annual budget.

Shortly afterwards, in early 1998, Kofi Annan went to Davos, Switzerland, for the annual meeting of the World Economic Forum, the glittering gathering of wealth and power that brings together business, finance and government leaders. He opened the question of closer ties between the United Nations and the private sector, but made clear the need for the UN to remain independent of business, and to remain accountable to the values on which it was founded.

The following year, with the UN's financial crisis in even more dire straits, Annan returned to Davos. He began with a warning of the looming threat of an international backlash against globalization because of the vast chasms between wealth and poverty it was creating and exacerbating. Just a day before the secretary-general spoke at Davos, South African President Nelson Mandela had asked the assembled leaders "is globalization only for the powerful? Does it offer nothing to men, women and children who are ravaged by the violence of poverty?"[58] This time Annan challenged international business leaders directly to enter a "compact" with the United Nations. If global corporations would promote human rights, labor rights and environmental protection the UN would provide political backing for free trade and open markets. He urged corporations to operate in accord with the Universal Declaration of Human Rights, the International Labor Organization's Declaration on Fundamental Principles and Rights and Work, and the Rio (Earth Summit) Declaration on Environment and Development. And he said that UN agencies were prepared to assist those corporations willing to adopt those standards.

Annan's proposed compact was cautiously drawn, and did not itself threaten the independence or credibility of the UN. But some UN constituent organizations took his proposal as license for far-reaching "partnerships" with global corporate giants that threatened the very basis for which those UN agencies were created.

Probably no UN agency went farther in recreating its identity as corporate partner than the UN Development Program. In early 1999, it created the Global Sustainable Development Facility, designed officially to show that "helping the poor in developing countries can also be profitable."[59] In fact, the corporations who joined the effort, for an insignificant $50,000 contribution, would gain access to UNDP's network of high-level contacts and, even more valuable, a chance to "greenwash" often appalling environmental, labor, and human rights records. Only days before his resignation, in a meeting with representatives of northern and southern-based NGOs concerned about the initiative, out-going UNDP chief Gus Speth went to great pains to describe the project (to which he had already assigned three full-time staff people) as still in the preliminary stages.

But however defensive the UNDP leadership, the planning and development of the GSDF project did not stop. And no UN leader, including Speth, was so eager to go as far in embracing corporate partnership as his successor, Mark Malloch Brown, who came to the agency in July 1999 directly from a career as a high-ranking public relations official for the World Bank.

Malloch Brown, a favorite in Washington, brought even the language of corporate culture directly to the development agency. In his inaugural speech on the day he took up his position as UNDP Administrator, he told the assembled UNDP headquarters staff and those in far-flung field postings brought in through video-conferencing, "We must work to develop a universal corporate focus and a corporate standard for country offices. We must overcome once and for all the image of a loose federation of development entrepreneurs lacking unity....Re-building UNDP's franchise and reputation for excellence starts with field entrepreneurship."

This from the new head of an institution whose own groundbreaking analysis, the *1999 UNDP Human Development Report*, cautioned of precisely the dangers inherent in the direction Mark Malloch Brown appeared to be heading. In early 2000, Nelson Mandela praised the *Report*'s warning that "when the profit motives of market players get out of hand, they challenge people's ethics and sacrifice respect for justice and human rights.... A simple reliance on the market to eradicate poverty and gross inequality is a grave fallacy. We all know that the market with all its benefits does not, as it were, sort it all out."

Mandela went on to describe the *Report*'s "specific figures highlighting the unequal and inequitable distribution. The top fifth of countries have 86 percent of GDP; the bottom fifth just 1 percent. The top fifth command 82 percent of the world export markets and 68 percent of foreign direct investment; the bottom fifth just 1 percent of each of these."[60] What the market didn't "sort out," of course, was precisely what UNDP was supposed to be doing.

But the corporate-friendly approach was not limited to partnerships. The UNDP's own financial crisis remained severe. Sparked largely by reductions in U.S. contributions, its core funding dropped to $750 million in 1999, down from $1.2 billion just five years earlier, one of the deepest cuts faced by any UN agency. Within three months, Malloch Brown had begun what the *Financial Times* called a "revolution" at the agency. Facing massive budget cuts and demands for management reforms, the UNDP's new PR-savvy leader did not attempt to hold Washington accountable through creative public campaigns. Instead, he chose a classic corporate-style downsizing, "preparing to embark on what looks likely to become the most radical overhaul yet."[61]

Malloch Brown seemed prepared to accept downsizing UNDP's leadership in development assistance relative to corporate, World Bank, IMF and other institutions' roles, as much as he relied on downsizing staff to deal with budget cuts. In an interview only a month after taking over, Malloch Brown said, "I believe UNDP's value-added lies in the area of advice and support for capacity building and not in funding many different projects that would be better financed by others with deeper pockets or more particular expertise. We have to be very tough-minded in choosing not just what to do but what not to do."[62] Malloch Brown had clearly accepted Bill Clinton's view on the importance of the UN learning to say no.

In his interview Malloch Brown said that UNDP's "partnerships with the private sector...cannot be about lending our good name to narrow commercial goals." But even the *New York Times* acknowledged that "companies know that if they help the United Nations with its pet projects, it will open doors ...[I]t is also a chance to introduce their brands to growing markets, while playing up to agencies that routinely buy their products.... [Malloch Brown said] 'It's not like we're saying Microsoft gets Botswana, Corel gets Ghana; we're stimulating competition.'"

Others soon followed Ted Turner's lead. In late 1999 the *New York Times* described how the Microsoft billionaire's "Bill and Melinda

Gates Foundation earmarked $26 million to help UNICEF wipe out tetanus in infants. But...[t]he new trend is for companies themselves to use UN collaboration as a marketing tool, not just a philanthropic one. 'Of course we want to help eradicate neonatal tetanus, but we also want to stimulate the use of nonreusable injection devices, and to build relationships with ministries of health that might buy other products from us as their economies develop,' said Gary M. Cohen, president of the medical systems unit of Becton Dickinson & Co. He is working with UNICEF—one of its biggest customers for syringes and other medical devices—to distribute the company's patented disposable syringes for the same anti-tetanus program the Gates Foundation is supporting."[63] The *Times* also noted another 1998 example, in which "Chevron, which had been drilling oil in Kazakhstan for five years, contributed $500,000 toward a business center, run by the UN Development Program, that helps Kazakhstanis set up new businesses." The *Times* didn't mention that also in 1998, the same Chevron Oil, across the world in the Niger Delta, had hired helicopters to ferry government soldiers to gun down peaceful protesters demanding environmental protection and Chevron's assistance to the development of the oil-rich but impoverished region. Two activists were killed, eleven others imprisoned and some tortured.[64] The UNDP seemed to find no contradiction.

International civil society organizations began mobilizing by 1998 against the new business orientation that increasingly undermined the UN's independence and particularly threatened the world organization's potential to serve as the focal point of a new internationalism that could counter corporate-driven globalization. The widespread protests during the World Trade Organization's Millennial Round in Seattle in December 1999, and the resulting inability of the WTO to craft its new corporate-friendly agenda, gave new hope. But it remained uncertain whether global activists, North and South, could stem the roaring tide of U.S.-orchestrated corporate threats to the United Nations.

UNILATERAL INTERVENTIONS AND INTERVENTIONIST UNILATERALISM

The law of empire is perhaps most clear of all in how the U.S., the only country in the world with the power to do so, has shifted decision-making on international interventions out of the hands of the United Nations, in favor of illegal reliance on NATO as an authorizing power, and ultimately on unilateral U.S. action.

In 1990 the U.S., however cynically, promoted the UN as its chosen instrument, orchestrating through bribes and threats and punishments the Security Council vote authorizing Washington's "coalition" war against Iraq. In the 1992–94 period of escalating crises and failures of international peacekeeping efforts in Bosnia, Somalia, Rwanda and elsewhere, the U.S. assigned the UN the most difficult tasks, then blamed its own and allied failures on the global organization. President Clinton continued, throughout his second term, to hold the UN responsible for the tragic deaths of U.S. Rangers in Somalia during Washington's non-UN-authorized, unilateral Pentagon mission in 1993.

At the end of the decade, former Bosnia troubleshooter and current U.S. Ambassador to the UN Richard Holbrooke was still blaming the UN for the disaster of Bosnia. "The UN was not the right organization," he said. "The fundamental mistake of the U.S. and the Europeans in 1991–94 was not to recognize at the outset that this was a NATO problem."[65] The mistake, for Holbrooke, wasn't that the U.S. and its European allies in the Security Council kept the UN mandate in Bosnia too narrow, or that they refused to provide the financial, personnel, political, and military support needed to implement even the limited mandate thus insuring that the blue helmets would be incapable of defending civilians in Srebrenica or other Council-identified "safe havens"—or that they denied the UN peacekeepers the forces necessary to do the job they were assigned. No, the problem according to Holbrooke was simple: the UN was the wrong organization. It was the UN's fault.

It was in 1999 that French Prime Minister Lionel Jospin announced that "we're confronted with a new problem on the international scene. The United States often behaves in a unilateral manner." His Foreign Minister, Hubert Vedrine went further, asserting that "the predominant weight of the United States and the absence for the moment of a counterweight...leads it to hegemony, and the idea it has of its mission to unilateralism. And that's inadmissible."[66]

Three months later, having denied the UN and European diplomatic organizations the authority and resources needed for serious preventive diplomacy in the escalating Kosovo crisis, Washington took the final step towards relinquishing whatever claim it still made to multilateralism. It abandoned the UN altogether, replacing the Charter-imposed legal requirement of UN authorization for the use of force, with the projection of the NATO military alliance as sponsor of yet another bombing campaign.

Vedrine described an approach to challenging U.S. unilateralism. "There are two opposing approaches: on one side, the dominant power with its means of influence; on the other side, a system both multilateral and multipolar associating all or part of the 185 countries of the world."[67] While Vedrine's proposals reflected France's limited definitions of multilateralism (focusing on "reform or reinforcement" of the Security Council, the WTO, the IMF, etc. rather than the General Assembly, the UN's ECOSOC, citizens' human rights, labor and environmental movements, etc.) he raises the right idea: unilateral power must be fought with engaged internationalism, not isolationist retreat.

There is no question that the U.S. should have accepted UN leadership and decision-making years ago, in Iraq, in Yugoslavia, in East Timor and elsewhere. There is no question that despite its flaws the UN represents a far more democratic expression of "the international community" than does Washington alone, or NATO's North Atlantic Council. There is no question that the U.S. should have paid its UN dues in full and on time all along; should have supported UN efforts (along with those of the OSCE, the OAU and other regional organizations) to respond pro-actively and collaboratively to emerging humanitarian crises; should have supported the creation of a UN Department of Preventive Diplomacy and a standing, independent UN-controlled rapid-response civilian/police/peacekeeping force.

There is no question that those things would have made the UN—a stronger, more democratic and more empowered UN bolstered by international social movements and far-flung citizens' organizations throughout the world—the centerpiece of a new internationalism. And that was certainly not the goal of Washington's law of empire.

A Welsh woman, writing at the beginning of the year 2000, admonished Americans that it may be that "President Clinton assures his people again, at the start of the 21st century, that they are the guiding light of the world, but the world does not invariably think so...To offer a last, best hope to the world, to be its guiding light, the United States must be powerful enough to impose its example on everyone else. In Lincoln's day, this might well have seemed an honorable intention, in a world still dominated by antique despotisms. Today, the example is not so compelling to many of us. We don't so often think of America as a matchless model of public liberty. So many of us live in democracies now and have given up such barbarities as the death penalty or such anachronisms as the right to carry guns. From far away in Wales, where I live, your country seems to us an increasingly unattractive exponent of capitalist neoimperialism."

"President Clinton," she went on, "surely must have noticed the uneasy stirring of the peoples before the prospects of global corporationism,...or of the ubiquitous influences of Disney and McDonalds. They are all threats to the individuality of lesser states, even to their sovereignty, and all of them, every one, are symptoms of that American dominance that once seemed the last best hope of Earth."

Finally, her message excoriated "America's evident contempt for the United Nations, its public air of self-righteous know-it-all-ism, its willfull interference in almost any political or military dispute anywhere across the globe."[68]

Madeleine Albright's and Jesse Helms' despicable efforts to make the UN a "tool of American foreign policy," however consistent with earlier U.S. history in the world organization, reflect exactly that kind of "self-righteous know-it-all-ism." Washington on its own is too rarely interested in, and too often does not know how to end wars or protect human rights. Bill Clinton's and Richard Holbrooke's machinations to set up the UN to take the fall for U.S. and NATO failures is no way to bring peace to Yugoslavia or East Timor. Civil war-wracked Sierra Leone, Colombia, Angola all need the UN—a UN empowered, financed, staffed and resourced to respond to those and other crises, not a UN called in as the scapegoat for Washington's failures. Being the richest and most powerful nation in the world does not give the U.S. the right to trample international law, to run endgames around the UN, to use or discard the global organization at the whim of superpower arrogance or the caprice of domestic politics.

At the turn of the twenty-first century, the world has had enough of empires writing their own rules.

Notes

[1] Catherine Toups, *Washington Times*, 13 December 1995.

[2] Justin Brown, "Rise of Armed Civilians Adds to Kosovo Dangers," *Christian Science Monitor,* 10 July 1998.

[3] Dalia Acosta & Patricia Grogg, "NATO's War Against Yugoslavia Has Dealt UN a 'Mortal Blow,'" *Third World Resurgence* no. 39.

[4] David Hoffman, "New Russian Security Plan Criticizes West," *Washington Post*, 15 January 2000.

[5] Eric Schmitt, "UN Drags Feet in Kosovo, Pentagon Leaders Declare," *New York Times,* 21 July 1999.

[6] Schmitt.

[7] "UN Needs Money, Manpower for Kosovo," Associated Press, 1 July 1999.

[8] T. Christian Miller & Ann M. Simmons, "Relief Camps for Africans, Kosovars Worlds Apart," 21 May 1999.

[9] Miller & Simmons.

[10] Miller & Simmons.

[11] Cited in Alexander Cockburn, "America's Sordid Past in East Timor," *Los Angeles Times*, 30 September 1999.

[12] Steven Mufson & Colum Lynch, "E. Timor Failure Puts UN on Spot," *Washington Post*, 26 September 1999.

[13] Steven Mufson & Bradley Graham, "U.S., IMF Move to Isolate Jakarta," *Washington Post*, 10 September 1999.

[14] "Another Messy Apartment," *Washington Post* editorial, 10 September 1999.

[15] Philip Shenon, "President Says Jakarta Must Act or Admit Troops," *New York Times,* 10 September 1999.

[16] Mufson & Lynch.

[17] Barbara Crossette, "Annan Says UN Must Take Over East Timor Rule," *New York Times*, 5 October 1999.

[18] *Singapore Straits Times*, 25 October 1999, cited in UNWire 25 October 1999.

[19] Philip Shenon, "Washington & Baghdad Agree on One Point: Sanctions Hurt," *Washington Post*, 22 November 1998.

[20] Barbara Crossette, "For Iraq, a Dog House With Many Rooms," *New York Times*, 23 November 1997.

[21] Steven Lee Myers, "U.S. Jets Strike Missile Sites 30 Miles Outside Baghdad," *New York Times*, 25 February 1999.

[22] Interview, Baghdad, August-September 1999.

[23] Butler meeting with UN-accredited disarmament organizations, New York, 12 February 1998.

[24] Tim Weiner, "The Case of the Spies Without a Country," 17 January 1999.

[25] 2 March 1998, outside Security Council chamber, UN Headquarters, New York.

[26] Laura Silber & David Buchan, "UN-Iraq Accord Faces Early Test," *Financial Times*, 4 March 1998.

[27] Lee Michael Katz, "UN Waffling on Threat of Force," *USA Today*, 3 March 1998.

[28] Jonathan Peterson, "Clinton to Iraq: U.S. 'Prepared to Act,'" *Los Angeles Times*, 4 March 1998.

[29] Meeting with Lt. Gen. Hal M. Hornburg, U.S. Air Force Academy, Colorado Springs, September 1999.

[30] Barbara Crossette, "America Moves Apart from the UN on Iraq," 26 December 1999.

[31] UNDP *Human Development Report*, cited in *Choices* (UNDP Magazine), December 1999.

[32] Alessandra Stanley, "U.S. Specifies Terms for War Crimes Court," *New York Times*, 10 July 1998.

[33] Richardson statement in Rome, 17 June 1998.

[34] Richardson.

[35] Thomas W. Lippman, "Worldwide War Crimes High Court is Approved: Delegates Overrule U.S. Objections," *Washington Post*, 18 July 1998.

[36] "Putting Limits on Lawlessness," *Washington Post*, 25 October 1998.

[37] Scheffer remarks issued by State Department, 31 August 1998.

[38] Steven Lee Myers, "After U.S. Reversal, Deal is Struck to Bar Using Child Soldiers, *New York Times*, 22 January 2000.

[39] Agencia de Informacion/Cubaweb, 6 December 1999, translation by UNWire, 21 December 1999.

[40] Atlanta *Journal -Constitution*, 23 October 1999, cited in UNWire, UN Foundation, 25 October 1999.

[41] Clifford Vellien, "Angola's Endless Agony," *The Guardian*, 25 Feb. 1999.

[42] "Horror in Rwanda, Shame in the UN," *New York Times*, 3 May 1994.

[43] "Report of the Independent Inquiry Into the Actions of the United Nations During the 1994 Genocide in Rwanda," 15 December 1999.

[44] Introduction, "Report to the Secretary-General Pursuant to General Assembly Resolution 53/35, United Nations.

[45] Report, 105.

[46] Report, 105.

[47] Report, 107.

[48] Report, 111.

[49] Gore speech to AIPAC, 23 May 1999.

[50] *New York Times*, 16 July 1999.

[51] *Washington Times*, June 1996 cited in Boutros Boutros-Ghali, *Unvanquished*, 1999.

[52] "U.S. pays $151 million to United Nations, saves Assembly vote," Reuters, December 21, 1999.

[53] Barbara Crossette, "Helms, in Visit to UN, Offers Harsh Message," *New York Times*, 21 January 2000.

[54] Better World Campaign survey conducted by Public Opinion Strategies & Talmey-Drake Research and Strategy, July 1999.

[55] *The InterDependent*, UN Association, Winter 1997-98.

[56] 20/20 Vision Poll, conducted by Bennett, Petts & Blumenthal, cited by UNWire, 21 January 2000.

[57] Harris Interactive release, 12 November 1999, cited by UNWire.

[58] James Flanigan, *Los Angeles Times*, 31 January 1999.

[59] Naomi Klein, *Toronto Star,* 26 March 1999.

[60] Nelson Mandela, "Globalizing Responsibility, " *Boston Globe*, 4 January 2000.

[61] Mark Suzman, *Financial Times*, 19 Oct. 1999.

[62] Ashali Varma, "INTERVIEW: Mark Malloch Brown on UNDP," *Choices*, August 1999.

[63] Claudia H. Deutsch, "Unlikely Allies Join With the United Nations," *New York Times,* 10 December 1999.

[64] Amy Goodman & Jeremy Scahill, "Drilling and Killing: Chevron & Nigeria's Oil Dictatorship," Democracy Now, 28 May 1998, Pacifica Radio.

[65] Richard Holbrook, 20 December 1999, National Public Radio.

[66] John Vinocur, "Going It Alone: U.S. Upsets France So Paris Begins a Campaign to Strengthen Multilateral Institutions," *International Herald-Tribune*, 3 February 1999.

[67] Vinocur.

[68] Jan Morris, "Mankind Stirs Uneasily at American Dominance," *Los Angeles Times,* 10 February 2000.

APPENDIX

Charter Of The United Nations

WE THE PEOPLES OF THE UNITED NATIONS, determined to save succeeding generations from the scourge of war, which twice in our lifetime has brought untold sorrow to mankind, and to reaffirm faith in fundamental human rights, in the dignity and worth of the human person, in the equal rights of men and women and of nations large and small, and to establish conditions under which justice and respect for the obligations arising from treaties and other sources of international law can be maintained, and to promote social progress and better standards of life in larger freedom, and for these ends to practice tolerance and live together in peace with one another as good neighbours, and to unite our strength to maintain international peace and security, and to ensure, by the acceptance of principles and the institution of methods, that armed force shall not be used, save in the common interest, and to employ international machinery for the promotion of the economic and social advancement of all peoples, have resolved to combine our efforts to accomplish these aims. Accordingly, our respective Governments, through representatives assembled in the city of San Francisco, who have exhibited their full powers found to be in good and due form, have agreed to the present Charter of the United Nations and do hereby establish an international organization to be known as the United Nations.

CHAPTER I
PURPOSES AND PRINCIPLES
ARTICLE 1
The Purposes of the United Nations are:

1. To maintain international peace and security, and to that end: to take effective collective measures for the prevention and removal of threats to the peace, and for the suppression of acts of aggression or other breaches of the peace, and to bring about by peaceful means, and in conformity with the principles of justice and international law, adjustment or settlement of international disputes or situations which might lead to a breach of the peace;
2. To develop friendly relations among nations based on respect for the principle of equal rights and self-determination of peoples, and to take other appropriate measures to strengthen universal peace;
3. To achieve international co-operation in solving international problems of an economic, social, cultural, or humanitarian character, and in promoting and encouraging respect for human rights and for fundamental freedoms for all without distinction as to race, sex, language, or religion; and
4. To be a centre for harmonizing the actions of nations in the attainment of these common ends.

ARTICLE 2

The Organization and its Members, in pursuit of the Purposes stated in Article 1, shall act in accordance with the following Principles:

1. The Organization is based on the principle of the sovereign equality of all its Members.
2. All Members, in order to ensure to all of them the rights and benefits resulting from membership, shall fulfil in good faith the obligations assumed by them in accordance with the present Charter.
3. All Members shall settle their international disputes by peaceful means in such a manner that international peace and security, and justice, are not endangered.
4. All Members shall refrain in their international relations from the threat or use of force against the territorial integrity or political independence of any state, or in any other manner inconsistent with the Purposes of the United Nations.
5. All Members shall give the United Nations every assistance in any action it takes in accordance with the present Charter, and shall refrain from giving assistance to any state against which the United Nations is taking preventive or enforcement action.
6. The Organization shall ensure that states which are not Members of the United Nations act in accordance with these Principles so far as may be necessary for the maintenance of international peace and security.
7. Nothing contained in the present Charter shall authorize the United Nations to intervene in matters which are essentially within the domestic jurisdiction of any state or shall require the Members to submit such matters to settlement under the present Charter; but this principle shall not prejudice the application of enforcement measures under Chapter VII.

CHAPTER II
MEMBERSHIP
ARTICLE 3

The original Members of the United Nations shall be the states which, having participated in the United Nations Conference on International Organization at San Francisco, or having previously signed the Declaration by United Nations of 1 January 1942, sign the present Charter and ratify it in accordance with Article 110.

ARTICLE 4

1. Membership in the United Nations is open to all other peace-loving states which accept the obligations contained in the present Charter and, in the judgment of the Organization, are able and willing to carry out these obligations.
2. The admission of any such state to membership in the United Nations will be effected by a decision of the General Assembly upon the recommendation of the Security Council.

ARTICLE 5

A Member of the United Nations against which preventive or enforcement action has been taken by the Security Council may be suspended from the exercise of the rights and privileges of membership by the General Assembly upon the recommendation of the Security Council. The exercise of these rights and privileges may be restored by the Security Council.

ARTICLE 6

A Member of the United Nations which has persistently violated the Principles contained in the present Charter may be expelled from the Organization by the General Assembly upon the recommendation of the Security Council.

CHAPTER III
ORGANS
ARTICLE 7

1. There are established as the principal organs of the United Nations: a General Assembly, a Security Council, an Economic and Social Council, a Trusteeship Council, an International Court of Justice, and a Secretariat.

2. Such subsidiary organs as may be found necessary may be established in accordance with the present Charter.

ARTICLE 8

The United Nations shall place no restrictions on the eligibility of men and women to participate in any capacity and under conditions of equality in its principal and subsidiary organs.

CHAPTER IV
THE GENERAL ASSEMBLY COMPOSITION
ARTICLE 9

1. The General Assembly shall consist of all the Members of the United Nations.

2. Each Member shall have not more than five representatives in the General Assembly.

FUNCTIONS AND POWERS
ARTICLE 10

The General Assembly may discuss any questions or any matters within the scope of the present Charter or relating to the powers and functions of any organs provided for in the present Charter, and, except as provided in Article 12, may make recommendations to the Members of the United Nations or to the Security Council or to both on any such questions or matters.

ARTICLE 11

1. The General Assembly may consider the general principles of co-operation in the maintenance of international peace and security, including the principles governing disarmament and the regulation of armaments, and may make recommendations with regard to such principles to the Members or to the Security Council or to both.

2. The General Assembly may discuss any questions relating to the maintenance of international peace and security brought before it by any Member of the United Nations, or by the Security Council, or by a state which is not a member of the United Nations in accordance with Article 35, paragraph 2, and except as provided in Article 12, may make recommendations with regard to any such questions to the state or states concerned or to the Security Council or to both. Any such question on which action is necessary shall be referred to the Security Council by the General Assembly either before or after discussion.

3. The General Assembly may call the attention of the Security Council to situations which are likely to endanger international peace and security.

4. The powers of the General Assembly set forth in this Article shall not limit the general scope of Article 10.

ARTICLE 12

1. While the Security Council is exercising in respect of any dispute or situation the functions assigned to it in the present Charter, the General Assembly shall not make any recommendation with regard to that dispute or situation unless the Security Council so requests.

2. The Secretary-General, with the consent of the Security Council, shall notify the General Assembly at each session of any matters relative to the maintenance of international peace and security which are being dealt with by the Security Council and

shall similarly notify the General Assembly, or the Members of the United Nations if the General Assembly is not in session, immediately the Security Council ceases to deal with such matters.

ARTICLE 13

1. The General Assembly shall initiate studies and make recommendations for the purpose of:

    a. promoting international co-operation in the political field and encouraging the progressive development of international law and its codification;

    b. promoting international co-operation in the economic, social, cultural, educational, and health fields, and assisting in the realization of human rights and fundamental freedoms for all without distinction as to race, sex, language, or religion.

2. The further responsibilities, functions and powers of the General Assembly with respect to matters mentioned in paragraph 1(b) above are set forth in Chapters IX and X.

ARTICLE 14

Subject to the provisions of Article 12, the General Assembly may recommend measures for the peaceful adjustment of any situation, regardless of origin, which it deems likely to impair the general welfare or friendly relations among nations, including situations resulting from a violation of the provisions of the present Charter setting forth the Purposes and Principles of the United Nations.

ARTICLE 15

1. The General Assembly shall receive and consider annual and special reports from the Security Council; these reports shall include an account of the measures that the Security Council has decided upon or taken to maintain international peace and security.

2. The General Assembly shall receive and consider reports from the other organs of the United Nations.

ARTICLE 16

The General Assembly shall perform such functions with respect to the international trusteeship system as are assigned to it under Chapters XII and XIII, including the approval of the trusteeship agreements for areas not designated as strategic.

ARTICLE 17

1. The General Assembly shall consider and approve the budget of the Organization.

2. The expenses of the Organization shall be borne by the Members as apportioned by the General Assembly.

3. The General Assembly shall consider and approve any financial and budgetary arrangements with specialized agencies referred to in Article 57 and shall examine the administrative budgets of such specialized agencies with a view to making recommendations to the agencies concerned.

VOTING

ARTICLE 18

1. Each member of the General Assembly shall have one vote.

2. Decisions of the General Assembly on important questions shall be made by a two-thirds majority of the members present and voting. These questions shall include: recommendations with respect to the maintenance of international peace and security, the election of the non-permanent members of the Security Council, the election of the members of the Economic and Social Council, the election of members of the Trusteeship Council in accordance with paragraph 1(c) of Article 86, the admission of new Members to the United Nations, the suspension of the rights and privileges of membership, the expulsion of Members, questions relating to the operation of the trusteeship system, and budgetary questions.

3. Decisions on other questions, including the determination of additional categories of questions to be decided by a two-thirds majority of the members present and voting.

ARTICLE 19

A Member of the United Nations which is in arrears in the payment of its financial contributions to the Organization shall have no vote in the General Assembly if the amount of its arrears equals or exceeds the amount of the contributions due from it for the preceding two full years. The General Assembly, may nevertheless, permit such a Member to vote if it is satisfied that the failure to pay is due to conditions beyond the control of the Member.

PROCEDURE
ARTICLE 20

The General Assembly shall meet in regular annual sessions and in such special sessions as occasion may require. Special sessions shall be convoked by the Secretary-General at the request of the Security Council or of a majority of the Members of the United Nations.

ARTICLE 21

The General Assembly shall adopt its own rules of procedure. It shall elect its President for each session.

ARTICLE 22

The General Assembly may establish such subsidiary organs as it deems necessary for the performance of its functions.

CHAPTER V
THE SECURITY COUNCIL COMPOSITION
ARTICLE 23

1. The Security Council shall consist of fifteen Members of the United Nations. The Republic of China, France, the Union of Soviet Socialist Republics, the United Kingdom of Great Britain and Northern Ireland, and the United States of America shall be permanent members of the Security Council. The General Assembly shall elect ten other Members of the United Nations to be non-permanent members of the Security Council, due regard being specially paid, in the first instance to the contribution of Members of the United Nations to the maintenance of international peace and security and to the other purposes of the Organization, and also to equitable geographical distribution.
2. The non-permanent members of the Security Council shall be elected for a term of two years. In the first election of the non-permanent members after the increase of the membership of the Security Council from eleven to fifteen, two of the four additional members shall be chosen for a term of one year. A retiring member shall not be eligible for immediate re-election.
3. Each member of the Security Council shall have one representative.

FUNCTIONS AND POWERS
ARTICLE 24

1. In order to ensure prompt and effective action by the United Nations, its Members confer on the Security Council primary responsibility for the maintenance of international peace and security, and agree that in carrying out its duties under this responsibility the Security Council acts on their behalf.
2. In discharging these duties the Security Council shall act in accordance with the Purposes and Principles of the United Nations. The specific powers granted to the Security Council for the discharge of these duties are laid down in Chapters VI, VII, VIII and XII.

3. The Security Council shall submit annual and, when necessary, special reports to the General Assembly for its consideration.

ARTICLE 25

The Members of the United Nations agree to accept and carry out the decisions of the Security Council in accordance with the present Charter.

ARTICLE 26

In order to promote the establishment and maintenance of international peace and security with the least diversion for armaments of the world's human and economic resources, the Security Council shall be responsible for formulating, with the assistance of the Military Staff Committee referred to in Article 47, plans to be submitted to the Members of the United Nations for the establishment of a system for the regulation of armaments.

VOTING
ARTICLE 27

1. Each member of the Security Council shall have one vote.

2. Decisions of the Security Council on procedural matters shall be made by an affirmative vote of nine members.

3. Decisions of the Security Council on all other matters shall be made by an affirmative vote of nine members including the concurring votes of the permanent members; provided that, in decisions under Chapter VI, and under paragraph 3 of Article 52, a party to a dispute shall abstain from voting.

PROCEDURE
ARTICLE 28

1. The Security Council shall be so organized as to be able to function continuously. Each member of the Security Council shall for this purpose be represented at all times at the seat of the Organization.

2. The Security Council shall hold periodic meetings at which each of its members may, if it so desires, be represented by a member of the government or by some other specially designated representative.

3. The Security Council may hold meetings at such places other than the seat of the Organization as in its judgment will best facilitate its work.

ARTICLE 29

The Security Council may establish such subsidiary organs as it deems necessary for the performance of its functions.

ARTICLE 30

The Security Council shall adopt its own rules of procedure, including the method of selecting its President.

ARTICLE 31

Any Member of the United Nations which is not a member of the Security Council may participate, without vote, in the discussion of any question brought before the Security Council whenever the latter considers that the interests of that Member are specially affected.

ARTICLE 32

Any Member of the United Nations which is not a member of the Security Council or any state which is not a Member of the United Nations, if it is a party to a dispute under consideration by the Security Council, shall be invited to participate, without vote, in the discussion relating to the dispute. The Security Council shall lay down such conditions as it deems just for the participation of a state which is not a Member of the United Nations.

CHAPTER VI
PACIFIC SETTLEMENT OF DISPUTES
ARTICLE 33

1. The parties to any dispute, the continuance of which is likely to endanger the maintenance of international peace and security, shall, first of all, seek a solution by negotiation, enquiry, mediation, conciliation, arbitration, judicial settlement, resort to regional agencies or arrangements, or other peaceful means of their own choice.
2. The Security Council shall, when it deems necessary, call upon the parties to settle their dispute by such means.

ARTICLE 34

The Security Council may investigate any dispute, or any situation which might lead to international friction or give rise to a dispute, in order to determine whether the continuance of the dispute or situation is likely to endanger the maintenance of international peace and security.

ARTICLE 35

1. Any Member of the United Nations may bring any dispute, or any situation of the nature referred to in Article 34, to the attention of the Security Council or of the General Assembly.
2. A state which is not a Member of the United Nations may bring to the attention of the Security Council or of the General Assembly any dispute to which it is a party if it accepts in advance, for the purposes of the dispute, the obligations of pacific settlement provided in the present Charter.
3. The proceedings of the General Assembly in respect of matters brought to its attention under this Article will be subject to the provisions of Articles 11 and 12.

ARTICLE 36

1. The Security Council may, at any stage of a dispute of the nature referred to in Article 33 or of a situation of like nature, recommend appropriate procedures or methods of adjustment.
2. The Security Council should take into consideration any procedures for the settlement of the dispute which have already been adopted by the Parties.
3. In making recommendations under this Article the Security Council should also take into consideration that legal disputes should as a general rule be referred by the Parties to the International Court of Justice in accordance with the provisions of the Statute of the Court.

ARTICLE 37

1. Should the parties to a dispute of the nature referred to in Article 33 fail to settle it by the means indicated in that Article, they shall refer it to the Security Council.
2. If the Security Council deems that the continuance of the dispute is in fact likely to endanger the maintenance of international peace and security, it shall decide whether to take action under Article 36 or to recommend such terms of settlement as it may consider appropriate.

ARTICLE 38

Without prejudice to the provisions of Articles 33 to 37, the Security Council may, if all the parties to any dispute so request, make recommendations to the parties with a view to a pacific settlement of the dispute.

CHAPTER VII
ACTION WITH RESPECT TO THREATS TO THE PEACE, BREACHES OF THE PEACE, AND ACTS OF AGGRESSION
ARTICLE 39

The Security Council shall determine the existence of any threat to the peace, breach of the peace, or act of aggression and shall make recommendations, or decide what measures shall be taken in accordance with Articles 41 and 42, to maintain or restore international peace and security.

ARTICLE 40

In order to prevent an aggravation of the situation, the Security Council may, before making the recommendations or deciding upon the measures provided for in Article 39, call upon the parties concerned to comply with such provisional measures as it deems necessary or desirable. Such provisional measures shall be without prejudice to the rights, claims, or position of the parties concerned. The Security Council shall duly take account of failure to comply with such provisional measures.

ARTICLE 41

The Security Council may decide what measures not involving the use of armed force are to be employed to give effect to its decisions, and it may call upon the Members of the United Nations to apply such measures. These may include complete or partial interruption of economic relations and of rail, sea, air, postal, telegraphic, radio, and other means of communication, and the severance of diplomatic relations.

ARTICLE 42

Should the Security Council consider the measures provided for in Article 41 would be inadequate or have proved to be inadequate, it may take such action by air, sea, or land forces as may be necessary to maintain or restore international peace and security. Such action may include demonstrations, blockade, and other operations by air, sea, or land forces of Members of the United Nations.

ARTICLE 43

1. All Members of the United Nations, in order to contribute to the maintenance of international peace and security, undertake to make available to the Security Council, on its call and in accordance with a special agreement or agreements, armed forces, assistance, and facilities, including rights of passage, necessary for the purpose of maintaining international peace and security.
2. Such agreement or agreements shall govern the numbers and types of forces, their degree of readiness and general location, and the nature of the facilities and assistance to be provided.
3. The agreement or agreements shall be negotiated as soon as possible on the initiative of the Security Council. They shall be concluded between the Security Council and Members or between the Security Council and groups of Members and shall be subject to ratification by the signatory states in accordance with their respective constitutional processes.

ARTICLE 44

When the Security Council has decided to use force it shall, before calling upon a Member not represented on it to provide armed forces in fulfilment of the obligations assumed under Article 43, invite the Member, if the Member so desires, to participate in the decisions of the Security Council concerning the employment of contingents of that Member's armed forces.

ARTICLE 45

In order to enable the United Nations to take urgent military measures, Members shall hold immediately available national air-force contingents for combined international enforcement action. The strength and degree of readiness of these contingents and plans for their combined action shall be determined, within the limits laid down in the special agreement or agreements referred to in Article 43, by the Security Council with the assistance of the Military Staff Committee.

ARTICLE 46

Plans for the application of armed force shall be made by the Security Council with the assistance of the Military Staff Committee.

ARTICLE 47

1. There shall be established a Military Staff Committee to advise and assist the Security Council on all questions relating to the Security Council's military requirements for the maintenance of international peace and security, the employment and command of forces placed at its disposal, the regulation of armaments, and possible disarmament.

2. The Military Staff Committee shall consist of the Chiefs of Staff of the permanent members of the Security Council or their representatives. Any Member of the United Nations not permanently represented on the Committee shall be invited by the Committee to be associated with it when the efficient discharge of the Committee's responsibilities requires the participation of that Member in its work.

3. The Military Staff Committee shall be responsible under the Security Council for the strategic direction of any armed forces placed at the disposal of the Security Council. Questions relating to the command of such forces shall be worked out subsequently.

4. The Military Staff Committee, with the authorization of the Security Council and after consultation with appropriate regional agencies, may establish regional sub-committees.

ARTICLE 48

1. The action required to carry out the decisions of the Security Council for the maintenance of international peace and security shall be taken by all the Members of the United Nations or by some of them, as the Security Council may determine.

2. Such decisions shall be carried out by the Members of the United Nations directly and through their action in the appropriate international agencies of which they are members.

ARTICLE 49

The Members of the United Nations shall join in affording mutual assistance in carrying out the measures decided upon by the Security Council.

ARTICLE 50

If preventive or enforcement measures against any state are taken by the Security Council, any other state, whether a Member of the United Nations or not, which finds itself confronted with special economic problems arising from the carrying out of those measures shall have the right to consult the Security Council with regard to a solution of those problems.

ARTICLE 51

Nothing in the present Charter shall impair the inherent right of individual or collective self-defense if an armed attack occurs against a Member of the United Nations, until the Security Council has taken measures necessary to maintain international peace and security. Measures taken by Members in the exercise of this right of self-defence shall be immediately reported to the Security Council and shall not in any way affect the authority and responsibility of the Security Council under the present Charter to take at any time such action as it deems necessary in order to maintain or restore international peace and security.

CHAPTER VIII
REGIONAL ARRANGEMENTS
ARTICLE 52

1. Nothing in the present Charter precludes the existence of regional arrangements or agencies for dealing with such matters relating to the maintenance of international peace and security as are appropriate for regional action, provided that such arrangements or agencies and their activities are consistent with the Purposes and Principles of the United Nations.

2. The Members of the United Nations entering into such arrangements or constituting such agencies shall make every effort to achieve pacific settlement of local disputes through such regional arrangements or by such regional agencies before referring them to the Security Council.

3. The Security Council shall encourage the development of pacific settlement of local disputes through such regional arrangements or by such regional agencies either on the initiative of the states concerned or by reference from the Security Council.

4. This Article in no way impairs the application of Articles 34 and 35.

ARTICLE 53

1. The Security Council shall, where appropriate, utilize such regional arrangements or agencies for enforcement action under its authority. But no enforcement action shall be taken under regional arrangements or by regional agencies without the authorization of the Security Council, with the exception of measures against any enemy state, as defined in paragraph 2 of this Article, provided for pursuant to Article 107 or in regional arrangements directed against renewal of aggressive policy on the part of any such state, until such time as the Organization may, on request of the Governments concerned, be charged with the responsibility for preventing further aggression by such a state.

2. The term enemy state as used in paragraph 1 of this Article applies to any state which during the Second World War has been an enemy of any signatory of the present Charter.

ARTICLE 54

The Security Council shall at all times be kept fully informed of activities undertaken or in contemplation under regional arrangements or by regional agencies for the maintenance of international peace and security.

CHAPTER IX
INTERNATIONAL ECONOMIC AND SOCIAL CO-OPERATION
ARTICLE 55

With a view to the creation of conditions of stability and well-being which are necessary for peaceful and friendly relations among nations based on respect for the principle of equal rights and self-determination of peoples, the United Nations shall promote:

a. higher standards of living, full employment, and conditions of economic and social progress and development;

b. solutions of international economic, social, health, and related problems; and international cultural and educational co-operation; and

c. universal respect for, and observance of, human rights and fundamental freedoms for all without distinction as to race, sex, language, or religion.

ARTICLE 56

All Members pledge themselves to take joint and separate action in co-operation with the Organization for the achievement of the purposes set forth in Article 55.

ARTICLE 57

1. The various specialized agencies, established by inter-governmental agreement and having wide international responsibilities, as defined in their basic instruments, in economic, social, cultural, educational, health, and related fields, shall be brought into relationship with the United Nations in accordance with the provisions of Article 63.
2. Such agencies thus brought into relationship with the United Nations are hereinafter referred to as specialized agencies.

ARTICLE 58

The Organization shall make recommendations for the co-ordination of the policies and activities of the specialized agencies.

ARTICLE 59

The Organization shall, where appropriate, initiate negotiations among the states concerned for the creation of any new specialized agencies required for the accomplishment of the purposes set forth in Article 55.

ARTICLE 60

Responsibility for the discharge of the functions of the Organization set forth in this Chapter shall be vested in the General Assembly and, under the authority of the General Assembly, in the Economic and Social Council, which shall have for this purpose the powers set forth in Chapter X.

CHAPTER X
THE ECONOMIC AND SOCIAL COUNCIL COMPOSITION
ARTICLE 61

1. The Economic and Social Council shall consist of fifty-four Members of the United Nations elected by the General Assembly.
2. Subject to the provisions of paragraph 3, eighteen members of the Economic and Social Council shall be elected each year for a term of three years. A retiring member shall be eligible for immediate re-election.
3. At the first election after the increase in the membership of the Economic and Social Council from twenty-seven to fifty-four members, in addition to the members elected in place of the nine members whose term of office expires at the end of that year, twenty-seven additional members shall be elected. Of these twenty-seven additional members, the term of office of nine members so elected shall expire at the end of one year, and of nine other members at the end of two years, in accordance with arrangements made by the General Assembly.
4. Each member of the Economic and Social Council shall have one representative.

FUNCTIONS AND POWERS
ARTICLE 62

1. The Economic and Social Council may make or initiate studies and reports with respect to international economic, social, cultural, educational, health, and related matters and may make recommendations with respect to any such matters to the General Assembly, to the Members of the United Nations, and to the specialized agencies concerned.
2. It may make recommendations for the purpose of promoting respect for, and observance of, human rights and fundamental freedoms for all.
3. It may prepare draft conventions for submission to the General Assembly, with respect to matters falling within its competence.
4. It may call, in accordance with the rules prescribed by the United Nations, international conferences on matters falling within its competence.

ARTICLE 63

1. The Economic and Social Council may enter into agreements with any of the agencies referred to in Article 57, defining the terms on which the agency concerned shall be brought into relationship with the United Nations. Such agreements shall be subject to approval by the General Assembly.

2. It may co-ordinate the activities of the specialized agencies and through recommendations to the General Assembly and to the Members of the United Nations.

ARTICLE 64

1. The Economic and Social Council may take appropriate steps to obtain regular reports from the specialized agencies. It may make arrangements with the Members of the United Nations and with the specialized agencies to obtain reports on the steps taken to give effect to its own recommendations and to recommendations on matters falling within its competence made by the General Assembly.

2. It may communicate its observations on these reports to the General Assembly.

ARTICLE 65

The Economic and Social Council may furnish information to the Security Council and shall assist the Security Council upon its request.

ARTICLE 66

1. The Economic and Social Council shall perform such functions as fall within its competence in connexion with the carrying out of the recommendations of the General Assembly.

2. It may, with the approval of the General Assembly, perform services at the request of Members of the United Nations and at the request of specialized agencies.

3. It shall perform such other functions as are specified elsewhere in the present Charter or as may be assigned to it by the General Assembly.

VOTING
ARTICLE 67

1. Each member of the Economic and Social Council shall have one vote.

2. Decisions of the Economic and Social Council shall be made by a majority of the members present and voting.

PROCEDURE
ARTICLE 68

The Economic and Social Council shall set up commissions in economic and social fields and for the promotion of human rights, and such other commissions as may be required for the performance of its functions.

ARTICLE 69

The Economic and Social Council shall invite any Member of the United Nations to participate, without vote, in its deliberations on any matter of particular concern to that Member.

ARTICLE 70

The Economic and Social Council may make arrangements for representatives of the specialized agencies to participate, without vote, in its deliberations and in those of the commissions established by it, and for its representatives to participate in the deliberations of the specialized agencies.

ARTICLE 71

The Economic and Social Council may make suitable arrangements for consultation with non-governmental organizations which are concerned with matters within its competence. Such arrangements may be made with international organizations and, where appropriate, with national organizations after consultation with the Member of the United Nations concerned.

ARTICLE 72

1. The Economic and Social Council shall adopt its own rules of procedure, including the method of selecting its President.

2. The Economic and Social Council shall meet as required in accordance with its rules, which shall include provision for the convening of meetings on the request of a majority of its members.

CHAPTER XI

DECLARATION REGARDING NON-SELF GOVERNING TERRITORIES
ARTICLE 73

Members of the United Nations which have or assume responsibilities for the administration of territories, whose peoples have not yet attained a full measure of self-government recognize the principle that the interests of the inhabitants of these territories are paramount, and accept as a sacred trust the obligation to promote to the utmost, within the system of international peace and security established by the present Charter, the well-being of the inhabitants of these territories, and, to this end:

a. to ensure, with due respect for the culture of the peoples concerned, their political, economic, social, and educational advancement, their just treatment, and their protection against abuses;

b. to develop self-government, to take due account of the political aspirations of the peoples, and to assist them in the progressive development of their free political institutions, according to the particular circumstances of each territory and its peoples and their varying stages of advancement;

c. to further international peace and security;

d. to promote constructive measures of development, to encourage research, and to co-operate with one another and, when and where appropriate, with specialized international bodies with a view to the practical achievement of the social, economic, and scientific purposes set forth in this Article: and

e. to transmit regularly to the Secretary-General for information purposes, subject to such limitation as security and constitutional considerations may require, statistical and other information of a technical nature relating to economic, social, and educational conditions in the territories for which they are respectively responsible other than those territories to which Chapter XII and XIII apply.

ARTICLE 74

Members of the United Nations also agree that their policy in respect of the territories to which this Chapter applies, no less than in respect of their metropolitan areas, must be based on the general principle of good-neighbourliness, due account being taken of the interests and well-being of the rest of the world, in social, economic, and commercial matters.

CHAPTER XII

INTERNATIONAL TRUSTEESHIP SYSTEM
ARTICLE 75

The United Nations shall establish under its authority an international trusteeship system for the administration and supervision of such territories as may be placed thereunder by subsequent individual agreements. These territories are hereinafter referred to as trust territories.

ARTICLE 76

The basic objectives of the trusteeship system, in accordance with the Purposes of the United Nations laid down in Article 1 of the present Charter, shall be:

a. to further international peace and security;
b. to promote the political, economic, social, and educational advancement of the inhabitants of the trust territories, and their progressive development towards self-government or independence as may be appropriate to the particular circumstances of each territory and its peoples and the freely expressed wishes of the peoples concerned, and as may be provided by the terms of each trusteeship agreement;
c. to encourage respect for human rights and for fundamental freedoms for all without distinction as to race, sex, language, or religion, and to encourage recognition of the interdependence of the peoples of the world; and
d. to ensure equal treatment in social, economic, and commercial matters for all Members of the United Nations and their nationals, and also equal treatment for the latter in the administration of justice, without prejudice to the attainment of the foregoing objectives and subject to the provisions of Article 80.

ARTICLE 77

1. The trusteeship system shall apply to such territories in the following categories as may be placed thereunder by means of trusteeship agreements:
a. territories now held under mandate;
b. territories which may be detached from enemy states as a result of the Second World War; and
c. territories voluntarily placed under the system by states responsible for their administration.

2. It will be a matter for subsequent agreement as to which territories in the foregoing categories will be brought under the trusteeship system and upon what terms.

ARTICLE 78

The trusteeship system shall not apply to territories which have become Members of the United Nations, relationship among which shall be based on respect for the principle of sovereign equality.

ARTICLE 79

The terms of trusteeship for each territory to be placed under the trusteeship system, including any alteration or amendment, shall be agreed upon by the states directly concerned, including the mandatory power in the case of territories held under mandate by a Member of the United Nations, and shall be approved as provided for in Articles 83 and 85.

ARTICLE 80

1. Except as may be agreed upon in individual trusteeship agreements, made under Articles 77, 79, and 81, placing each territory under the trusteeship system, and until such agreements have been concluded, nothing in this Chapter shall be construed in or of itself to alter in any manner the rights whatsoever of any states or any peoples or the terms of existing international instruments to which Members of the United Nations may respectively be parties.

2. Paragraph 1 of this Article shall not be interpreted as giving grounds for delay or postponement of the negotiation and conclusion of agreements for placing mandated and other territories under the trusteeship system as provided for in Article 77.

ARTICLE 81

The trusteeship agreement shall in each case include the terms under which the trust territory will be administered and designate the authority which will exercise the administration of the trust territory. Such authority, hereinafter called the administering authority, may be one or more states or the Organization itself.

ARTICLE 82

There may be designated, in any trusteeship agreement, a strategic area or areas which may include part or all of the trust territory to which the agreement applies, without prejudice to any special agreement or agreements made under Article 43.

ARTICLE 83

1. All functions of the United Nations relating to strategic areas, including the approval of the terms of the trusteeship agreements and of their alteration or amendment, shall be exercised by the Security Council.
2. The basic objectives set forth in Article 76 shall be applicable to the people of each strategic area.
3. The Security Council shall, subject to the provisions of the trusteeship agreements and without prejudice to security considerations, avail itself of the assistance of the Trusteeship Council to perform those functions of the United Nations under the trusteeship system relating to political, economic, social, and educational matters in the strategic areas.

ARTICLE 84

It shall be the duty of the administering authority to ensure that the trust territory shall play its part in the maintenance of international peace and security. To this end the administering authority may make use of volunteer forces, facilities, and assistance from the trust territory in carrying out the obligations towards the Security Council undertaken in this regard by the administering authority, as well as for local defence and the maintenance of law and order within the trust territory.

ARTICLE 85

1. The functions of the United Nations with regard to trusteeship agreements for all areas not designated as strategic, including the approval of the terms of the trusteeship agreements and of their alteration or amendment, shall be exercised by the General Assembly.
2. The Trusteeship Council, operating under the authority of the General Assembly, shall assist the General Assembly in carrying out these functions.

CHAPTER XIII
THE TRUSTEESHIP COUNCIL COMPOSITION
ARTICLE 86

1. The Trusteeship Council shall consist of the following Members of the United Nations:
   a. those Members administering trust territories;
   b. such of those Members mentioned by name in Article 23 as are not administering trust territories; and
   c. as many other Members elected for three-year terms by the General Assembly as may be necessary to ensure that the total number of members of the Trusteeship Council is equally divided between those Members of the United Nations which administer trust territories and those which do not.
2. Each member of the Trusteeship Council shall designate one specially qualified person to represent it therein.

FUNCTIONS AND POWERS
ARTICLE 87

The General Assembly and, under its authority, the Trusteeship Council, in carrying out their functions, may:
   a. consider reports submitted by the administering authority;
   b. accept petitions and examine them in consultation with the administering authority;
   c. provide for periodic visits to the respective trust territories at times agreed upon with the administering authority; and

d. take these and other actions in conformity with the terms of the trusteeship agreements.

ARTICLE 88

The Trusteeship Council shall formulate a questionnaire on the political, economic, social, and educational advancement of the inhabitants of each trust territory, and the administering authority for each trust territory within the competence of the General Assembly shall make an annual report to the General Assembly upon the basis of such questionnaire.

VOTING
ARTICLE 89

1. Each member of the Trusteeship Council shall have one vote.
2. Decisions of the Trusteeship Council shall be made by a majority of the members present and voting.

PROCEDURE
ARTICLE 90

1. The Trusteeship Council shall adopt its own rules of procedure, including the method of selecting its President.
2. The Trusteeship Council shall meet as required in accordance with its rules, which shall include provision for the convening of meetings on the request of a majority of its members.

ARTICLE 91

The Trusteeship Council shall, when appropriate, avail itself of the assistance of the Economic and Social Council and of the specialized agencies in regard to matters with which they are respectively concerned.

CHAPTER XIV
THE INTERNATIONAL COURT OF JUSTICE
ARTICLE 92

The International Court of Justice shall be the principal judicial organ of the United Nations. It shall function in accordance with the annexed Statute, which is based upon the Statute of the Permanent Court of International Justice and forms an integral part of the present Charter.

ARTICLE 93

1. All Members of the United Nations are *ipso facto* parties to the Statute of the International Court of Justice.
2. A state which is not a Member of the United Nations may become a party to the Statute of the International Court of Justice on conditions to be determined in each case by the General Assembly upon the recommendation of the Security Council.

ARTICLE 94

1. Each Member of the United Nations undertakes to comply with the decision of the International Court of Justice in any case to which it is a party.
2. If any party to a case fails to perform the obligations incumbent upon it under a judgement rendered by the Court, the other party may have recourse to the Security Council, which may, if it deems necessary, make recommendations or decide upon measures to be taken to give effect to the judgement.

ARTICLE 95

Nothing in the present Charter shall prevent Members of the United Nations from entrusting the solution of their differences to other tribunals by virtue of agreements already in existence or which may be concluded in the future.

ARTICLE 96

1. The General Assembly or the Security Council may request the International Court of Justice to give an advisory opinion on any legal question.

2. Other organs of the United Nations and specialized agencies, which may at any time be so authorized by the General Assembly, may also request advisory opinions of the Court on legal questions arising within the scope of their activities.

CHAPTER XV

THE SECRETARIAT

ARTICLE 97

The Secretariat shall comprise a Secretary-General and such staff as the Organization may require. The Secretary-General shall be appointed by the General Assembly upon the recommendation of the Security Council. He shall be the chief administrative officer of the Organization.

ARTICLE 98

The Secretary-General shall act in that capacity in all meetings of the General Assembly, of the Security Council, of the Economic and Social Council, and of the Trusteeship Council, and shall perform such other functions as are entrusted to him by these organs. The Secretary-General shall make an annual report to the General Assembly on the work of the Organization.

ARTICLE 99

The Secretary-General may bring to the attention of the Security Council any matter which in his opinion may threaten the maintenance of international peace and security.

ARTICLE 100

1. In the performance of their duties the Secretary-General and the staff shall not seek or receive instructions from any government or from any other authority external to the Organization. They shall refrain from any action which might reflect on their position as international officials responsible only to the Organization.

2. Each Member of the United Nations undertakes to respect the exclusively international character of the responsibilities of the Secretary-General and the staff and not to seek to influence them in the discharge of their responsibilities.

ARTICLE 101

1. The staff shall be appointed by the Secretary-General under regulations established by the General Assembly.

2. Appropriate staffs shall be permanently assigned to the Economic and Social Council, the Trusteeship Council, and, as required, to other organs of the United Nations. These staffs shall form a part of the Secretariat.

3. The paramount consideration in the employment of the staff and in the determination of the conditions of service shall be the necessity of securing the highest standards of efficiency, competence, and integrity. Due regard shall be paid to the importance of recruiting the staff on as wide a geographical basis as possible.

CHAPTER XVI

MISCELLANEOUS PROVISIONS

ARTICLE 102

1. Every treaty and every international agreement entered into by any Member of the United Nations after the present Charter comes into force shall as soon as possible be registered with the Secretariat and published by it.

2. No party to any such treaty or international agreement which has not been registered in accordance with the provisions of paragraph 1 of this Article may invoke that treaty or agreement before any organ of the United Nations.

ARTICLE 103

In the event of a conflict between the obligations of the Members of the United Nations under the present Charter and their obligations under any other international agreement, their obligations under the present Charter shall prevail.

ARTICLE 104

The Organization shall enjoy in the territory of each of its Members such legal capacity as may be necessary for the exercise of its functions and the fulfillment of its purposes.

ARTICLE 105

1. The Organization shall enjoy in the territory of each of its Members such privileges and immunities as are necessary for the fulfillment of its purposes.

2. Representatives of the Members of the United Nations and officials of the Organization shall similarly enjoy such privileges and immunities as are necessary for the independent exercise of their functions in connexion with the Organization.

3. The General Assembly may make recommendations with a view to determining the details of the application of paragraphs 1 and 2 of this Article or may propose conventions to the Members of the United Nations for this purpose.

CHAPTER XVII
TRANSITIONAL SECURITY ARRANGEMENTS
ARTICLE 106

Pending the coming into force of such special agreements referred to in Article 43 as in the opinion of the Security Council enable it to begin the exercise of its responsibilities under Article 42, the parties to the Four-Nation Declaration, signed at Moscow, 30 October 1943, and France, shall, in accordance with the provisions of paragraph 5 of that Declaration, consult with one another and as occasion requires with other Members of the United Nations with a view to such joint action on behalf of the Organization as may be necessary for the purpose of maintaining international peace and security.

ARTICLE 107

Nothing in the present Charter shall invalidate or preclude action, in relation to any state which during the Second World War has been an enemy of any signatory to the present Charter, taken or authorized as a result of that war by the Governments having responsibility for such action.

CHAPTER XVIII
AMENDMENTS
ARTICLE 108

Amendments to the present Charter shall come into force for all Members of the United Nations when they have been adopted by a vote of two-thirds of the members of the General Assembly and ratified in accordance with their respective constitutional processes by two-thirds of the Members of the United Nations, including all the permanent members of the Security Council.

ARTICLE 109

1. A General Conference of the Members of the United Nations for the purpose of reviewing the present Charter may be held at a date and place to be fixed by a two-thirds vote of the members of the General Assembly and by a vote of any nine members of the Security Council. Each Member of the United Nations shall have one vote in the conference.

2. Any alteration of the present Charter recommended by a two-thirds vote of the con-

ference shall take effect when ratified in accordance with their respective constitutional processes by two-thirds of the Members of the United Nations including all the permanent members of the Security Council.

3. If such a conference has not been held before the tenth annual session of the General Assembly following the coming into force of the present Charter, the proposal to call such a conference shall be placed on the agenda of that session of the General Assembly, and the conference shall be held if so decided by a majority vote of the members of the General Assembly and by a vote of any seven members of the Security Council.

CHAPTER XIX
RATIFICATION AND SIGNATURE
ARTICLE 110

1. The present Charter shall be ratified by the signatory states in accordance with their respective constitutional processes.

2. The ratifications shall be deposited with the Government of the United States of America, which shall notify all the signatory states of each deposit as well as the Secretary-General of the Organization when he has been appointed.

3. The present Charter shall come into force upon the deposit of ratifications by the Republic of China, France, the Union of Soviet Socialist Republics, the United Kingdom of Great Britain and Northern Ireland, and the United States of America, and by a majority of the other signatory states. A protocol of the ratifications deposited shall thereupon be drawn up by the Government of the United States of America which shall communicate copies thereof to all the signatory states.

4. The states signatory to the present Charter which ratify if after it has come into force will become original Members of the United Nations on the date of the deposit of their respective ratifications.

ARTICLE 111

The present Charter, of which the Chinese, French, Russian, English, and Spanish texts are equally authentic, shall remain deposited in the archives of the Government of the United States of America. Duly certified copies thereof shall be transmitted by that Government to the Governments of the other signatory states.

IN FAITH WHEREOF the representatives of the Governments of the United Nations have signed the present Charter.

DONE at the city of San Francisco the twenty-sixth day of June, one thousand nine hundred and forty-five.

THE UNITED NATIONS: Principal Organs of the United Nations

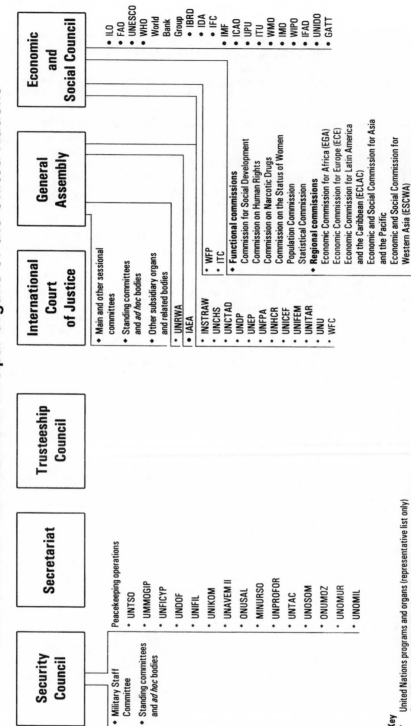

Security Council
- Military Staff Committee
- Standing committees and *ad hoc* bodies

Peacekeeping operations
- UNTSO
- UNMOGIP
- UNFICYP
- UNDOF
- UNIFIL
- UNIKOM
- UNAVEM II
- ONUSAL
- MINURSO
- UNPROFOR
- UNTAC
- UNOSOM
- ONUMOZ
- UNOMUR
- UNOMIL

Secretariat

Trusteeship Council

International Court of Justice

- UNRWA
- IAEA

General Assembly
- Main and other sessional committees
- Standing committees and *ad hoc* bodies
- Other subsidiary organs and related bodies

- INSTRAW
- UNCHS
- UNCTAD
- UNDP
- UNEP
- UNFPA
- UNHCR
- UNICEF
- UNIFEM
- UNITAR
- UNU
- WFC

Economic and Social Council
- ILO
- FAO
- UNESCO
- WHO
- World Bank Group
  - IBRD
  - IDA
  - IFC
- IMF
- ICAO
- UPU
- ITU
- WMO
- IMO
- WIPO
- IFAD
- UNIDO
- GATT

- WFP
- ITC
- **Functional commissions**
  - Commission for Social Development
  - Commission on Human Rights
  - Commission on Narcotic Drugs
  - Commission on the Status of Women
  - Population Commission
  - Statistical Commission
- **Regional commissions**
  - Economic Commission for Africa (EGA)
  - Economic Commission for Europe (ECE)
  - Economic Commission for Latin America and the Caribbean (ECLAC)
  - Economic and Social Commission for Asia and the Pacific
  - Economic and Social Commission for Western Asia (ESCWA)
- **Sessional and standing committees**
- **Expert, *ad hoc*, and related bodies**

Key
- ✦ United Nations programs and organs (representative list only)
- ● Specialised agencies and other autonomous organisations within the system
- ◆ Other commissions, committees and *ad hoc* and related bodies

Glossary

ACC	Administrative Coordinating Committee
ECOSOC	UN Economic and Social Council
ESC	Economic and Social Council
FAO	Food and Agriculture Organization of the UN
G-7	Group of Seven most industrialized nations (Canada, France, Germany, Italy, Japan, United Kingdom and United States)
GA	General Assembly
GATT	General Agreement on Tariffs and Trade
IAEA	International Atomic Energy Agency
IBRD	International Bank for Reconstruction and Development
ICAO	International Civil Aviation Organization
IDA	International Development Association
IFAD	International Fund for Agricultural Development
IFC	International Finance Corporation
ILO	International Labor Office
IMF	International Monetary Fund
IMO	International Maritime Organization
INSTRAW	International Research and Training Institute for the Advancement of Women
ITC	International Trade Center (UNCTAD/GATT)
ITO	International Trade Organization
ITU	International Telecommunication Union
MINURSO	UN Mission for the Referendum in Western Sahara
OECD	Organization for Economic Cooperation and Development
ONUMOZ	UN Operation in Mozambique
ONUSAL	UN Observer Mission in El Salvador
SC	Security Council
UN	United Nations
UNAVEM II	UN Angola Verification Mission II
UNCHS	UN Center for Human Settlements (Habitat)
UNCTAD	UN Conference on Trade and Development
UNDCP	UN International Drug Control Program
UNDOF	UN Disengagement Observer Force
UNDP	UN Development Program
UNEP	UN Environment Program
UNESCO	UN Educational, Scientific and Cultural Organization
UNFICYP	UN Peace-Keeping Force in Cyprus
UNFPA	UN Population Fund
UNHCR	Office of the UN High Commissioner for Refugees
UNICEF	UN Children's Fund
UNIDO	UN Industrial Development Organization
UNIFEM	UN Development Fund for Women
UNIFIL	UN Interim Force in Lebanon
UNIKOM	UN Iraq-Kuwait Observation Mission
UNITAR	UN Institute for Training and Research
UNMOGIP	UN Military Observer Group in India and Pakistan
UNOMIL	UN Observer Mission in Liberia
UNOMUR	UN Observer Mission in Uganda-Rwanda
UNOSOM	UN Operation in Somalia
UNPROFOR	UN Protection Force
UNRWA	UN Relief and Works Agency for Palestine Refugees in the Near East
UNTACX	UN Transnational Authority in Cambodia
UNTSO	UN Truce Supervision Organization
UNU	UN University
UPU	Universal Postal Union
WFC	World Food Council
WFP	World Food Program
WHO	World Health Organization
WIPO	World Intellectual Property Organization
WMO	World Meteorological Organization

BIBLIOGRAPHY

Rabia Ali and Lawrence Lifschultz (eds.), *Why Bosnia: Writings on the Balkan War* (Stony Creek, Conn.: Pamphleteer's Press, 1993).

Phyllis Bennis and Michel Moushabeck (eds.), *Altered States: A Reader in the New World Order* (New York: Olive Branch Press/Interlink, 1993).

Bennis and Moushabeck (eds.), *Beyond the Storm: A Gulf Crisis Reader* (New York: Olive Branch Press/Interlink, 1991).

Carnegie Endowment National Commission, *Changing Our Ways: America and the New World* (Washington, D.C.: Brookings Institution, 1992).

Erskine Childers (ed.), *Challenges to the United Nations: Building a Safer World* (London and New York: CIIR/St. Martin's Press, 1994).

Erskine Childers with Brian Urquhart, *Renewing the United Nations System* (Uppsala, Sweden: Dag Hammarskjold Foundation, 1994).

Childers and Urquhart, *Towards a More Effective United Nations* (Uppsala, Sweden: Dag Hammarskjold Foundation, 1992).

Harlan Cleveland, *Birth of a New World: An Open Moment for International Leadership* (San Francisco: Jossey-Bass Publishers, 1993).

Michael Cranna, *The True Cost of Conflict: Seven Recent Wars and Their Effects on Society* (New York: The New Press, 1994).

Omar Dahbour and Micheline R. Ishay (eds.), *The Nationalism Reader* (Atlantic Highlands, N.J.: Humanities Press, 1995).

Gareth Evans, *Cooperating for Peace: The Global Agenda for the 1990s and Beyond* (St. Leonards, Australia: Allen & Unwin, 1993).

Elizabeth G. Ferris (ed.), *The Challenge to Intervene: A New Role for the United Nations?* (Uppsala, Sweden: Life and Peace Institute, 1992).

Thomas M. Frank, *Nation Against Nation: What Happened to the UN Dream and What the U.S. Can Do About It* (New York: Oxford University Press, 1985).

Hilary F. French, *After the Earth Summit: The Future of Environmental Governance* (Washington, D.C.: Worldwatch Institute, 1992).

Peter J. Fromuth (ed.), *A Successor Vision: The United Nations of Tomorrow* (New York: United Nations Association, 1988).

Allan Gerson, *The Kirkpatrick Mission: Diplomacy Without Apology: America at the United Nations, 1981-1985* (New York: The Free Press, 1991).

Jochen Hippler, *Pax Americana? Hegemony or Decline* (London: Pluto Press, 1994).

Human Rights Watch, *The Lost Agenda: Human Rights and UN Field Operations* (New York: Human Rights Watch, 1993).

Independent Working Group on the Future of the United Nations, *The United Nations in Its Second Half-Century* (New York: Ford Foundation/Yale University, 1995).

International Committee of the Red Cross, *Annual Report* (Geneva, 1992).

Hans Kochler (ed.), *Studies in International Relations: The United Nations and the New World Order* (Vienna: International Conference on a More Democratic United Nations, 1992).

Michael Krinsky and David Golove (eds.), *United States Economic Measures Against Cuba: Proceedings in the United Nations and International Law Issues* (Northampton, Mass.: Aletheia Press, 1993).

Josdin Landell-Mills, *Helping the Poor: The IMF's New Facilities for Structural Adjustment* (Washington, D.C.: IMF External Relations Dept., 1988/92).

NGO Division, Canadian Partnership Branch, *The Role of NGOs in the Peacebuilding Process* (Hull, Quebec: Canadian International Develoment Agency, March 1994).

Michael Renner, *Critical Juncture: The Future of Peacekeeping* (Washington, D.C.: Worldwatch Institute, 1993).

Adam Roberts and Benedict Kingsbury (eds.), *United Nations, Divided World: The UN's Role in International Relations* (New York: Clarendon Press, 1993).

Michael Shuman and Julia Sweig (eds.), *Conditions of Peace: An Inquiry: Security, Democracy, Ecology, Economics, Community* (Washington, D.C.: Expro Press, 1991).

South Center, *Facing the Challenge: Responses to the Report of the South Commission* (London: Zed Books, 1993).

South Commission, *The Challenge to the South* (New York: Oxford University Press, 1990).

Harold Stassen, *United Nations: A Working Paper for Restructuring* (Minneapolis: Lerner Publications Co., 1994).

United Nations, *Basic Facts About the United Nations* (New York: UN Department of Public Information, 1992, 1995).

United Nations, *The Blue Helmets: A Review of United Nations Peacekeeping* (New York: UN Department of Public Information, 1990).

United Nations, *Disarmament: Strengthening the NPT and the Nuclear Non-Proliferation Regime* (New York: UN Office for Disarmament Affairs, 1993).

UN Department of Economic & Social Information and Policy Analysis, *World Economic and Social Survey 1994* (New York: United Nations, 1994).

UN Development Program, *Human Development Report 1994* (New York: Oxford University Press, 1994).

UN High Commissioner for Refugees, *The State of the World's Refugees: The Challenge of Protection* (London: Penguin Books, 1993).

U.S. Committee for Refugees, *World Refugee Survey 1992* (Washington, D.C.: American Council for Nationalities Service, 1992).

David Wurmser and Nancy Bearg Dyke, *The Professionalization of Peacekeeping* (Washington, D.C.: U.S. Institute of Peace, 1993).

Index